Let's Dance, Snoopy

Let's Dance, Snoopy

Charles M. Schulz

Ballantine Books
New York

A Ballantine Books Trade Paperback Original

Copyright © 2015 by Peanuts Worldwide LLC

Published in the United States by Ballantine Books,
an imprint of Random House,
a division of Random House LLC,
a Penguin Random House Company, New York.

BALLANTINE and the HOUSE colophon are registered trademarks of Random House LLC.

The comic strips in this book were originally published in newspapers worldwide.

ISBN 978-0-8041-7947-8

eBook ISBN 978-0-8041-7948-5

Printed in the United States of America on acid-free paper

www.ballantinebooks.com

2 4 6 8 9 7 5 3 1

Book design by Diane Hobbing

Let's Dance, Snoopy

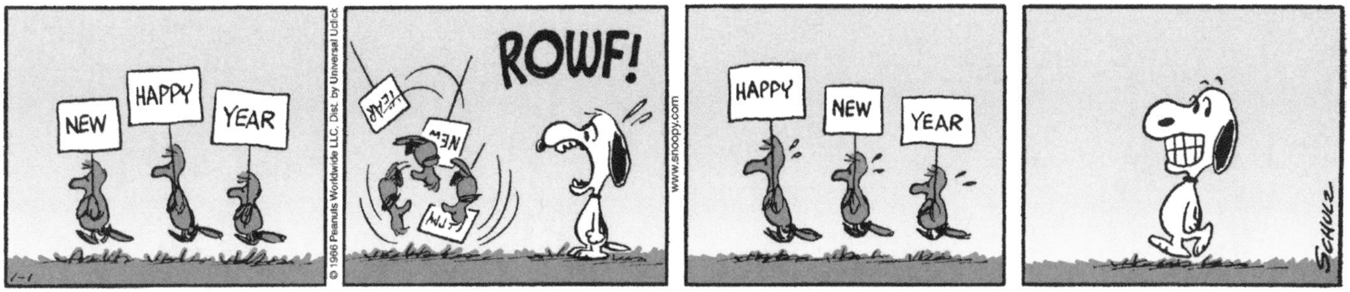
NEW
HAPPY
YEAR
© 1966 Peanuts Worldwide LLC, Dist. by Universal Uclick
ROWF!
www.snoopy.com
HAPPY
NEW
YEAR
SCHULZ

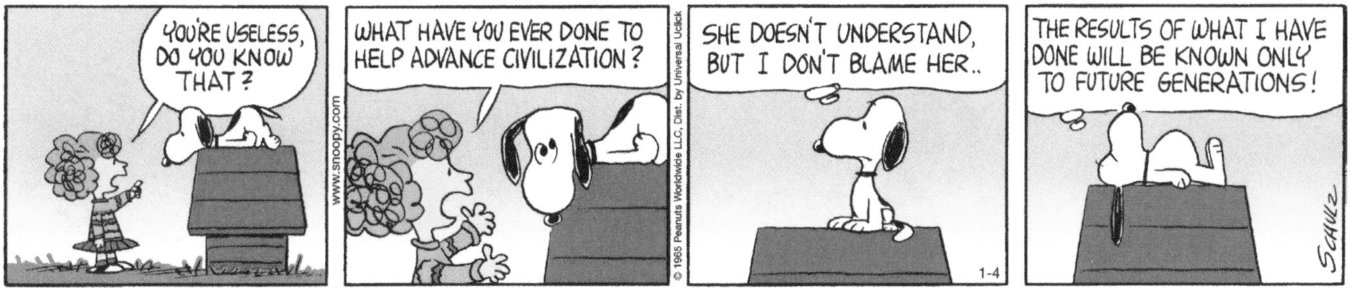
YOU'RE USELESS, DO YOU KNOW THAT?
www.snoopy.com
WHAT HAVE YOU EVER DONE TO HELP ADVANCE CIVILIZATION?
© 1965 Peanuts Worldwide LLC, Dist. by Universal Uclick
SHE DOESN'T UNDERSTAND, BUT I DON'T BLAME HER..
1-4
THE RESULTS OF WHAT I HAVE DONE WILL BE KNOWN ONLY TO FUTURE GENERATIONS!
SCHULZ

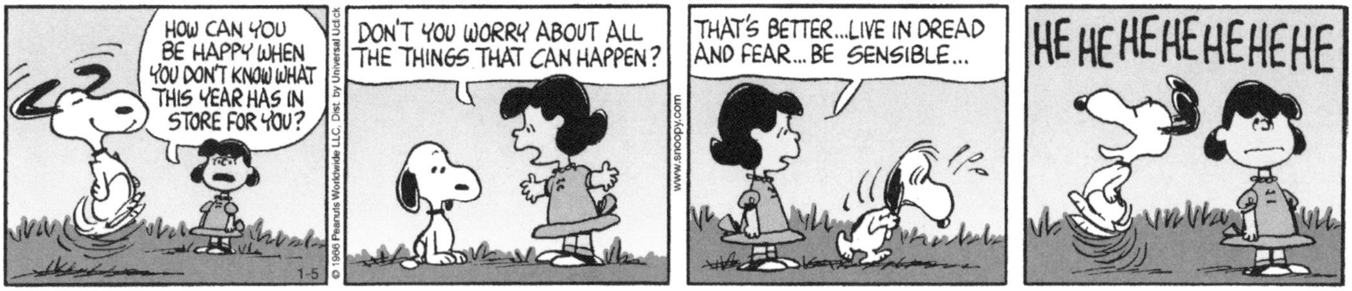
HOW CAN YOU BE HAPPY WHEN YOU DON'T KNOW WHAT THIS YEAR HAS IN STORE FOR YOU?
1-5
© 1966 Peanuts Worldwide LLC, Dist. by Universal Uclick
DON'T YOU WORRY ABOUT ALL THE THINGS THAT CAN HAPPEN?
www.snoopy.com
THAT'S BETTER...LIVE IN DREAD AND FEAR... BE SENSIBLE...
HE HE HE HE HE HE HE HE

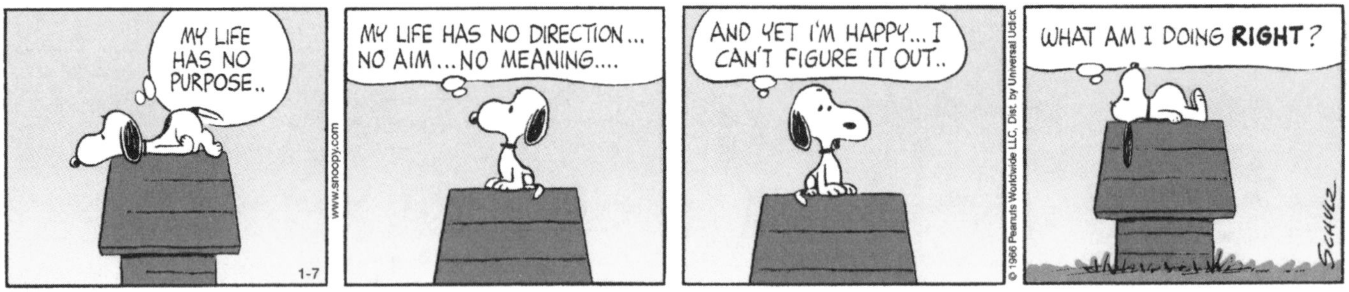
MY LIFE HAS NO PURPOSE..
www.snoopy.com
1-7
MY LIFE HAS NO DIRECTION... NO AIM...NO MEANING....
AND YET I'M HAPPY... I CAN'T FIGURE IT OUT..
© 1966 Peanuts Worldwide LLC. Dist. by Universal Udick
WHAT AM I DOING **RIGHT**?
SCHULZ

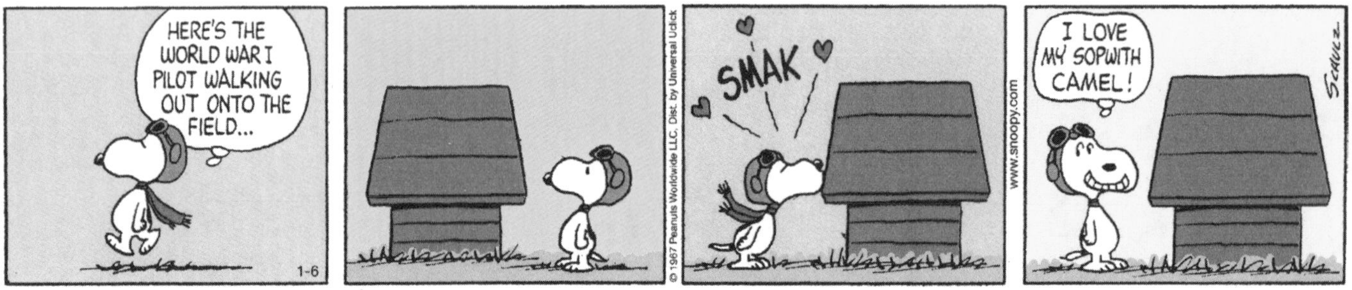
HERE'S THE WORLD WAR I PILOT WALKING OUT ONTO THE FIELD...
1-6
© 1967 Peanuts Worldwide LLC. Dist. by Universal Udick
SMAK
www.snoopy.com
I LOVE MY SOPWITH CAMEL!
SCHULZ

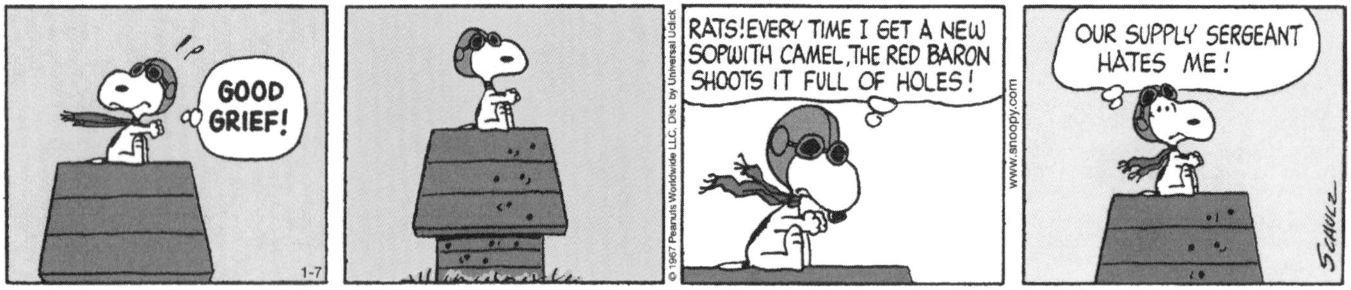
GOOD GRIEF!
1-7
© 1967 Peanuts Worldwide LLC. Dist. by Universal Udick
RATS! EVERY TIME I GET A NEW SOPWITH CAMEL, THE RED BARON SHOOTS IT FULL OF HOLES!
www.snoopy.com
OUR SUPPLY SERGEANT HATES ME!
SCHULZ

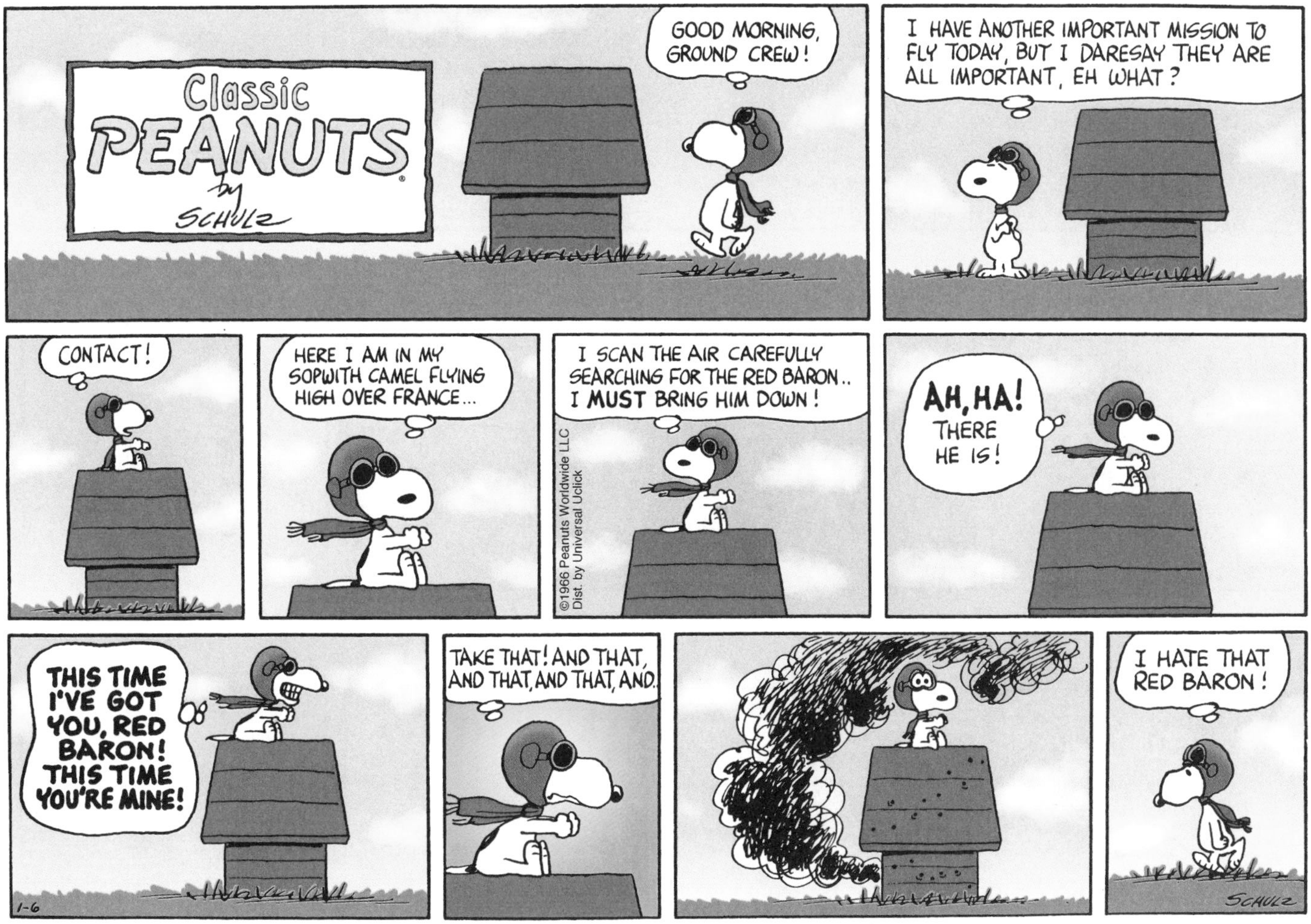
Classic PEANUTS by SCHULZ
GOOD MORNING, GROUND CREW!
I HAVE ANOTHER IMPORTANT MISSION TO FLY TODAY, BUT I DARESAY THEY ARE ALL IMPORTANT, EH WHAT?
CONTACT!
HERE I AM IN MY SOPWITH CAMEL FLYING HIGH OVER FRANCE...
I SCAN THE AIR CAREFULLY SEARCHING FOR THE RED BARON.. I MUST BRING HIM DOWN!
©1966 Peanuts Worldwide LLC
Dist. by Universal Uclick
AH, HA! THERE HE IS!
THIS TIME I'VE GOT YOU, RED BARON! THIS TIME YOU'RE MINE!
1-6
TAKE THAT! AND THAT, AND THAT, AND THAT, AND.
I HATE THAT RED BARON!
SCHULZ

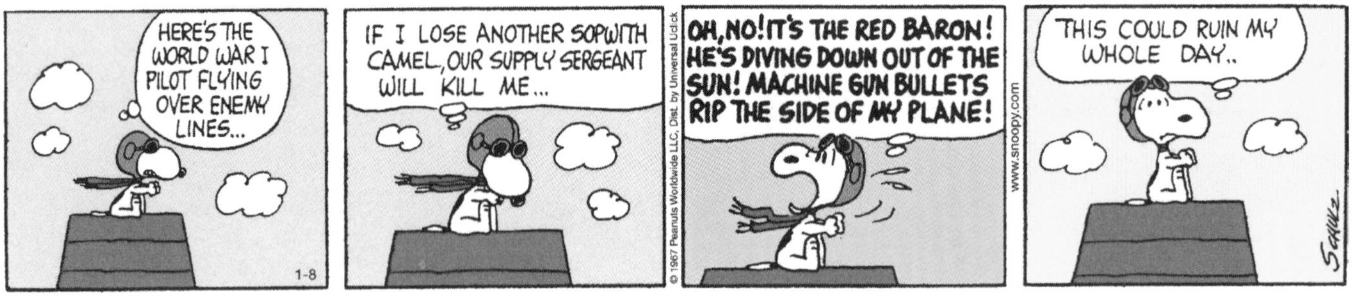
HERE'S THE WORLD WAR I PILOT FLYING OVER ENEMY LINES...
1-8
IF I LOSE ANOTHER SOPWITH CAMEL, OUR SUPPLY SERGEANT WILL KILL ME...
© 1967 Peanuts Worldwide LLC, Dist. by Universal Uclick
OH, NO! IT'S THE RED BARON! HE'S DIVING DOWN OUT OF THE SUN! MACHINE GUN BULLETS RIP THE SIDE OF MY PLANE!
www.snoopy.com
THIS COULD RUIN MY WHOLE DAY..
SCHULZ

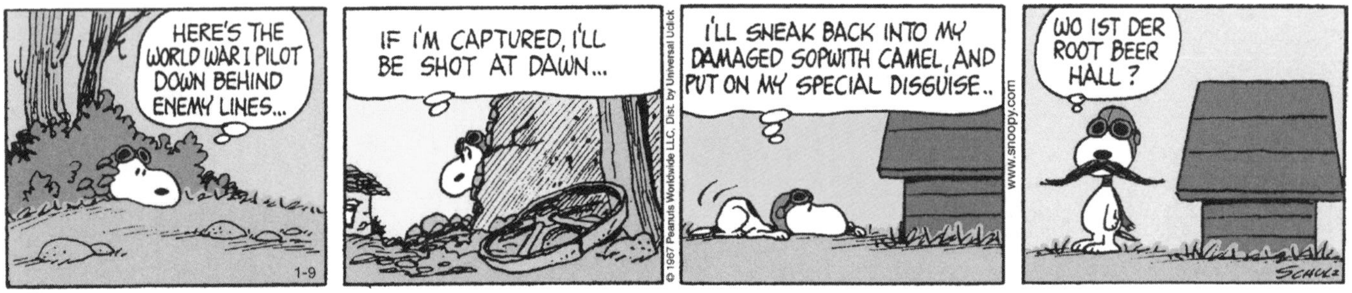
HERE'S THE WORLD WAR I PILOT DOWN BEHIND ENEMY LINES...
1-9
IF I'M CAPTURED, I'LL BE SHOT AT DAWN...
© 1967 Peanuts Worldwide LLC, Dist. by Universal Uclick
I'LL SNEAK BACK INTO MY DAMAGED SOPWITH CAMEL, AND PUT ON MY SPECIAL DISGUISE..
www.snoopy.com
WO IST DER ROOT BEER HALL?
SCHULZ

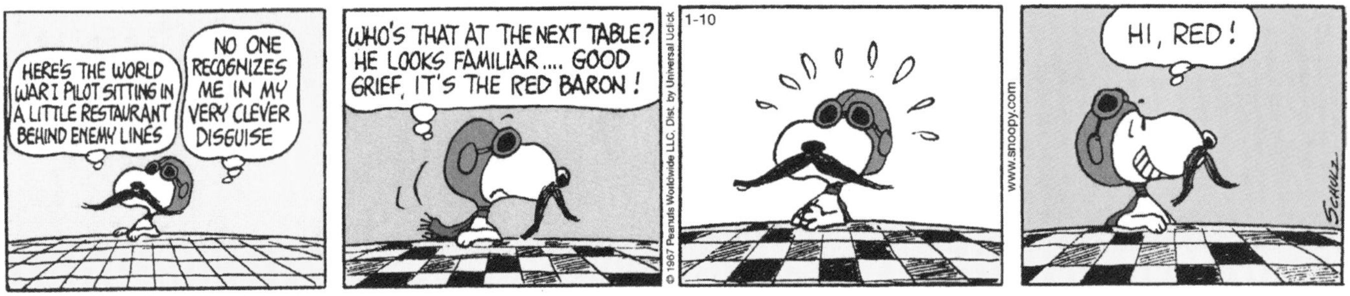
HERE'S THE WORLD WAR I PILOT SITTING IN A LITTLE RESTAURANT BEHIND ENEMY LINES
NO ONE RECOGNIZES ME IN MY VERY CLEVER DISGUISE
WHO'S THAT AT THE NEXT TABLE? HE LOOKS FAMILIAR.... GOOD GRIEF, IT'S THE RED BARON!
© 1967 Peanuts Worldwide LLC, Dist. by Universal Uclick
1-10
www.snoopy.com
HI, RED!
SCHULZ

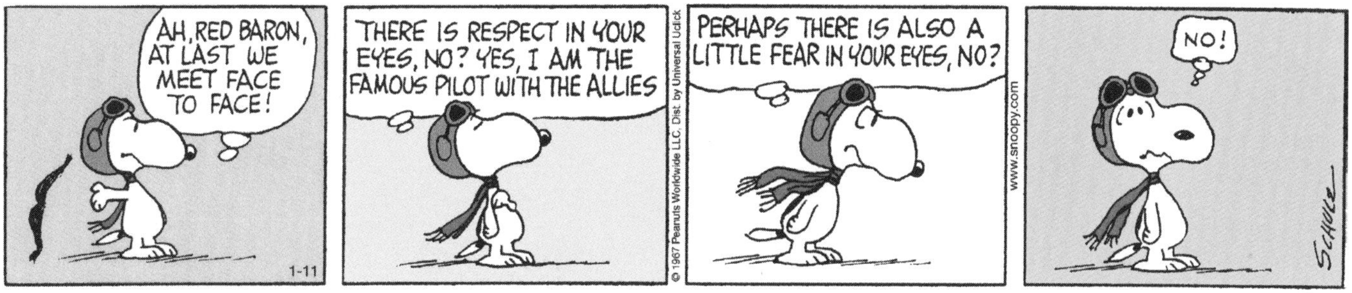
AH, RED BARON, AT LAST WE MEET FACE TO FACE!
1-11
THERE IS RESPECT IN YOUR EYES, NO? YES, I AM THE FAMOUS PILOT WITH THE ALLIES
© 1967 Peanuts Worldwide LLC. Dist. by Universal Uclick
PERHAPS THERE IS ALSO A LITTLE FEAR IN YOUR EYES, NO?
www.snoopy.com
NO!
SCHULZ

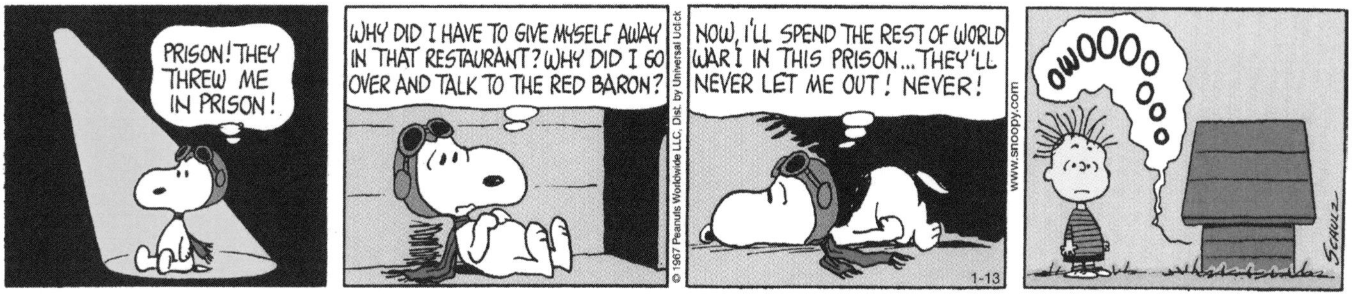
PRISON! THEY THREW ME IN PRISON!
WHY DID I HAVE TO GIVE MYSELF AWAY IN THAT RESTAURANT? WHY DID I GO OVER AND TALK TO THE RED BARON?
© 1967 Peanuts Worldwide LLC. Dist. by Universal Uclick
NOW, I'LL SPEND THE REST OF WORLD WAR I IN THIS PRISON... THEY'LL NEVER LET ME OUT! NEVER!
1-13
www.snoopy.com
OWOOOOOOOO
SCHULZ

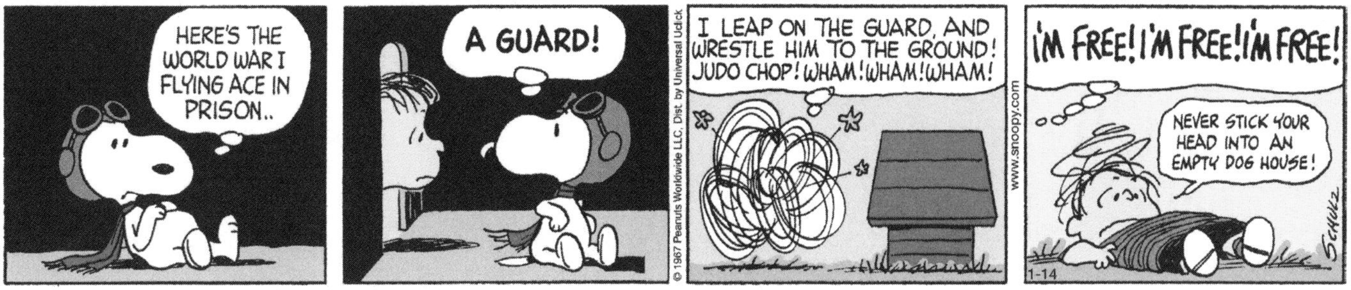
HERE'S THE WORLD WAR I FLYING ACE IN PRISON..
A GUARD!
© 1967 Peanuts Worldwide LLC. Dist. by Universal Uclick
I LEAP ON THE GUARD, AND WRESTLE HIM TO THE GROUND! JUDO CHOP! WHAM! WHAM! WHAM!
www.snoopy.com
I'M FREE! I'M FREE! I'M FREE!
NEVER STICK YOUR HEAD INTO AN EMPTY DOG HOUSE!
1-14
SCHULZ

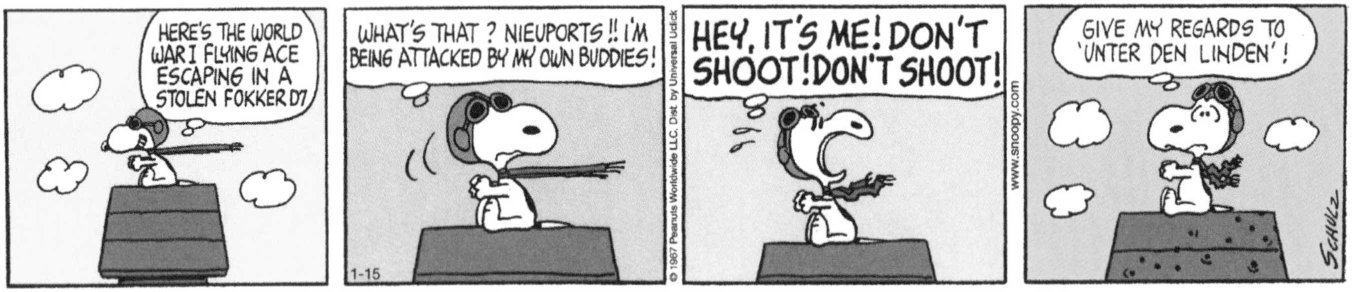
HERE'S THE WORLD WAR I FLYING ACE ESCAPING IN A STOLEN FOKKER D7
WHAT'S THAT ? NIEUPORTS !! I'M BEING ATTACKED BY MY OWN BUDDIES !
HEY, IT'S ME! DON'T SHOOT! DON'T SHOOT!
GIVE MY REGARDS TO 'UNTER DEN LINDEN' !
1-15
© 1967 Peanuts Worldwide LLC, Dist. by Universal Uclick
www.snoopy.com
SCHULZ

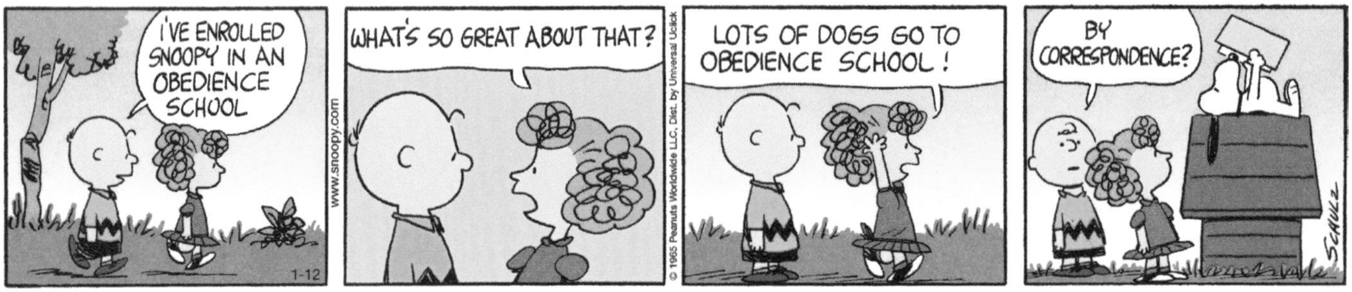
I'VE ENROLLED SNOOPY IN AN OBEDIENCE SCHOOL
WHAT'S SO GREAT ABOUT THAT ?
LOTS OF DOGS GO TO OBEDIENCE SCHOOL !
BY CORRESPONDENCE ?
1-12
www.snoopy.com
© 1965 Peanuts Worldwide LLC, Dist. by Universal Uclick
SCHULZ

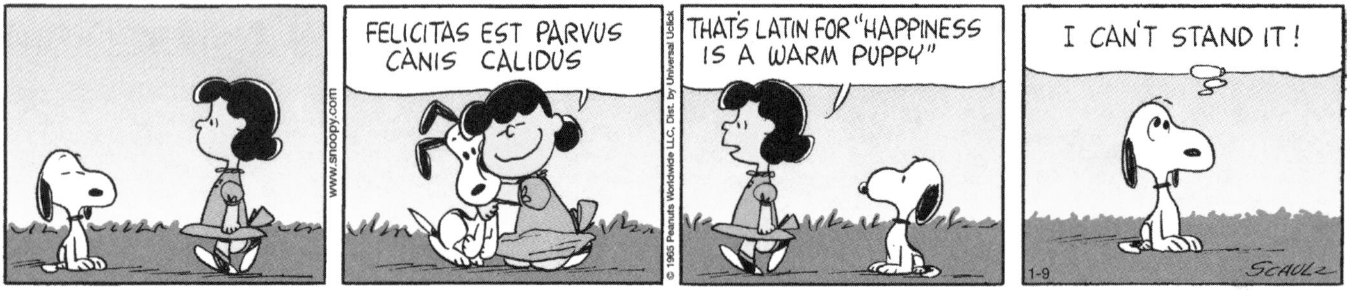
FELICITAS EST PARVUS CANIS CALIDUS
THAT'S LATIN FOR "HAPPINESS IS A WARM PUPPY"
I CAN'T STAND IT !
www.snoopy.com
© 1965 Peanuts Worldwide LLC, Dist. by Universal Uclick
1-9
SCHULZ

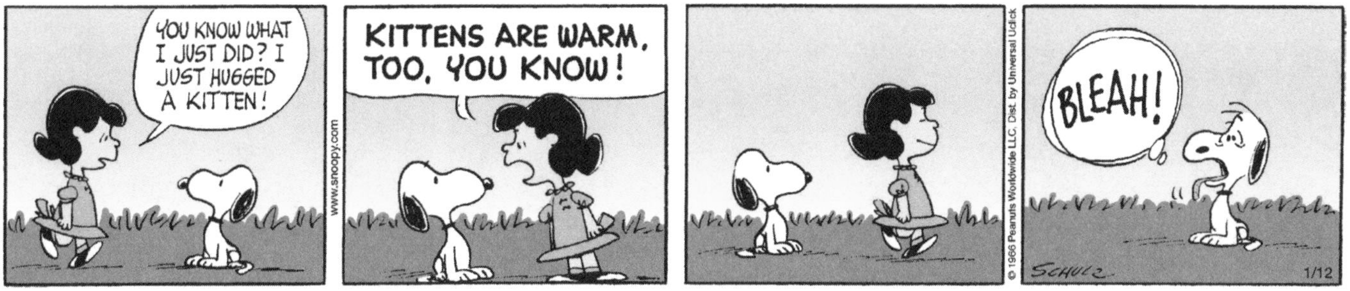
YOU KNOW WHAT I JUST DID? I JUST HUGGED A KITTEN!
KITTENS ARE WARM, TOO, YOU KNOW!
BLEAH!
www.snoopy.com
© 1966 Peanuts Worldwide LLC, Dist. by Universal Uclick
SCHULZ
1/12

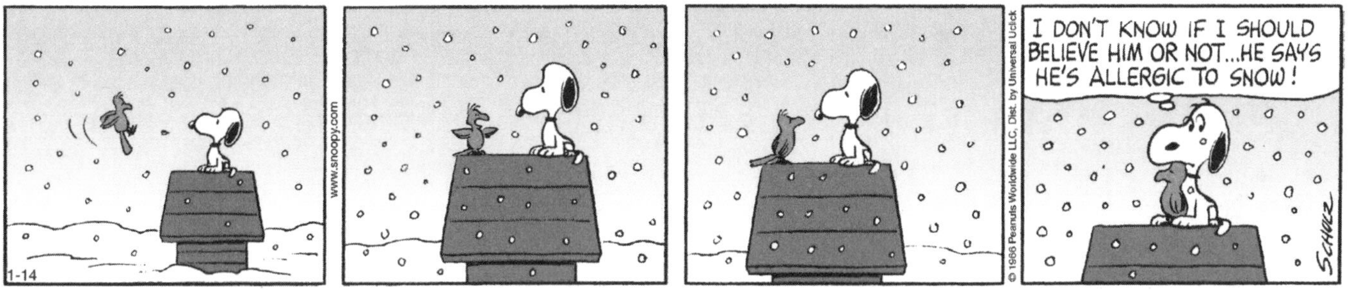
I DON'T KNOW IF I SHOULD BELIEVE HIM OR NOT...HE SAYS HE'S ALLERGIC TO SNOW!
1-14
www.snoopy.com
© 1966 Peanuts Worldwide LLC, Dist. by Universal Uclick
SCHULZ

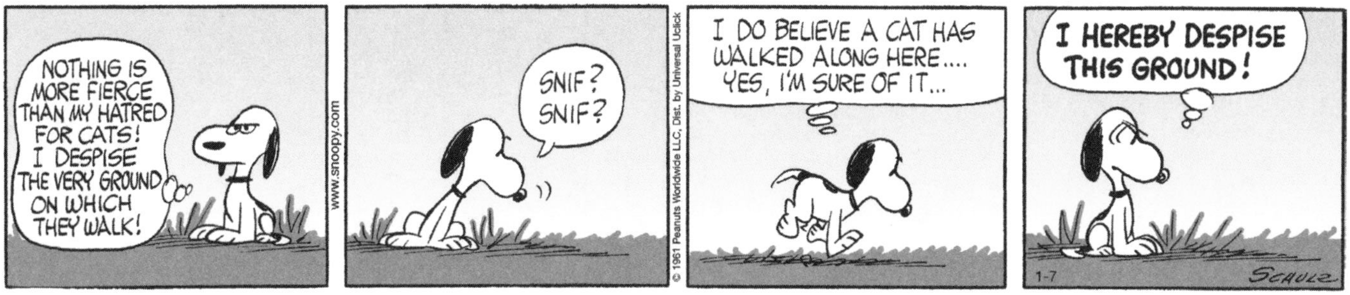
NOTHING IS MORE FIERCE THAN MY HATRED FOR CATS! I DESPISE THE VERY GROUND ON WHICH THEY WALK!
SNIF? SNIF?
I DO BELIEVE A CAT HAS WALKED ALONG HERE.... YES, I'M SURE OF IT...
I HEREBY DESPISE THIS GROUND!
www.snoopy.com
© 1961 Peanuts Worldwide LLC, Dist. by Universal Uclick
1-7
SCHULZ

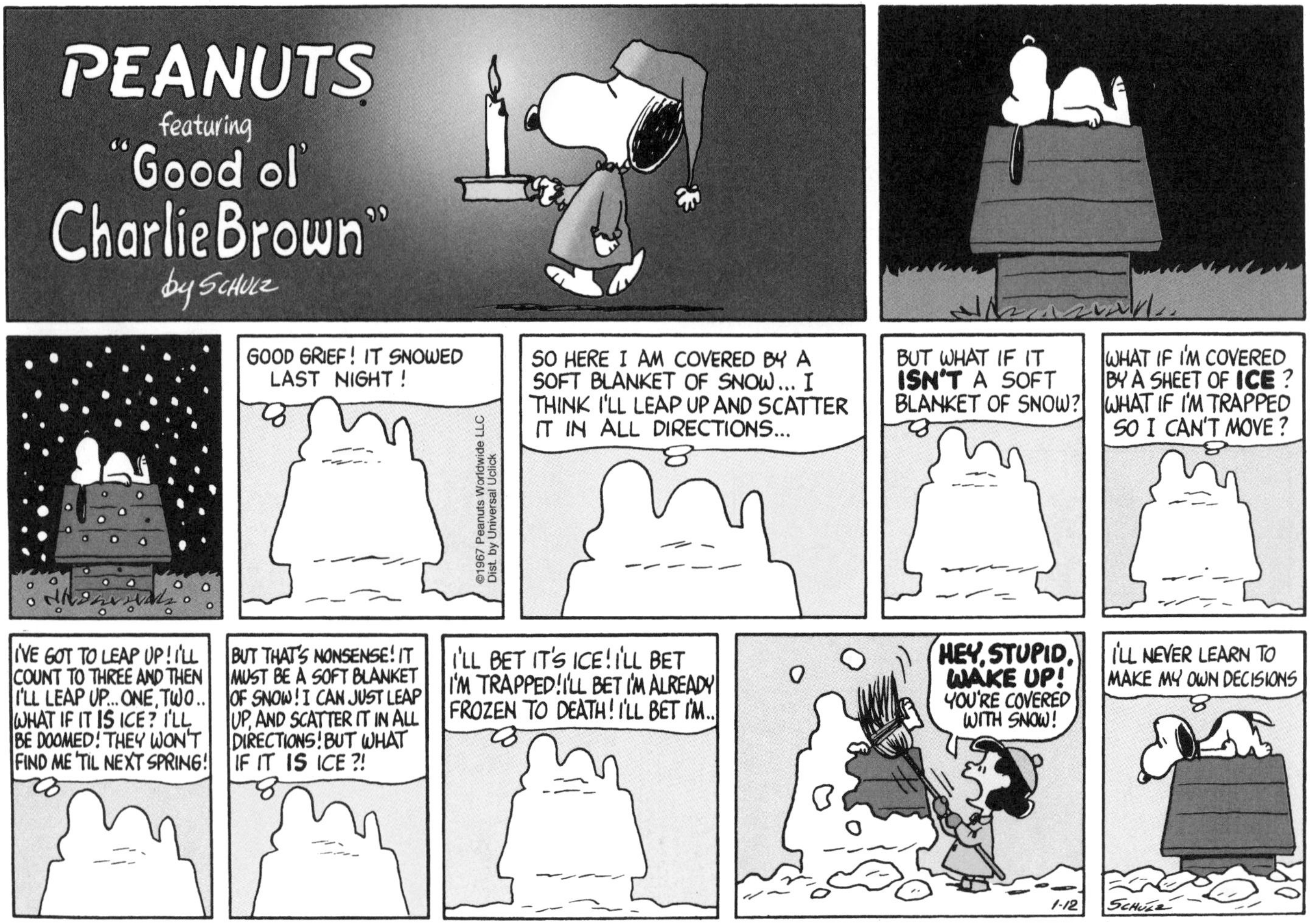
PEANUTS
featuring
"Good ol' Charlie Brown"
by SCHULZ
©1967 Peanuts Worldwide LLC
Dist. by Universal Uclick
GOOD GRIEF! IT SNOWED LAST NIGHT!
SO HERE I AM COVERED BY A SOFT BLANKET OF SNOW... I THINK I'LL LEAP UP AND SCATTER IT IN ALL DIRECTIONS...
BUT WHAT IF IT **ISN'T** A SOFT BLANKET OF SNOW?
WHAT IF I'M COVERED BY A SHEET OF **ICE**? WHAT IF I'M TRAPPED SO I CAN'T MOVE?
I'VE GOT TO LEAP UP! I'LL COUNT TO THREE AND THEN I'LL LEAP UP... ONE, TWO.. WHAT IF IT **IS** ICE? I'LL BE DOOMED! THEY WON'T FIND ME 'TIL NEXT SPRING!
BUT THAT'S NONSENSE! IT MUST BE A SOFT BLANKET OF SNOW! I CAN JUST LEAP UP, AND SCATTER IT IN ALL DIRECTIONS! BUT WHAT IF IT **IS** ICE?!
I'LL BET IT'S ICE! I'LL BET I'M TRAPPED! I'LL BET I'M ALREADY FROZEN TO DEATH! I'LL BET I'M..
HEY, STUPID, WAKE UP! YOU'RE COVERED WITH SNOW!
1-12
I'LL NEVER LEARN TO MAKE MY OWN DECISIONS
SCHULZ

www.snoopy.com
© 1965 Peanuts Worldwide LLC, Dist. by Universal Uclick
Z
FORTUNATELY, I'M PRACTICING A PIECE WHERE I CAN PLAY **AROUND** HIS NOSE!
Z
1-10
SCHULZ

www.snoopy.com
© 1965 Peanuts Worldwide LLC, Dist. by Universal Uclick
BLEAH!
WITHHOLD MY COMPLIMENTS TO THE CHEF!
1-14
SCHULZ

OH, NO!
1-16
www.snoopy.com
THIS IS GOING TO BE ONE OF THOSE "TOSS AND TURN" NIGHTS WHERE I CAN'T GET TO SLEEP...
© 1965 Peanuts Worldwide LLC, Dist. by Universal Uclick
WHEN NONE OF THE NORMAL SLEEPING POSITIONS WORK, YOU HAVE TO TRY UNUSUAL ONES...
Z
SCHULZ

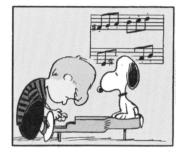

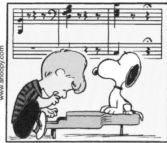

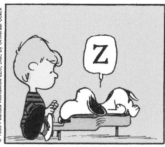

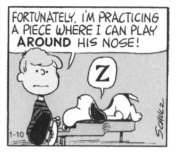

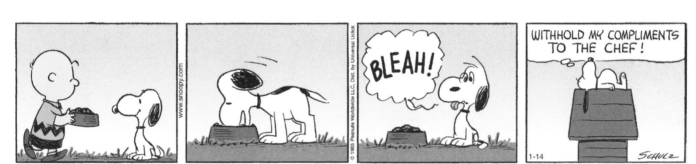

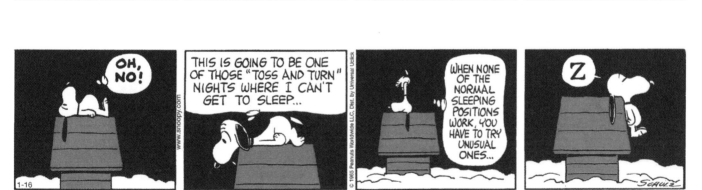

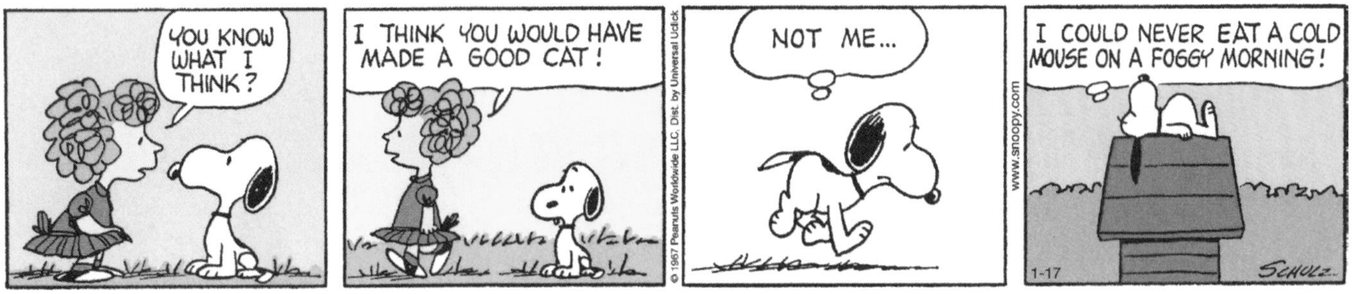
YOU KNOW WHAT I THINK?
I THINK YOU WOULD HAVE MADE A GOOD CAT!
© 1967 Peanuts Worldwide LLC. Dist. by Universal Uclick
NOT ME...
I COULD NEVER EAT A COLD MOUSE ON A FOGGY MORNING!
www.snoopy.com
1-17
SCHULZ

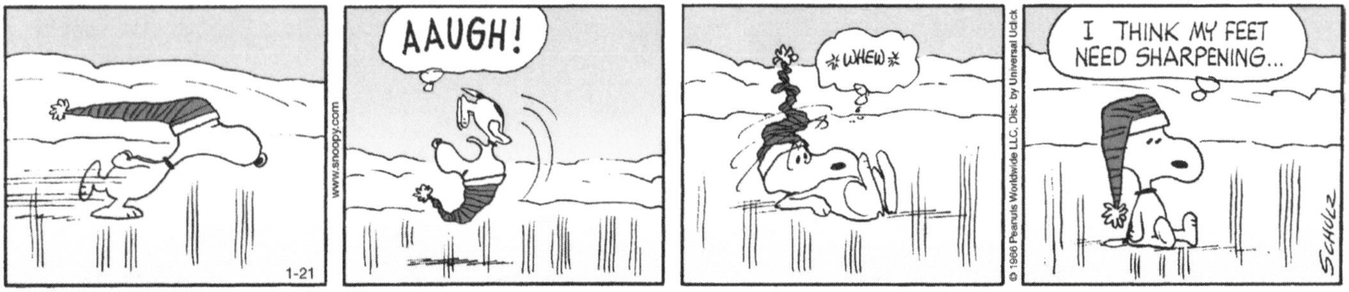
1-21
www.snoopy.com
AAUGH!
WHEW
© 1966 Peanuts Worldwide LLC. Dist. by Universal Uclick
I THINK MY FEET NEED SHARPENING...
SCHULZ

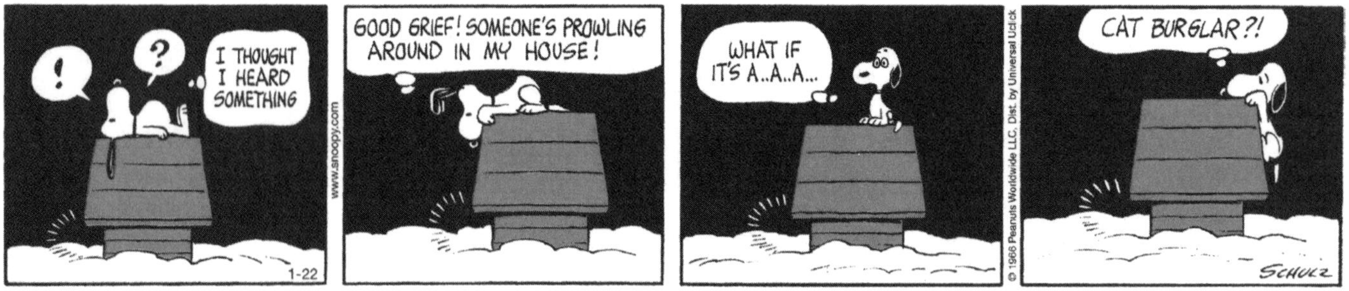
!
?
I THOUGHT I HEARD SOMETHING
1-22
www.snoopy.com
GOOD GRIEF! SOMEONE'S PROWLING AROUND IN MY HOUSE!
WHAT IF IT'S A..A..A...
© 1966 Peanuts Worldwide LLC. Dist. by Universal Uclick
CAT BURGLAR?!
SCHULZ

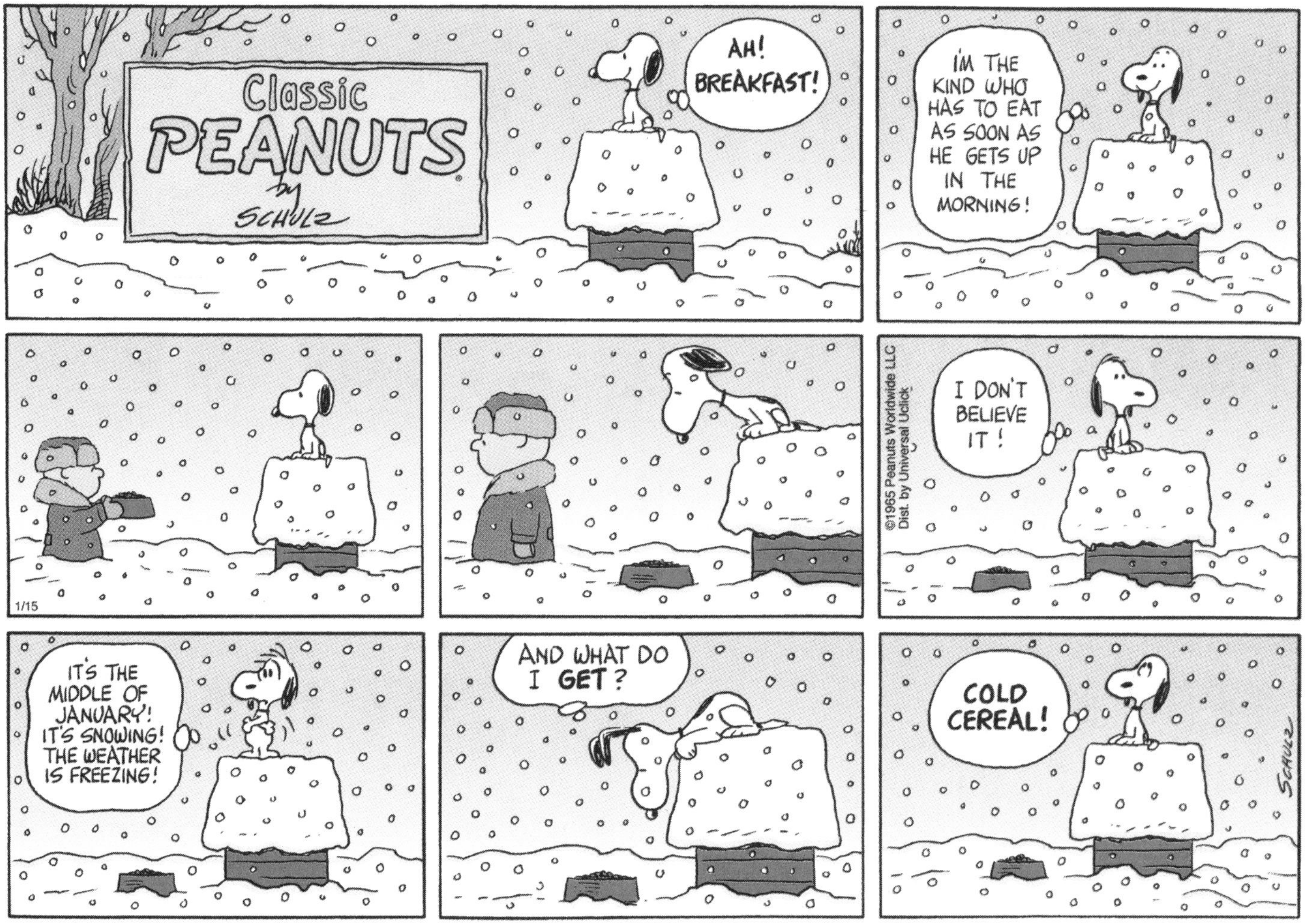
Classic
PEANUTS
by
SCHULZ
AH! BREAKFAST!
I'M THE KIND WHO HAS TO EAT AS SOON AS HE GETS UP IN THE MORNING!
1/15
©1965 Peanuts Worldwide LLC
Dist. by Universal Uclick
I DON'T BELIEVE IT!
IT'S THE MIDDLE OF JANUARY! IT'S SNOWING! THE WEATHER IS FREEZING!
AND WHAT DO I GET?
COLD CEREAL!
SCHULZ

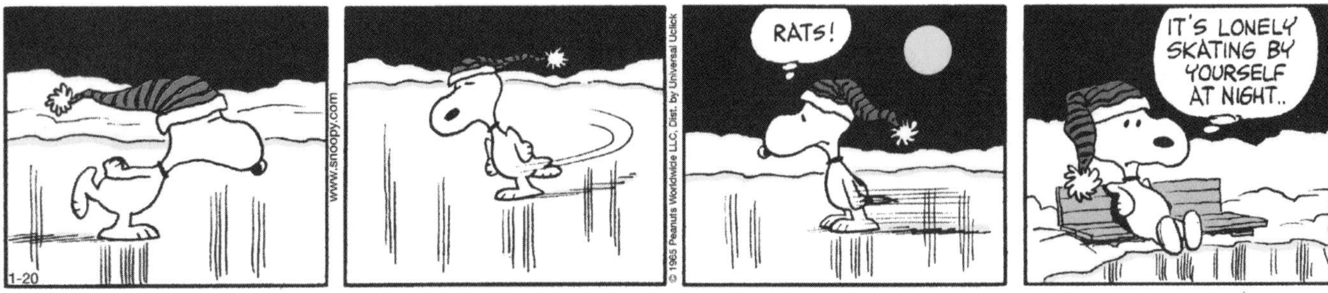
1-20
www.snoopy.com
© 1965 Peanuts Worldwide LLC, Dist. by Universal Uclick
RATS!
IT'S LONELY SKATING BY YOURSELF AT NIGHT..
SCHULZ

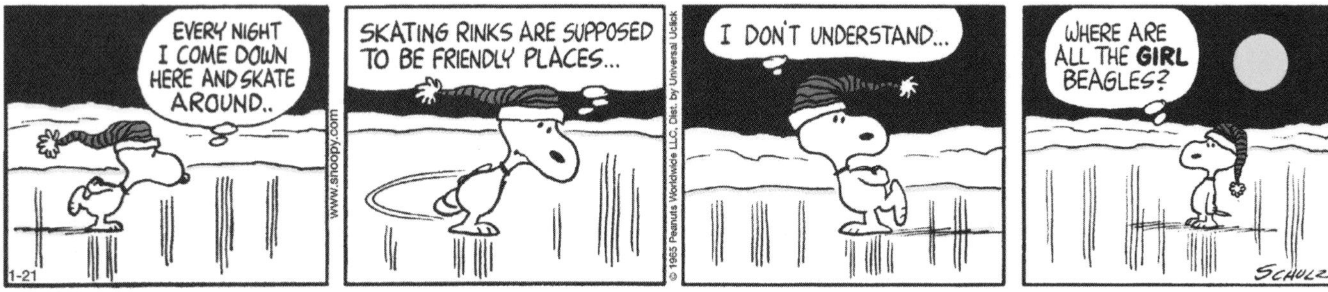
EVERY NIGHT I COME DOWN HERE AND SKATE AROUND..
1-21
www.snoopy.com
SKATING RINKS ARE SUPPOSED TO BE FRIENDLY PLACES...
© 1965 Peanuts Worldwide LLC, Dist. by Universal Uclick
I DON'T UNDERSTAND...
WHERE ARE ALL THE **GIRL** BEAGLES?
SCHULZ

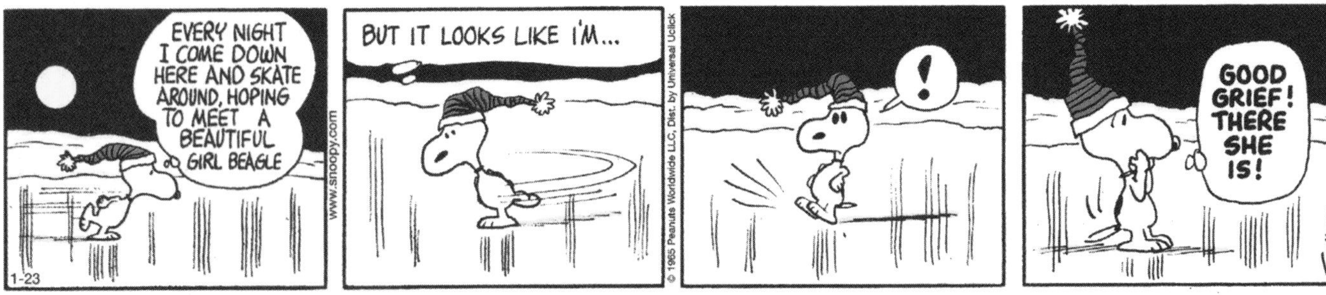
EVERY NIGHT I COME DOWN HERE AND SKATE AROUND, HOPING TO MEET A BEAUTIFUL GIRL BEAGLE
1-23
www.snoopy.com
BUT IT LOOKS LIKE I'M...
© 1965 Peanuts Worldwide LLC, Dist. by Universal Uclick
!
GOOD GRIEF! THERE SHE IS!
SCHULZ

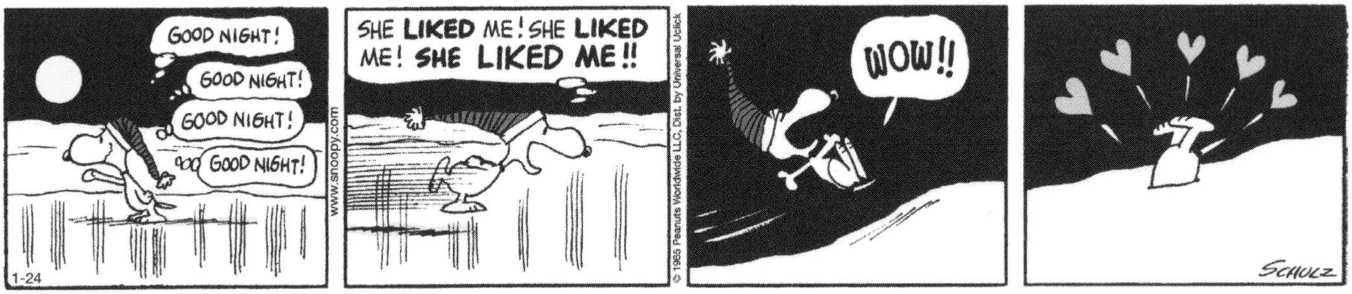
GOOD NIGHT!
GOOD NIGHT!
GOOD NIGHT!
GOOD NIGHT!
1-24
www.snoopy.com
SHE LIKED ME! SHE LIKED ME! SHE LIKED ME!!
© 1965 Peanuts Worldwide LLC, Dist. by Universal Uclick
WOW!!
SCHULZ

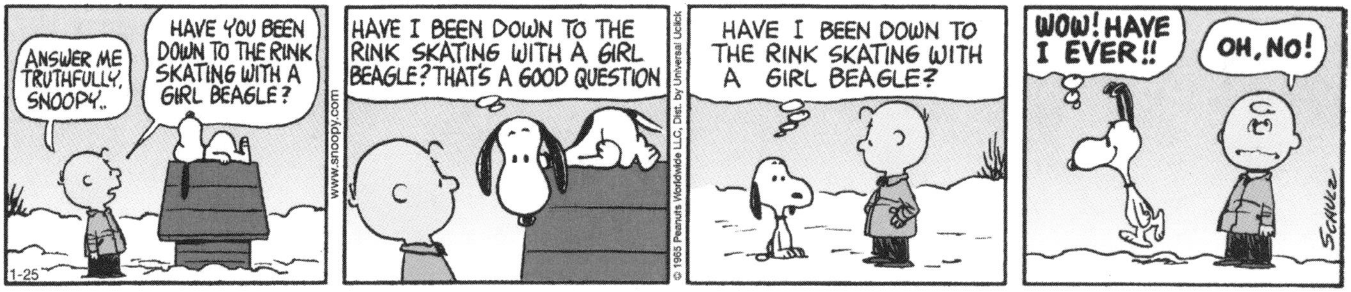
ANSWER ME TRUTHFULLY, SNOOPY..
HAVE YOU BEEN DOWN TO THE RINK SKATING WITH A GIRL BEAGLE?
1-25
www.snoopy.com
HAVE I BEEN DOWN TO THE RINK SKATING WITH A GIRL BEAGLE? THAT'S A GOOD QUESTION
© 1965 Peanuts Worldwide LLC, Dist. by Universal Uclick
HAVE I BEEN DOWN TO THE RINK SKATING WITH A GIRL BEAGLE?
WOW! HAVE I EVER!!
OH, NO!
SCHULZ

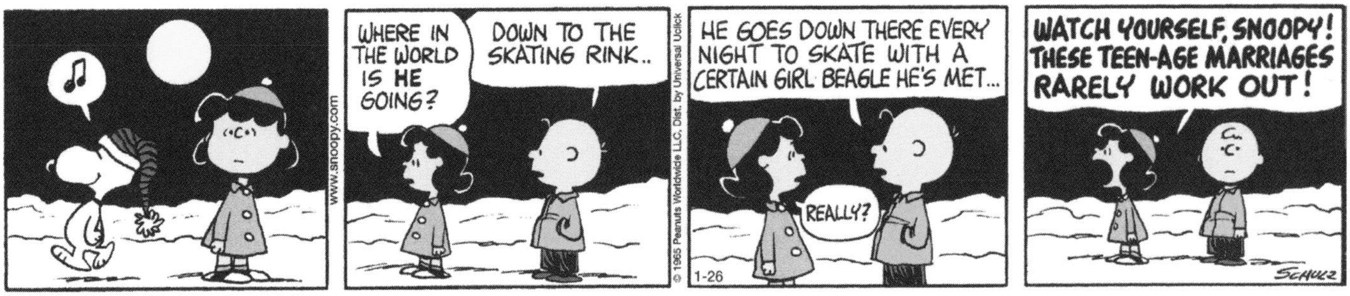
www.snoopy.com
WHERE IN THE WORLD IS HE GOING?
DOWN TO THE SKATING RINK..
© 1965 Peanuts Worldwide LLC, Dist. by Universal Uclick
HE GOES DOWN THERE EVERY NIGHT TO SKATE WITH A CERTAIN GIRL BEAGLE HE'S MET...
REALLY?
1-26
WATCH YOURSELF, SNOOPY! THESE TEEN-AGE MARRIAGES RARELY WORK OUT!
SCHULZ

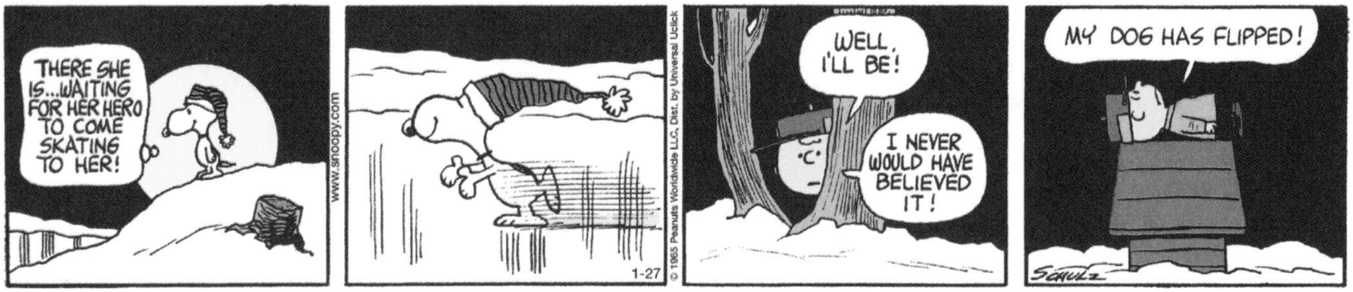
THERE SHE IS...WAITING FOR HER HERO TO COME SKATING TO HER!
www.snoopy.com
1-27
© 1965 Peanuts Worldwide LLC, Dist. by Universal Uclick
WELL, I'LL BE!
I NEVER WOULD HAVE BELIEVED IT!
MY DOG HAS FLIPPED!
SCHULZ

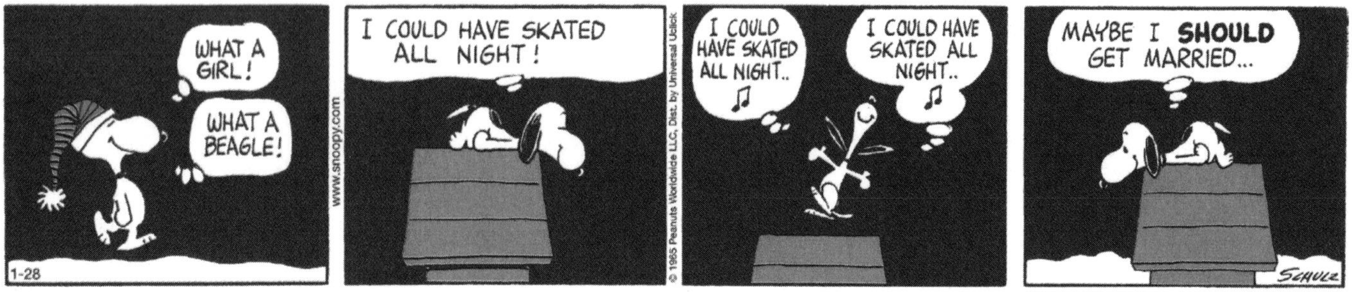
WHAT A GIRL!
WHAT A BEAGLE!
1-28
www.snoopy.com
I COULD HAVE SKATED ALL NIGHT!
© 1965 Peanuts Worldwide LLC, Dist. by Universal Uclick
I COULD HAVE SKATED ALL NIGHT.. ♫
I COULD HAVE SKATED ALL NIGHT.. ♫
MAYBE I **SHOULD** GET MARRIED...
SCHULZ

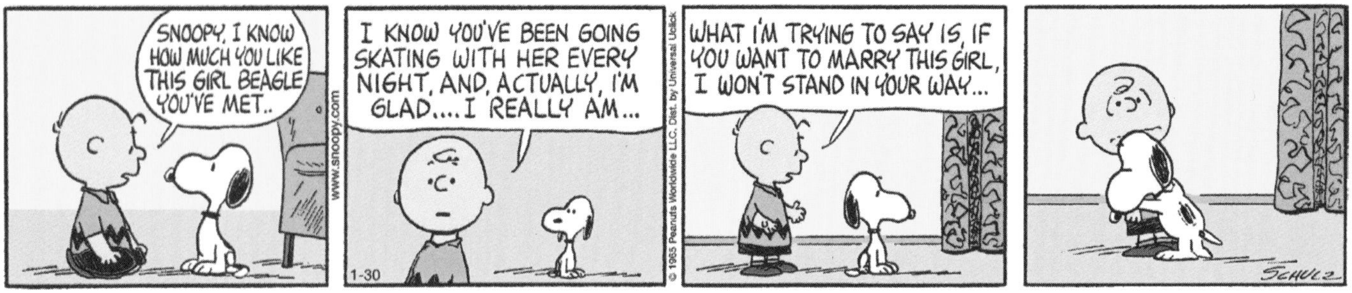
SNOOPY, I KNOW HOW MUCH YOU LIKE THIS GIRL BEAGLE YOU'VE MET..
www.snoopy.com
I KNOW YOU'VE BEEN GOING SKATING WITH HER EVERY NIGHT, AND, ACTUALLY, I'M GLAD.... I REALLY AM...
1-30
© 1965 Peanuts Worldwide LLC, Dist. by Universal Uclick
WHAT I'M TRYING TO SAY IS, IF YOU WANT TO MARRY THIS GIRL, I WON'T STAND IN YOUR WAY...
SCHULZ

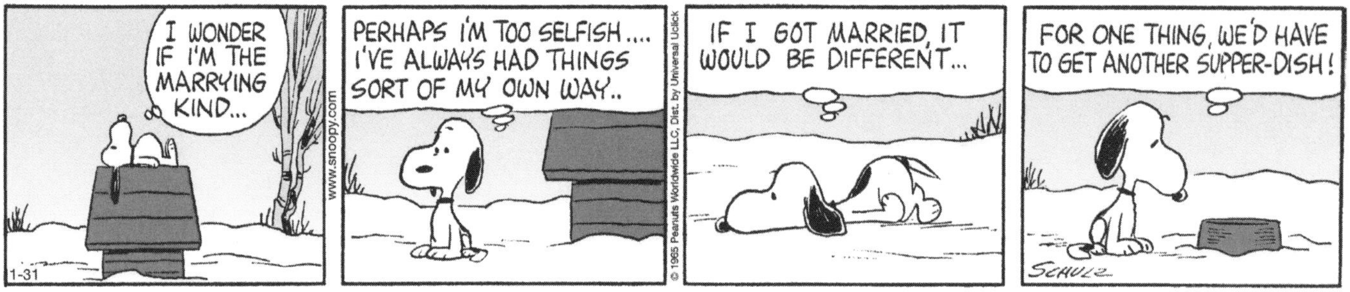
I WONDER IF I'M THE MARRYING KIND...
1-31
www.snoopy.com
PERHAPS I'M TOO SELFISH.... I'VE ALWAYS HAD THINGS SORT OF MY OWN WAY..
© 1965 Peanuts Worldwide LLC, Dist. by Universal Uclick
IF I GOT MARRIED, IT WOULD BE DIFFERENT...
FOR ONE THING, WE'D HAVE TO GET ANOTHER SUPPER-DISH!
SCHULZ

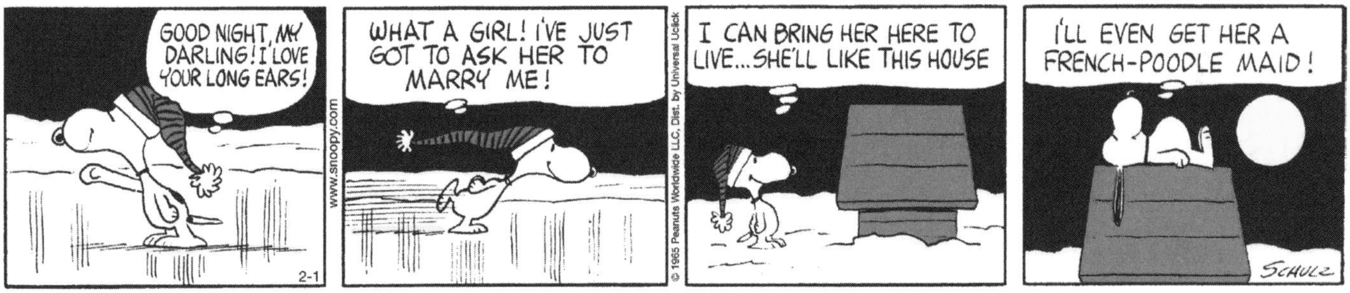
GOOD NIGHT, MY DARLING! I LOVE YOUR LONG EARS!
2-1
www.snoopy.com
WHAT A GIRL! I'VE JUST GOT TO ASK HER TO MARRY ME!
© 1965 Peanuts Worldwide LLC, Dist. by Universal Uclick
I CAN BRING HER HERE TO LIVE...SHE'LL LIKE THIS HOUSE
I'LL EVEN GET HER A FRENCH-POODLE MAID!
SCHULZ

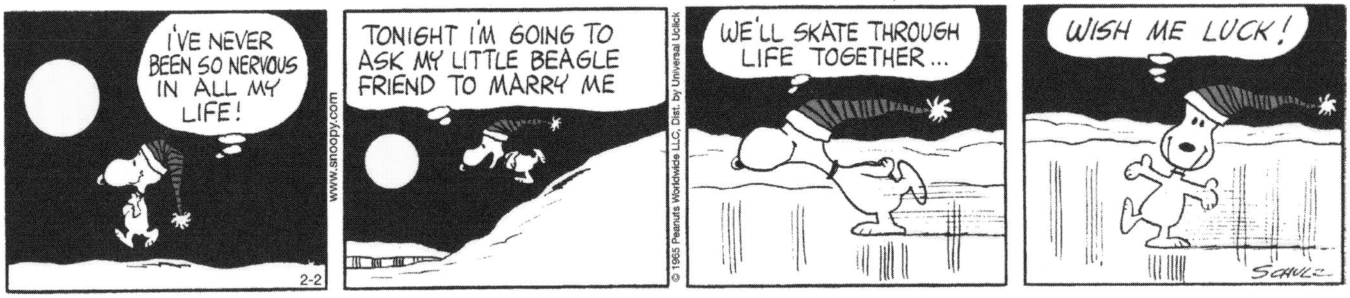
I'VE NEVER BEEN SO NERVOUS IN ALL MY LIFE!
2-2
www.snoopy.com
TONIGHT I'M GOING TO ASK MY LITTLE BEAGLE FRIEND TO MARRY ME
© 1965 Peanuts Worldwide LLC, Dist. by Universal Uclick
WE'LL SKATE THROUGH LIFE TOGETHER...
WISH ME LUCK!
SCHULZ

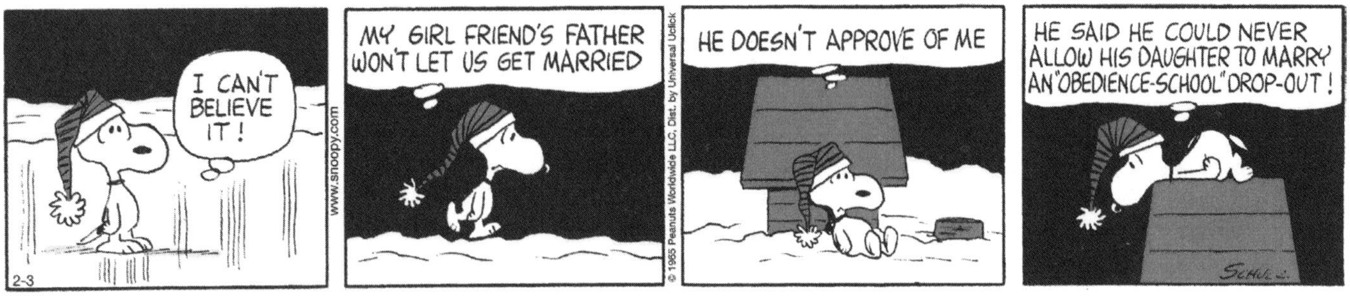
2-3
I CAN'T BELIEVE IT!
MY GIRL FRIEND'S FATHER WON'T LET US GET MARRIED
HE DOESN'T APPROVE OF ME
HE SAID HE COULD NEVER ALLOW HIS DAUGHTER TO MARRY AN "OBEDIENCE-SCHOOL" DROP-OUT!
www.snoopy.com
© 1965 Peanuts Worldwide LLC, Dist. by Universal Uclick

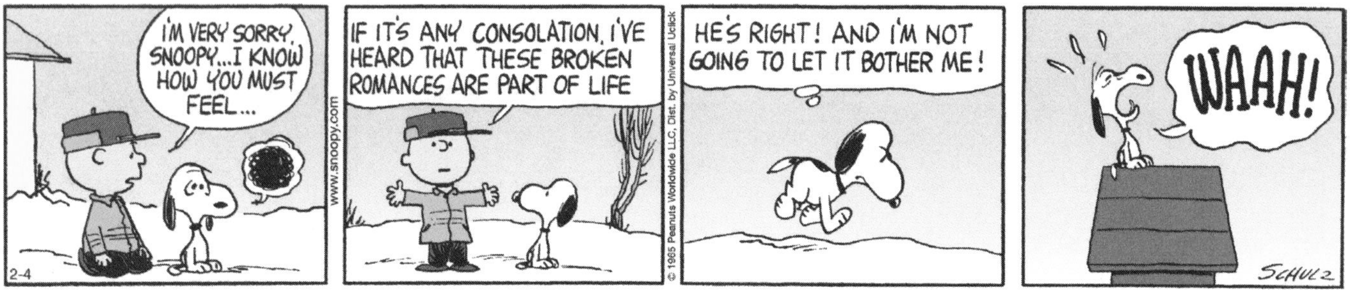
2-4
I'M VERY SORRY, SNOOPY... I KNOW HOW YOU MUST FEEL...
IF IT'S ANY CONSOLATION, I'VE HEARD THAT THESE BROKEN ROMANCES ARE PART OF LIFE
HE'S RIGHT! AND I'M NOT GOING TO LET IT BOTHER ME!
WAAH!
SCHULZ
www.snoopy.com
© 1965 Peanuts Worldwide LLC, Dist. by Universal Uclick

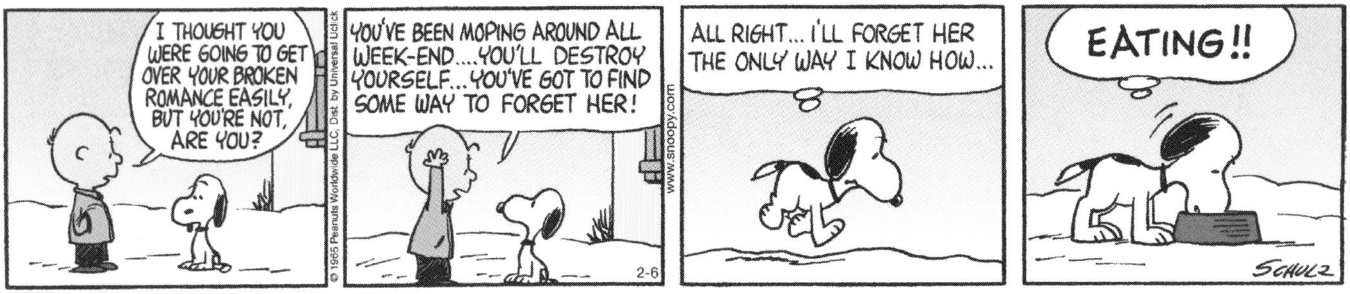
I THOUGHT YOU WERE GOING TO GET OVER YOUR BROKEN ROMANCE EASILY, BUT YOU'RE NOT, ARE YOU?
YOU'VE BEEN MOPING AROUND ALL WEEK-END.... YOU'LL DESTROY YOURSELF... YOU'VE GOT TO FIND SOME WAY TO FORGET HER!
2-6
ALL RIGHT... I'LL FORGET HER THE ONLY WAY I KNOW HOW...
EATING!!
SCHULZ
© 1965 Peanuts Worldwide LLC, Dist. by Universal Uclick
www.snoopy.com

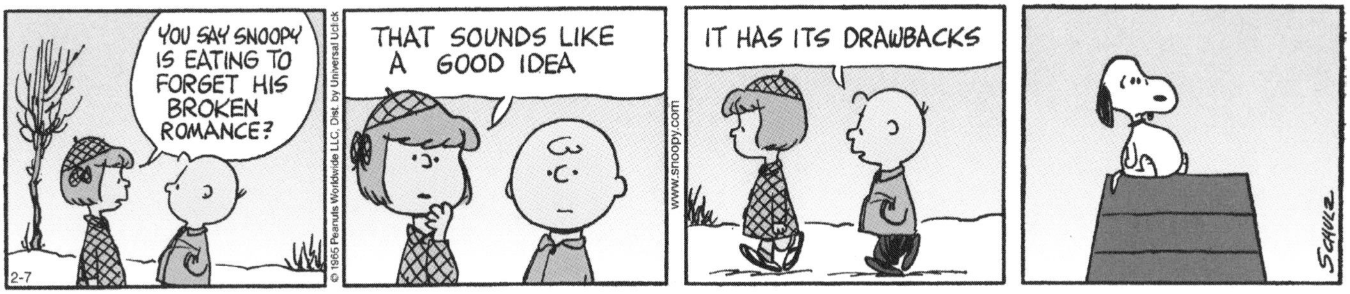
YOU SAY SNOOPY IS EATING TO FORGET HIS BROKEN ROMANCE?
THAT SOUNDS LIKE A GOOD IDEA
IT HAS ITS DRAWBACKS
2-7
© 1965 Peanuts Worldwide LLC, Dist. by Universal Uclick
www.snoopy.com
SCHULZ

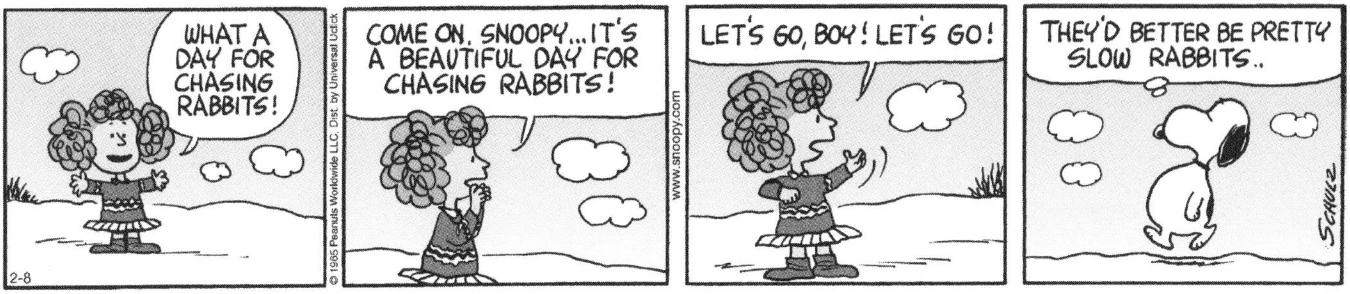
WHAT A DAY FOR CHASING RABBITS!
COME ON, SNOOPY...IT'S A BEAUTIFUL DAY FOR CHASING RABBITS!
LET'S GO, BOY! LET'S GO!
THEY'D BETTER BE PRETTY SLOW RABBITS..
2-8
© 1965 Peanuts Worldwide LLC, Dist. by Universal Uclick
www.snoopy.com
SCHULZ

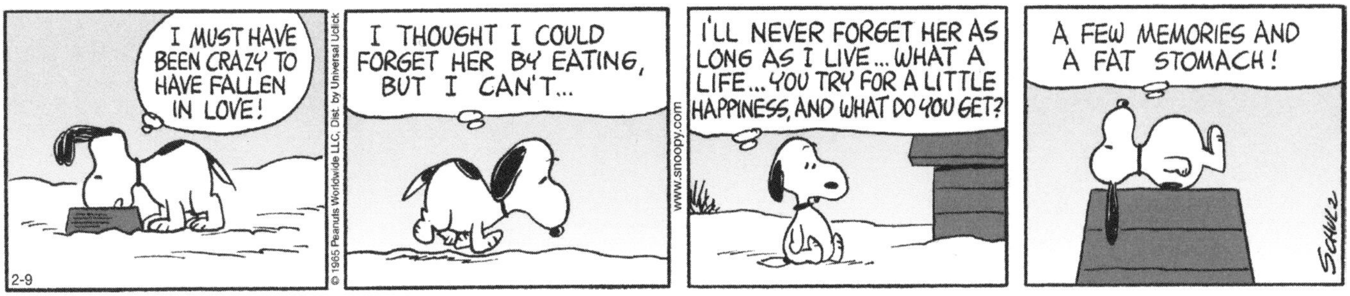
I MUST HAVE BEEN CRAZY TO HAVE FALLEN IN LOVE!
I THOUGHT I COULD FORGET HER BY EATING, BUT I CAN'T...
I'LL NEVER FORGET HER AS LONG AS I LIVE...WHAT A LIFE...YOU TRY FOR A LITTLE HAPPINESS, AND WHAT DO YOU GET?
A FEW MEMORIES AND A FAT STOMACH!
2-9
© 1965 Peanuts Worldwide LLC, Dist. by Universal Uclick
www.snoopy.com
SCHULZ

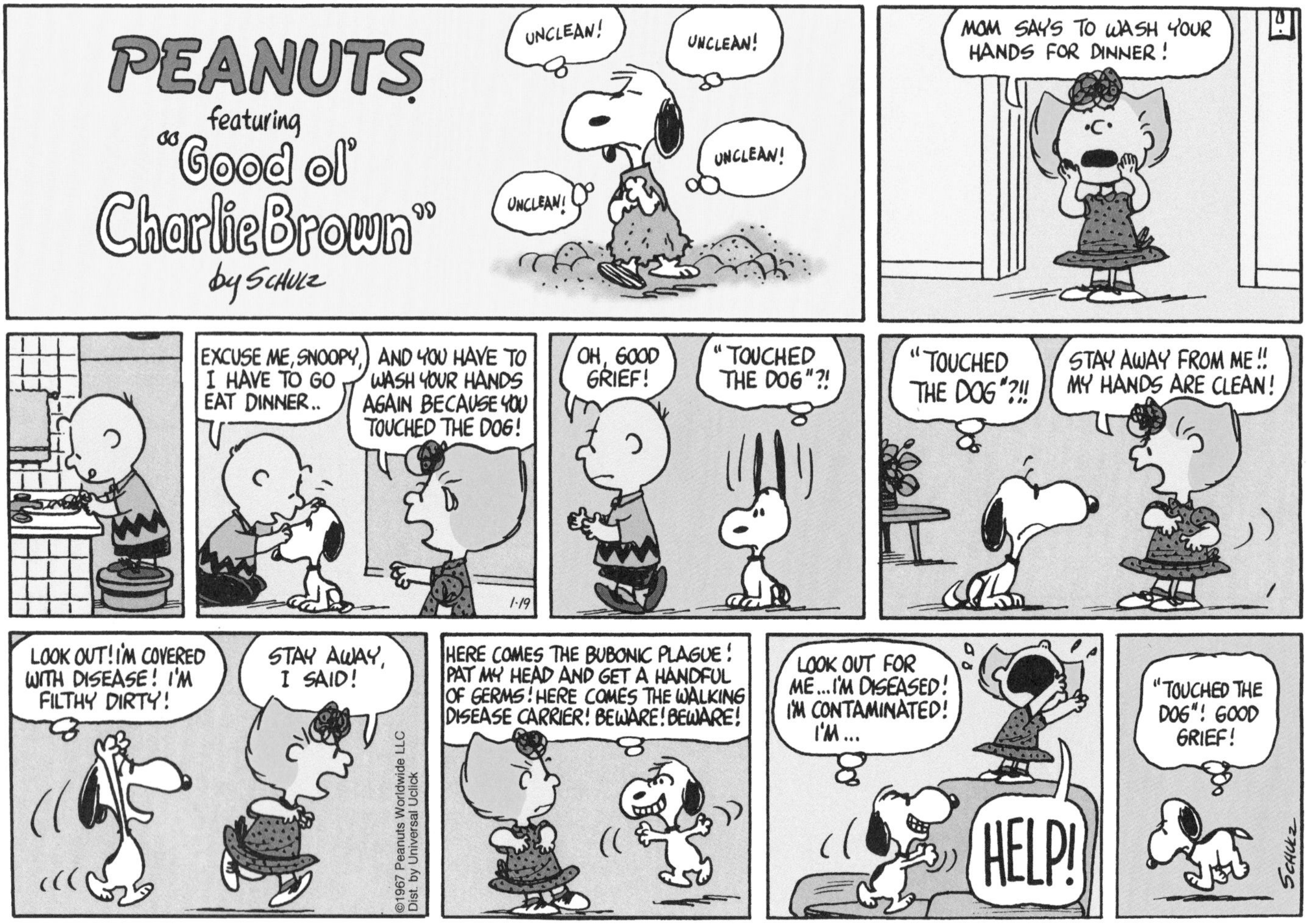
PEANUTS
featuring "Good ol' CharlieBrown"
by SCHULZ
UNCLEAN!
UNCLEAN!
UNCLEAN!
UNCLEAN!
MOM SAYS TO WASH YOUR HANDS FOR DINNER!
EXCUSE ME, SNOOPY, I HAVE TO GO EAT DINNER..
AND YOU HAVE TO WASH YOUR HANDS AGAIN BECAUSE YOU TOUCHED THE DOG!
1-19
OH, GOOD GRIEF!
"TOUCHED THE DOG"?!
"TOUCHED THE DOG"?!!
STAY AWAY FROM ME!! MY HANDS ARE CLEAN!
LOOK OUT! I'M COVERED WITH DISEASE! I'M FILTHY DIRTY!
STAY AWAY, I SAID!
HERE COMES THE BUBONIC PLAGUE! PAT MY HEAD AND GET A HANDFUL OF GERMS! HERE COMES THE WALKING DISEASE CARRIER! BEWARE! BEWARE!
LOOK OUT FOR ME...I'M DISEASED! I'M CONTAMINATED! I'M...
HELP!
"TOUCHED THE DOG"! GOOD GRIEF!
SCHULZ

THERE'S A BURGLAR IN MY HOUSE!
OH, WHY DO I LIVE ALONE? I COULD HAVE BEEN MURDERED IN MY BED! THIS IS AWFUL!
HOW DID HE GET IN? WHY DIDN'T ANYONE SOUND THE ALARM? WHAT'S WRONG WITH THE STUPID WATCHDOG?
I'M THE STUPID WATCHDOG!
www.snoopy.com
1-23
© 1966 Peanuts Worldwide LLC. Dist. by Universal Uclick
SCHULZ

THERE'S A BURGLAR DOWN THERE...I CAN HEAR HIM!
I CAN HEAR TWO OF THEM! I WONDER WHAT THEY'RE AFTER.. MAYBE MY SILVER CANDLESTICKS...
THEY'RE COMING UP THE STAIRWAY!
THEY'RE STEALING MY VAN GOGH!
www.snoopy.com
1-24
© 1966 Peanuts Worldwide LLC. Dist. by Universal Uclick
SCHULZ

ART THIEVES!
CAN YOU IMAGINE THOSE TWO BIRDS? THEY THOUGHT THEY COULD SNEAK INTO MY HOME, AND STEAL MY VALUABLE VAN GOGH!
WELL, I SURE SHOWED THEM! A LITTLE MANUAL LABOR WILL TEACH THEM A LESSON...
DIG, THIEVES, DIG!
www.snoopy.com
1-25
© 1966 Peanuts Worldwide LLC. Dist. by Universal Uclick
SCHULZ

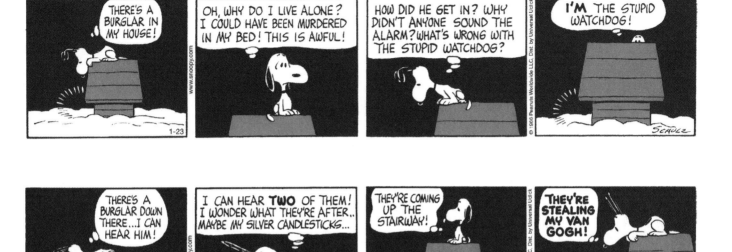

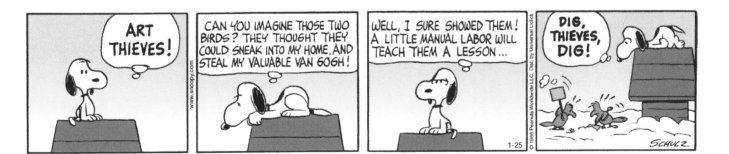

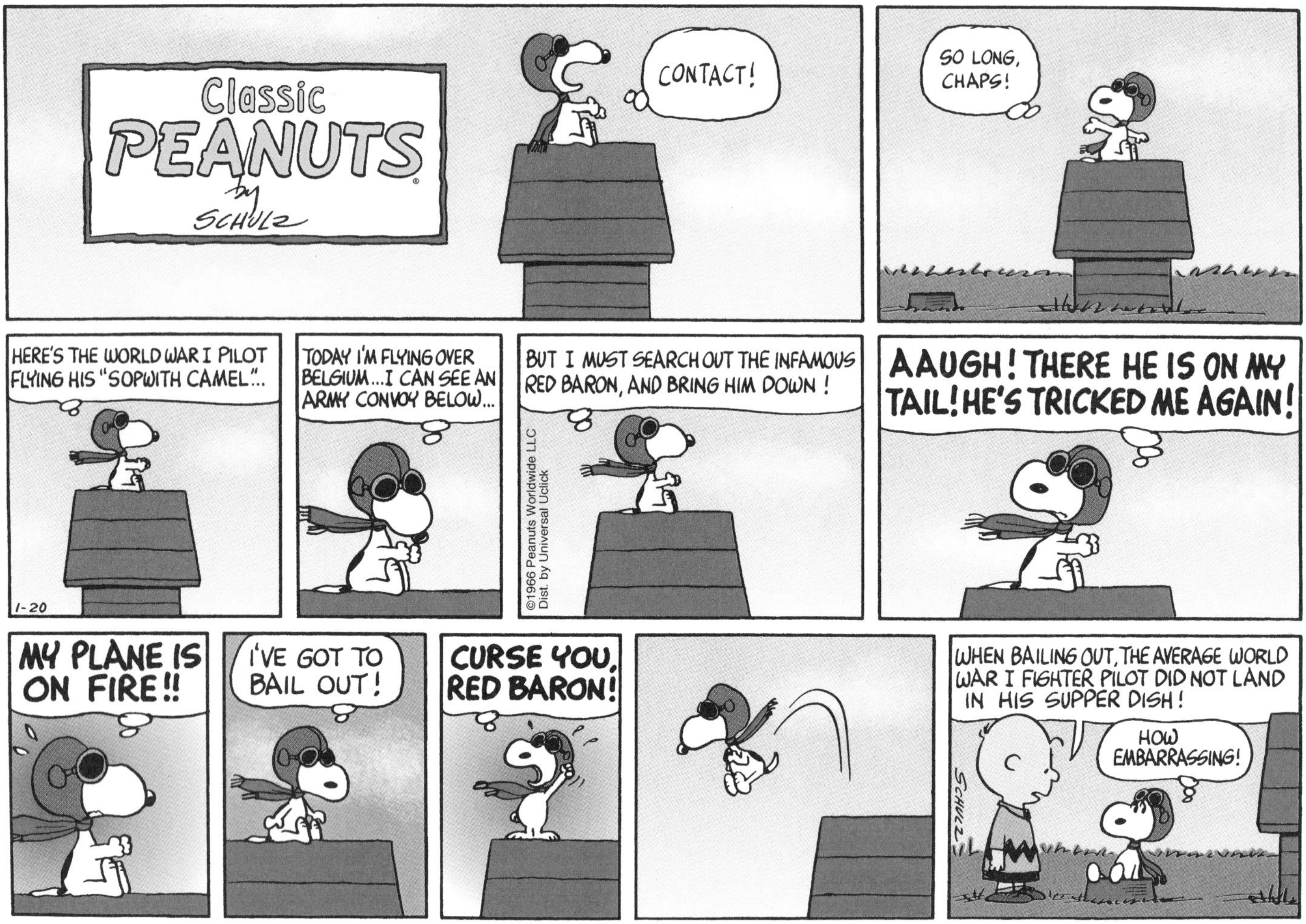
Classic PEANUTS by SCHULZ
CONTACT!
SO LONG, CHAPS!
HERE'S THE WORLD WAR I PILOT FLYING HIS "SOPWITH CAMEL"...
1-20
TODAY I'M FLYING OVER BELGIUM...I CAN SEE AN ARMY CONVOY BELOW...
BUT I MUST SEARCH OUT THE INFAMOUS RED BARON, AND BRING HIM DOWN!
©1966 Peanuts Worldwide LLC
Dist. by Universal Uclick
AAUGH! THERE HE IS ON MY TAIL! HE'S TRICKED ME AGAIN!
MY PLANE IS ON FIRE!!
I'VE GOT TO BAIL OUT!
CURSE YOU, RED BARON!
SCHULZ
WHEN BAILING OUT, THE AVERAGE WORLD WAR I FIGHTER PILOT DID NOT LAND IN HIS SUPPER DISH!
HOW EMBARRASSING!

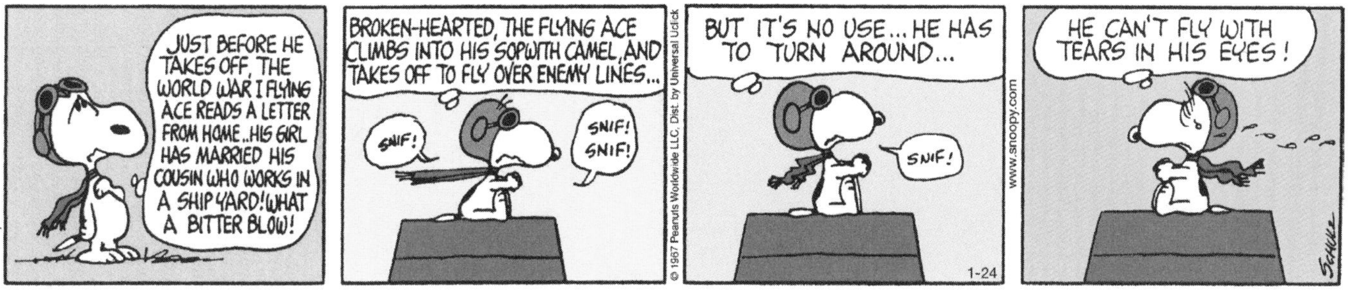
JUST BEFORE HE TAKES OFF, THE WORLD WAR I FLYING ACE READS A LETTER FROM HOME..HIS GIRL HAS MARRIED HIS COUSIN WHO WORKS IN A SHIPYARD! WHAT A BITTER BLOW!
BROKEN-HEARTED, THE FLYING ACE CLIMBS INTO HIS SOPWITH CAMEL, AND TAKES OFF TO FLY OVER ENEMY LINES...
SNIF!
SNIF! SNIF!
© 1967 Peanuts Worldwide LLC, Dist. by Universal Uclick
BUT IT'S NO USE... HE HAS TO TURN AROUND...
SNIF!
1-24
www.snoopy.com
HE CAN'T FLY WITH TEARS IN HIS EYES!
SCHULZ

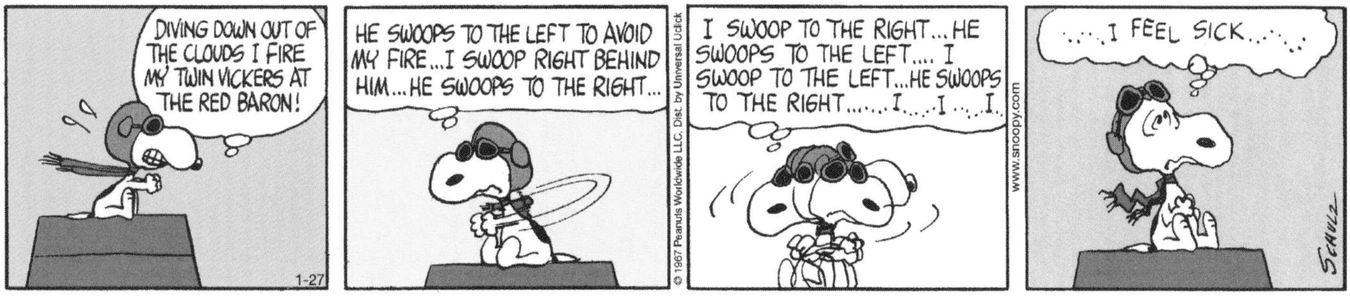
DIVING DOWN OUT OF THE CLOUDS I FIRE MY TWIN VICKERS AT THE RED BARON!
1-27
HE SWOOPS TO THE LEFT TO AVOID MY FIRE...I SWOOP RIGHT BEHIND HIM...HE SWOOPS TO THE RIGHT...
© 1967 Peanuts Worldwide LLC, Dist. by Universal Uclick
I SWOOP TO THE RIGHT... HE SWOOPS TO THE LEFT.... I SWOOP TO THE LEFT...HE SWOOPS TO THE RIGHT....... I...... I I
www.snoopy.com
......I FEEL SICK.........
SCHULZ

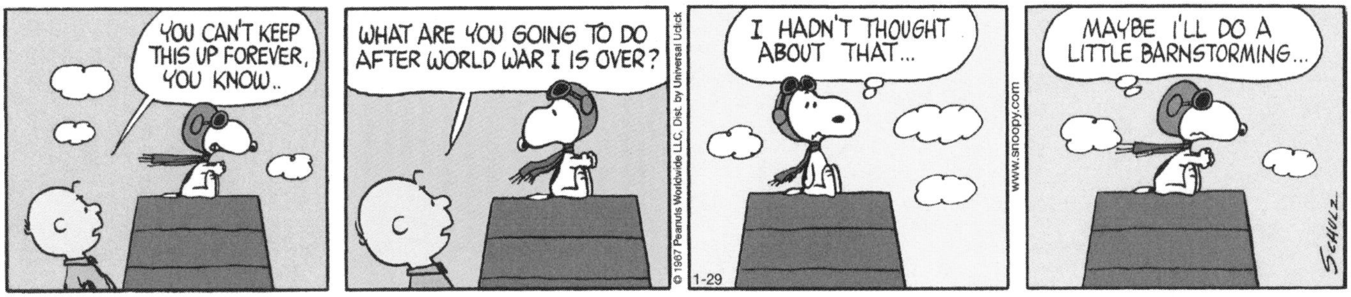
YOU CAN'T KEEP THIS UP FOREVER, YOU KNOW..
WHAT ARE YOU GOING TO DO AFTER WORLD WAR I IS OVER?
© 1967 Peanuts Worldwide LLC, Dist. by Universal Uclick
I HADN'T THOUGHT ABOUT THAT...
1-29
www.snoopy.com
MAYBE I'LL DO A LITTLE BARNSTORMING...
SCHULZ

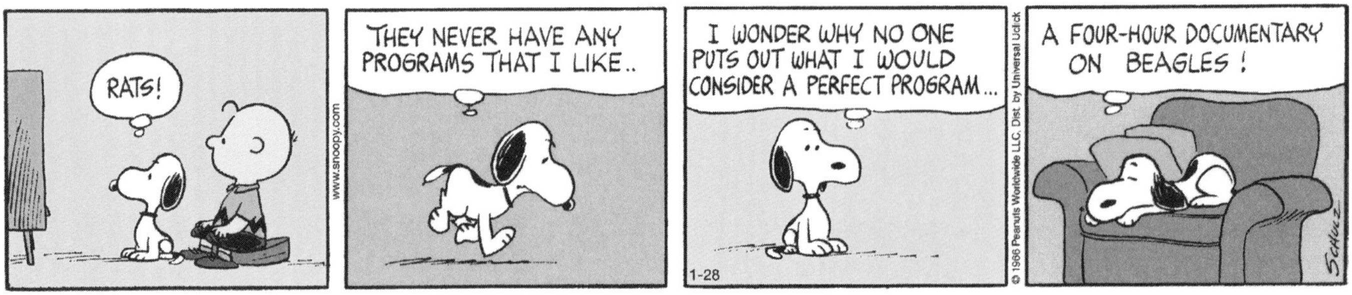
RATS!
www.snoopy.com
THEY NEVER HAVE ANY PROGRAMS THAT I LIKE..
I WONDER WHY NO ONE PUTS OUT WHAT I WOULD CONSIDER A PERFECT PROGRAM...
1-28
© 1966 Peanuts Worldwide LLC. Dist. by Universal Uclick
A FOUR-HOUR DOCUMENTARY ON BEAGLES!
SCHULZ

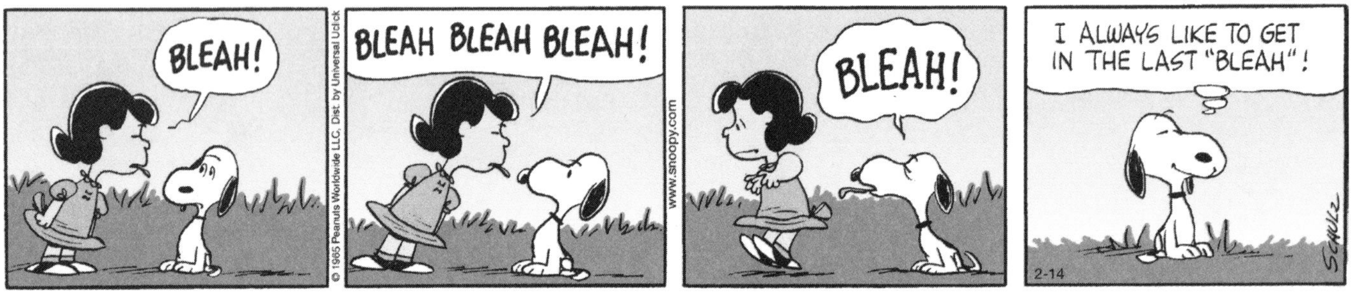
BLEAH!
© 1965 Peanuts Worldwide LLC. Dist. by Universal Uclick
BLEAH BLEAH BLEAH!
www.snoopy.com
BLEAH!
I ALWAYS LIKE TO GET IN THE LAST "BLEAH"!
2-14
SCHULZ

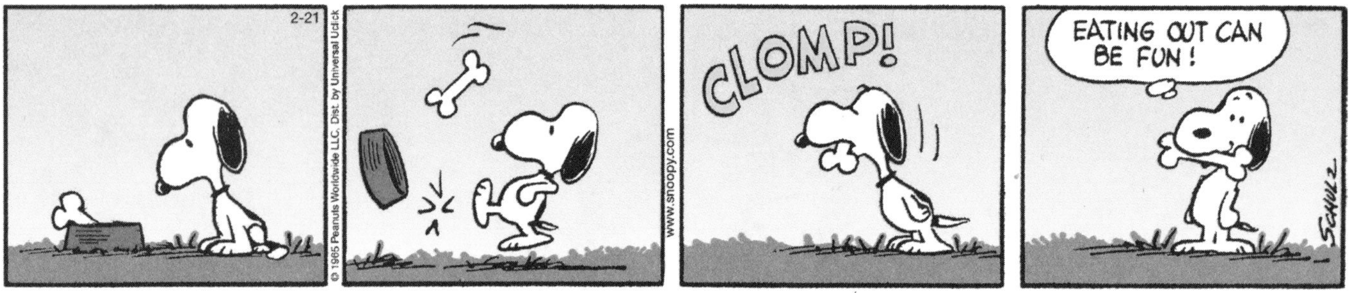
2-21
© 1965 Peanuts Worldwide LLC. Dist. by Universal Uclick
www.snoopy.com
CLOMP!
EATING OUT CAN BE FUN!
SCHULZ

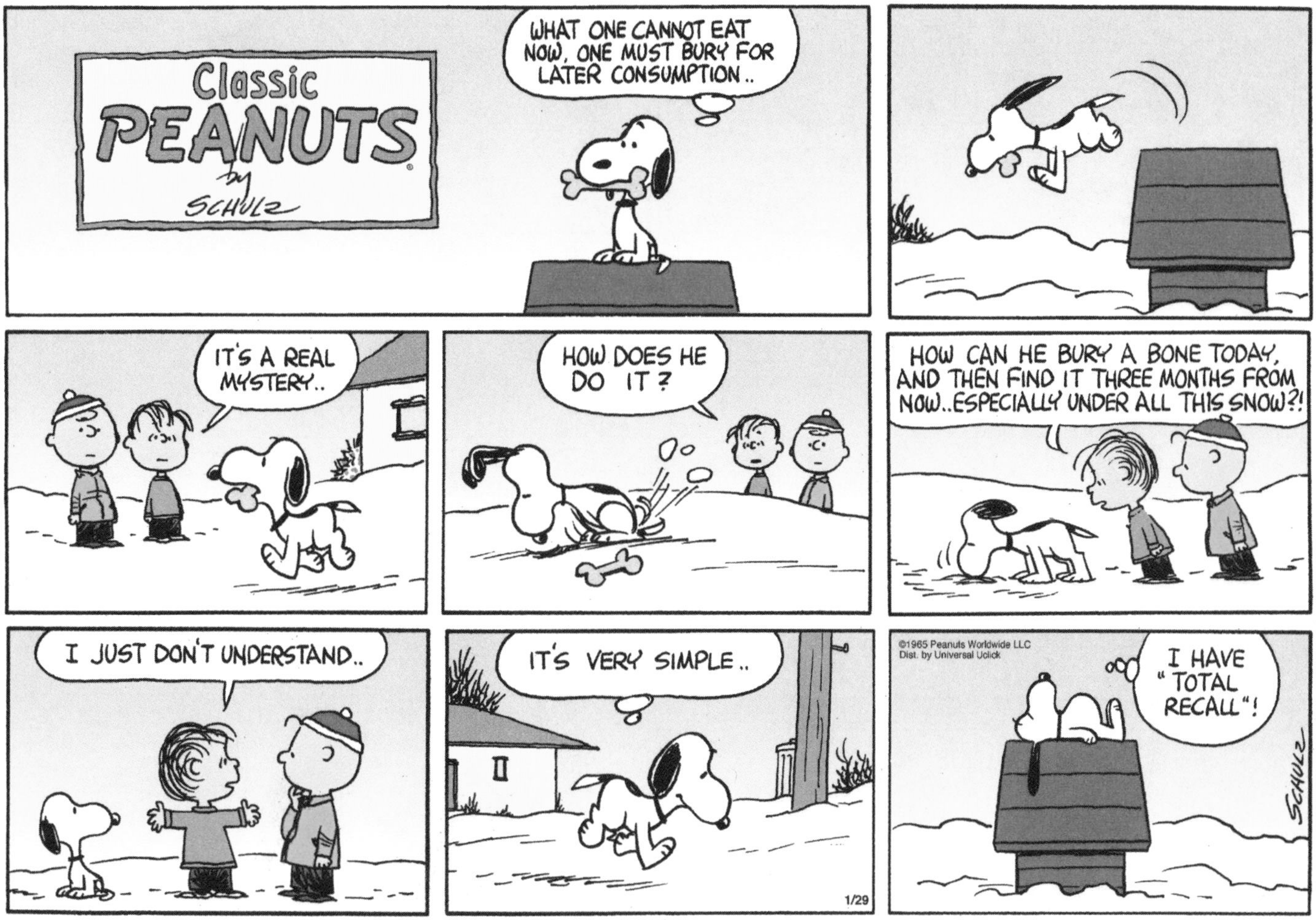
Classic PEANUTS by SCHULZ
WHAT ONE CANNOT EAT NOW, ONE MUST BURY FOR LATER CONSUMPTION..
IT'S A REAL MYSTERY..
HOW DOES HE DO IT?
HOW CAN HE BURY A BONE TODAY, AND THEN FIND IT THREE MONTHS FROM NOW..ESPECIALLY UNDER ALL THIS SNOW?!
I JUST DON'T UNDERSTAND..
IT'S VERY SIMPLE..
1/29
©1965 Peanuts Worldwide LLC Dist. by Universal Uclick
I HAVE "TOTAL RECALL"!
SCHULZ

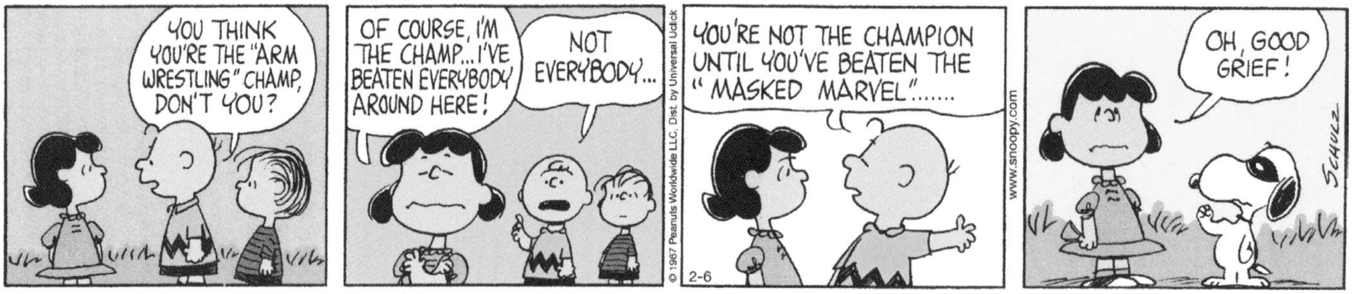
YOU THINK YOU'RE THE "ARM WRESTLING" CHAMP, DON'T YOU?
OF COURSE, I'M THE CHAMP... I'VE BEATEN EVERYBODY AROUND HERE!
NOT EVERYBODY...
© 1967 Peanuts Worldwide LLC, Dist. by Universal Uclick
2-6
YOU'RE NOT THE CHAMPION UNTIL YOU'VE BEATEN THE "MASKED MARVEL".......
www.snoopy.com
OH, GOOD GRIEF!
SCHULZ

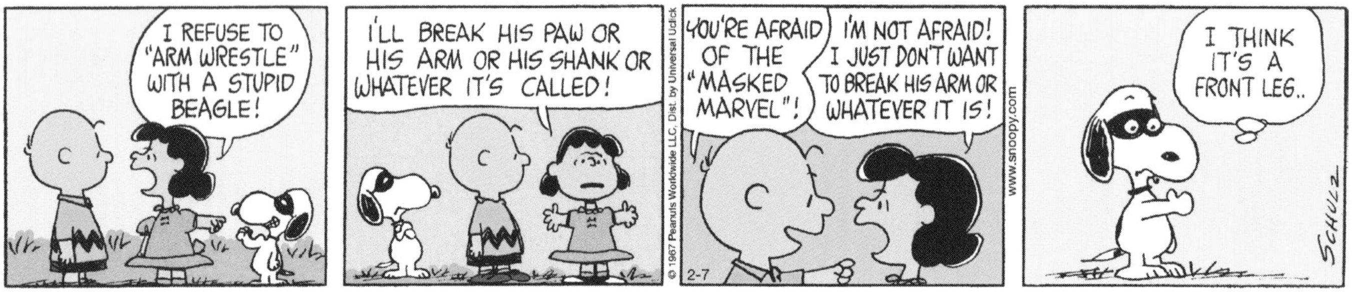
I REFUSE TO "ARM WRESTLE" WITH A STUPID BEAGLE!
I'LL BREAK HIS PAW OR HIS ARM OR HIS SHANK OR WHATEVER IT'S CALLED!
© 1967 Peanuts Worldwide LLC, Dist. by Universal Uclick
2-7
YOU'RE AFRAID OF THE "MASKED MARVEL"!
I'M NOT AFRAID! I JUST DON'T WANT TO BREAK HIS ARM OR WHATEVER IT IS!
www.snoopy.com
I THINK IT'S A FRONT LEG..
SCHULZ

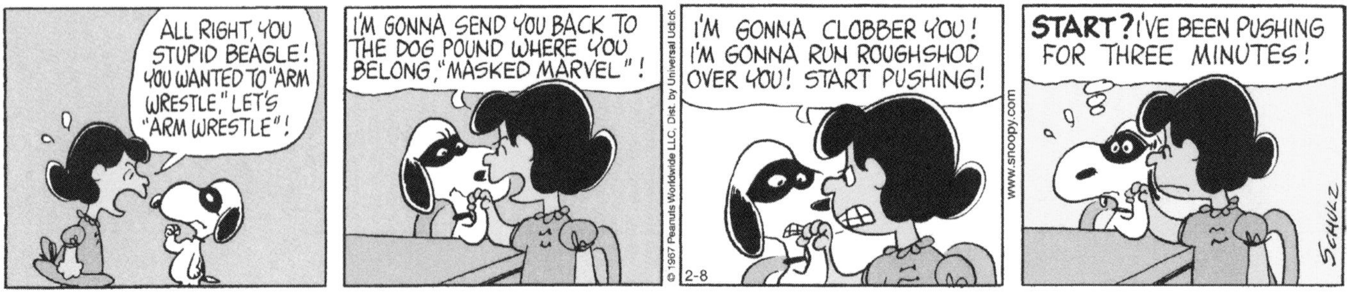
ALL RIGHT, YOU STUPID BEAGLE! YOU WANTED TO "ARM WRESTLE," LET'S "ARM WRESTLE"!
I'M GONNA SEND YOU BACK TO THE DOG POUND WHERE YOU BELONG, "MASKED MARVEL"!
© 1967 Peanuts Worldwide LLC, Dist. by Universal Uclick
2-8
I'M GONNA CLOBBER YOU! I'M GONNA RUN ROUGHSHOD OVER YOU! START PUSHING!
www.snoopy.com
START? I'VE BEEN PUSHING FOR THREE MINUTES!
SCHULZ

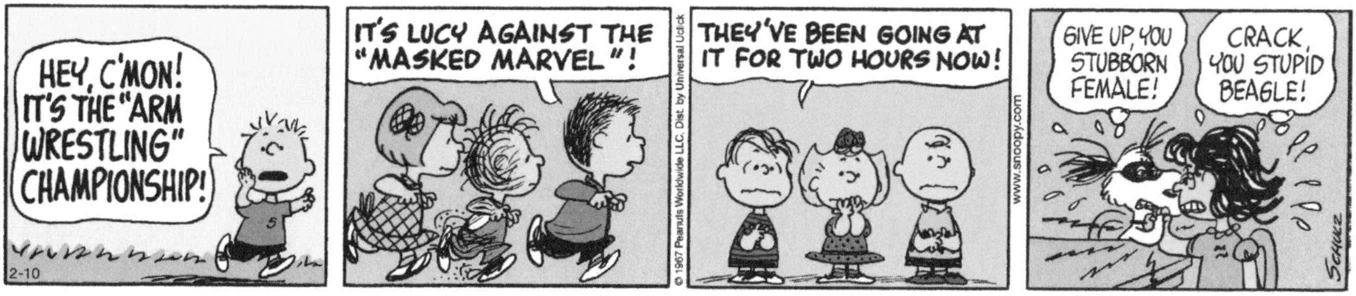
HEY, C'MON! IT'S THE "ARM WRESTLING" CHAMPIONSHIP!
2-10
IT'S LUCY AGAINST THE "MASKED MARVEL"!
© 1967 Peanuts Worldwide LLC. Dist. by Universal Uclick
THEY'VE BEEN GOING AT IT FOR TWO HOURS NOW!
www.snoopy.com
GIVE UP, YOU STUBBORN FEMALE!
CRACK, YOU STUPID BEAGLE!
SCHULZ

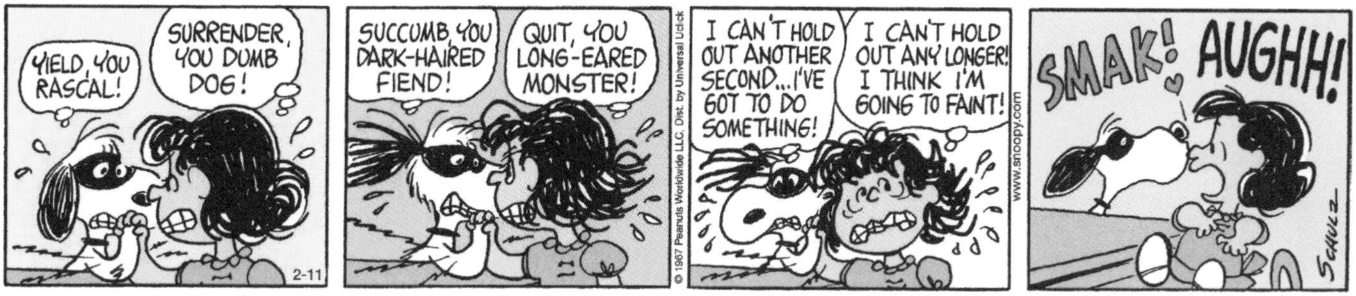
YIELD, YOU RASCAL!
SURRENDER, YOU DUMB DOG!
2-11
SUCCUMB, YOU DARK-HAIRED FIEND!
QUIT, YOU LONG-EARED MONSTER!
© 1967 Peanuts Worldwide LLC. Dist. by Universal Uclick
I CAN'T HOLD OUT ANOTHER SECOND...I'VE GOT TO DO SOMETHING!
I CAN'T HOLD OUT ANY LONGER! I THINK I'M GOING TO FAINT!
www.snoopy.com
SMAK!
AUGHH!
SCHULZ

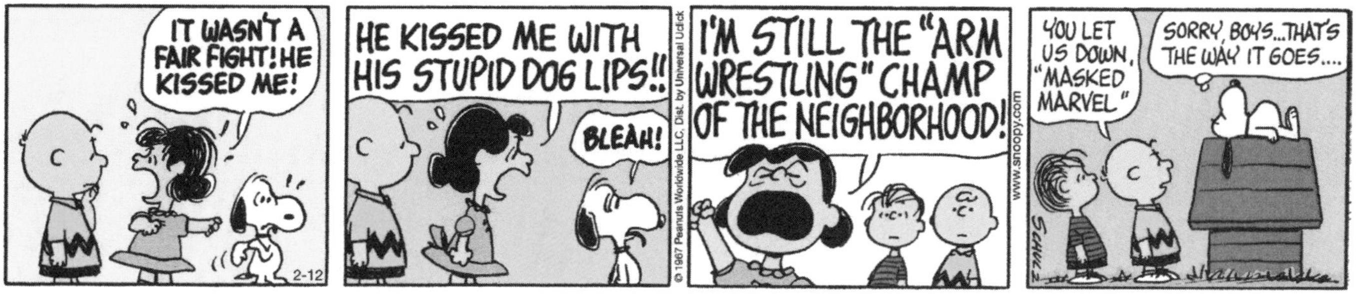
IT WASN'T A FAIR FIGHT! HE KISSED ME!
2-12
HE KISSED ME WITH HIS STUPID DOG LIPS!!
BLEAH!
© 1967 Peanuts Worldwide LLC. Dist. by Universal Uclick
I'M STILL THE "ARM WRESTLING" CHAMP OF THE NEIGHBORHOOD!
www.snoopy.com
YOU LET US DOWN, "MASKED MARVEL"
SORRY, BOYS...THAT'S THE WAY IT GOES....
SCHULZ

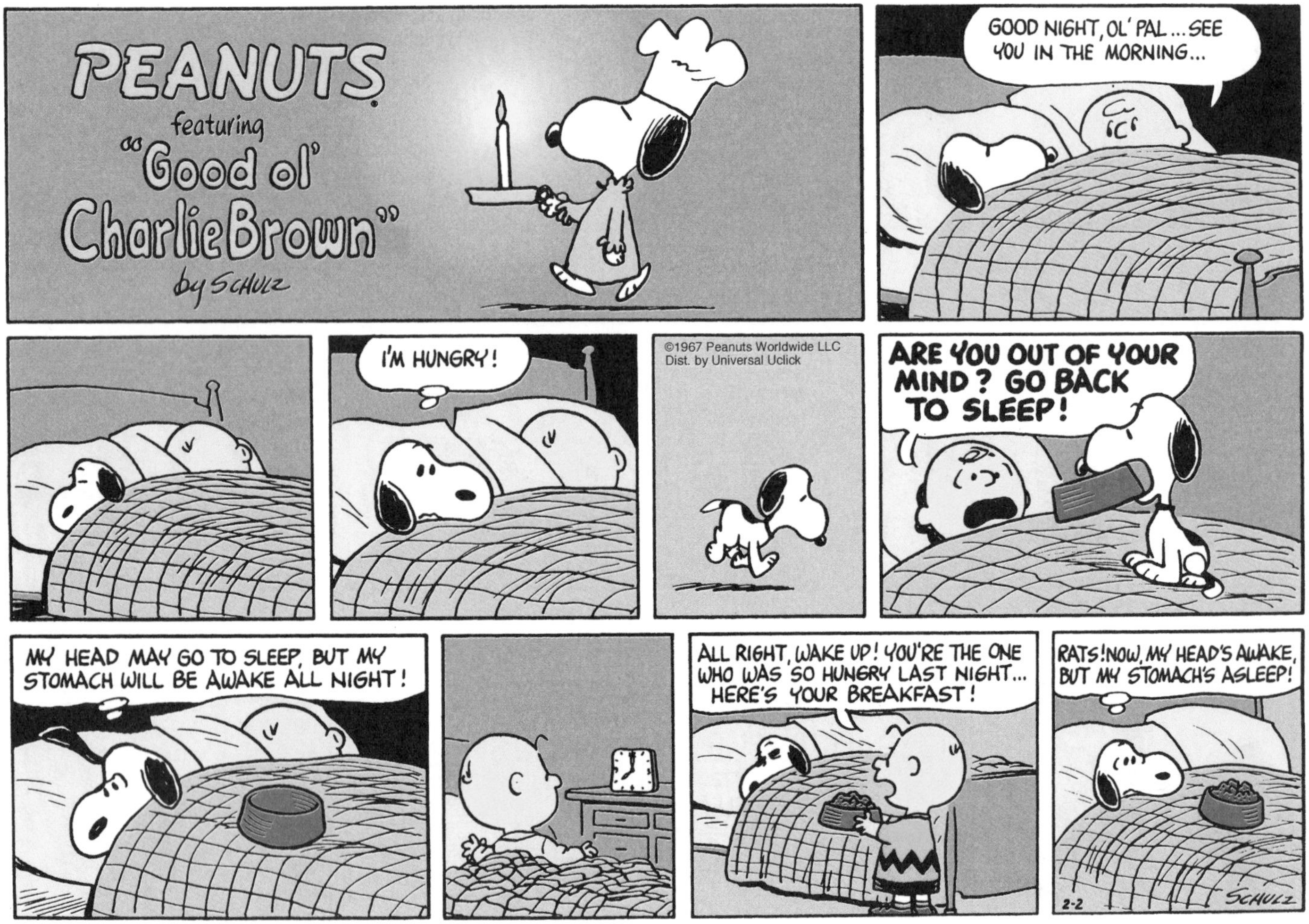
PEANUTS
featuring
"Good ol' Charlie Brown"
by SCHULZ
GOOD NIGHT, OL' PAL...SEE YOU IN THE MORNING...
I'M HUNGRY!
©1967 Peanuts Worldwide LLC
Dist. by Universal Uclick
ARE YOU OUT OF YOUR MIND? GO BACK TO SLEEP!
MY HEAD MAY GO TO SLEEP, BUT MY STOMACH WILL BE AWAKE ALL NIGHT!
ALL RIGHT, WAKE UP! YOU'RE THE ONE WHO WAS SO HUNGRY LAST NIGHT... HERE'S YOUR BREAKFAST!
RATS! NOW, MY HEAD'S AWAKE, BUT MY STOMACH'S ASLEEP!
2-2
SCHULZ

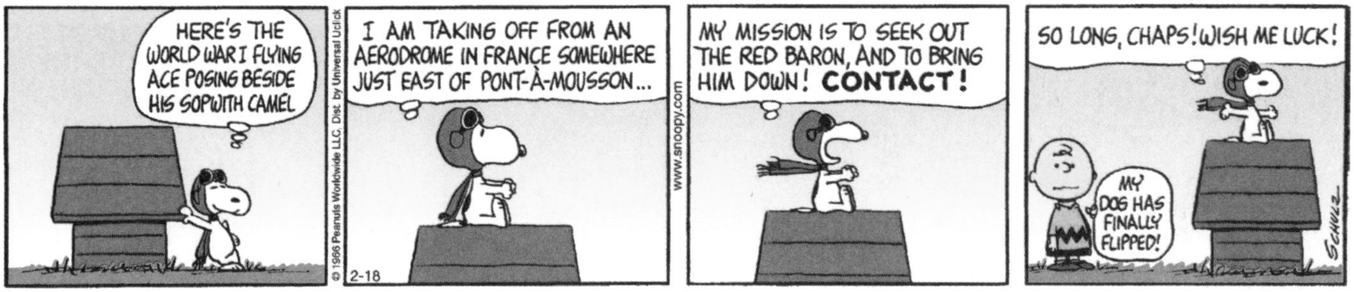
HERE'S THE WORLD WAR I FLYING ACE POSING BESIDE HIS SOPWITH CAMEL
© 1966 Peanuts Worldwide LLC, Dist. by Universal Uclick
2-18
I AM TAKING OFF FROM AN AERODROME IN FRANCE SOMEWHERE JUST EAST OF PONT-À-MOUSSON...
www.snoopy.com
MY MISSION IS TO SEEK OUT THE RED BARON, AND TO BRING HIM DOWN! CONTACT!
SO LONG, CHAPS! WISH ME LUCK!
MY DOG HAS FINALLY FLIPPED!
SCHULZ

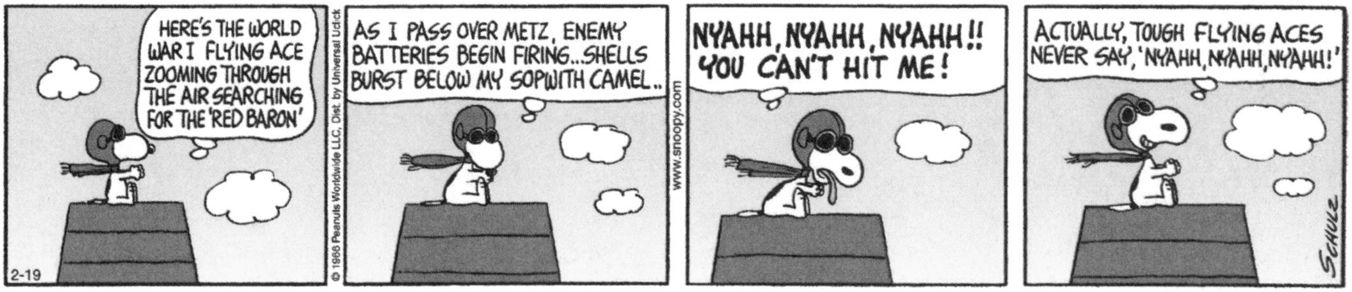
HERE'S THE WORLD WAR I FLYING ACE ZOOMING THROUGH THE AIR SEARCHING FOR THE 'RED BARON'
2-19
© 1966 Peanuts Worldwide LLC, Dist. by Universal Uclick
AS I PASS OVER METZ, ENEMY BATTERIES BEGIN FIRING...SHELLS BURST BELOW MY SOPWITH CAMEL..
www.snoopy.com
NYAHH, NYAHH, NYAHH!! YOU CAN'T HIT ME!
ACTUALLY, TOUGH FLYING ACES NEVER SAY, 'NYAHH, NYAHH, NYAHH!'
SCHULZ

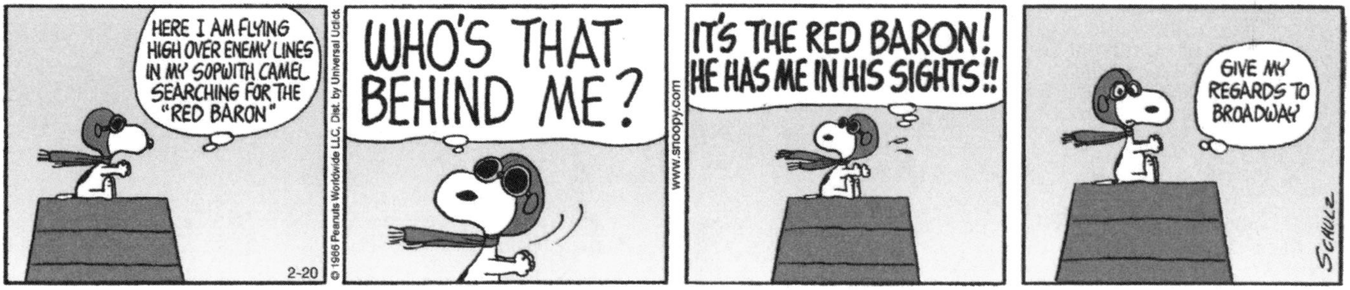
HERE I AM FLYING HIGH OVER ENEMY LINES IN MY SOPWITH CAMEL SEARCHING FOR THE "RED BARON"
2-20
© 1966 Peanuts Worldwide LLC, Dist. by Universal Uclick
WHO'S THAT BEHIND ME?
www.snoopy.com
IT'S THE RED BARON! HE HAS ME IN HIS SIGHTS!!
GIVE MY REGARDS TO BROADWAY
SCHULZ

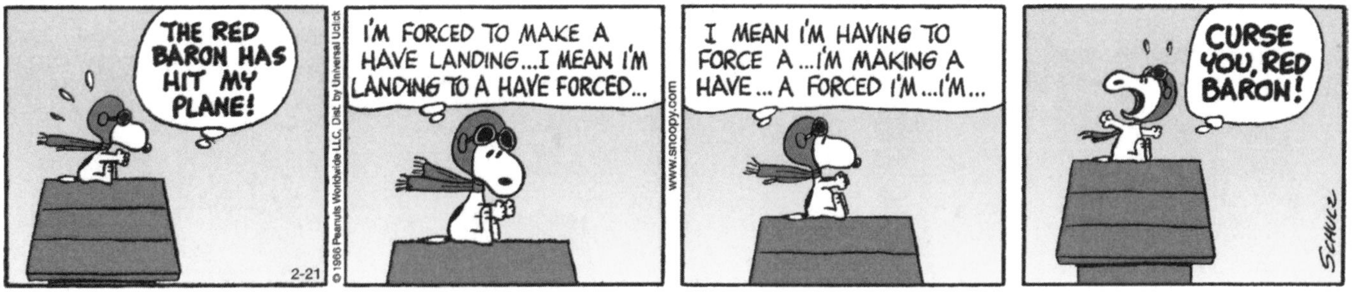
THE RED BARON HAS HIT MY PLANE!
2-21
© 1966 Peanuts Worldwide LLC. Dist. by Universal Uclick
I'M FORCED TO MAKE A HAVE LANDING...I MEAN I'M LANDING TO A HAVE FORCED...
www.snoopy.com
I MEAN I'M HAVING TO FORCE A ...I'M MAKING A HAVE... A FORCED I'M...I'M...
CURSE YOU, RED BARON!
SCHULZ

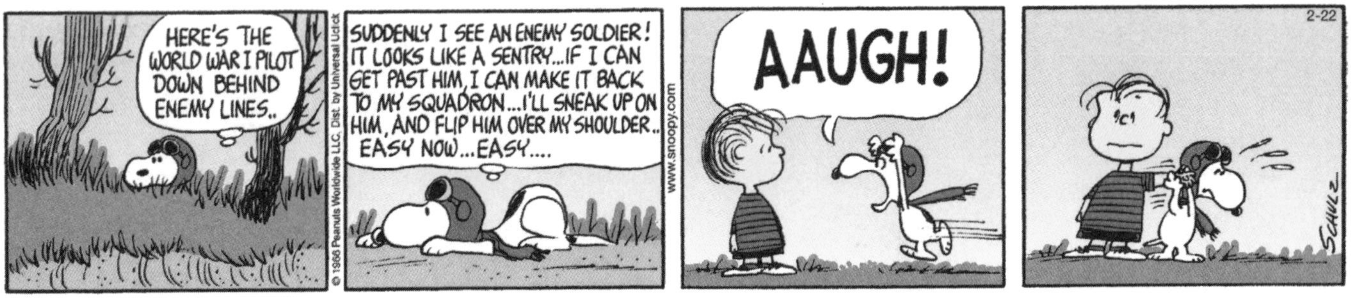
HERE'S THE WORLD WAR I PILOT DOWN BEHIND ENEMY LINES..
© 1966 Peanuts Worldwide LLC. Dist. by Universal Uclick
SUDDENLY I SEE AN ENEMY SOLDIER! IT LOOKS LIKE A SENTRY...IF I CAN GET PAST HIM, I CAN MAKE IT BACK TO MY SQUADRON...I'LL SNEAK UP ON HIM, AND FLIP HIM OVER MY SHOULDER.. EASY NOW...EASY....
www.snoopy.com
AAUGH!
2-22
SCHULZ

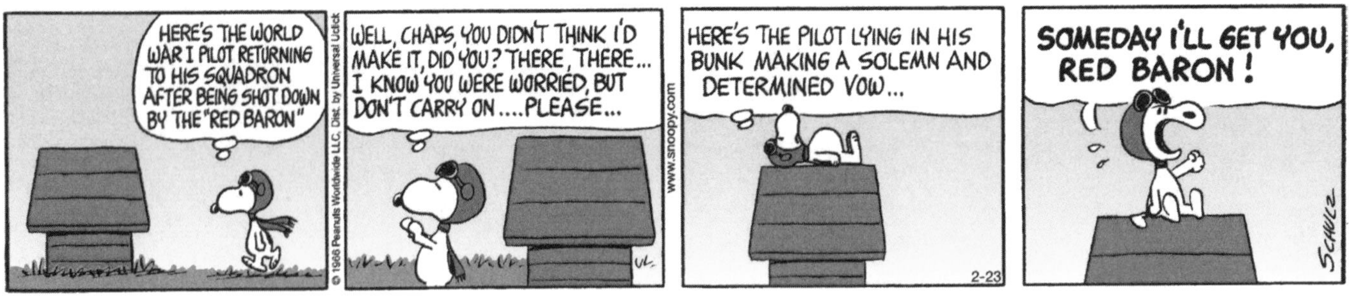
HERE'S THE WORLD WAR I PILOT RETURNING TO HIS SQUADRON AFTER BEING SHOT DOWN BY THE "RED BARON"
© 1966 Peanuts Worldwide LLC. Dist. by Universal Uclick
WELL, CHAPS, YOU DIDN'T THINK I'D MAKE IT, DID YOU? THERE, THERE... I KNOW YOU WERE WORRIED, BUT DON'T CARRY ON ....PLEASE...
www.snoopy.com
HERE'S THE PILOT LYING IN HIS BUNK MAKING A SOLEMN AND DETERMINED VOW...
2-23
SOMEDAY I'LL GET YOU, RED BARON!
SCHULZ

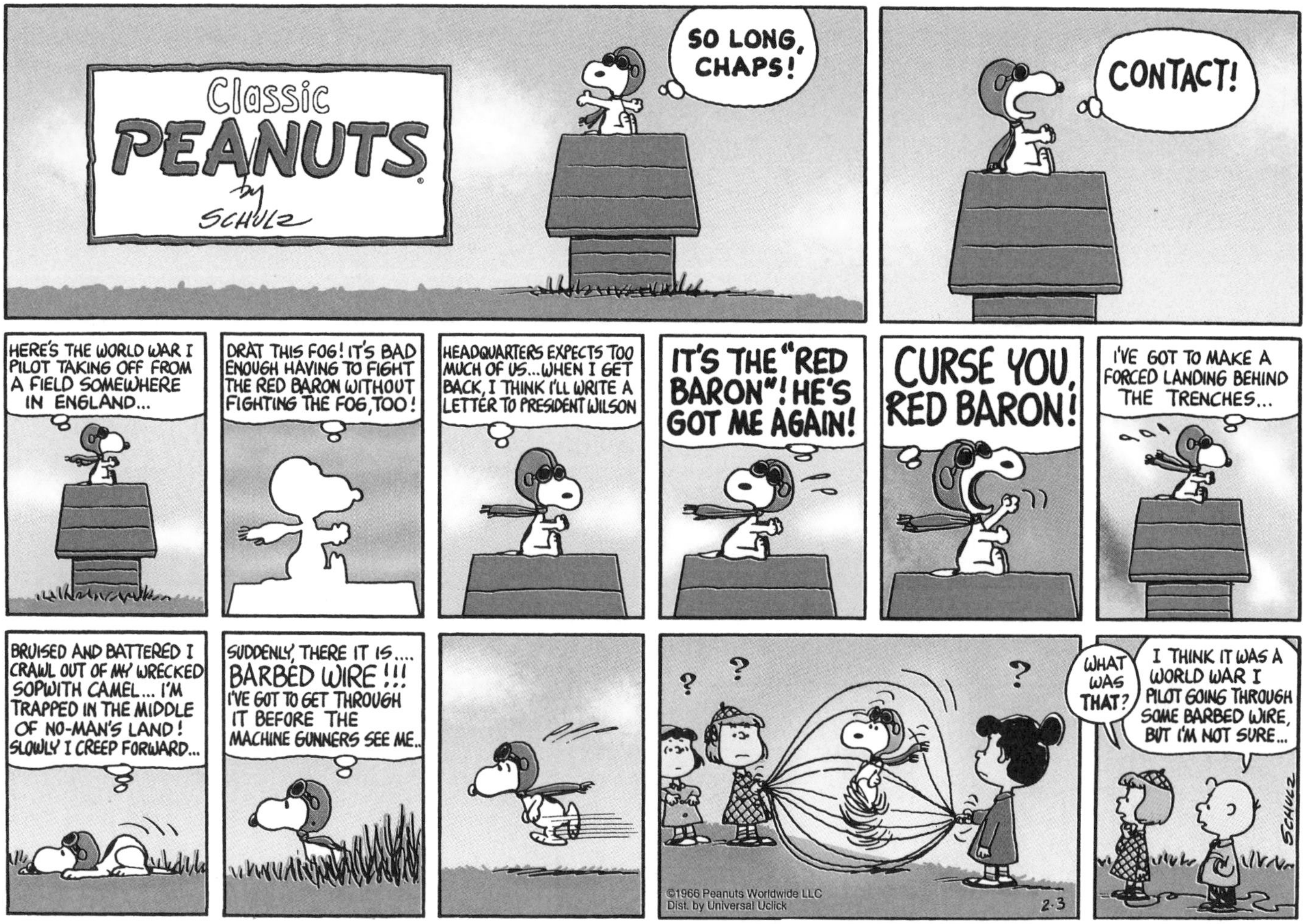
Classic
PEANUTS
by SCHULZ
SO LONG, CHAPS!
CONTACT!
HERE'S THE WORLD WAR I PILOT TAKING OFF FROM A FIELD SOMEWHERE IN ENGLAND...
DRAT THIS FOG! IT'S BAD ENOUGH HAVING TO FIGHT THE RED BARON WITHOUT FIGHTING THE FOG, TOO!
HEADQUARTERS EXPECTS TOO MUCH OF US...WHEN I GET BACK, I THINK I'LL WRITE A LETTER TO PRESIDENT WILSON
IT'S THE "RED BARON"! HE'S GOT ME AGAIN!
CURSE YOU, RED BARON!
I'VE GOT TO MAKE A FORCED LANDING BEHIND THE TRENCHES...
BRUISED AND BATTERED I CRAWL OUT OF MY WRECKED SOPWITH CAMEL... I'M TRAPPED IN THE MIDDLE OF NO-MAN'S LAND! SLOWLY I CREEP FORWARD...
SUDDENLY, THERE IT IS.... BARBED WIRE!!! I'VE GOT TO GET THROUGH IT BEFORE THE MACHINE GUNNERS SEE ME..
?
?
?
©1966 Peanuts Worldwide LLC
Dist. by Universal Uclick
2-3
WHAT WAS THAT?
I THINK IT WAS A WORLD WAR I PILOT GOING THROUGH SOME BARBED WIRE, BUT I'M NOT SURE...
SCHULZ

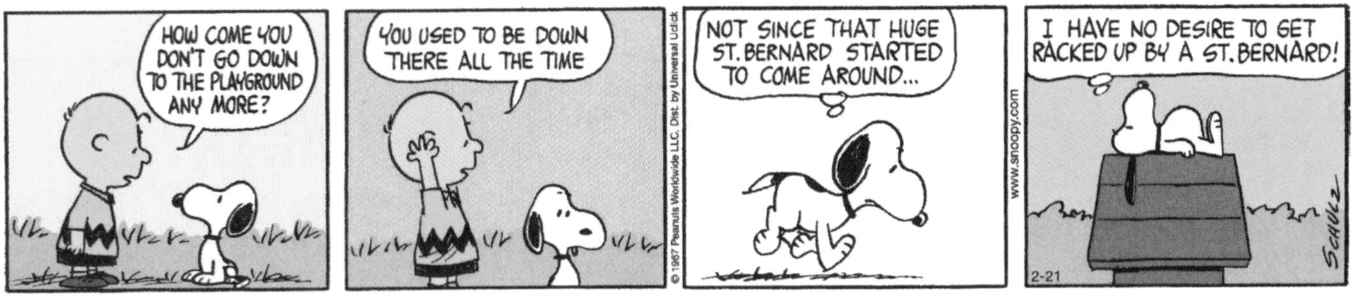
HOW COME YOU DON'T GO DOWN TO THE PLAYGROUND ANY MORE?
YOU USED TO BE DOWN THERE ALL THE TIME
NOT SINCE THAT HUGE ST. BERNARD STARTED TO COME AROUND...
I HAVE NO DESIRE TO GET RACKED UP BY A ST. BERNARD!
© 1967 Peanuts Worldwide LLC, Dist. by Universal Uclick
www.snoopy.com
2-21
SCHULZ

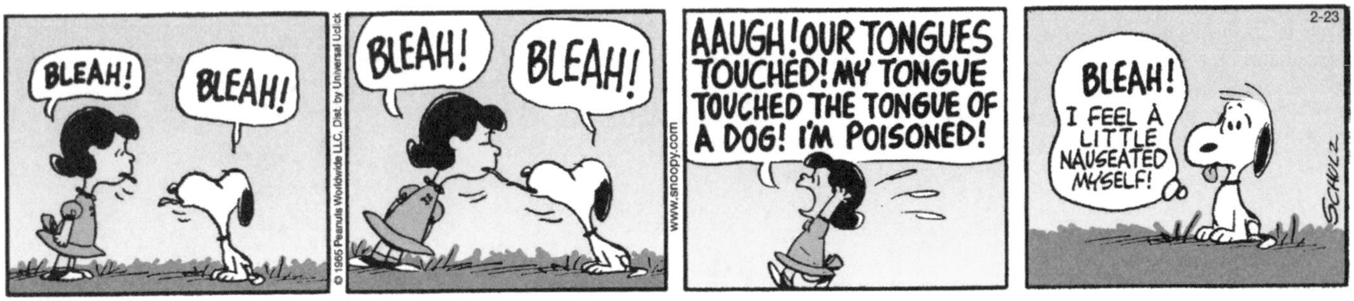
BLEAH!
BLEAH!
BLEAH!
BLEAH!
AAUGH! OUR TONGUES TOUCHED! MY TONGUE TOUCHED THE TONGUE OF A DOG! I'M POISONED!
BLEAH! I FEEL A LITTLE NAUSEATED MYSELF!
© 1965 Peanuts Worldwide LLC, Dist. by Universal Uclick
www.snoopy.com
2-23
SCHULZ

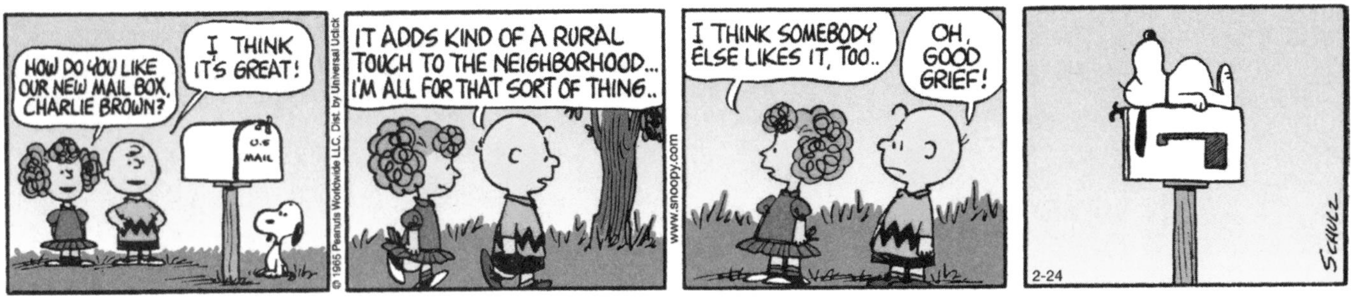
HOW DO YOU LIKE OUR NEW MAIL BOX, CHARLIE BROWN?
I THINK IT'S GREAT!
IT ADDS KIND OF A RURAL TOUCH TO THE NEIGHBORHOOD... I'M ALL FOR THAT SORT OF THING..
I THINK SOMEBODY ELSE LIKES IT, TOO..
OH, GOOD GRIEF!
© 1965 Peanuts Worldwide LLC, Dist. by Universal Uclick
www.snoopy.com
2-24
SCHULZ

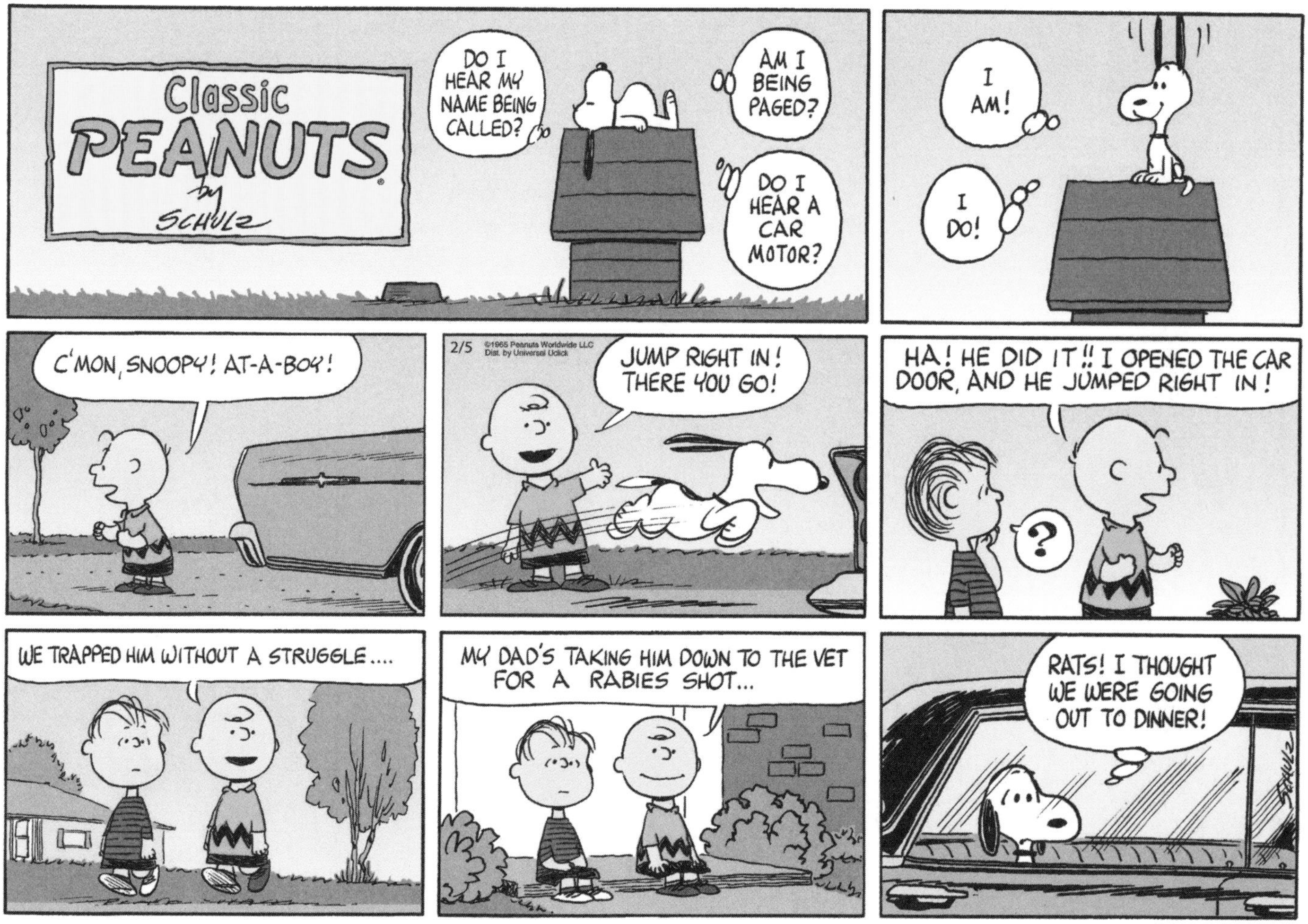
Classic PEANUTS by SCHULZ
DO I HEAR MY NAME BEING CALLED?
AM I BEING PAGED?
DO I HEAR A CAR MOTOR?
I AM!
I DO!
C'MON, SNOOPY! AT-A-BOY!
2/5 ©1965 Peanuts Worldwide LLC Dist. by Universal Uclick
JUMP RIGHT IN! THERE YOU GO!
HA! HE DID IT!! I OPENED THE CAR DOOR, AND HE JUMPED RIGHT IN!
?
WE TRAPPED HIM WITHOUT A STRUGGLE....
MY DAD'S TAKING HIM DOWN TO THE VET FOR A RABIES SHOT...
RATS! I THOUGHT WE WERE GOING OUT TO DINNER!
SCHULZ

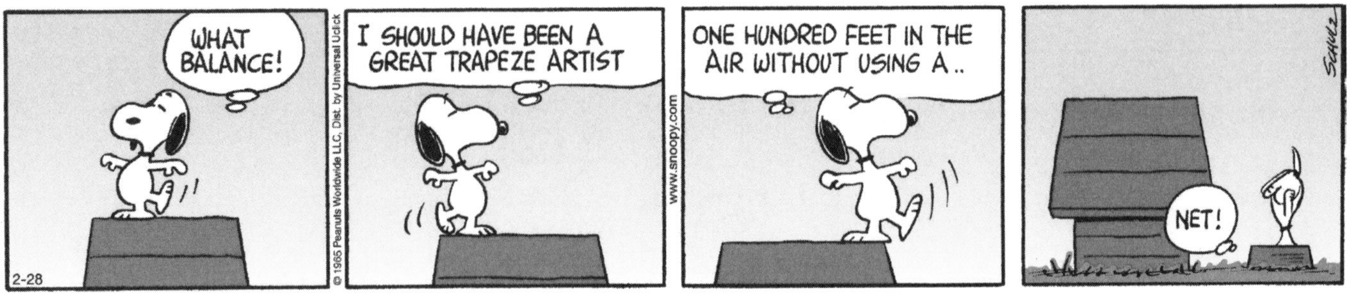
WHAT BALANCE!
2-28
© 1965 Peanuts Worldwide LLC. Dist. by Universal Uclick
I SHOULD HAVE BEEN A GREAT TRAPEZE ARTIST
www.snoopy.com
ONE HUNDRED FEET IN THE AIR WITHOUT USING A ..
SCHULZ
NET!

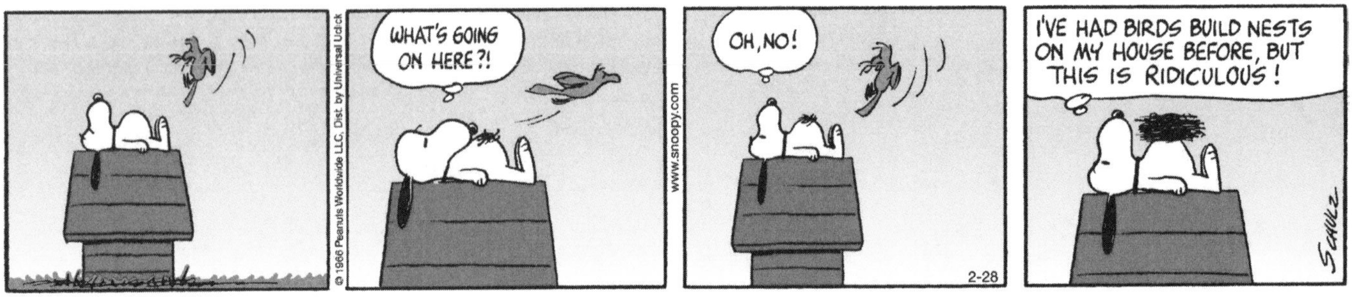
© 1966 Peanuts Worldwide LLC. Dist. by Universal Uclick
WHAT'S GOING ON HERE?!
www.snoopy.com
OH, NO!
2-28
I'VE HAD BIRDS BUILD NESTS ON MY HOUSE BEFORE, BUT THIS IS RIDICULOUS!
SCHULZ

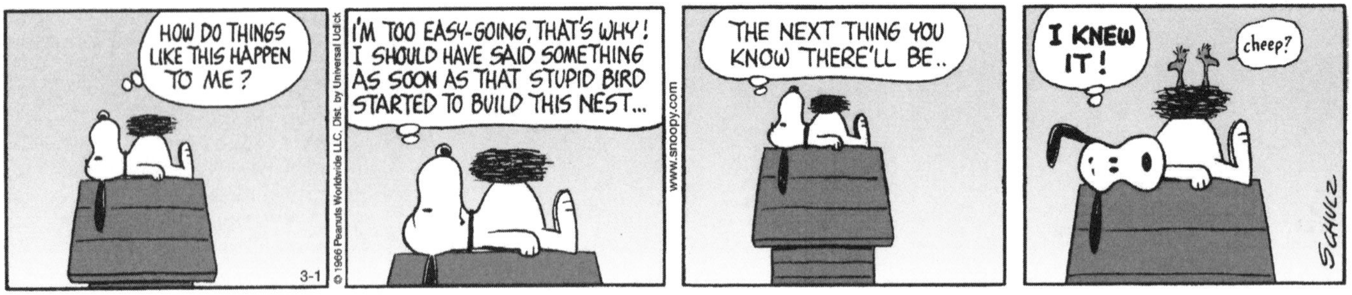
HOW DO THINGS LIKE THIS HAPPEN TO ME?
3-1
© 1966 Peanuts Worldwide LLC. Dist. by Universal Uclick
I'M TOO EASY-GOING, THAT'S WHY! I SHOULD HAVE SAID SOMETHING AS SOON AS THAT STUPID BIRD STARTED TO BUILD THIS NEST...
www.snoopy.com
THE NEXT THING YOU KNOW THERE'LL BE..
I KNEW IT!
cheep?
SCHULZ

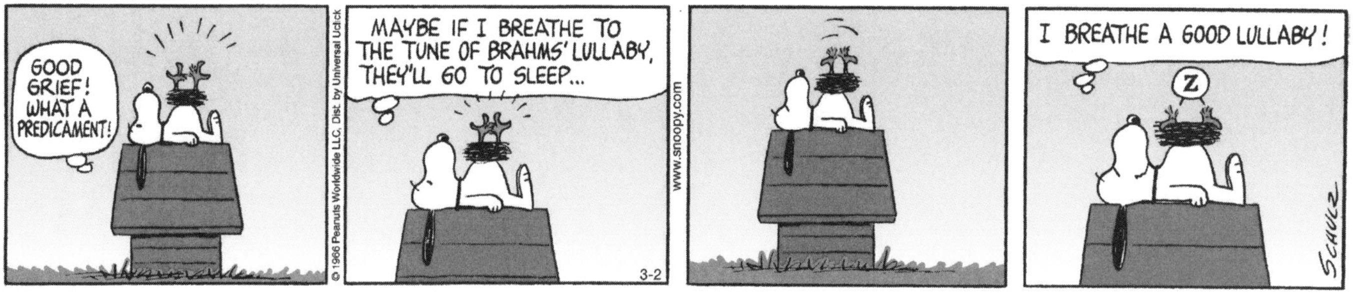
GOOD GRIEF! WHAT A PREDICAMENT!
© 1966 Peanuts Worldwide LLC, Dist. by Universal Uclick
MAYBE IF I BREATHE TO THE TUNE OF BRAHMS' LULLABY, THEY'LL GO TO SLEEP...
3-2
www.snoopy.com
I BREATHE A GOOD LULLABY!
Z
SCHULZ

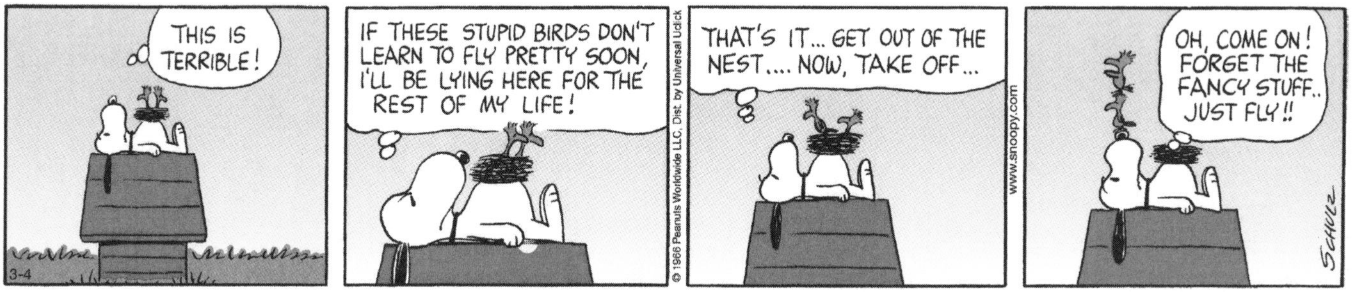
THIS IS TERRIBLE!
3-4
IF THESE STUPID BIRDS DON'T LEARN TO FLY PRETTY SOON, I'LL BE LYING HERE FOR THE REST OF MY LIFE!
© 1966 Peanuts Worldwide LLC, Dist. by Universal Uclick
THAT'S IT... GET OUT OF THE NEST.... NOW, TAKE OFF...
www.snoopy.com
OH, COME ON! FORGET THE FANCY STUFF.. JUST FLY!!
SCHULZ

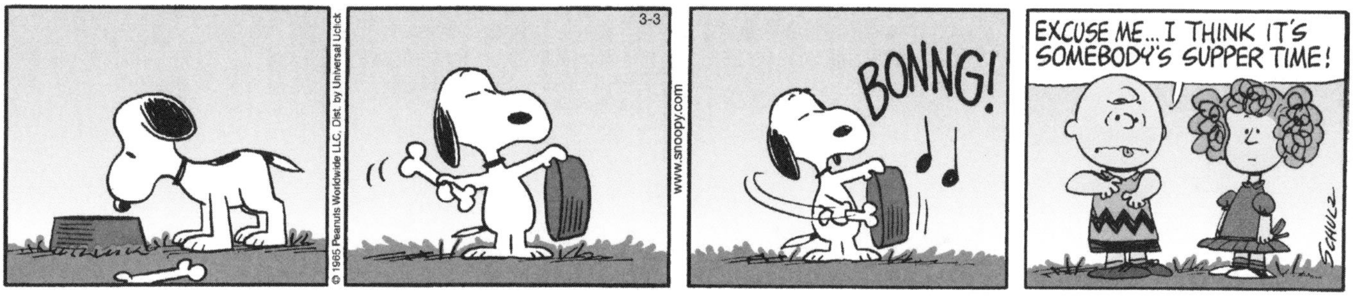
© 1965 Peanuts Worldwide LLC, Dist. by Universal Uclick
3-3
www.snoopy.com
BONNG!
EXCUSE ME... I THINK IT'S SOMEBODY'S SUPPER TIME!
SCHULZ

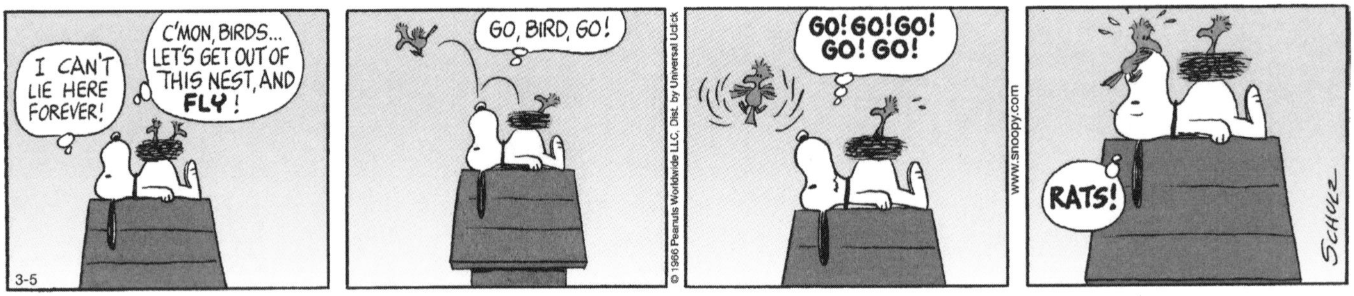
I CAN'T LIE HERE FOREVER!
C'MON, BIRDS... LET'S GET OUT OF THIS NEST, AND FLY!
3-5
GO, BIRD, GO!
© 1966 Peanuts Worldwide LLC, Dist. by Universal Uclick
GO! GO! GO! GO! GO!
www.snoopy.com
RATS!
SCHULZ

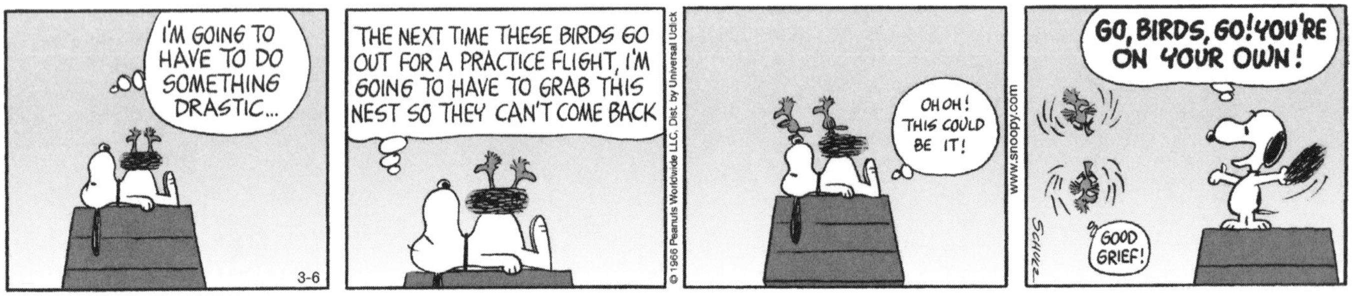
I'M GOING TO HAVE TO DO SOMETHING DRASTIC...
3-6
THE NEXT TIME THESE BIRDS GO OUT FOR A PRACTICE FLIGHT, I'M GOING TO HAVE TO GRAB THIS NEST SO THEY CAN'T COME BACK
© 1966 Peanuts Worldwide LLC, Dist. by Universal Uclick
OH OH! THIS COULD BE IT!
www.snoopy.com
GO, BIRDS, GO! YOU'RE ON YOUR OWN!
GOOD GRIEF!
SCHULZ

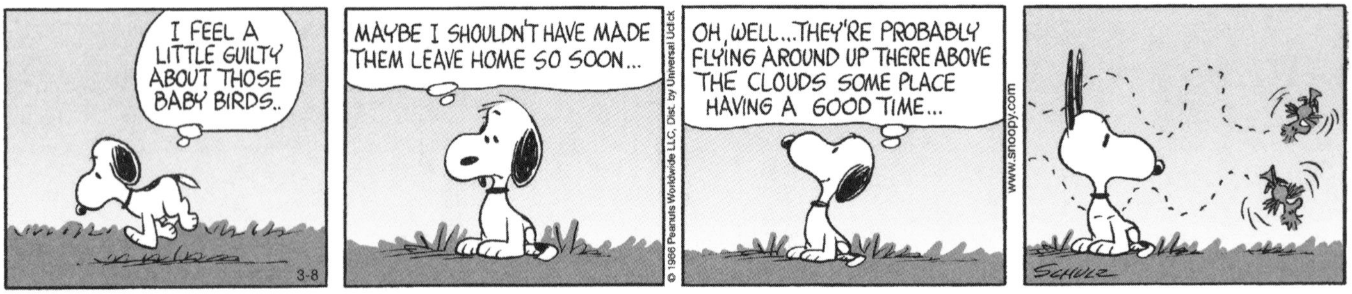
I FEEL A LITTLE GUILTY ABOUT THOSE BABY BIRDS..
3-8
MAYBE I SHOULDN'T HAVE MADE THEM LEAVE HOME SO SOON...
© 1966 Peanuts Worldwide LLC, Dist. by Universal Uclick
OH, WELL...THEY'RE PROBABLY FLYING AROUND UP THERE ABOVE THE CLOUDS SOME PLACE HAVING A GOOD TIME...
www.snoopy.com
SCHULZ

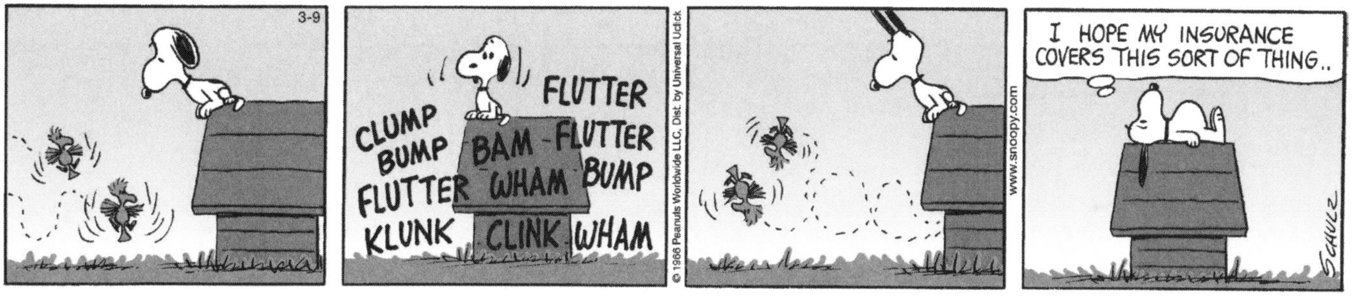
3-9
CLUMP
BUMP
FLUTTER
BAM
WHAM
KLUNK
CLINK
FLUTTER
FLUTTER
BUMP
WHAM
© 1966 Peanuts Worldwide LLC, Dist. by Universal Uclick
www.snoopy.com
I HOPE MY INSURANCE COVERS THIS SORT OF THING..
SCHULZ

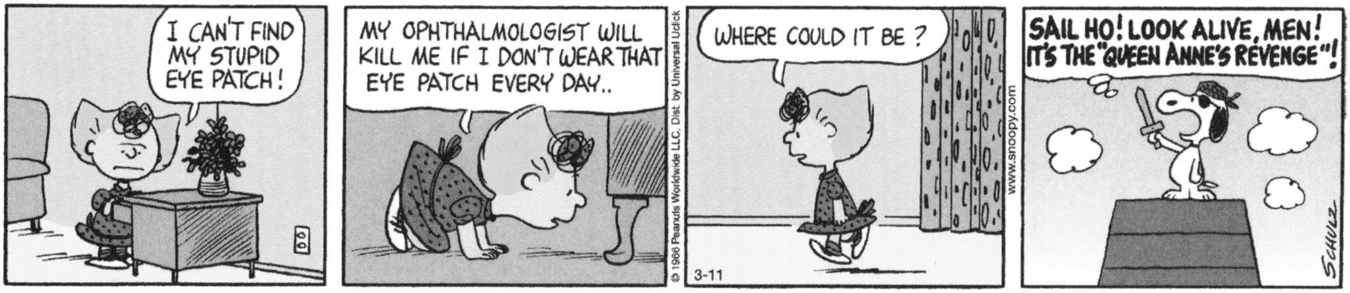
I CAN'T FIND MY STUPID EYE PATCH!
MY OPHTHALMOLOGIST WILL KILL ME IF I DON'T WEAR THAT EYE PATCH EVERY DAY..
© 1966 Peanuts Worldwide LLC, Dist. by Universal Uclick
3-11
WHERE COULD IT BE ?
www.snoopy.com
SAIL HO! LOOK ALIVE, MEN! IT'S THE "QUEEN ANNE'S REVENGE"!
SCHULZ

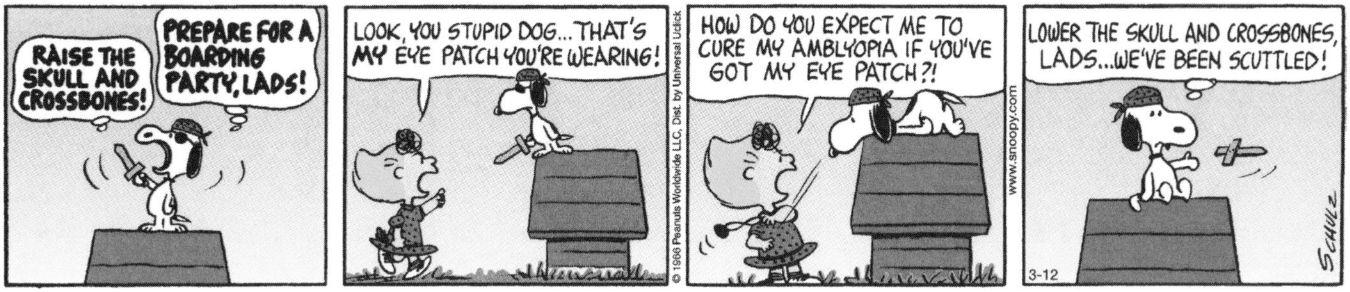
RAISE THE SKULL AND CROSSBONES!
PREPARE FOR A BOARDING PARTY, LADS!
LOOK, YOU STUPID DOG... THAT'S MY EYE PATCH YOU'RE WEARING!
© 1966 Peanuts Worldwide LLC, Dist. by Universal Uclick
HOW DO YOU EXPECT ME TO CURE MY AMBLYOPIA IF YOU'VE GOT MY EYE PATCH?!
www.snoopy.com
LOWER THE SKULL AND CROSSBONES, LADS...WE'VE BEEN SCUTTLED!
3-12
SCHULZ

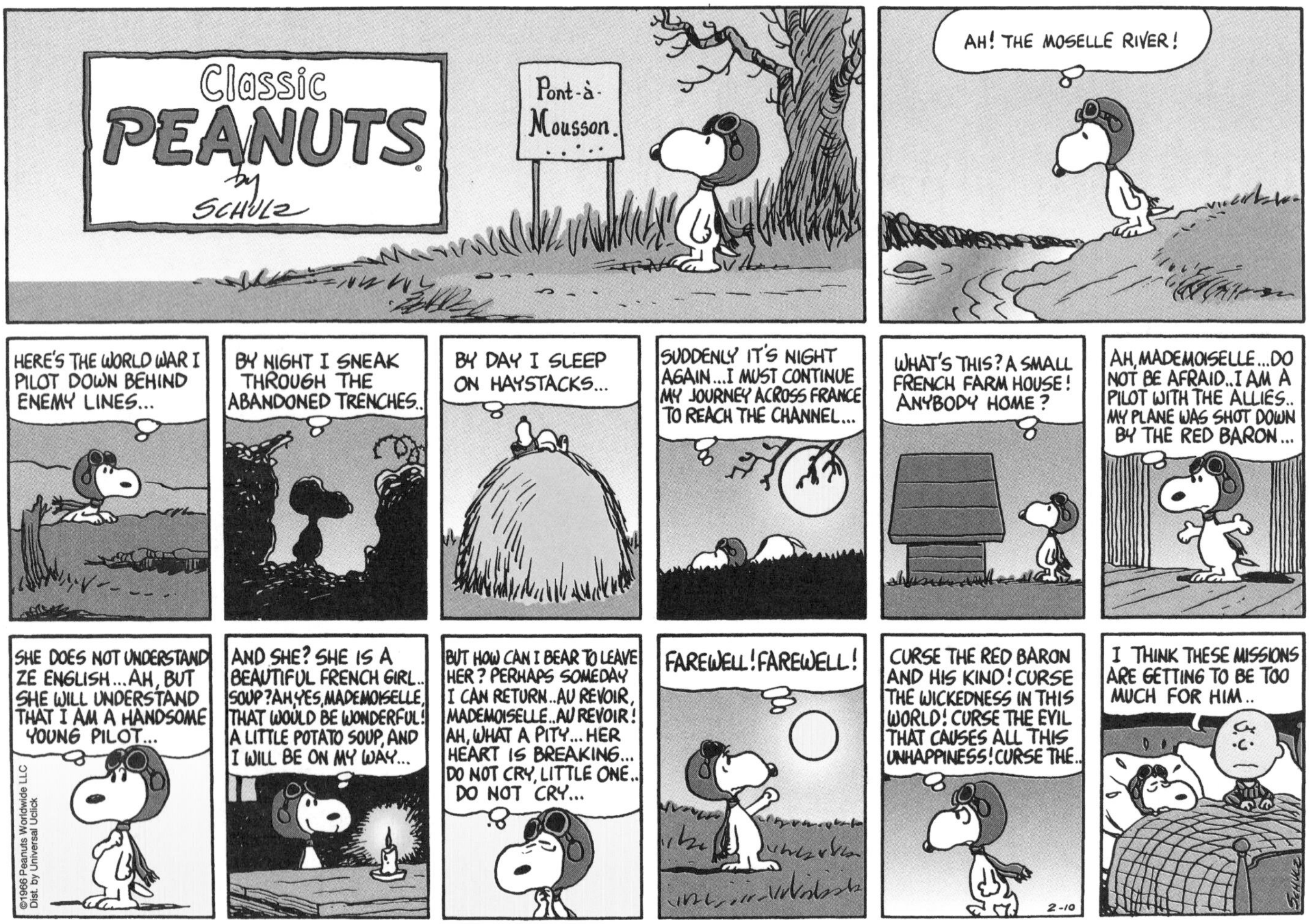
Classic
PEANUTS
by SCHULZ
Pont-à-Mousson
AH! THE MOSELLE RIVER!
HERE'S THE WORLD WAR I PILOT DOWN BEHIND ENEMY LINES...
BY NIGHT I SNEAK THROUGH THE ABANDONED TRENCHES..
BY DAY I SLEEP ON HAYSTACKS...
SUDDENLY IT'S NIGHT AGAIN...I MUST CONTINUE MY JOURNEY ACROSS FRANCE TO REACH THE CHANNEL...
WHAT'S THIS? A SMALL FRENCH FARM HOUSE! ANYBODY HOME?
AH, MADEMOISELLE...DO NOT BE AFRAID..I AM A PILOT WITH THE ALLIES.. MY PLANE WAS SHOT DOWN BY THE RED BARON...
SHE DOES NOT UNDERSTAND ZE ENGLISH...AH, BUT SHE WILL UNDERSTAND THAT I AM A HANDSOME YOUNG PILOT...
©1966 Peanuts Worldwide LLC
Dist. by Universal Uclick
AND SHE? SHE IS A BEAUTIFUL FRENCH GIRL.. SOUP? AH, YES, MADEMOISELLE, THAT WOULD BE WONDERFUL! A LITTLE POTATO SOUP, AND I WILL BE ON MY WAY...
BUT HOW CAN I BEAR TO LEAVE HER? PERHAPS SOMEDAY I CAN RETURN..AU REVOIR, MADEMOISELLE..AU REVOIR! AH, WHAT A PITY...HER HEART IS BREAKING... DO NOT CRY, LITTLE ONE.. DO NOT CRY...
FAREWELL! FAREWELL!
CURSE THE RED BARON AND HIS KIND! CURSE THE WICKEDNESS IN THIS WORLD! CURSE THE EVIL THAT CAUSES ALL THIS UNHAPPINESS! CURSE THE..
2-10
I THINK THESE MISSIONS ARE GETTING TO BE TOO MUCH FOR HIM..
SCHULZ

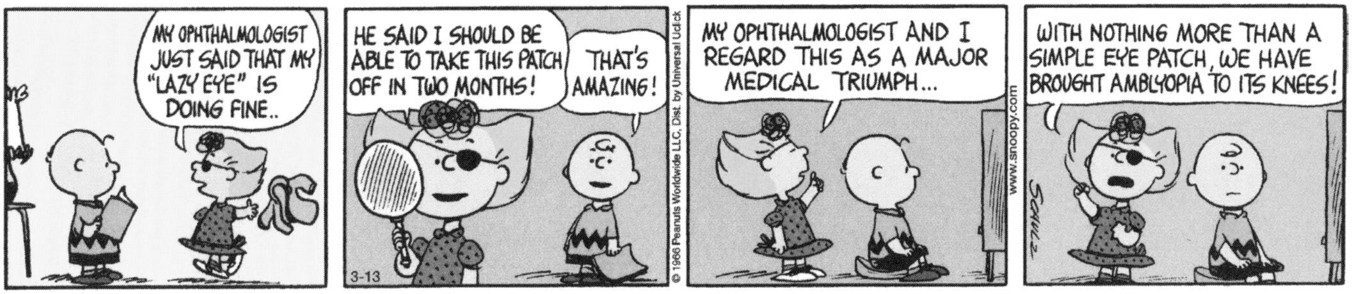
MY OPHTHALMOLOGIST JUST SAID THAT MY "LAZY EYE" IS DOING FINE..
HE SAID I SHOULD BE ABLE TO TAKE THIS PATCH OFF IN TWO MONTHS!
THAT'S AMAZING!
3-13
© 1966 Peanuts Worldwide LLC, Dist. by Universal Uclick
MY OPHTHALMOLOGIST AND I REGARD THIS AS A MAJOR MEDICAL TRIUMPH...
www.snoopy.com
SCHULZ
WITH NOTHING MORE THAN A SIMPLE EYE PATCH, WE HAVE BROUGHT AMBLYOPIA TO ITS KNEES!

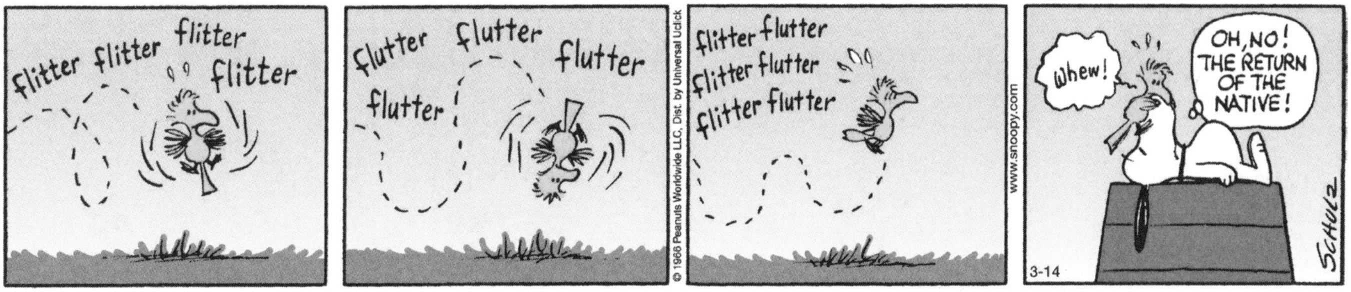
flitter flitter flitter flitter
flutter flutter flutter flutter
© 1966 Peanuts Worldwide LLC, Dist. by Universal Uclick
flitter flutter flitter flutter flitter flutter
www.snoopy.com
Whew!
OH, NO! THE RETURN OF THE NATIVE!
3-14
SCHULZ

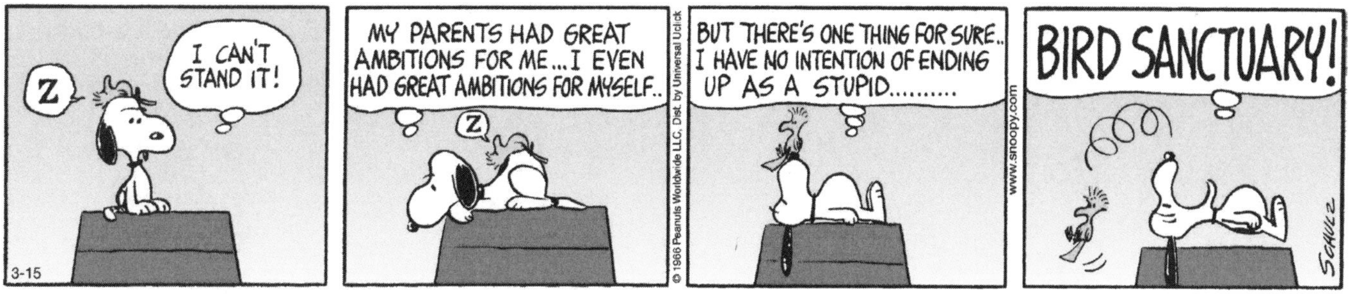
Z
I CAN'T STAND IT!
3-15
MY PARENTS HAD GREAT AMBITIONS FOR ME...I EVEN HAD GREAT AMBITIONS FOR MYSELF..
Z
© 1966 Peanuts Worldwide LLC, Dist. by Universal Uclick
BUT THERE'S ONE THING FOR SURE.. I HAVE NO INTENTION OF ENDING UP AS A STUPID..........
www.snoopy.com
BIRD SANCTUARY!
SCHULZ

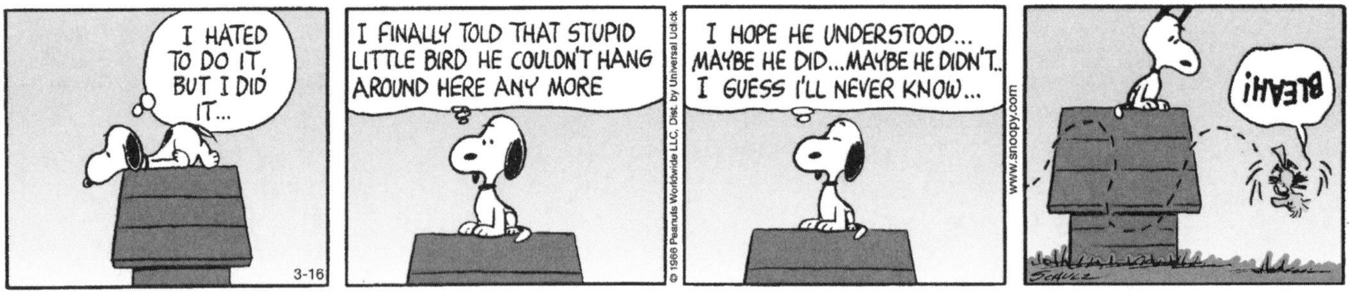
I HATED TO DO IT, BUT I DID IT...
3-16
I FINALLY TOLD THAT STUPID LITTLE BIRD HE COULDN'T HANG AROUND HERE ANY MORE
© 1966 Peanuts Worldwide LLC, Dist. by Universal Uclick
I HOPE HE UNDERSTOOD... MAYBE HE DID...MAYBE HE DIDN'T.. I GUESS I'LL NEVER KNOW...
www.snoopy.com
BLEAH!
SCHULZ

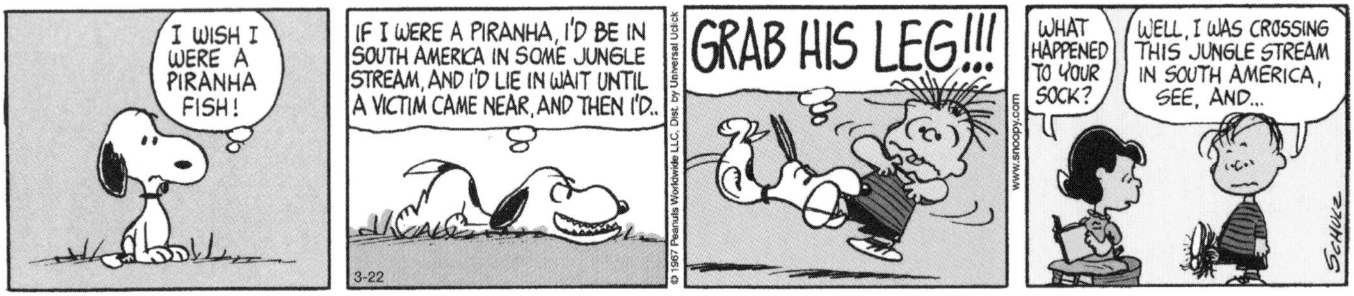
I WISH I WERE A PIRANHA FISH!
IF I WERE A PIRANHA, I'D BE IN SOUTH AMERICA IN SOME JUNGLE STREAM, AND I'D LIE IN WAIT UNTIL A VICTIM CAME NEAR, AND THEN I'D..
3-22
© 1967 Peanuts Worldwide LLC, Dist. by Universal Uclick
GRAB HIS LEG!!!...
www.snoopy.com
WHAT HAPPENED TO YOUR SOCK?
WELL, I WAS CROSSING THIS JUNGLE STREAM IN SOUTH AMERICA, SEE, AND...
SCHULZ

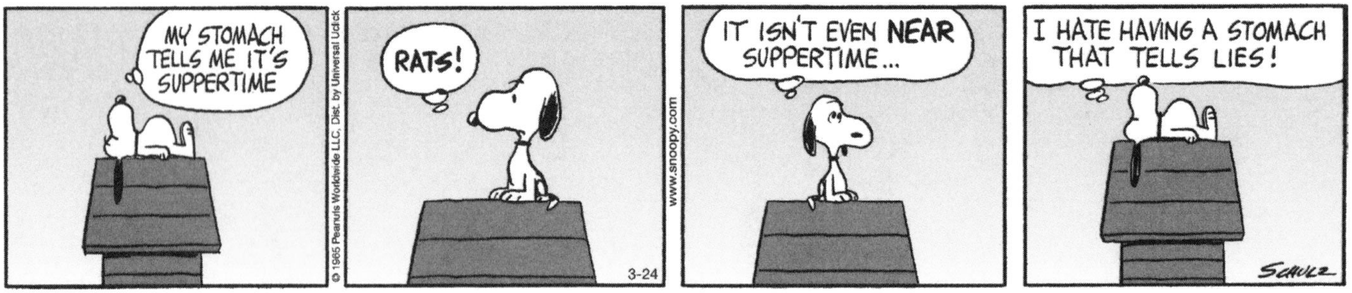
MY STOMACH TELLS ME IT'S SUPPERTIME
© 1965 Peanuts Worldwide LLC, Dist. by Universal Uclick
RATS!
3-24
www.snoopy.com
IT ISN'T EVEN NEAR SUPPERTIME...
I HATE HAVING A STOMACH THAT TELLS LIES!
SCHULZ

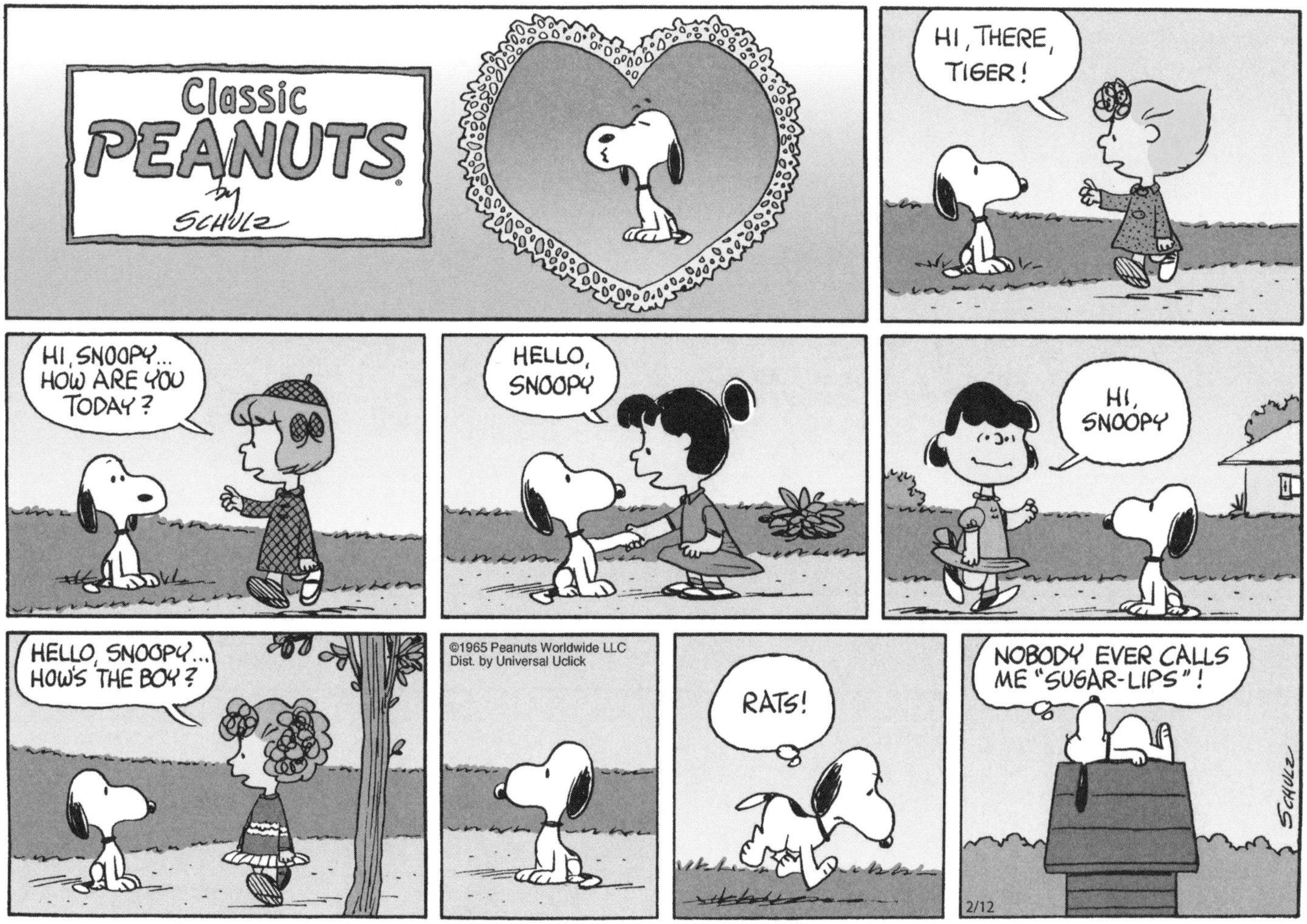
Classic PEANUTS by SCHULZ
HI, THERE, TIGER!
HI, SNOOPY... HOW ARE YOU TODAY?
HELLO, SNOOPY
HI, SNOOPY
HELLO, SNOOPY... HOW'S THE BOY?
©1965 Peanuts Worldwide LLC
Dist. by Universal Uclick
RATS!
NOBODY EVER CALLS ME "SUGAR-LIPS"!
2/12
SCHULZ

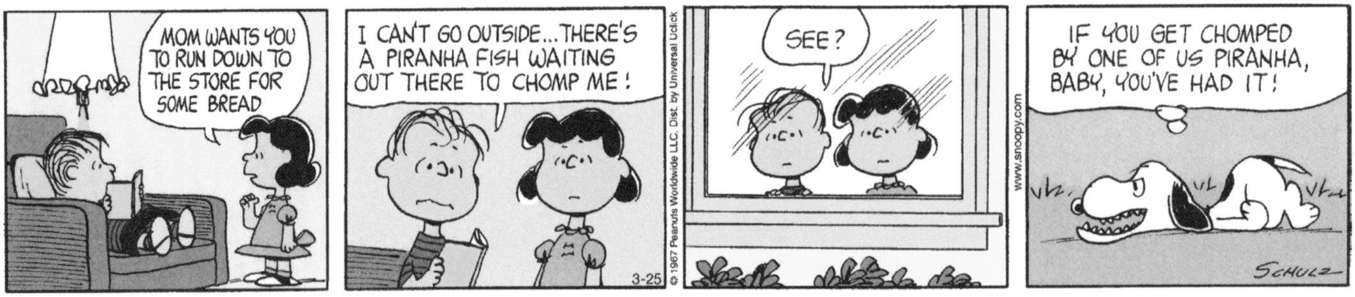
MOM WANTS YOU TO RUN DOWN TO THE STORE FOR SOME BREAD
I CAN'T GO OUTSIDE...THERE'S A PIRANHA FISH WAITING OUT THERE TO CHOMP ME!
3-25
© 1967 Peanuts Worldwide LLC. Dist. by Universal Uclick
SEE?
www.snoopy.com
IF YOU GET CHOMPED BY ONE OF US PIRANHA, BABY, YOU'VE HAD IT!
SCHULZ

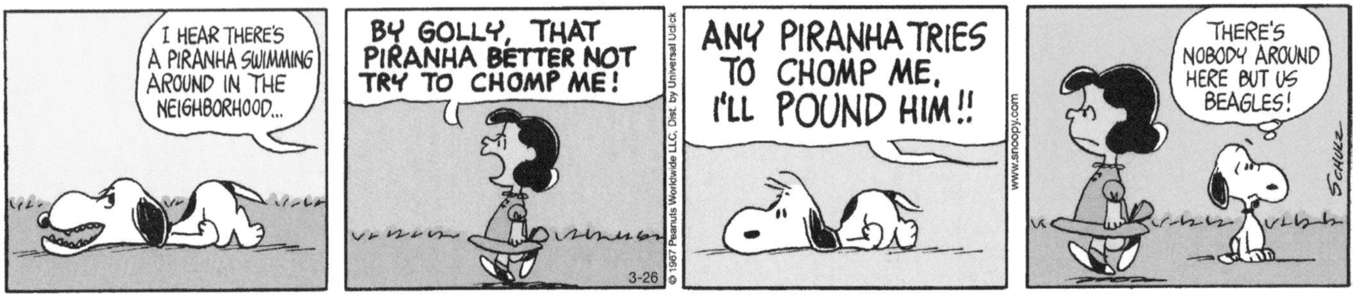
I HEAR THERE'S A PIRANHA SWIMMING AROUND IN THE NEIGHBORHOOD...
BY GOLLY, THAT PIRANHA BETTER NOT TRY TO CHOMP ME!
3-26
© 1967 Peanuts Worldwide LLC. Dist. by Universal Uclick
ANY PIRANHA TRIES TO CHOMP ME, I'LL POUND HIM!!
www.snoopy.com
THERE'S NOBODY AROUND HERE BUT US BEAGLES!
SCHULZ

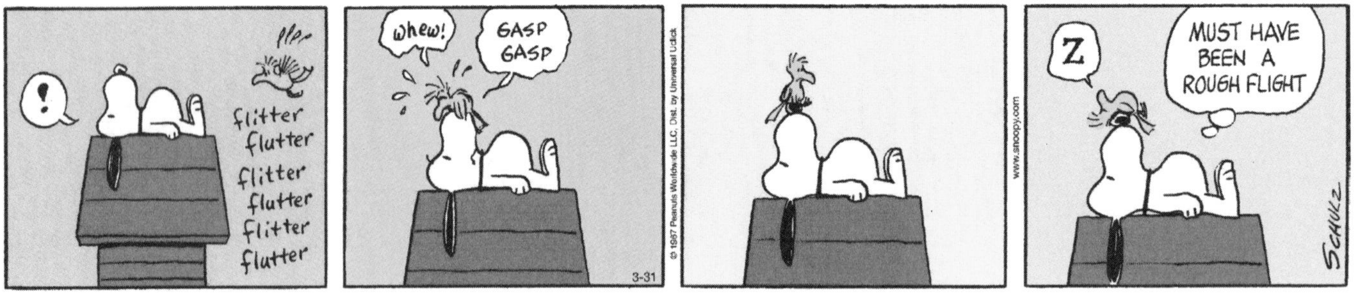
!
flitter flutter flitter flutter flitter flutter
whew!
GASP GASP
3-31
© 1967 Peanuts Worldwide LLC. Dist. by Universal Uclick
www.snoopy.com
Z
MUST HAVE BEEN A ROUGH FLIGHT
SCHULZ

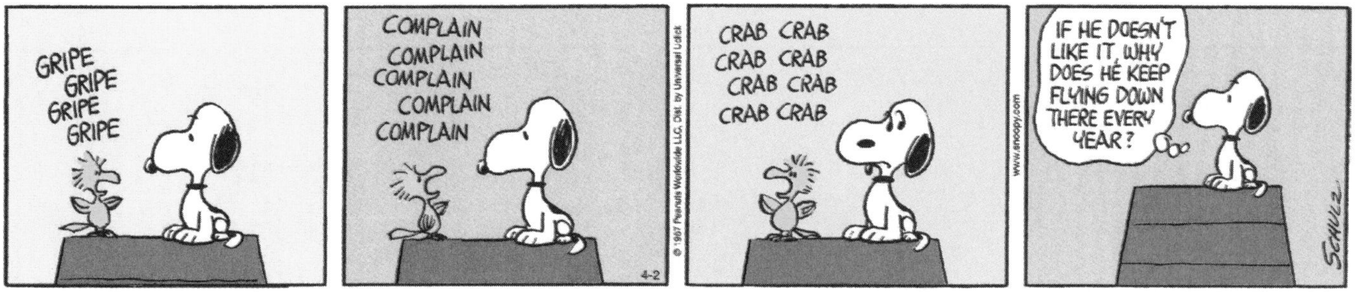
GRIPE GRIPE GRIPE GRIPE
COMPLAIN COMPLAIN COMPLAIN COMPLAIN COMPLAIN
© 1967 Peanuts Worldwide LLC. Dist. by Universal Uclick
4-2
CRAB CRAB CRAB CRAB CRAB CRAB CRAB CRAB
www.snoopy.com
IF HE DOESN'T LIKE IT, WHY DOES HE KEEP FLYING DOWN THERE EVERY YEAR?
SCHULZ

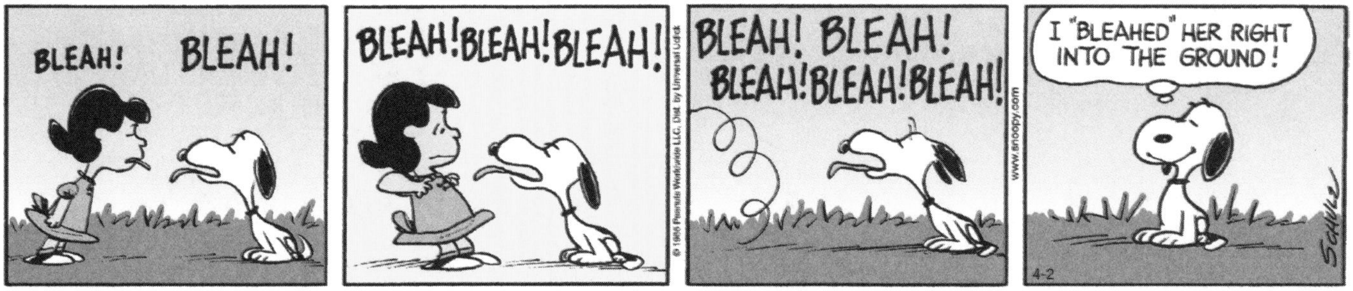
BLEAH! BLEAH!
BLEAH! BLEAH! BLEAH!
© 1966 Peanuts Worldwide LLC. Dist. by Universal Uclick
BLEAH! BLEAH! BLEAH! BLEAH! BLEAH!
www.snoopy.com
I "BLEAHED" HER RIGHT INTO THE GROUND!
4-2
SCHULZ

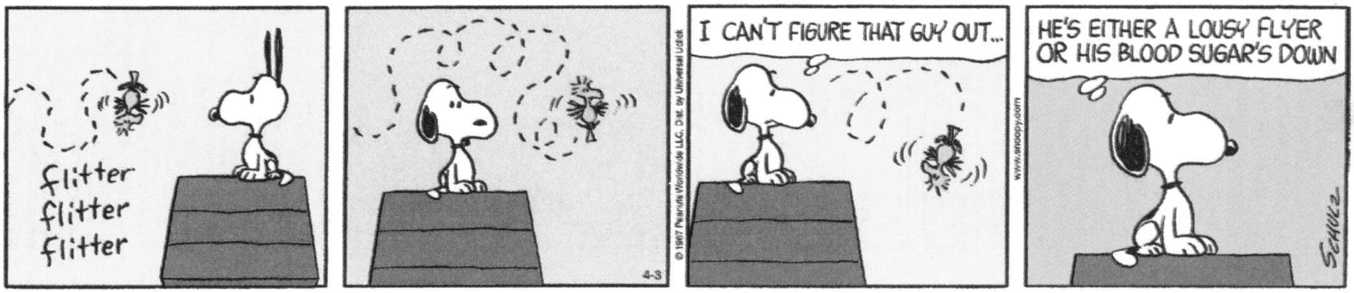
flitter flitter flitter
4-3
© 1967 Peanuts Worldwide LLC. Dist. by Universal Uclick
I CAN'T FIGURE THAT GUY OUT...
www.snoopy.com
HE'S EITHER A LOUSY FLYER OR HIS BLOOD SUGAR'S DOWN
SCHULZ

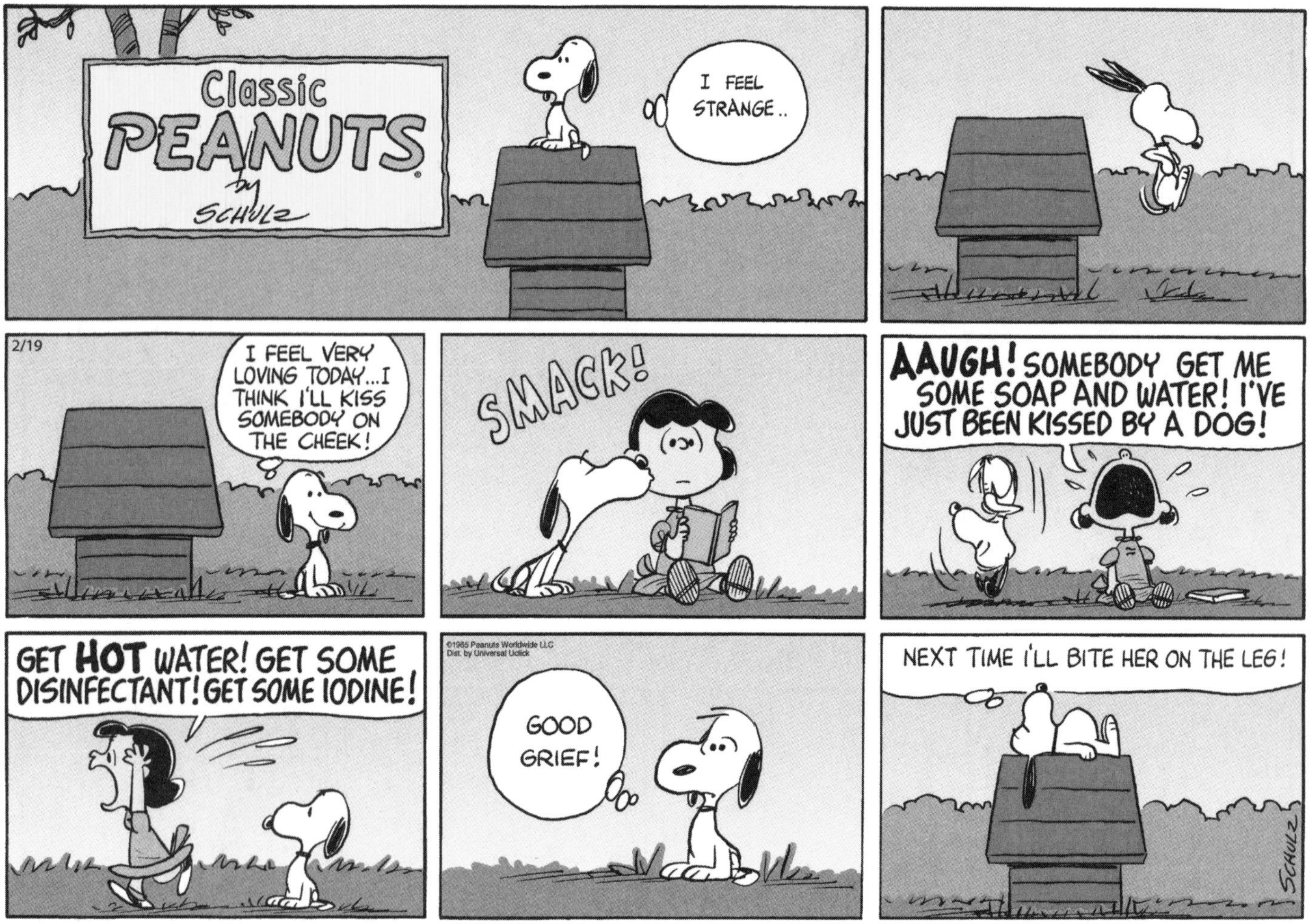
Classic PEANUTS by SCHULZ
I FEEL STRANGE..
2/19
I FEEL VERY LOVING TODAY...I THINK I'LL KISS SOMEBODY ON THE CHEEK!
SMACK!
AAUGH! SOMEBODY GET ME SOME SOAP AND WATER! I'VE JUST BEEN KISSED BY A DOG!
GET HOT WATER! GET SOME DISINFECTANT! GET SOME IODINE!
©1965 Peanuts Worldwide LLC
Dist. by Universal Uclick
GOOD GRIEF!
NEXT TIME I'LL BITE HER ON THE LEG!
SCHULZ

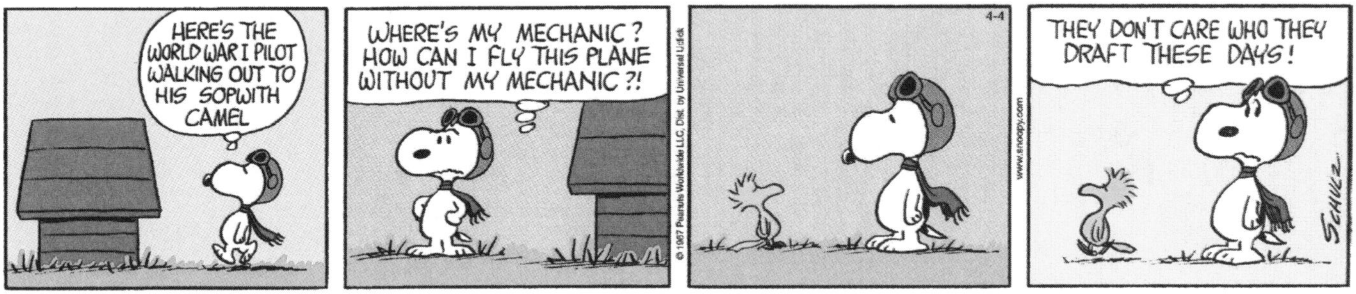
HERE'S THE WORLD WAR I PILOT WALKING OUT TO HIS SOPWITH CAMEL
WHERE'S MY MECHANIC? HOW CAN I FLY THIS PLANE WITHOUT MY MECHANIC?!
© 1987 Peanuts Worldwide LLC. Dist. by Universal Uclick
4-4
www.snoopy.com
THEY DON'T CARE WHO THEY DRAFT THESE DAYS!
SCHULZ

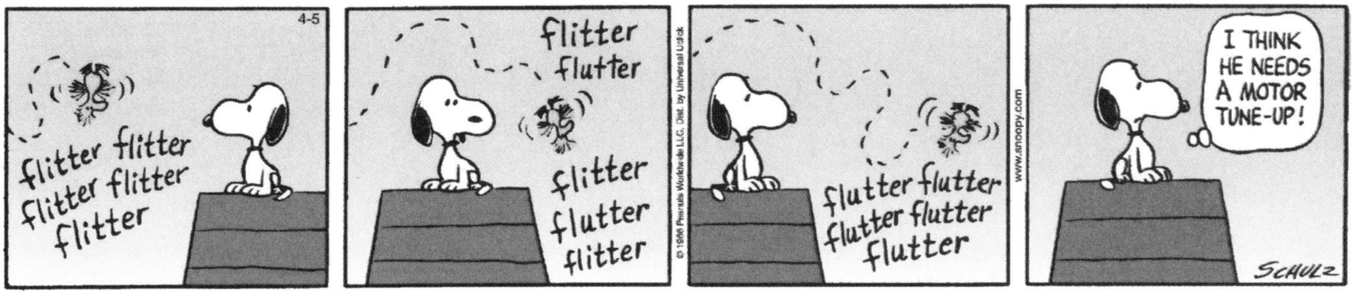
4-5
flitter flitter flitter flitter flitter
flitter flutter
flitter flutter flitter
© 1988 Peanuts Worldwide LLC. Dist. by Universal Uclick
flutter flutter flutter flutter flutter
www.snoopy.com
I THINK HE NEEDS A MOTOR TUNE-UP!
SCHULZ

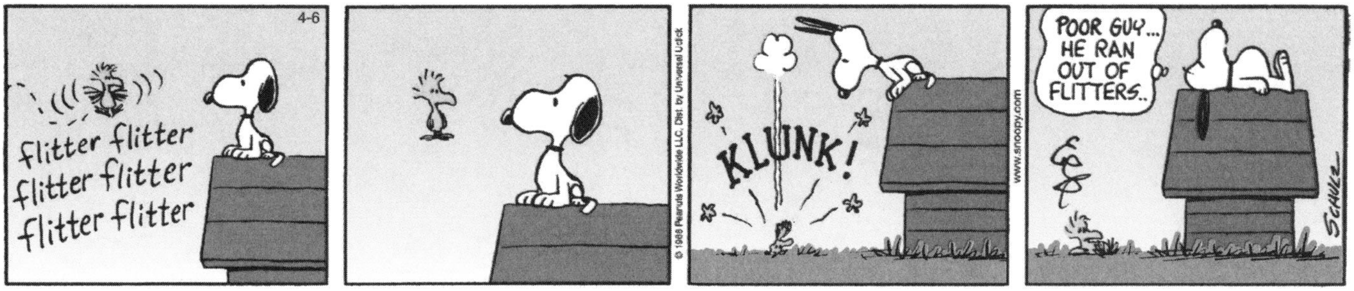
4-6
flitter flitter flitter flitter flitter flitter
© 1988 Peanuts Worldwide LLC. Dist. by Universal Uclick
KLUNK!
www.snoopy.com
POOR GUY... HE RAN OUT OF FLITTERS..
SCHULZ

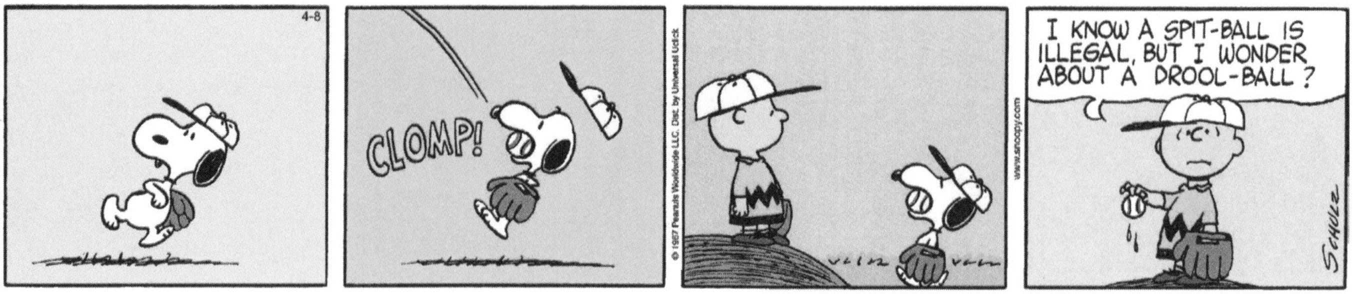
4-8
CLOMP!
© 1987 Peanuts Worldwide LLC. Dist. by Universal Uclick
www.snoopy.com
I KNOW A SPIT-BALL IS ILLEGAL, BUT I WONDER ABOUT A DROOL-BALL ?
SCHULZ

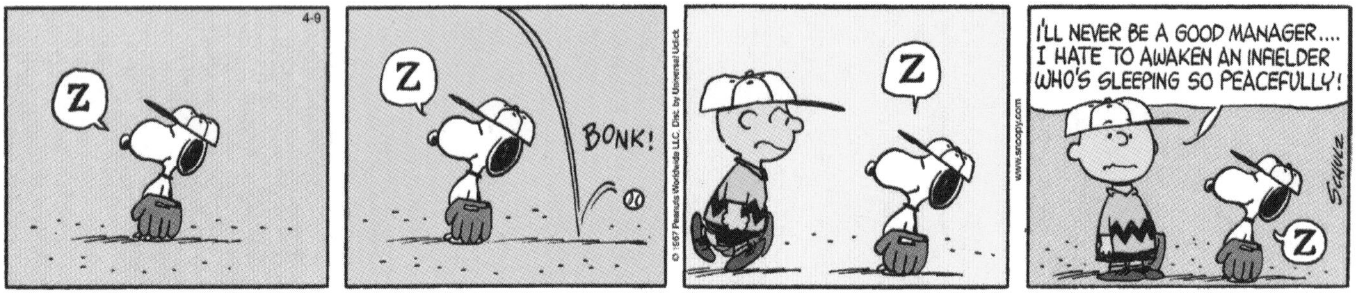
4-9
Z
Z
BONK!
© 1987 Peanuts Worldwide LLC. Dist. by Universal Uclick
Z
www.snoopy.com
I'LL NEVER BE A GOOD MANAGER.... I HATE TO AWAKEN AN INFIELDER WHO'S SLEEPING SO PEACEFULLY!
Z
SCHULZ

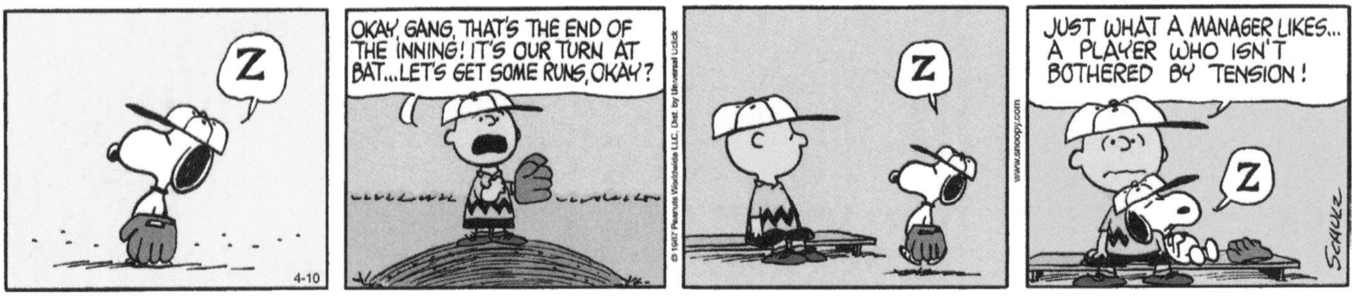
Z
4-10
OKAY, GANG, THAT'S THE END OF THE INNING! IT'S OUR TURN AT BAT...LET'S GET SOME RUNS, OKAY?
© 1987 Peanuts Worldwide LLC. Dist. by Universal Uclick
Z
www.snoopy.com
JUST WHAT A MANAGER LIKES... A PLAYER WHO ISN'T BOTHERED BY TENSION!
Z
SCHULZ

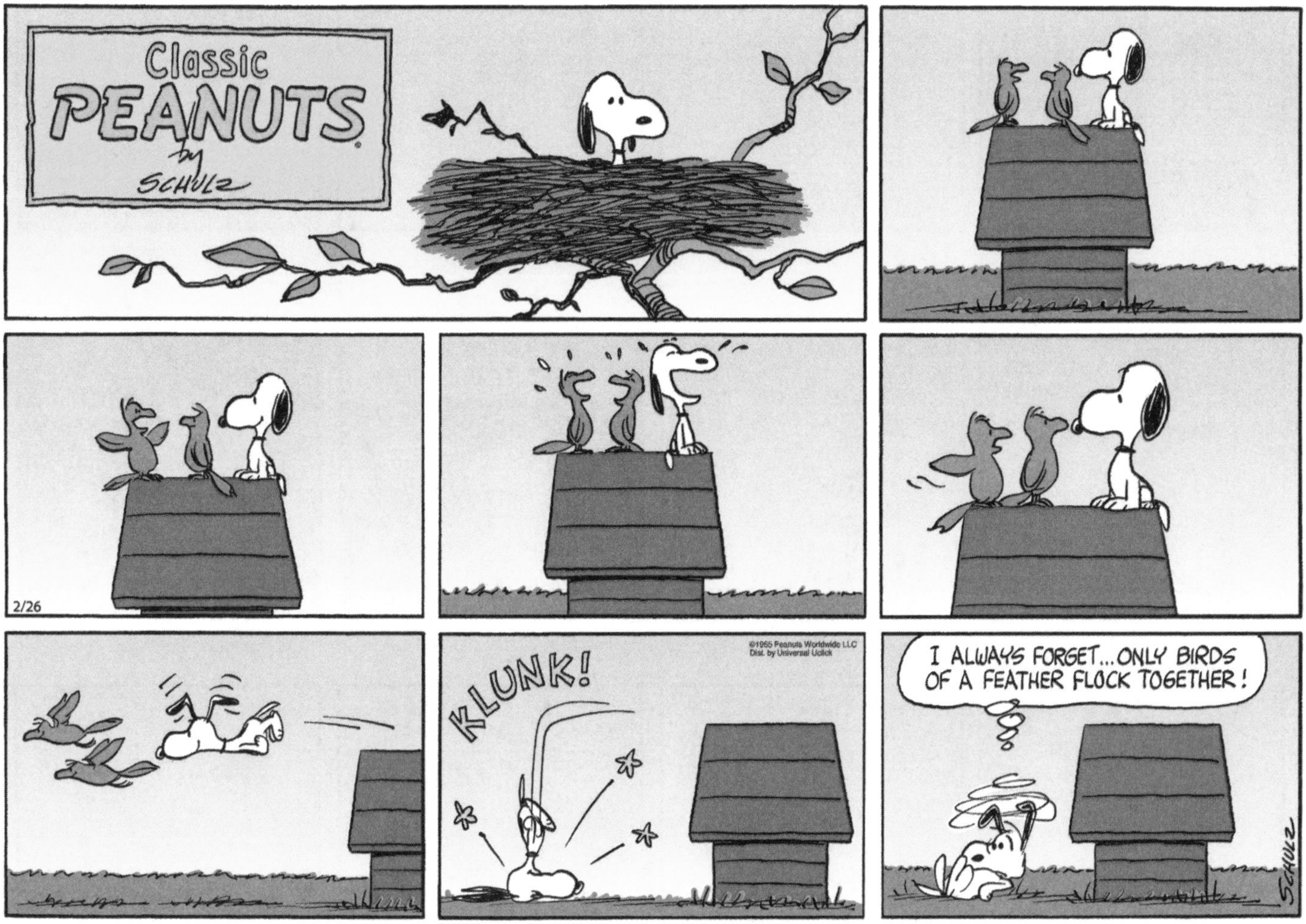
Classic PEANUTS by SCHULZ
2/26
KLUNK!
©1955 Peanuts Worldwide LLC
Dist. by Universal Uclick
I ALWAYS FORGET...ONLY BIRDS OF A FEATHER FLOCK TOGETHER!
SCHULZ

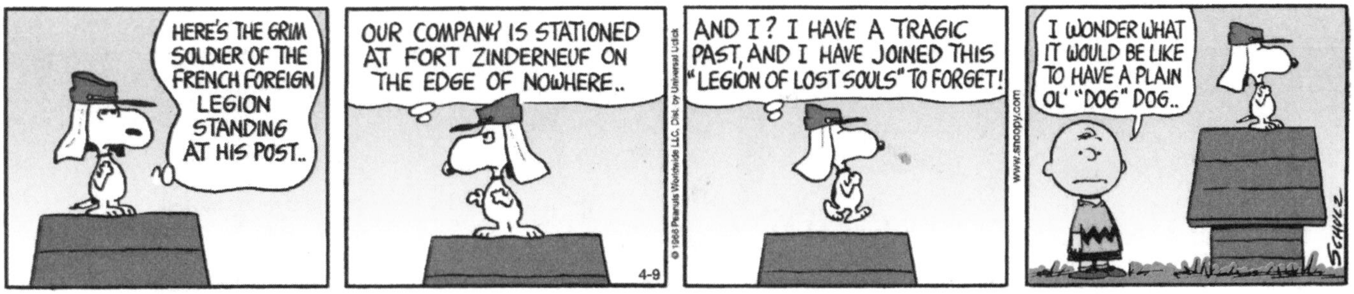
HERE'S THE GRIM SOLDIER OF THE FRENCH FOREIGN LEGION STANDING AT HIS POST..
OUR COMPANY IS STATIONED AT FORT ZINDERNEUF ON THE EDGE OF NOWHERE..
4-9
© 1966 Peanuts Worldwide LLC, Dist. by Universal Uclick
AND I ? I HAVE A TRAGIC PAST, AND I HAVE JOINED THIS "LEGION OF LOST SOULS" TO FORGET!
www.snoopy.com
I WONDER WHAT IT WOULD BE LIKE TO HAVE A PLAIN OL' "DOG" DOG..
SCHULZ

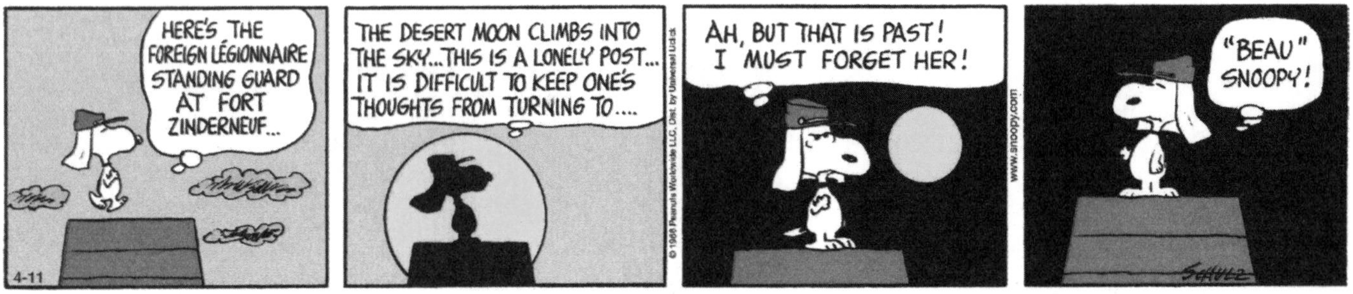
HERE'S THE FOREIGN LÉGIONNAIRE STANDING GUARD AT FORT ZINDERNEUF...
4-11
THE DESERT MOON CLIMBS INTO THE SKY...THIS IS A LONELY POST... IT IS DIFFICULT TO KEEP ONE'S THOUGHTS FROM TURNING TO....
© 1966 Peanuts Worldwide LLC, Dist. by Universal Uclick
AH, BUT THAT IS PAST! I MUST FORGET HER!
www.snoopy.com
"BEAU" SNOOPY!
SCHULZ

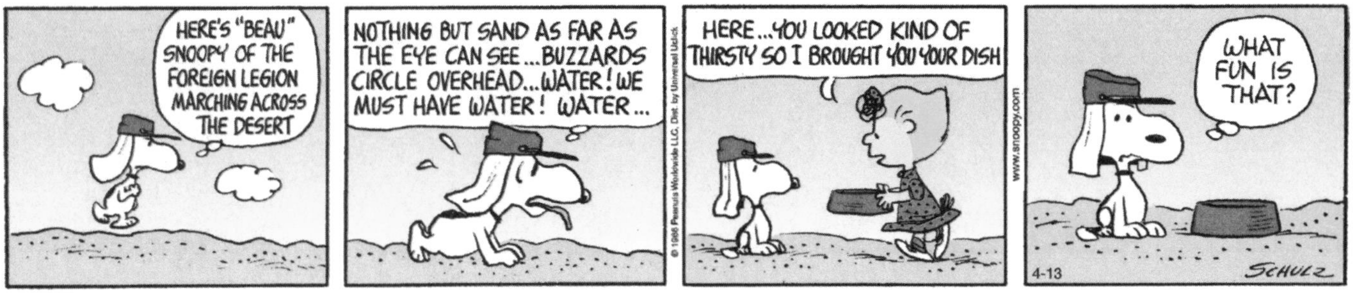
HERE'S "BEAU" SNOOPY OF THE FOREIGN LEGION MARCHING ACROSS THE DESERT
NOTHING BUT SAND AS FAR AS THE EYE CAN SEE...BUZZARDS CIRCLE OVERHEAD...WATER! WE MUST HAVE WATER! WATER...
© 1966 Peanuts Worldwide LLC, Dist. by Universal Uclick
HERE...YOU LOOKED KIND OF THIRSTY SO I BROUGHT YOU YOUR DISH
www.snoopy.com
WHAT FUN IS THAT?
4-13
SCHULZ

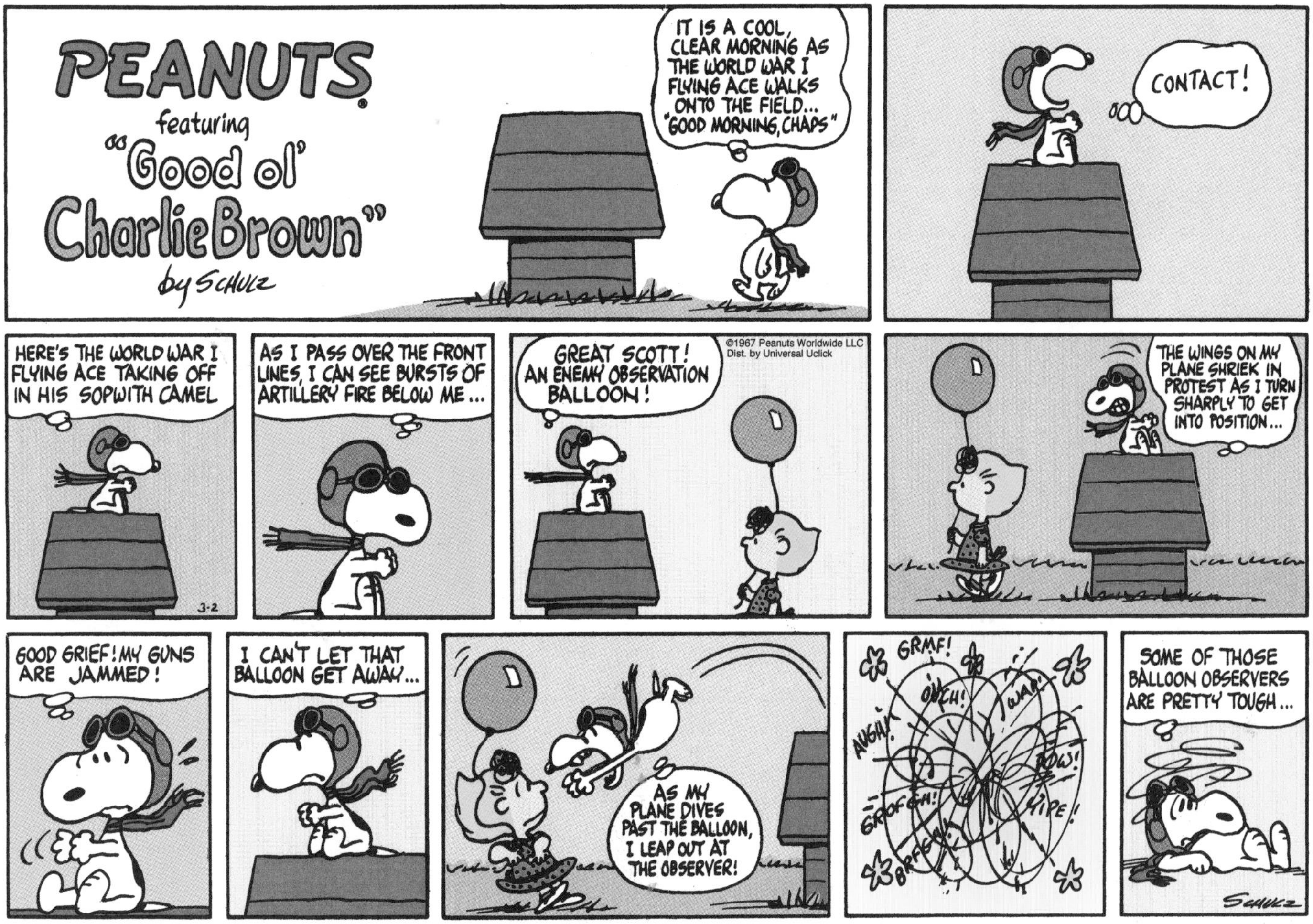
PEANUTS
featuring "Good ol' CharlieBrown"
by SCHULZ
IT IS A COOL, CLEAR MORNING AS THE WORLD WAR I FLYING ACE WALKS ONTO THE FIELD... "GOOD MORNING, CHAPS"
CONTACT!
HERE'S THE WORLD WAR I FLYING ACE TAKING OFF IN HIS SOPWITH CAMEL
3-2
AS I PASS OVER THE FRONT LINES, I CAN SEE BURSTS OF ARTILLERY FIRE BELOW ME...
GREAT SCOTT! AN ENEMY OBSERVATION BALLOON!
©1967 Peanuts Worldwide LLC
Dist. by Universal Uclick
THE WINGS ON MY PLANE SHRIEK IN PROTEST AS I TURN SHARPLY TO GET INTO POSITION...
GOOD GRIEF! MY GUNS ARE JAMMED!
I CAN'T LET THAT BALLOON GET AWAY...
AS MY PLANE DIVES PAST THE BALLOON, I LEAP OUT AT THE OBSERVER!
GRMF!
OUCH!
WAP!
AUGH!
POW!
SOME OF THOSE BALLOON OBSERVERS ARE PRETTY TOUGH...
SCHULZ

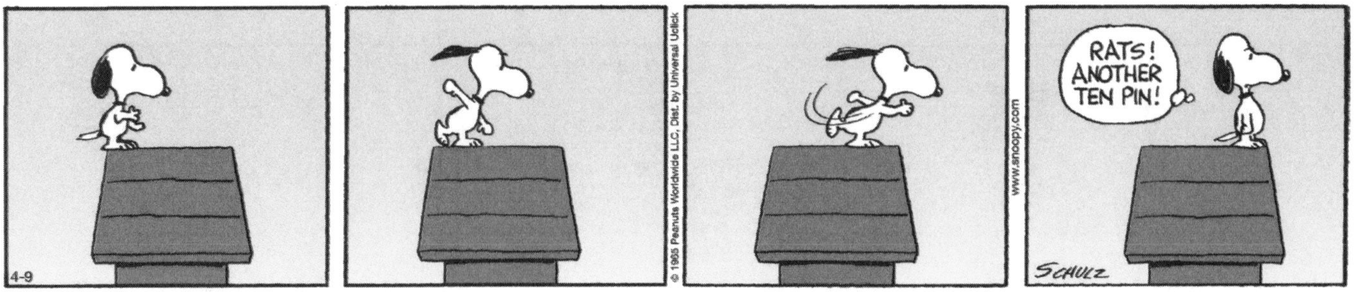
4-9
© 1965 Peanuts Worldwide LLC, Dist. by Universal Uclick
www.snoopy.com
RATS! ANOTHER TEN PIN!
SCHULZ

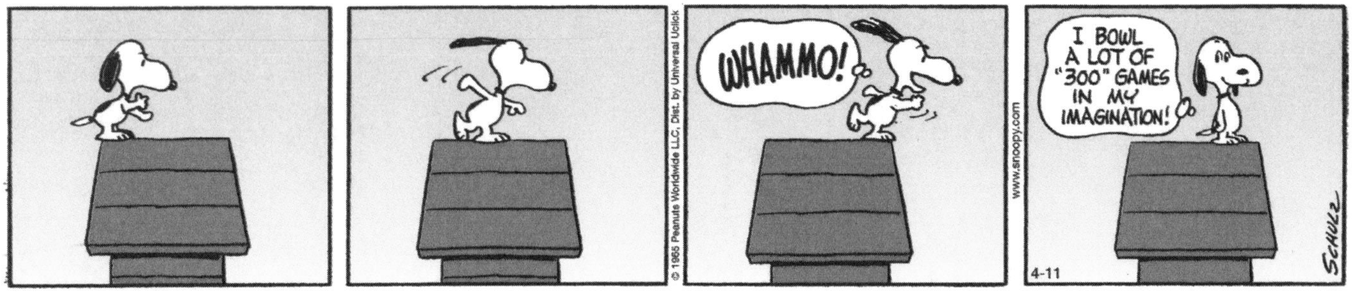
© 1965 Peanuts Worldwide LLC, Dist. by Universal Uclick
WHAMMO!
www.snoopy.com
I BOWL A LOT OF "300" GAMES IN MY IMAGINATION!
4-11
SCHULZ

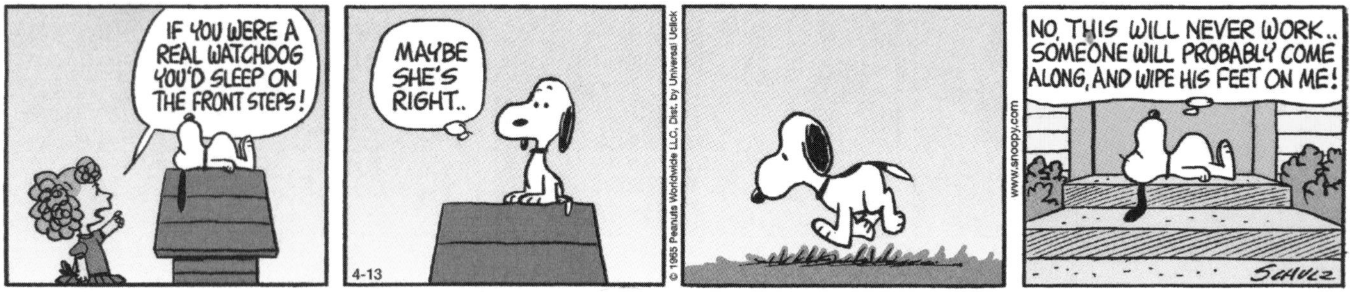
IF YOU WERE A REAL WATCHDOG YOU'D SLEEP ON THE FRONT STEPS!
MAYBE SHE'S RIGHT..
4-13
© 1965 Peanuts Worldwide LLC, Dist. by Universal Uclick
www.snoopy.com
NO, THIS WILL NEVER WORK.. SOMEONE WILL PROBABLY COME ALONG, AND WIPE HIS FEET ON ME!
SCHULZ

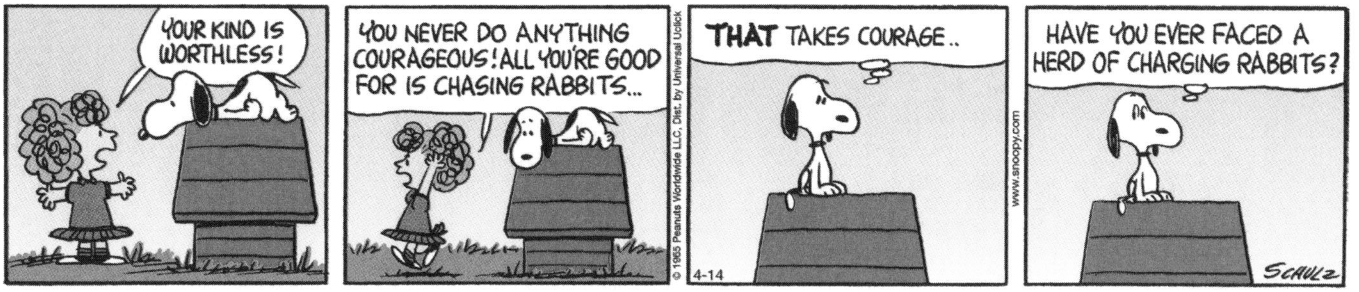
YOUR KIND IS WORTHLESS!
YOU NEVER DO ANYTHING COURAGEOUS! ALL YOU'RE GOOD FOR IS CHASING RABBITS...
THAT TAKES COURAGE..
HAVE YOU EVER FACED A HERD OF CHARGING RABBITS?
SCHULZ

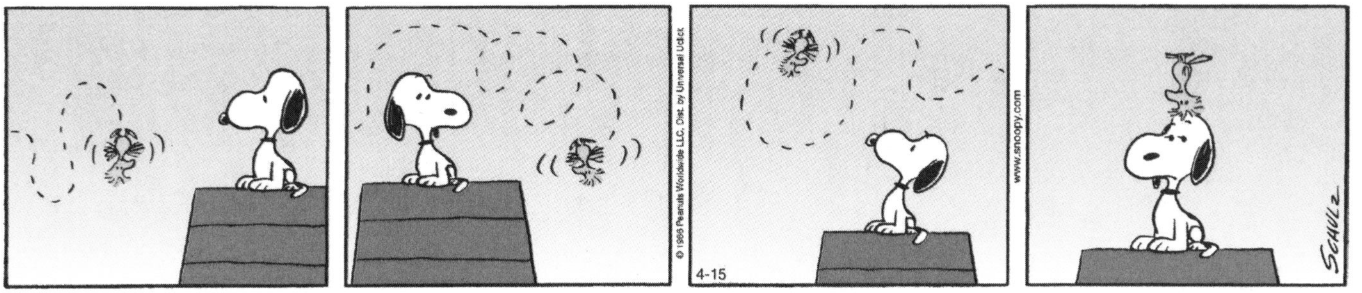
SCHULZ

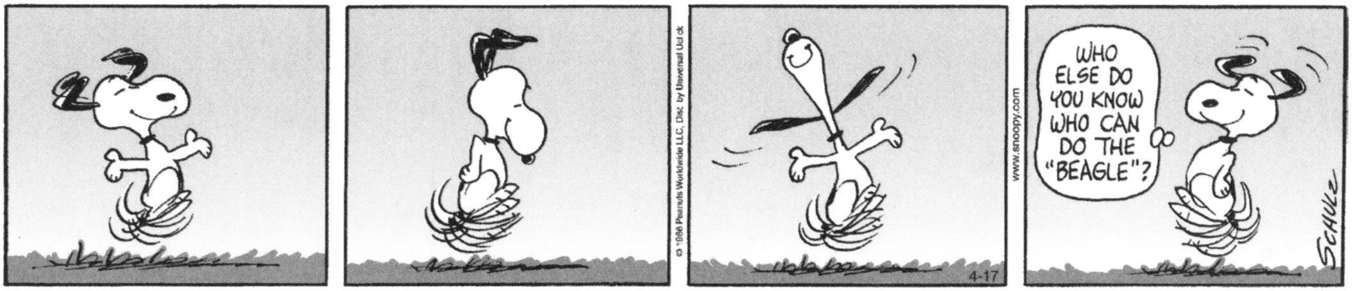
WHO ELSE DO YOU KNOW WHO CAN DO THE "BEAGLE"?
SCHULZ

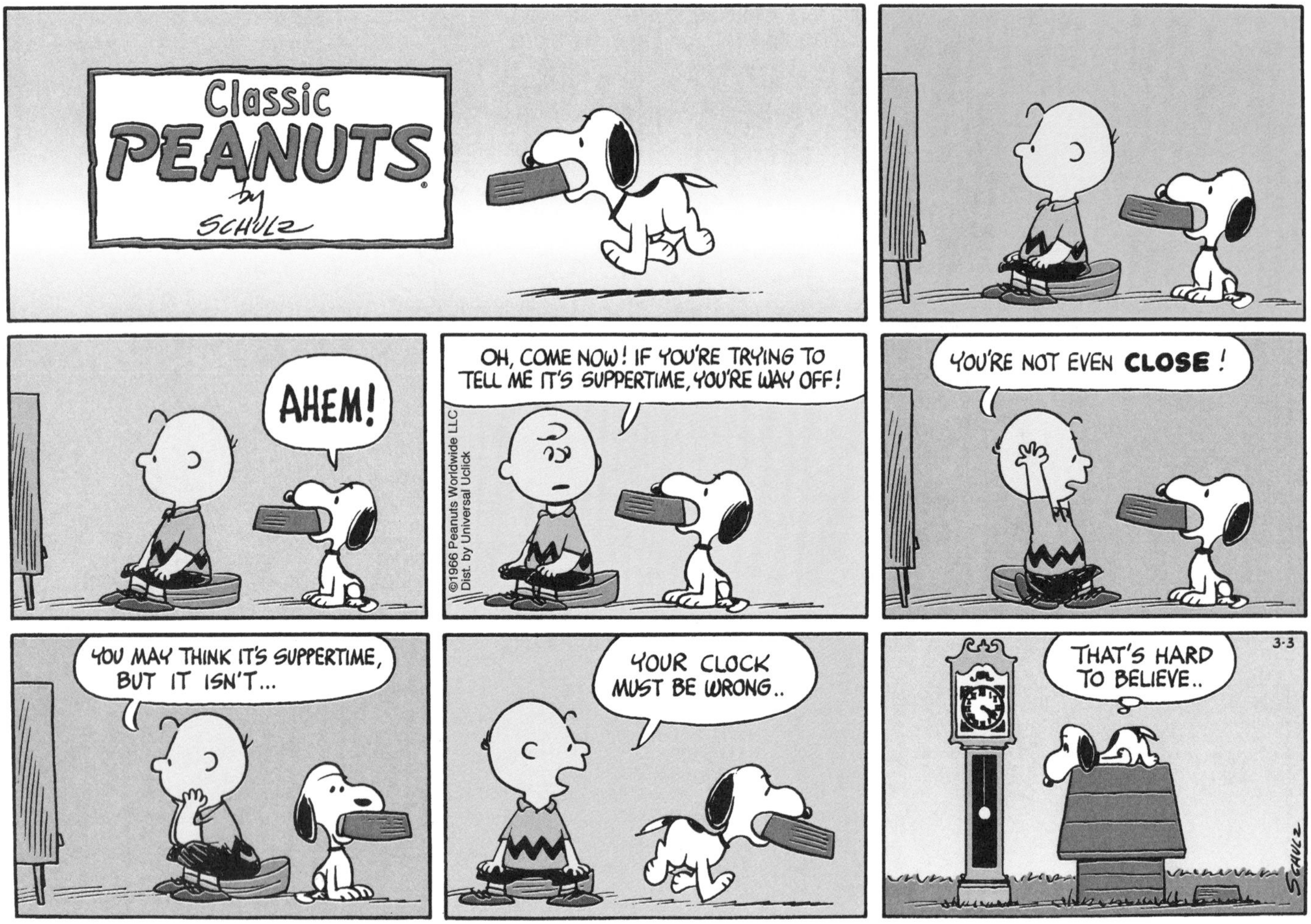
Classic PEANUTS by SCHULZ
AHEM!
OH, COME NOW! IF YOU'RE TRYING TO TELL ME IT'S SUPPERTIME, YOU'RE WAY OFF!
©1966 Peanuts Worldwide LLC Dist. by Universal Uclick
YOU'RE NOT EVEN CLOSE!
YOU MAY THINK IT'S SUPPERTIME, BUT IT ISN'T...
YOUR CLOCK MUST BE WRONG..
THAT'S HARD TO BELIEVE..
3-3
SCHULZ

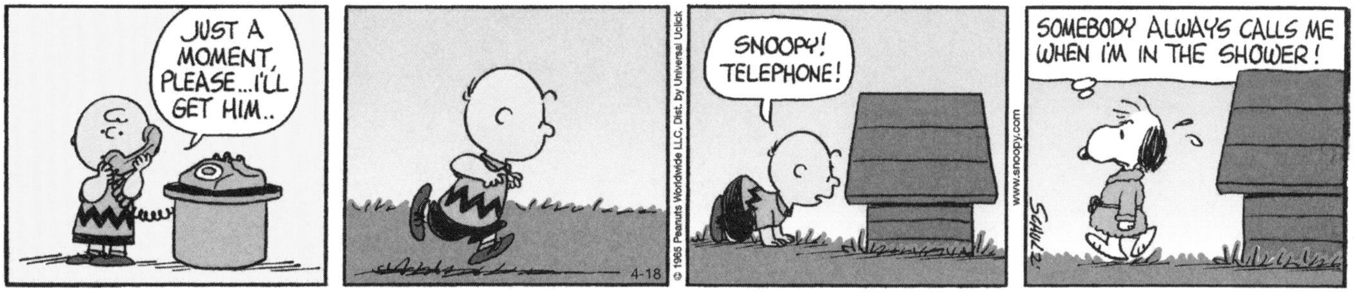
JUST A MOMENT, PLEASE...I'LL GET HIM..
4-18
SNOOPY! TELEPHONE!
SOMEBODY ALWAYS CALLS ME WHEN I'M IN THE SHOWER!
SCHULZ

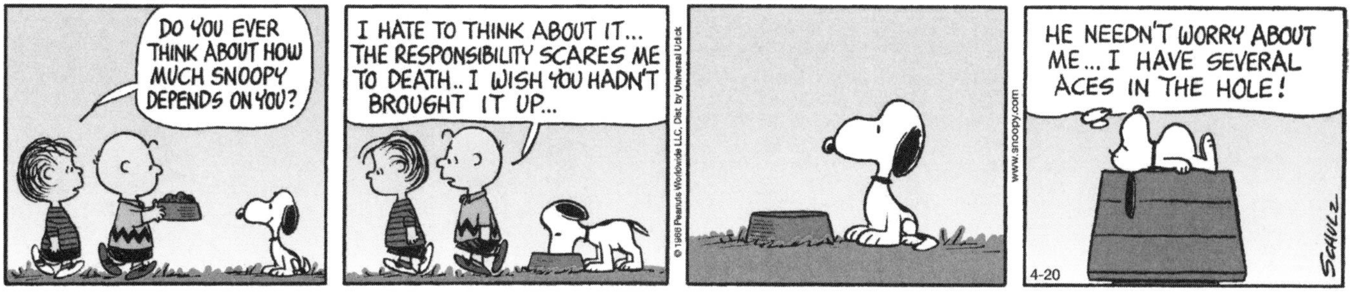
DO YOU EVER THINK ABOUT HOW MUCH SNOOPY DEPENDS ON YOU?
I HATE TO THINK ABOUT IT... THE RESPONSIBILITY SCARES ME TO DEATH.. I WISH YOU HADN'T BROUGHT IT UP...
HE NEEDN'T WORRY ABOUT ME... I HAVE SEVERAL ACES IN THE HOLE!
4-20
SCHULZ

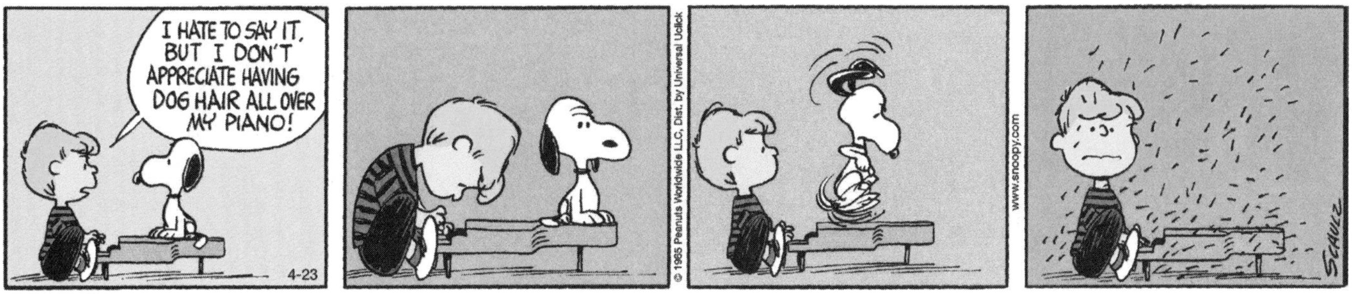
I HATE TO SAY IT, BUT I DON'T APPRECIATE HAVING DOG HAIR ALL OVER MY PIANO!
4-23
SCHULZ

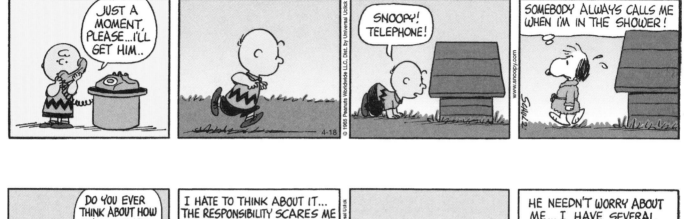

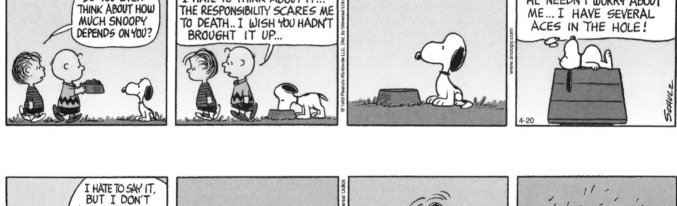

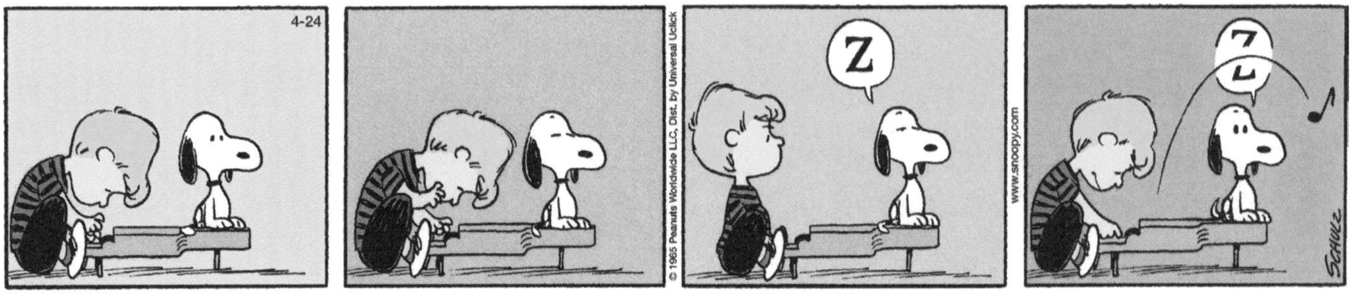
4-24
© 1965 Peanuts Worldwide LLC, Dist. by Universal Uclick
Z
www.snoopy.com
Z
SCHULZ

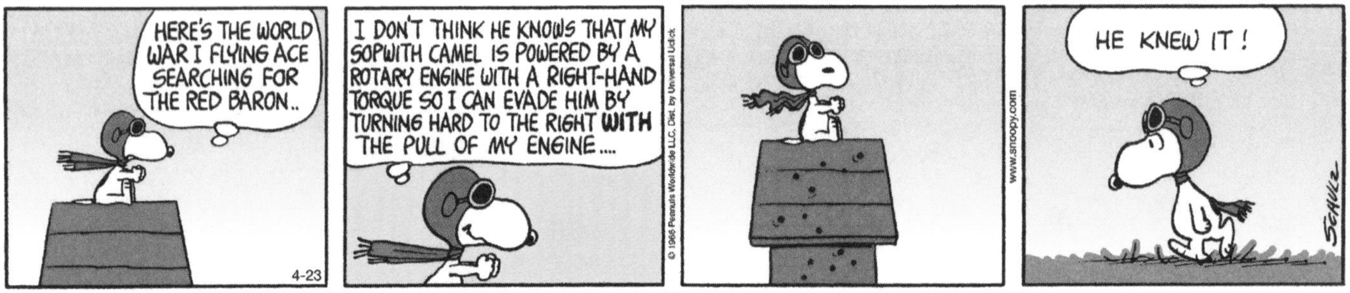
HERE'S THE WORLD WAR I FLYING ACE SEARCHING FOR THE RED BARON..
4-23
I DON'T THINK HE KNOWS THAT MY SOPWITH CAMEL IS POWERED BY A ROTARY ENGINE WITH A RIGHT-HAND TORQUE SO I CAN EVADE HIM BY TURNING HARD TO THE RIGHT **WITH** THE PULL OF MY ENGINE....
© 1966 Peanuts Worldwide LLC, Dist. by Universal Uclick
www.snoopy.com
HE KNEW IT!
SCHULZ

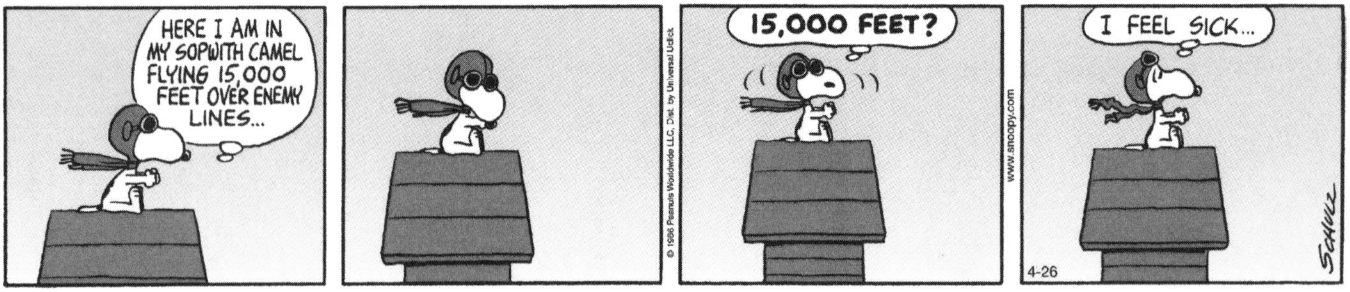
HERE I AM IN MY SOPWITH CAMEL FLYING 15,000 FEET OVER ENEMY LINES...
© 1966 Peanuts Worldwide LLC, Dist. by Universal Uclick
15,000 FEET?
www.snoopy.com
I FEEL SICK...
4-26
SCHULZ

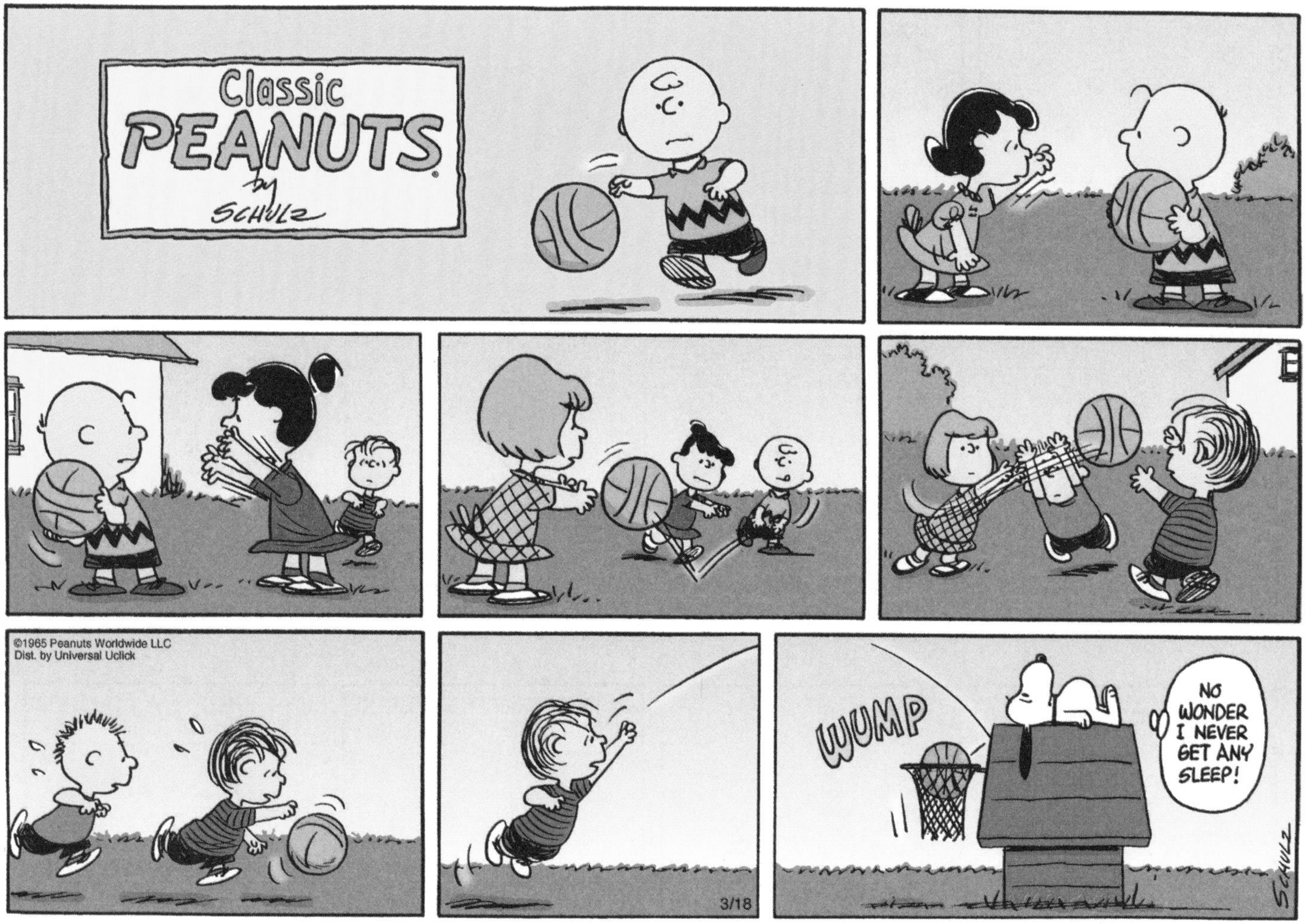
Classic PEANUTS by SCHULZ
©1965 Peanuts Worldwide LLC
Dist. by Universal Uclick
3/18
WUMP
NO WONDER I NEVER GET ANY SLEEP!
SCHULZ

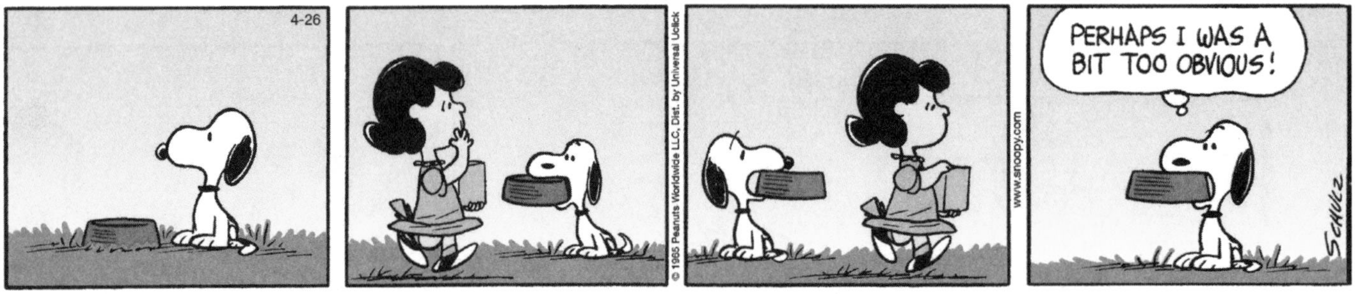
4-26
© 1965 Peanuts Worldwide LLC, Dist. by Universal Uclick
www.snoopy.com
PERHAPS I WAS A BIT TOO OBVIOUS!

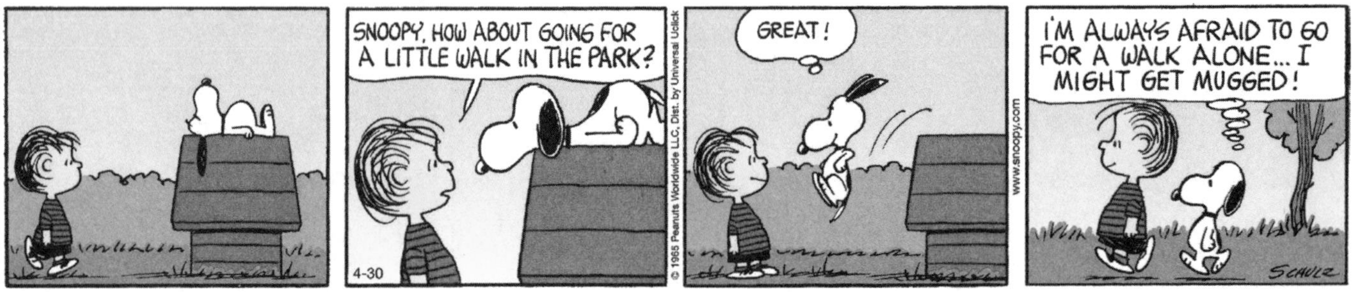
SNOOPY, HOW ABOUT GOING FOR A LITTLE WALK IN THE PARK?
4-30
© 1965 Peanuts Worldwide LLC, Dist. by Universal Uclick
GREAT!
www.snoopy.com
I'M ALWAYS AFRAID TO GO FOR A WALK ALONE... I MIGHT GET MUGGED!

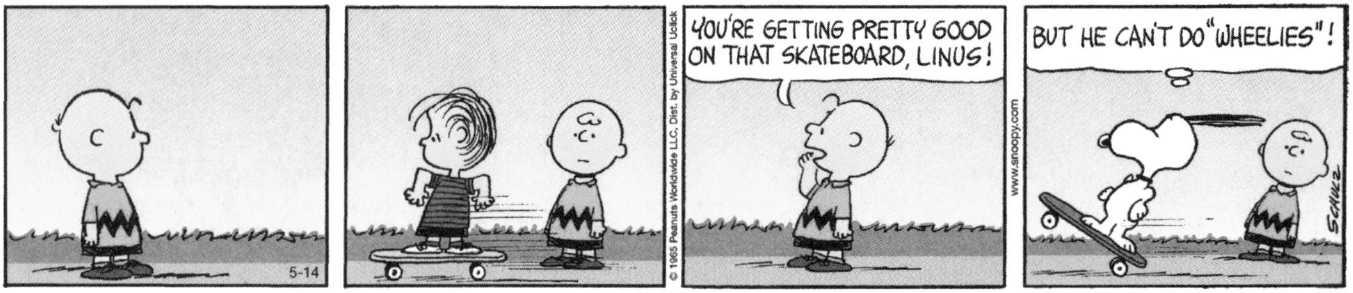
5-14
© 1965 Peanuts Worldwide LLC, Dist. by Universal Uclick
YOU'RE GETTING PRETTY GOOD ON THAT SKATEBOARD, LINUS!
www.snoopy.com
BUT HE CAN'T DO "WHEELIES"!

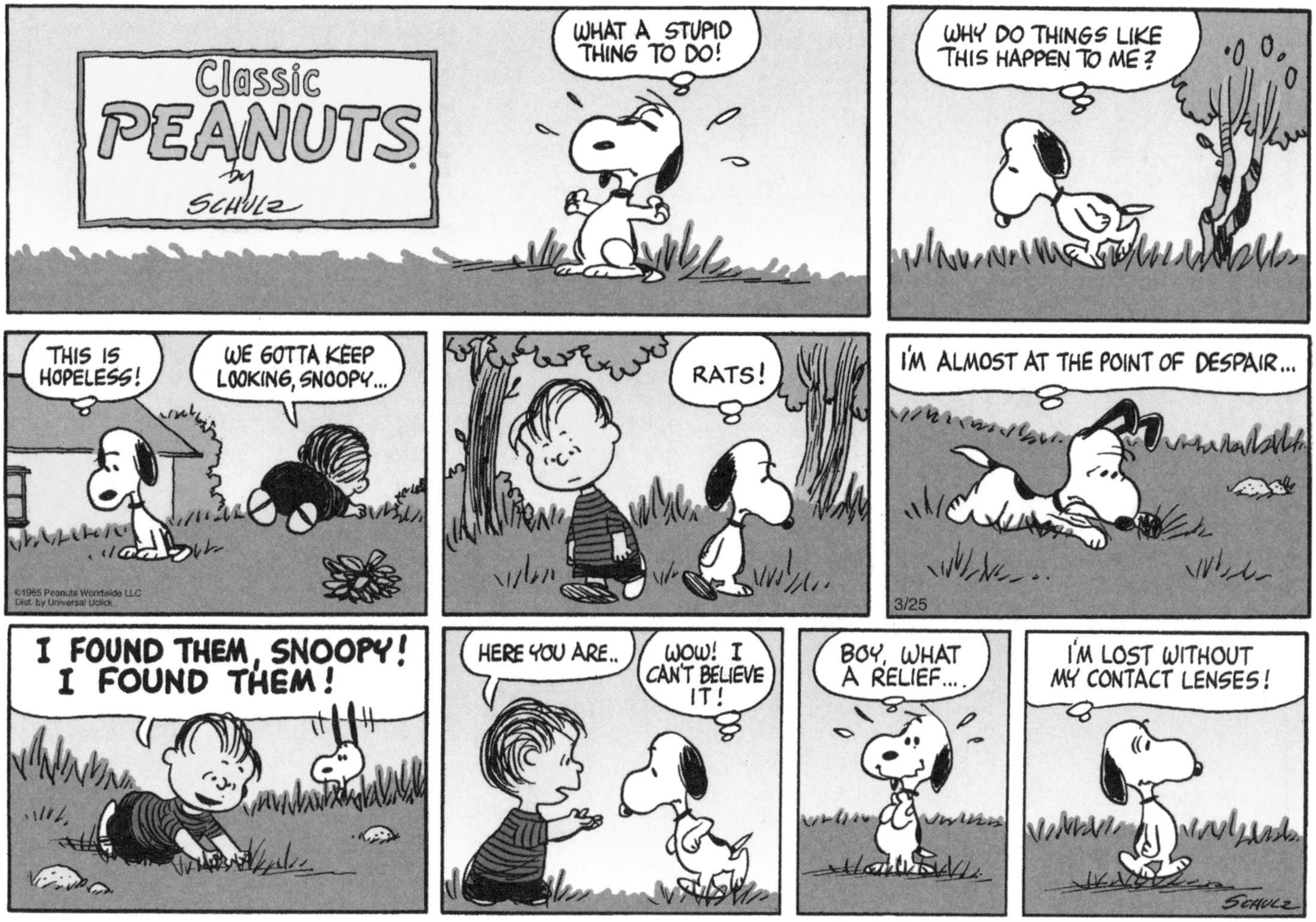
Classic PEANUTS by SCHULZ
WHAT A STUPID THING TO DO!
WHY DO THINGS LIKE THIS HAPPEN TO ME?
THIS IS HOPELESS!
WE GOTTA KEEP LOOKING, SNOOPY...
©1965 Peanuts Worldwide LLC Dist. by Universal Uclick
RATS!
I'M ALMOST AT THE POINT OF DESPAIR...
3/25
I FOUND THEM, SNOOPY! I FOUND THEM!
HERE YOU ARE..
WOW! I CAN'T BELIEVE IT!
BOY, WHAT A RELIEF....
I'M LOST WITHOUT MY CONTACT LENSES!
SCHULZ

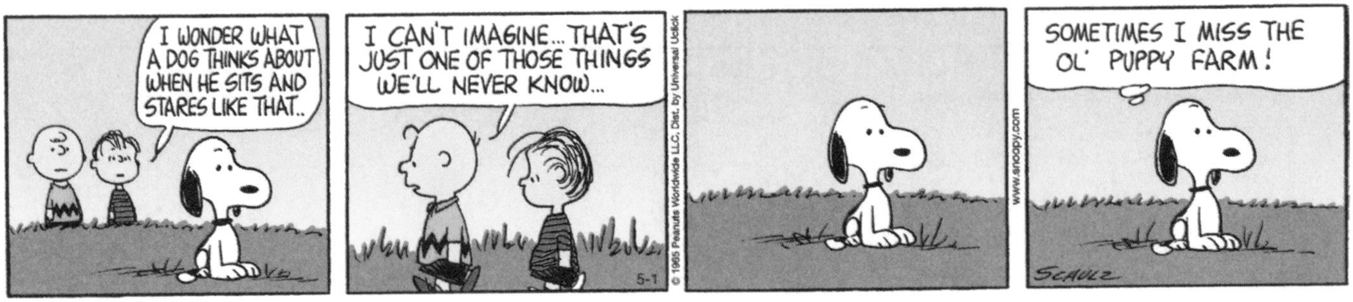
I WONDER WHAT A DOG THINKS ABOUT WHEN HE SITS AND STARES LIKE THAT..
I CAN'T IMAGINE... THAT'S JUST ONE OF THOSE THINGS WE'LL NEVER KNOW...
SOMETIMES I MISS THE OL' PUPPY FARM!
5-1
© 1965 Peanuts Worldwide LLC, Dist. by Universal Uclick
www.snoopy.com
SCHULZ

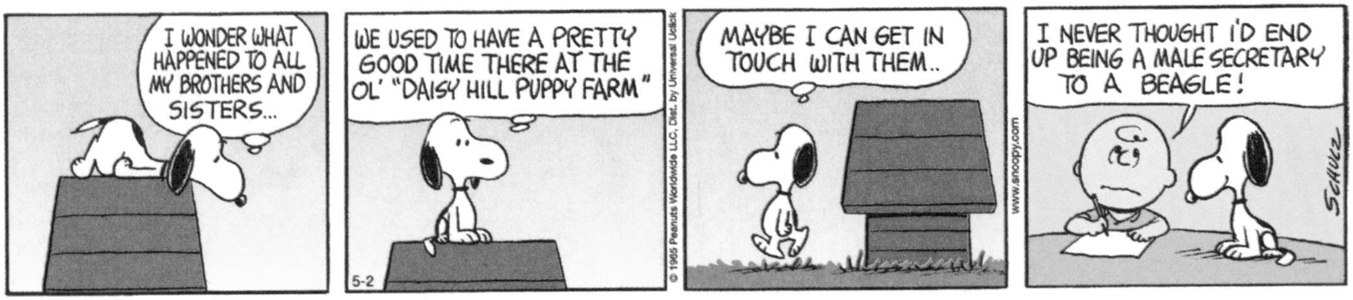
I WONDER WHAT HAPPENED TO ALL MY BROTHERS AND SISTERS...
WE USED TO HAVE A PRETTY GOOD TIME THERE AT THE OL' "DAISY HILL PUPPY FARM"
MAYBE I CAN GET IN TOUCH WITH THEM..
I NEVER THOUGHT I'D END UP BEING A MALE SECRETARY TO A BEAGLE!
5-2
© 1965 Peanuts Worldwide LLC, Dist. by Universal Uclick
www.snoopy.com
SCHULZ

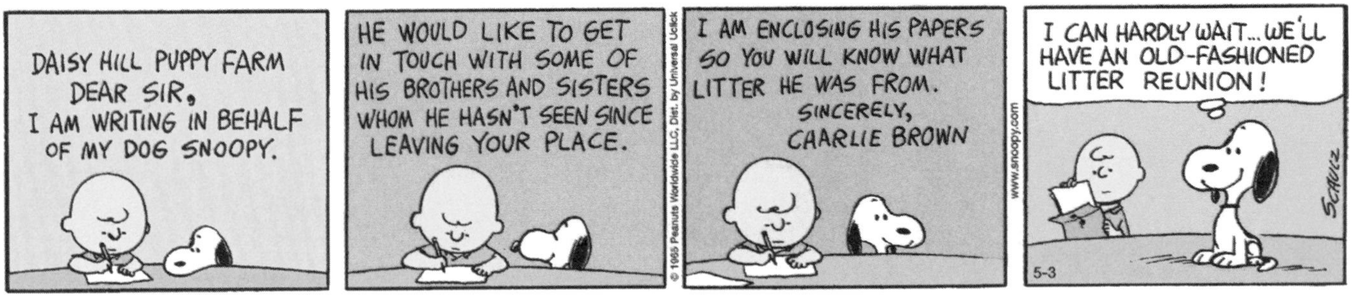
DAISY HILL PUPPY FARM
DEAR SIR,
I AM WRITING IN BEHALF OF MY DOG SNOOPY.
HE WOULD LIKE TO GET IN TOUCH WITH SOME OF HIS BROTHERS AND SISTERS WHOM HE HASN'T SEEN SINCE LEAVING YOUR PLACE.
I AM ENCLOSING HIS PAPERS SO YOU WILL KNOW WHAT LITTER HE WAS FROM.
SINCERELY,
CAARLIE BROWN
I CAN HARDLY WAIT... WE'LL HAVE AN OLD-FASHIONED LITTER REUNION!
5-3
© 1965 Peanuts Worldwide LLC, Dist. by Universal Uclick
www.snoopy.com
SCHULZ

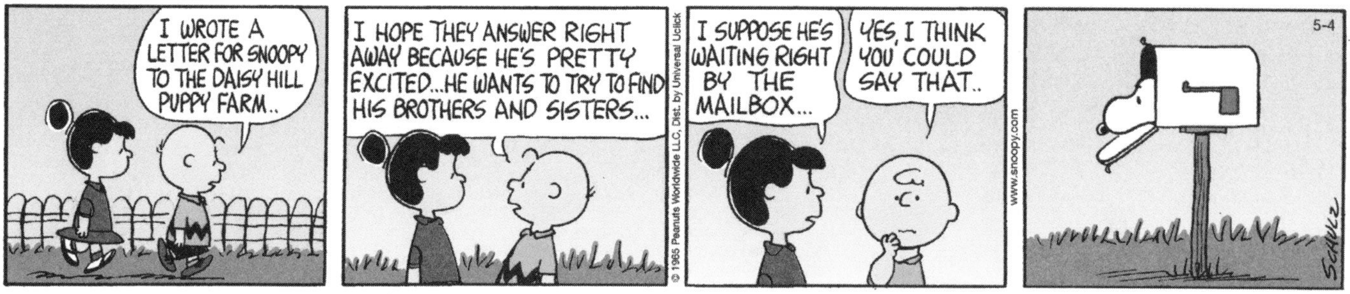
I WROTE A LETTER FOR SNOOPY TO THE DAISY HILL PUPPY FARM..
I HOPE THEY ANSWER RIGHT AWAY BECAUSE HE'S PRETTY EXCITED...HE WANTS TO TRY TO FIND HIS BROTHERS AND SISTERS...
© 1965 Peanuts Worldwide LLC, Dist. by Universal Uclick
I SUPPOSE HE'S WAITING RIGHT BY THE MAILBOX...
YES, I THINK YOU COULD SAY THAT..
www.snoopy.com
5-4
SCHULZ

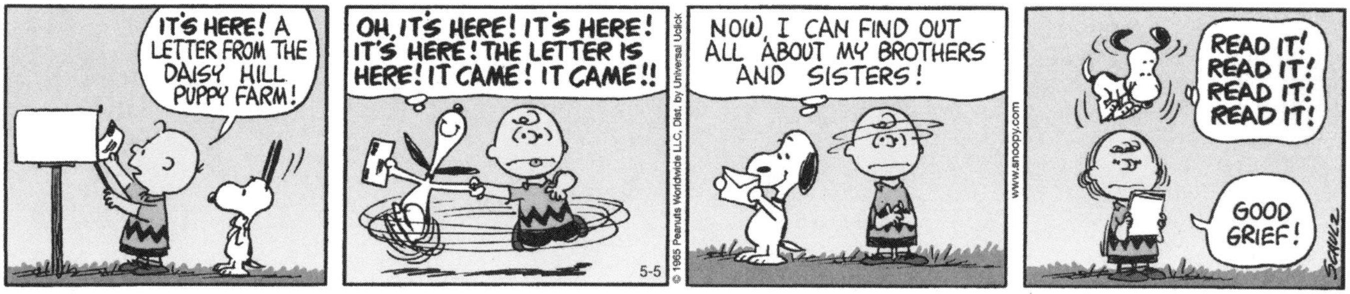
IT'S HERE! A LETTER FROM THE DAISY HILL PUPPY FARM!
OH, IT'S HERE! IT'S HERE! IT'S HERE! THE LETTER IS HERE! IT CAME! IT CAME!!
5-5
© 1965 Peanuts Worldwide LLC, Dist. by Universal Uclick
NOW, I CAN FIND OUT ALL ABOUT MY BROTHERS AND SISTERS!
www.snoopy.com
READ IT! READ IT! READ IT! READ IT!
GOOD GRIEF!
SCHULZ

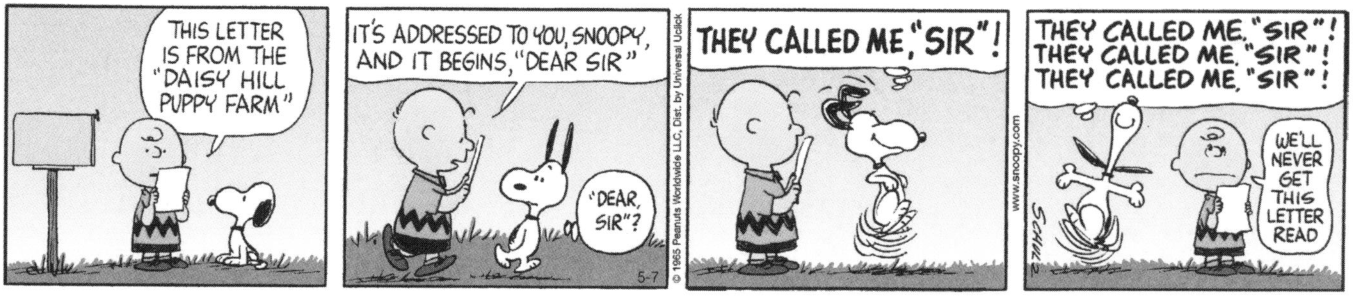
THIS LETTER IS FROM THE "DAISY HILL PUPPY FARM"
IT'S ADDRESSED TO YOU, SNOOPY, AND IT BEGINS, "DEAR SIR"
"DEAR, SIR"?
5-7
© 1965 Peanuts Worldwide LLC, Dist. by Universal Uclick
THEY CALLED ME, "SIR"!
www.snoopy.com
THEY CALLED ME, "SIR"! THEY CALLED ME, "SIR"! THEY CALLED ME, "SIR"!
WE'LL NEVER GET THIS LETTER READ
SCHULZ

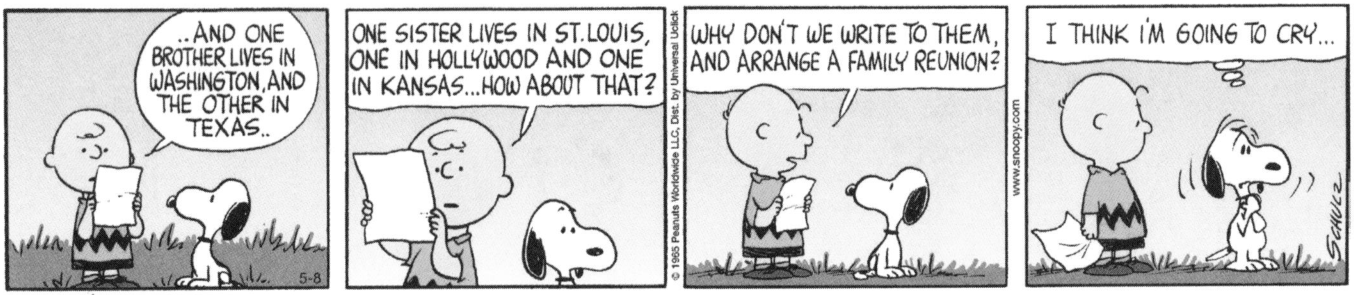
..AND ONE BROTHER LIVES IN WASHINGTON, AND THE OTHER IN TEXAS..
5-8
ONE SISTER LIVES IN ST. LOUIS, ONE IN HOLLYWOOD AND ONE IN KANSAS...HOW ABOUT THAT?
© 1965 Peanuts Worldwide LLC, Dist. by Universal Uclick
WHY DON'T WE WRITE TO THEM, AND ARRANGE A FAMILY REUNION?
www.snoopy.com
I THINK I'M GOING TO CRY...
SCHULZ

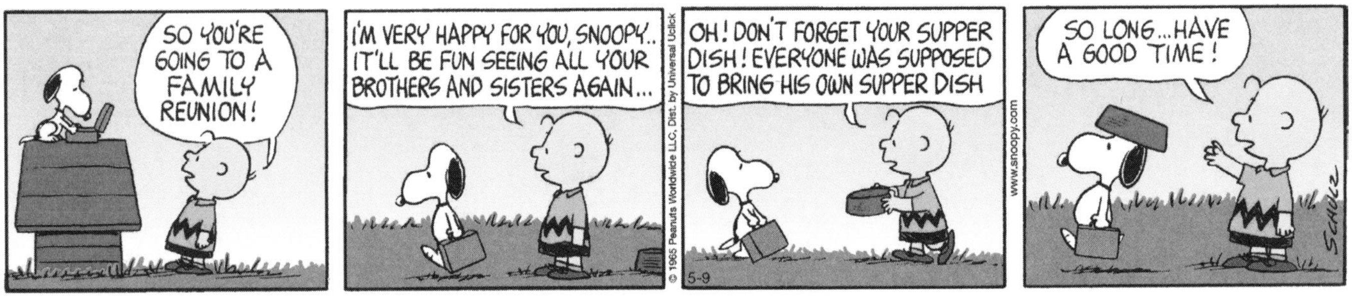
SO YOU'RE GOING TO A FAMILY REUNION!
I'M VERY HAPPY FOR YOU, SNOOPY.. IT'LL BE FUN SEEING ALL YOUR BROTHERS AND SISTERS AGAIN...
© 1965 Peanuts Worldwide LLC, Dist. by Universal Uclick
OH! DON'T FORGET YOUR SUPPER DISH! EVERYONE WAS SUPPOSED TO BRING HIS OWN SUPPER DISH
5-9
www.snoopy.com
SO LONG...HAVE A GOOD TIME!
SCHULZ

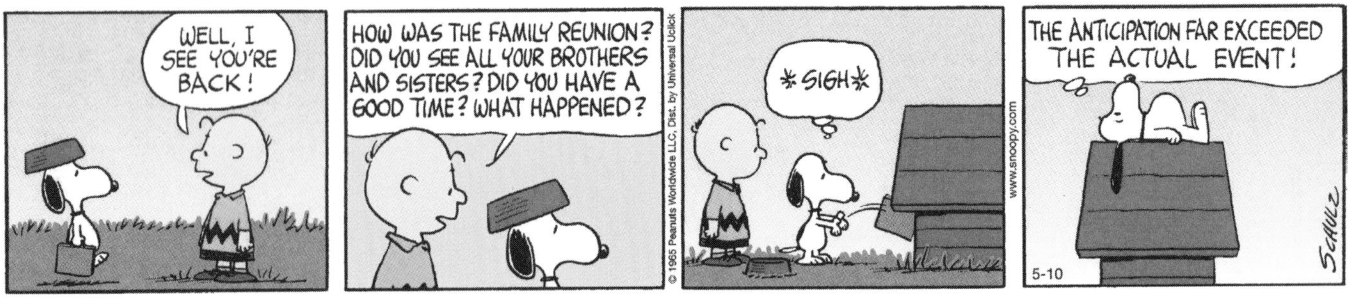
WELL, I SEE YOU'RE BACK!
HOW WAS THE FAMILY REUNION? DID YOU SEE ALL YOUR BROTHERS AND SISTERS? DID YOU HAVE A GOOD TIME? WHAT HAPPENED?
© 1965 Peanuts Worldwide LLC, Dist. by Universal Uclick
SIGH
www.snoopy.com
THE ANTICIPATION FAR EXCEEDED THE ACTUAL EVENT!
5-10
SCHULZ

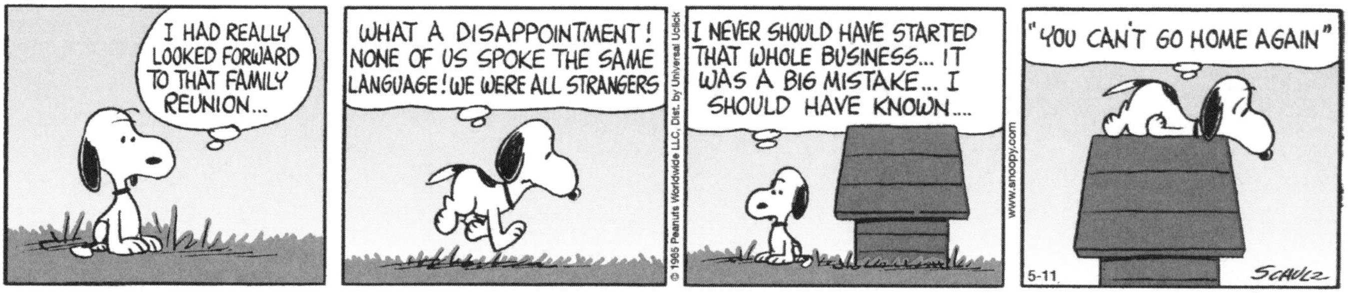
I HAD REALLY LOOKED FORWARD TO THAT FAMILY REUNION...
WHAT A DISAPPOINTMENT! NONE OF US SPOKE THE SAME LANGUAGE! WE WERE ALL STRANGERS
© 1985 Peanuts Worldwide LLC, Dist. by Universal Uclick
I NEVER SHOULD HAVE STARTED THAT WHOLE BUSINESS... IT WAS A BIG MISTAKE... I SHOULD HAVE KNOWN....
www.snoopy.com
"YOU CAN'T GO HOME AGAIN"
5-11
SCHULZ

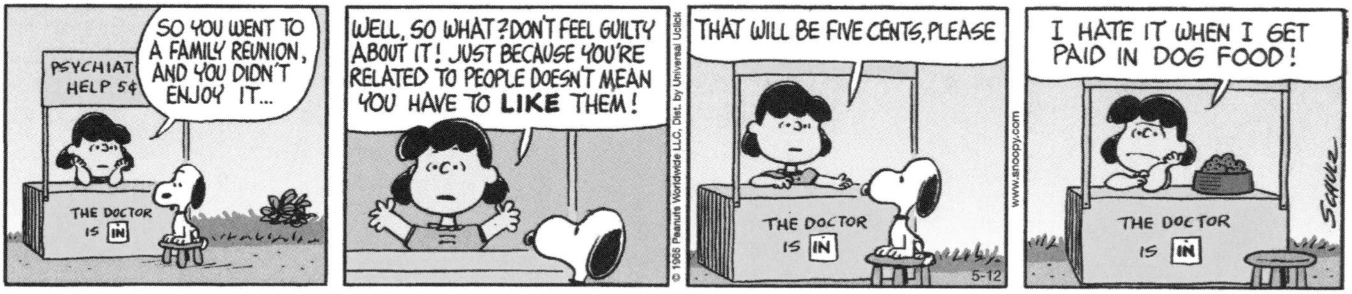
PSYCHIAT HELP 5¢
THE DOCTOR IS IN
SO YOU WENT TO A FAMILY REUNION, AND YOU DIDN'T ENJOY IT...
WELL, SO WHAT? DON'T FEEL GUILTY ABOUT IT! JUST BECAUSE YOU'RE RELATED TO PEOPLE DOESN'T MEAN YOU HAVE TO **LIKE** THEM!
© 1985 Peanuts Worldwide LLC, Dist. by Universal Uclick
THAT WILL BE FIVE CENTS, PLEASE
THE DOCTOR IS IN
5-12
www.snoopy.com
I HATE IT WHEN I GET PAID IN DOG FOOD!
THE DOCTOR IS IN
SCHULZ

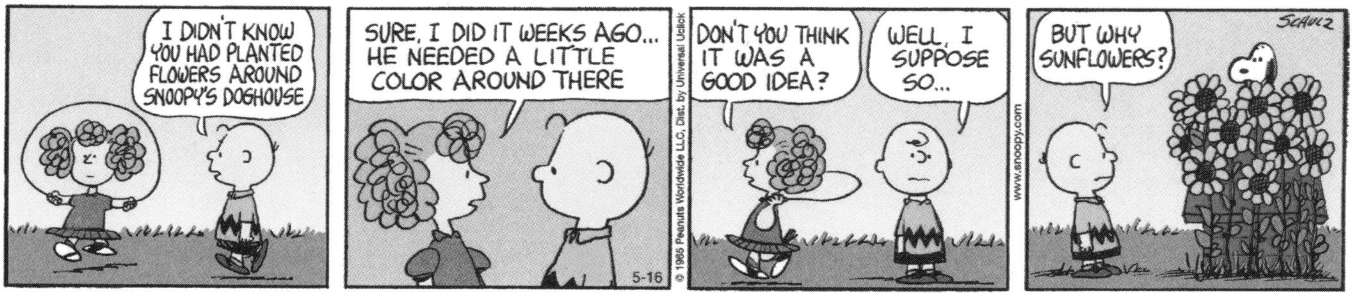
I DIDN'T KNOW YOU HAD PLANTED FLOWERS AROUND SNOOPY'S DOGHOUSE
SURE, I DID IT WEEKS AGO... HE NEEDED A LITTLE COLOR AROUND THERE
5-16
© 1985 Peanuts Worldwide LLC, Dist. by Universal Uclick
DON'T YOU THINK IT WAS A GOOD IDEA?
WELL, I SUPPOSE SO...
www.snoopy.com
SCHULZ
BUT WHY SUNFLOWERS?

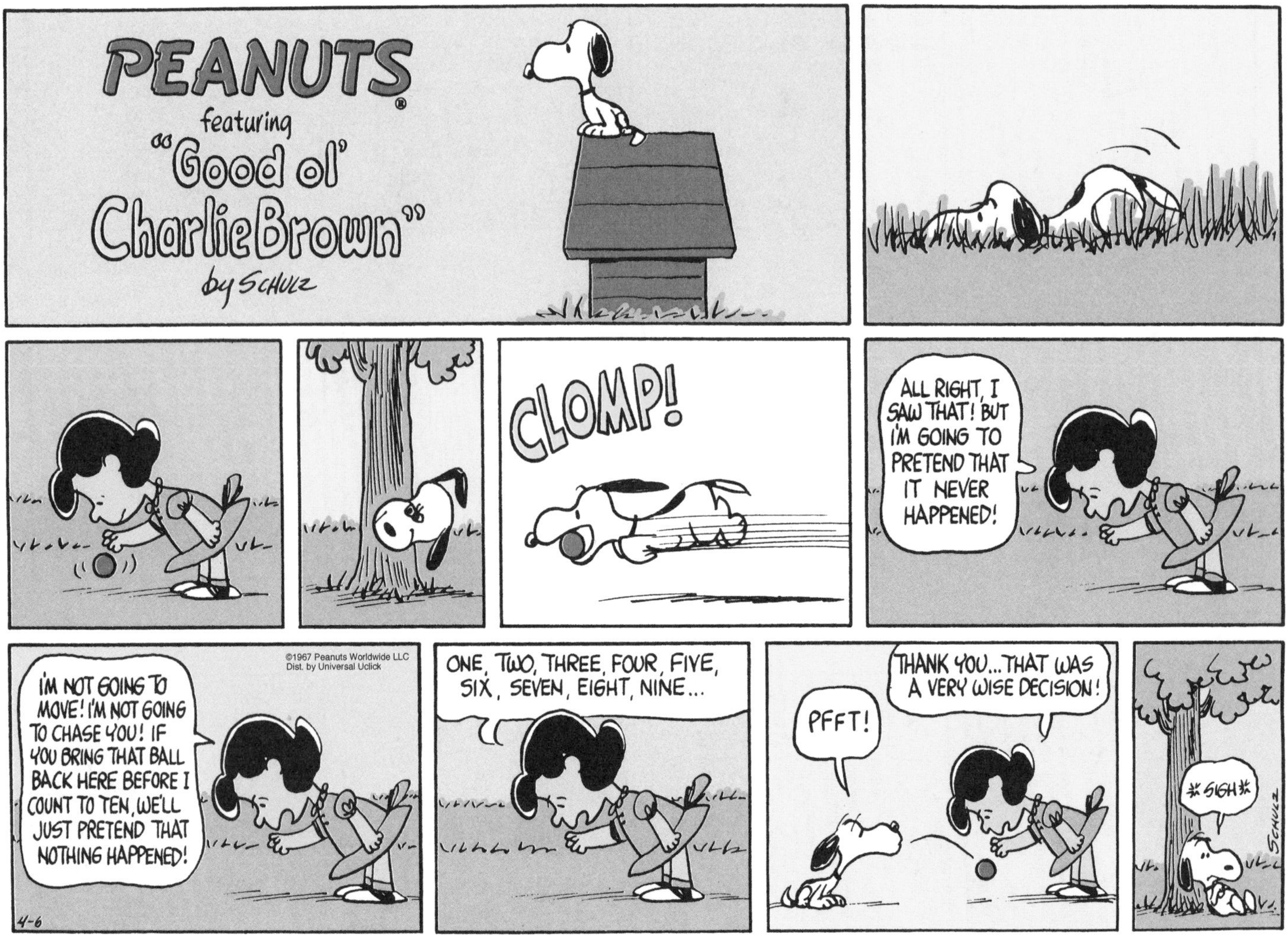
PEANUTS
featuring "Good ol' Charlie Brown"
by SCHULZ
CLOMP!
ALL RIGHT, I SAW THAT! BUT I'M GOING TO PRETEND THAT IT NEVER HAPPENED!
©1967 Peanuts Worldwide LLC Dist. by Universal Uclick
I'M NOT GOING TO MOVE! I'M NOT GOING TO CHASE YOU! IF YOU BRING THAT BALL BACK HERE BEFORE I COUNT TO TEN, WE'LL JUST PRETEND THAT NOTHING HAPPENED!
4-6
ONE, TWO, THREE, FOUR, FIVE, SIX, SEVEN, EIGHT, NINE...
PFFT!
THANK YOU... THAT WAS A VERY WISE DECISION!
SIGH
SCHULZ

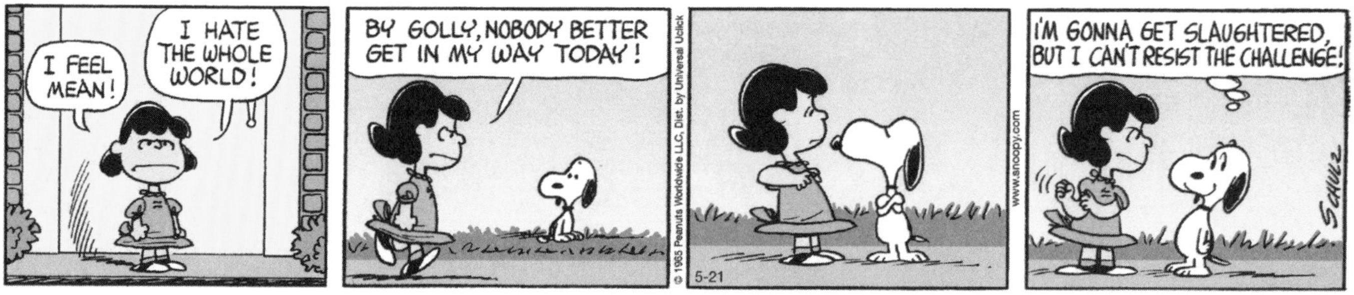
I FEEL MEAN!
I HATE THE WHOLE WORLD!
BY GOLLY, NOBODY BETTER GET IN MY WAY TODAY!
© 1965 Peanuts Worldwide LLC, Dist. by Universal Uclick
5-21
www.snoopy.com
I'M GONNA GET SLAUGHTERED, BUT I CAN'T RESIST THE CHALLENGE!
SCHULZ

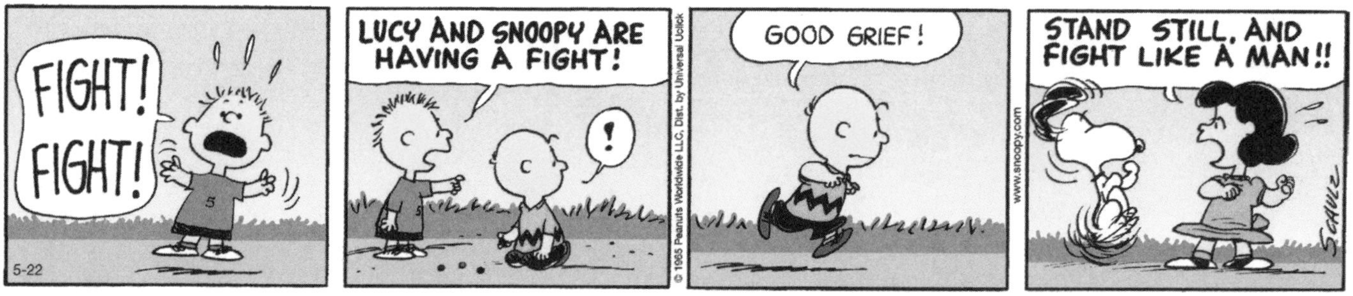
FIGHT! FIGHT!
5-22
LUCY AND SNOOPY ARE HAVING A FIGHT!
!
© 1965 Peanuts Worldwide LLC, Dist. by Universal Uclick
GOOD GRIEF!
www.snoopy.com
STAND STILL, AND FIGHT LIKE A MAN!!
SCHULZ

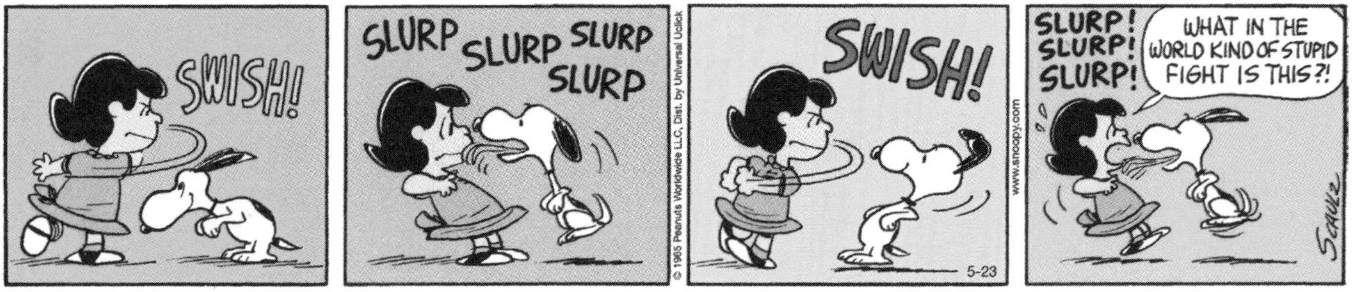
SWISH!
SLURP SLURP SLURP SLURP
© 1965 Peanuts Worldwide LLC, Dist. by Universal Uclick
SWISH!
5-23
www.snoopy.com
SLURP! SLURP! SLURP!
WHAT IN THE WORLD KIND OF STUPID FIGHT IS THIS?!
SCHULZ

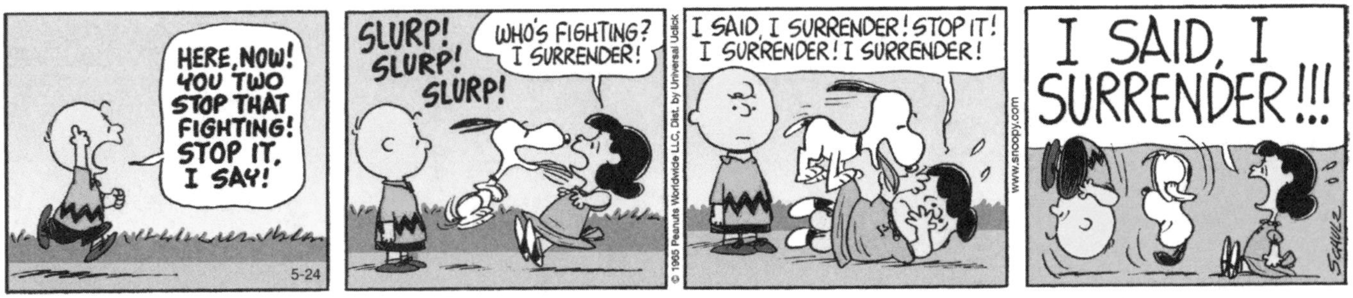
HERE, NOW! YOU TWO STOP THAT FIGHTING! STOP IT, I SAY!
5-24
SLURP! SLURP! SLURP!
WHO'S FIGHTING? I SURRENDER!
© 1965 Peanuts Worldwide LLC, Dist. by Universal Uclick
I SAID, I SURRENDER! STOP IT! I SURRENDER! I SURRENDER!
www.snoopy.com
I SAID, I SURRENDER!!!
SCHULZ

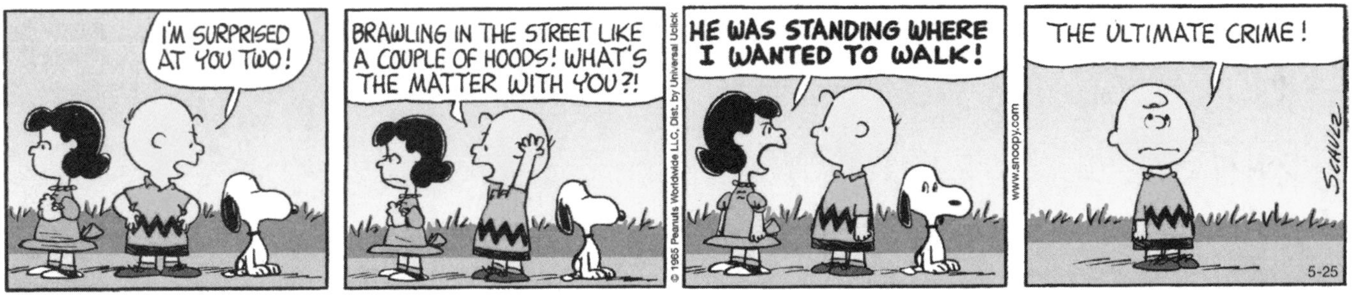
I'M SURPRISED AT YOU TWO!
BRAWLING IN THE STREET LIKE A COUPLE OF HOODS! WHAT'S THE MATTER WITH YOU?!
© 1965 Peanuts Worldwide LLC, Dist. by Universal Uclick
HE WAS STANDING WHERE I WANTED TO WALK!
www.snoopy.com
THE ULTIMATE CRIME!
SCHULZ
5-25

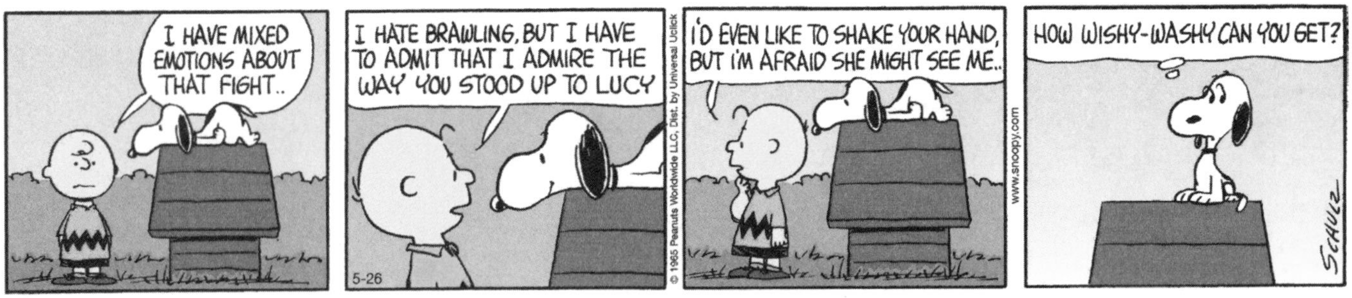
I HAVE MIXED EMOTIONS ABOUT THAT FIGHT..
I HATE BRAWLING, BUT I HAVE TO ADMIT THAT I ADMIRE THE WAY YOU STOOD UP TO LUCY
5-26
© 1965 Peanuts Worldwide LLC, Dist. by Universal Uclick
I'D EVEN LIKE TO SHAKE YOUR HAND, BUT I'M AFRAID SHE MIGHT SEE ME..
www.snoopy.com
HOW WISHY-WASHY CAN YOU GET?
SCHULZ

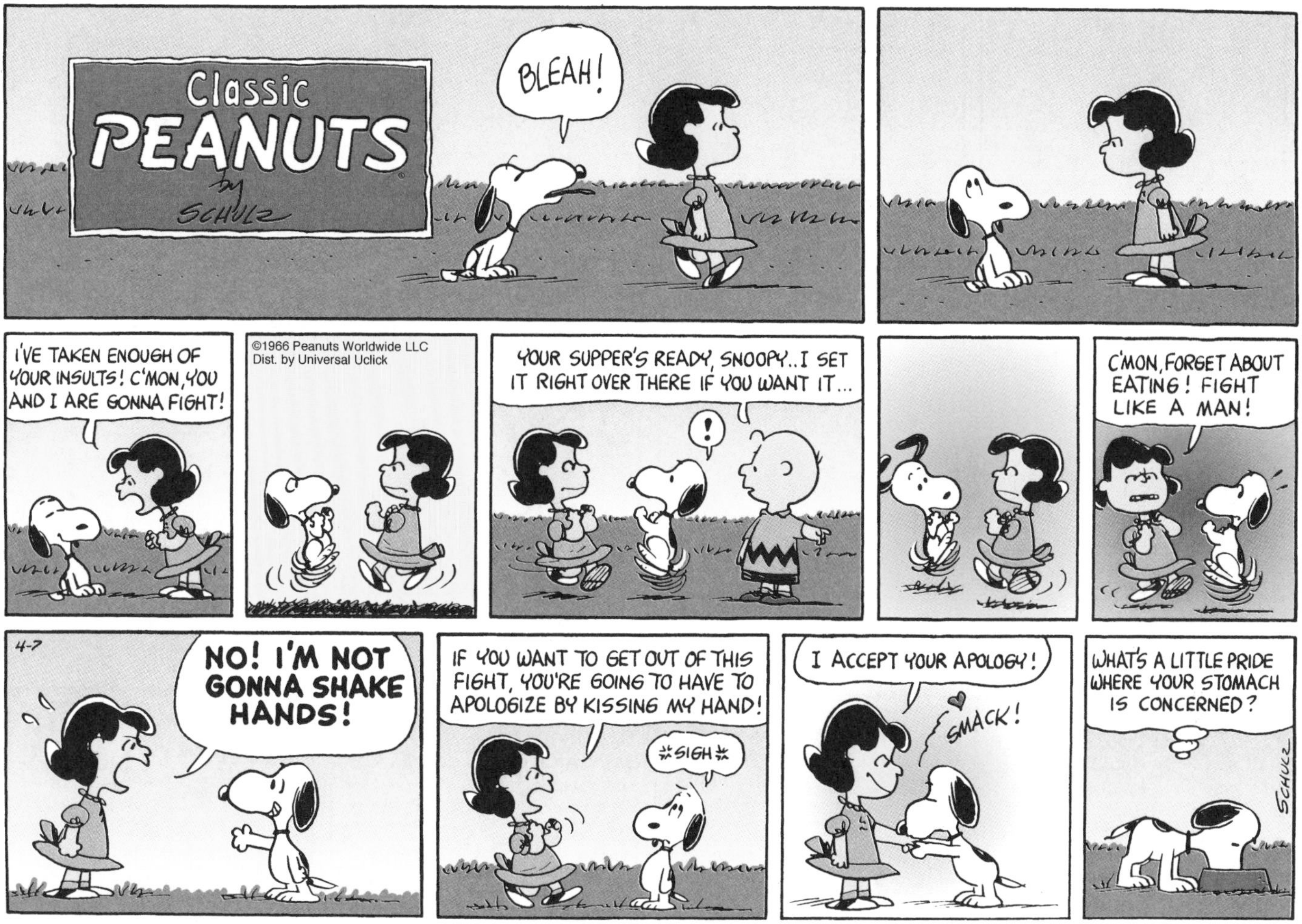

Classic PEANUTS by SCHULZ
BLEAH!
I'VE TAKEN ENOUGH OF YOUR INSULTS! C'MON, YOU AND I ARE GONNA FIGHT!
©1966 Peanuts Worldwide LLC
Dist. by Universal Uclick
YOUR SUPPER'S READY, SNOOPY.. I SET IT RIGHT OVER THERE IF YOU WANT IT...
!
C'MON, FORGET ABOUT EATING! FIGHT LIKE A MAN!
4-7
NO! I'M NOT GONNA SHAKE HANDS!
IF YOU WANT TO GET OUT OF THIS FIGHT, YOU'RE GOING TO HAVE TO APOLOGIZE BY KISSING MY HAND!
SIGH
I ACCEPT YOUR APOLOGY!
SMACK!
WHAT'S A LITTLE PRIDE WHERE YOUR STOMACH IS CONCERNED?
SCHULZ

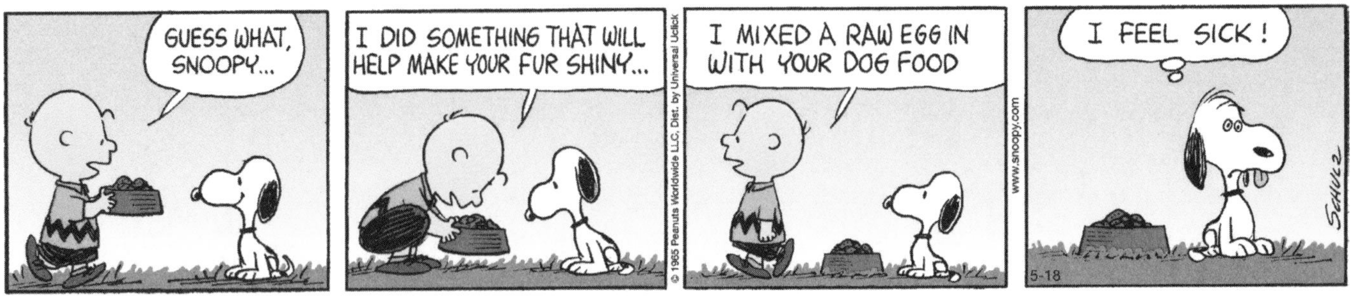
GUESS WHAT, SNOOPY...
I DID SOMETHING THAT WILL HELP MAKE YOUR FUR SHINY...
I MIXED A RAW EGG IN WITH YOUR DOG FOOD
I FEEL SICK!
SCHULZ
5-18
© 1965 Peanuts Worldwide LLC. Dist. by Universal Uclick
www.snoopy.com

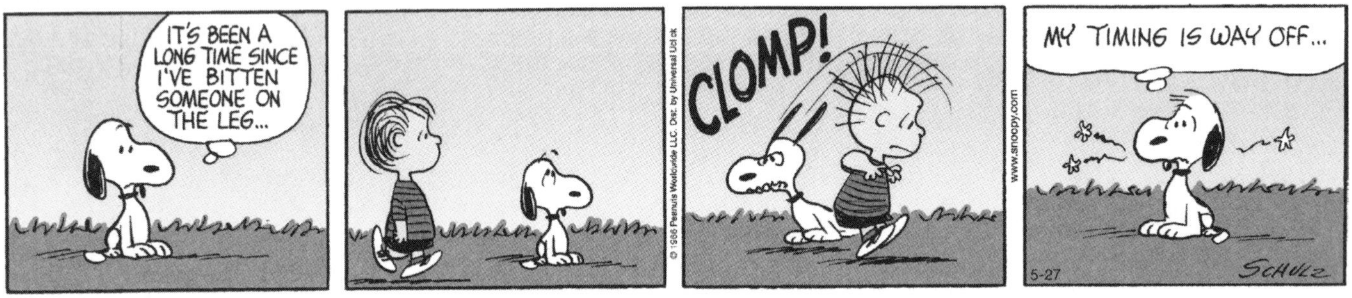
IT'S BEEN A LONG TIME SINCE I'VE BITTEN SOMEONE ON THE LEG...
CLOMP!
MY TIMING IS WAY OFF...
SCHULZ
5-27
© 1966 Peanuts Worldwide LLC. Dist. by Universal Uclick
www.snoopy.com

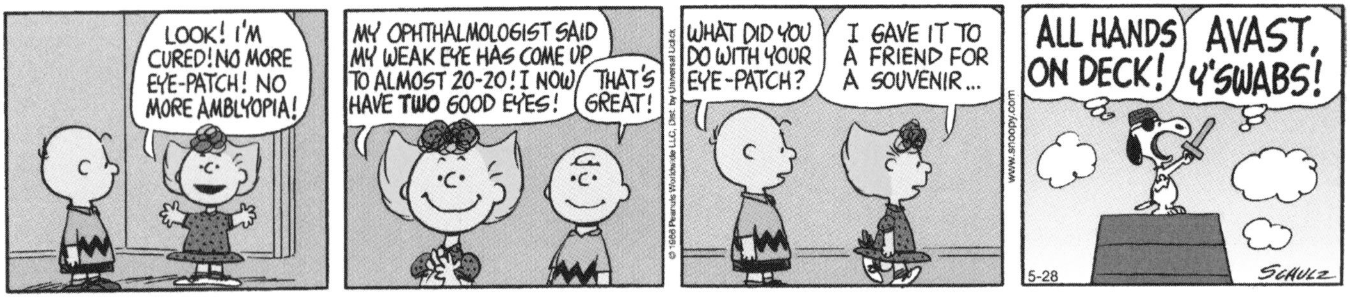
LOOK! I'M CURED! NO MORE EYE-PATCH! NO MORE AMBLYOPIA!
MY OPHTHALMOLOGIST SAID MY WEAK EYE HAS COME UP TO ALMOST 20-20! I NOW HAVE **TWO** GOOD EYES!
THAT'S GREAT!
WHAT DID YOU DO WITH YOUR EYE-PATCH?
I GAVE IT TO A FRIEND FOR A SOUVENIR...
ALL HANDS ON DECK!
AVAST, Y'SWABS!
SCHULZ
5-28
© 1966 Peanuts Worldwide LLC. Dist. by Universal Uclick
www.snoopy.com

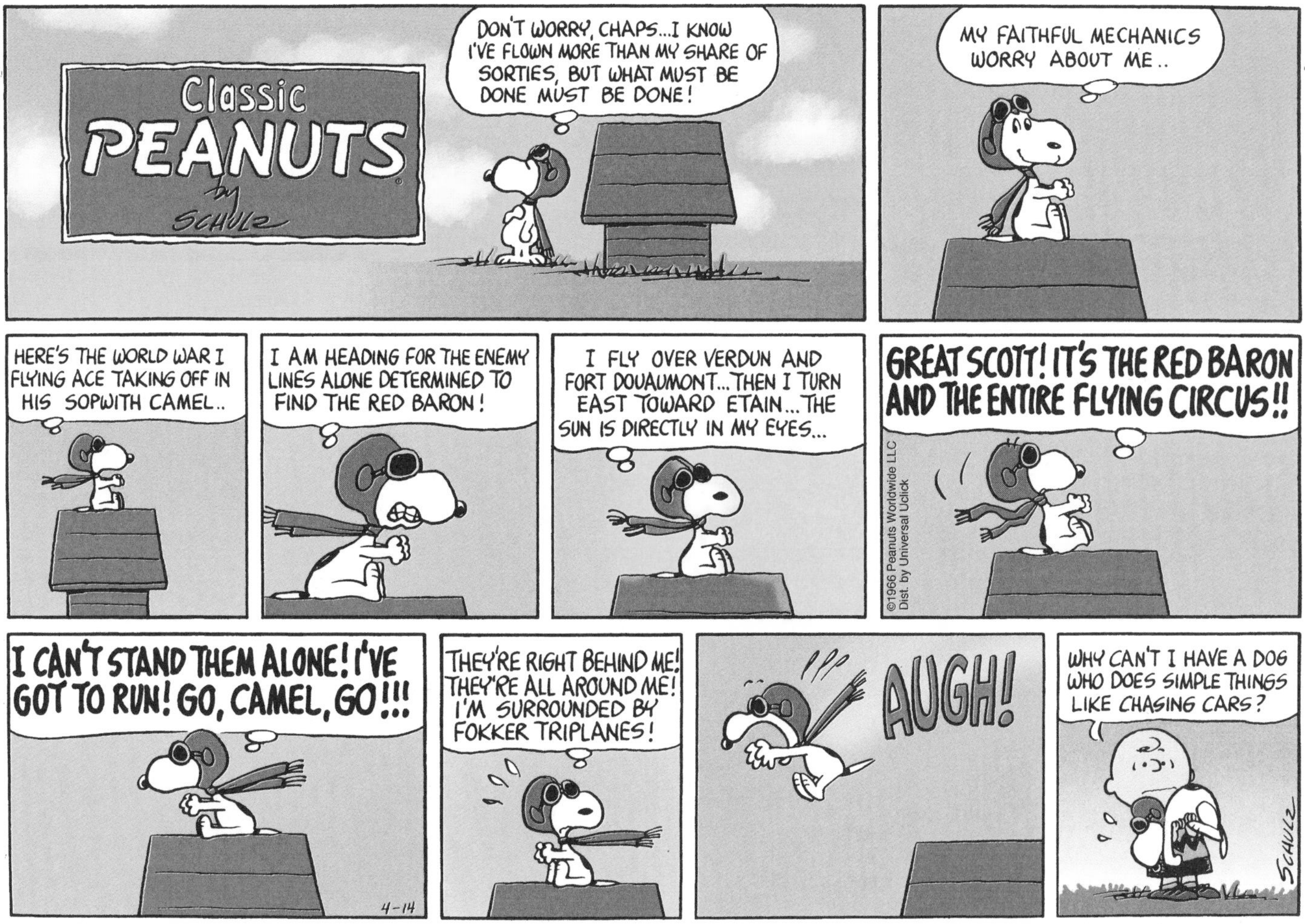
Classic PEANUTS by SCHULZ
DON'T WORRY, CHAPS...I KNOW I'VE FLOWN MORE THAN MY SHARE OF SORTIES, BUT WHAT MUST BE DONE MUST BE DONE!
MY FAITHFUL MECHANICS WORRY ABOUT ME..
HERE'S THE WORLD WAR I FLYING ACE TAKING OFF IN HIS SOPWITH CAMEL..
I AM HEADING FOR THE ENEMY LINES ALONE DETERMINED TO FIND THE RED BARON!
I FLY OVER VERDUN AND FORT DOUAUMONT...THEN I TURN EAST TOWARD ETAIN...THE SUN IS DIRECTLY IN MY EYES...
©1966 Peanuts Worldwide LLC
Dist. by Universal Uclick
GREAT SCOTT! IT'S THE RED BARON AND THE ENTIRE FLYING CIRCUS!!
I CAN'T STAND THEM ALONE! I'VE GOT TO RUN! GO, CAMEL, GO!!!
4-14
THEY'RE RIGHT BEHIND ME! THEY'RE ALL AROUND ME! I'M SURROUNDED BY FOKKER TRIPLANES!
AUGH!
WHY CAN'T I HAVE A DOG WHO DOES SIMPLE THINGS LIKE CHASING CARS?
SCHULZ

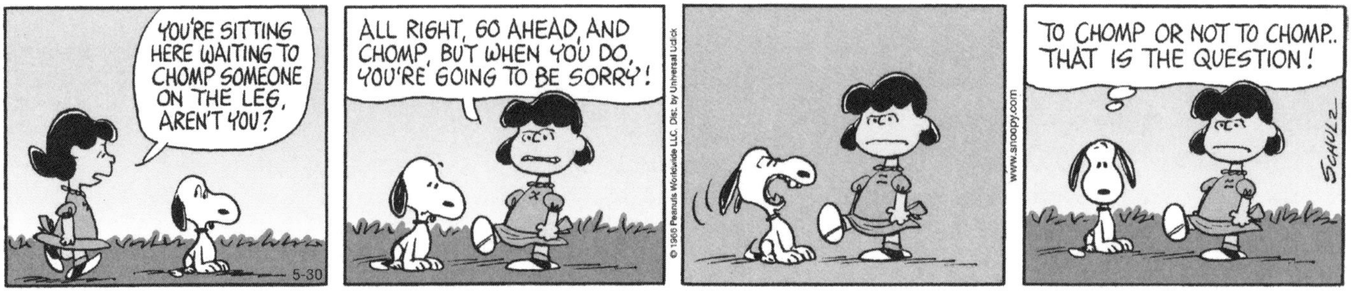
YOU'RE SITTING HERE WAITING TO CHOMP SOMEONE ON THE LEG, AREN'T YOU?
5-30
ALL RIGHT, GO AHEAD, AND CHOMP, BUT WHEN YOU DO, YOU'RE GOING TO BE SORRY!
© 1966 Peanuts Worldwide LLC. Dist. by Universal Uclick
www.snoopy.com
TO CHOMP OR NOT TO CHOMP.. THAT IS THE QUESTION!
SCHULZ

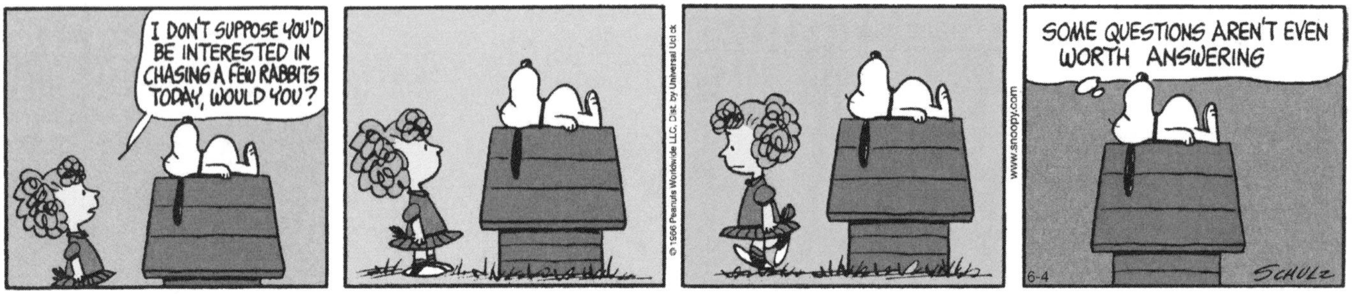
I DON'T SUPPOSE YOU'D BE INTERESTED IN CHASING A FEW RABBITS TODAY, WOULD YOU?
© 1966 Peanuts Worldwide LLC. Dist. by Universal Uclick
www.snoopy.com
SOME QUESTIONS AREN'T EVEN WORTH ANSWERING
6-4
SCHULZ

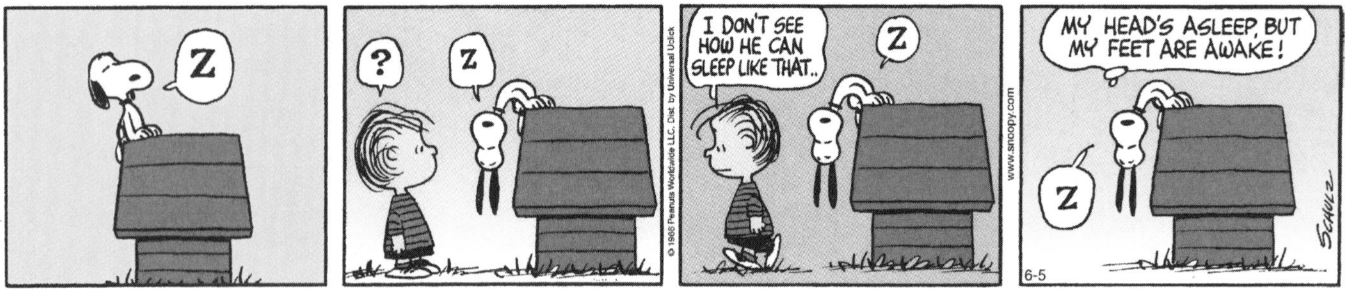
Z
?
Z
© 1966 Peanuts Worldwide LLC. Dist. by Universal Uclick
I DON'T SEE HOW HE CAN SLEEP LIKE THAT..
Z
www.snoopy.com
MY HEAD'S ASLEEP, BUT MY FEET ARE AWAKE!
Z
6-5
SCHULZ

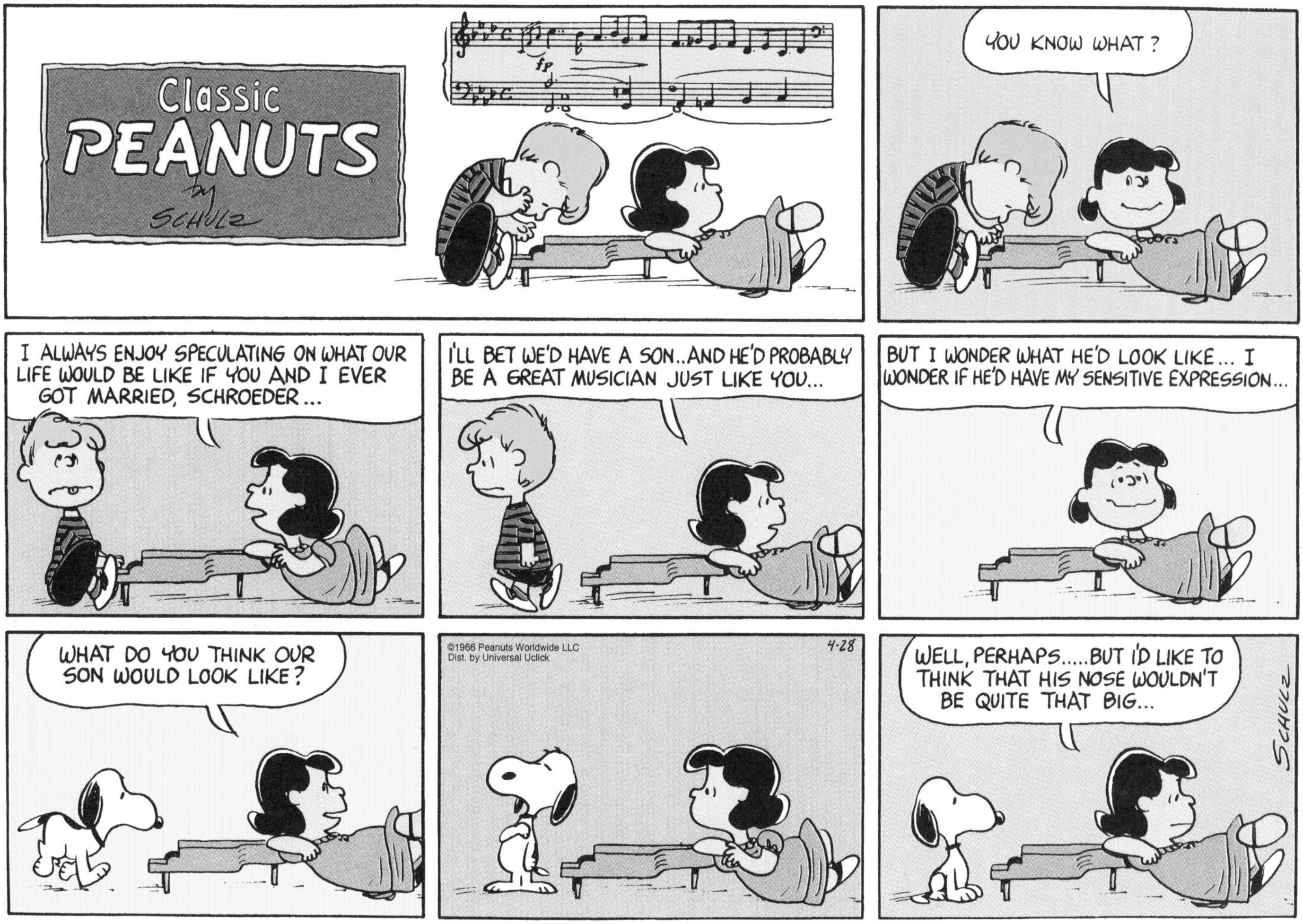
Classic PEANUTS by SCHULZ
fp
YOU KNOW WHAT?
I ALWAYS ENJOY SPECULATING ON WHAT OUR LIFE WOULD BE LIKE IF YOU AND I EVER GOT MARRIED, SCHROEDER...
I'LL BET WE'D HAVE A SON..AND HE'D PROBABLY BE A GREAT MUSICIAN JUST LIKE YOU...
BUT I WONDER WHAT HE'D LOOK LIKE... I WONDER IF HE'D HAVE MY SENSITIVE EXPRESSION...
WHAT DO YOU THINK OUR SON WOULD LOOK LIKE?
©1966 Peanuts Worldwide LLC
Dist. by Universal Uclick
4-28
WELL, PERHAPS.....BUT I'D LIKE TO THINK THAT HIS NOSE WOULDN'T BE QUITE THAT BIG...
SCHULZ

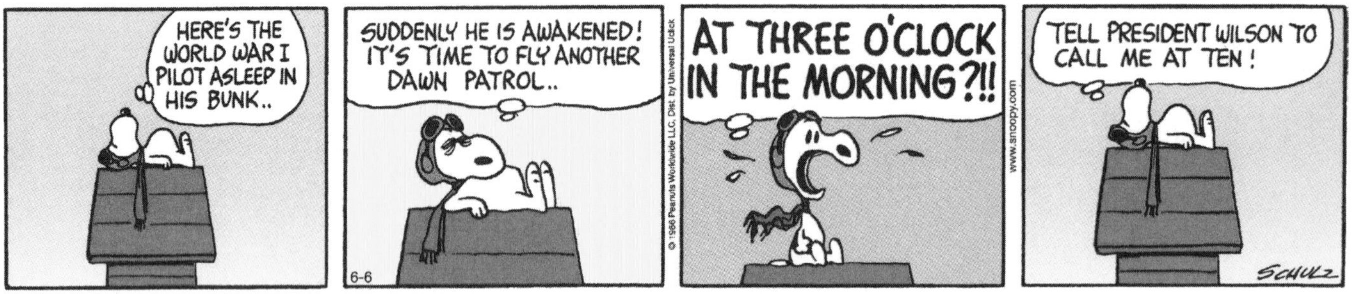
HERE'S THE WORLD WAR I PILOT ASLEEP IN HIS BUNK..
SUDDENLY HE IS AWAKENED! IT'S TIME TO FLY ANOTHER DAWN PATROL..
6-6
AT THREE O'CLOCK IN THE MORNING?!!
TELL PRESIDENT WILSON TO CALL ME AT TEN!
SCHULZ
© 1966 Peanuts Worldwide LLC. Dist. by Universal Uclick
www.snoopy.com

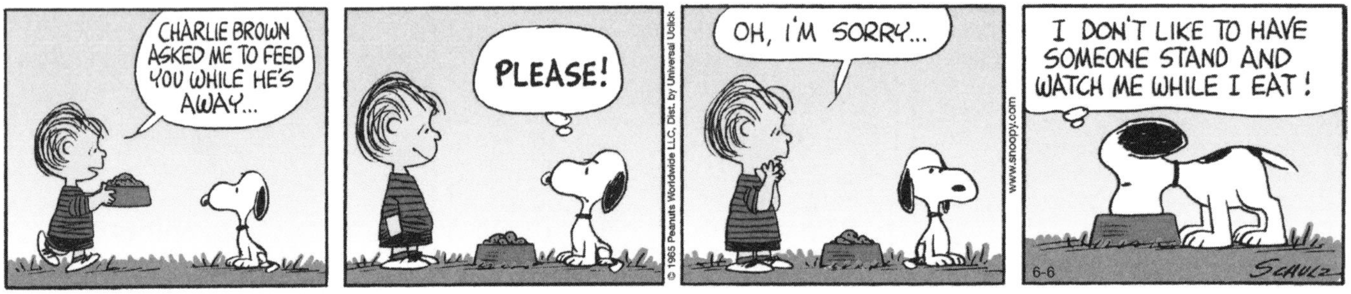
CHARLIE BROWN ASKED ME TO FEED YOU WHILE HE'S AWAY...
PLEASE!
OH, I'M SORRY...
I DON'T LIKE TO HAVE SOMEONE STAND AND WATCH ME WHILE I EAT!
6-6
SCHULZ
© 1965 Peanuts Worldwide LLC. Dist. by Universal Uclick
www.snoopy.com

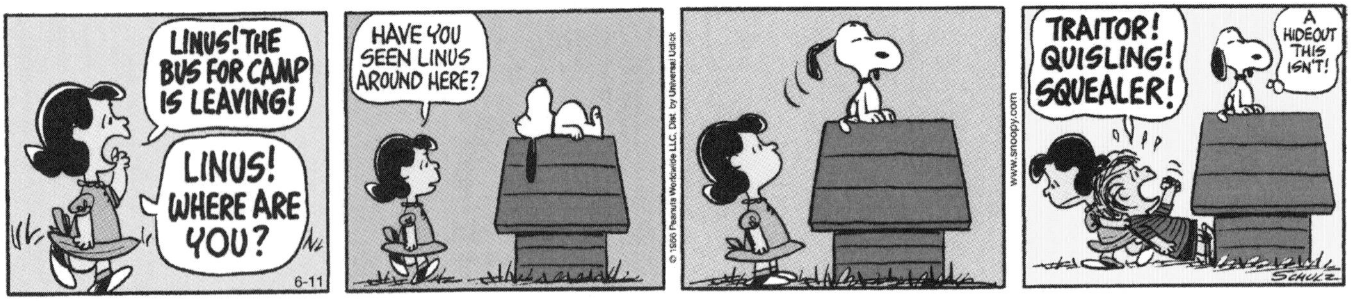
LINUS! THE BUS FOR CAMP IS LEAVING!
LINUS! WHERE ARE YOU?
6-11
HAVE YOU SEEN LINUS AROUND HERE?
TRAITOR! QUISLING! SQUEALER!
A HIDEOUT THIS ISN'T!
SCHULZ
© 1966 Peanuts Worldwide LLC. Dist. by Universal Uclick
www.snoopy.com

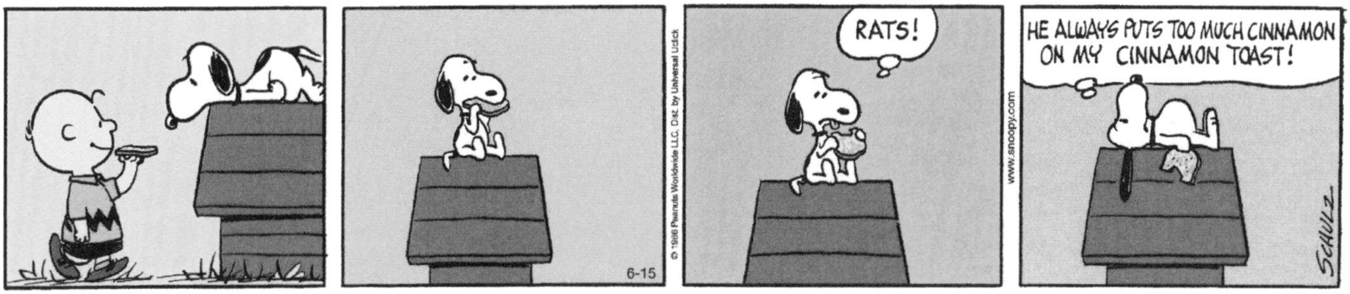
6-15
RATS!
HE ALWAYS PUTS TOO MUCH CINNAMON ON MY CINNAMON TOAST!
www.snoopy.com
SCHULZ

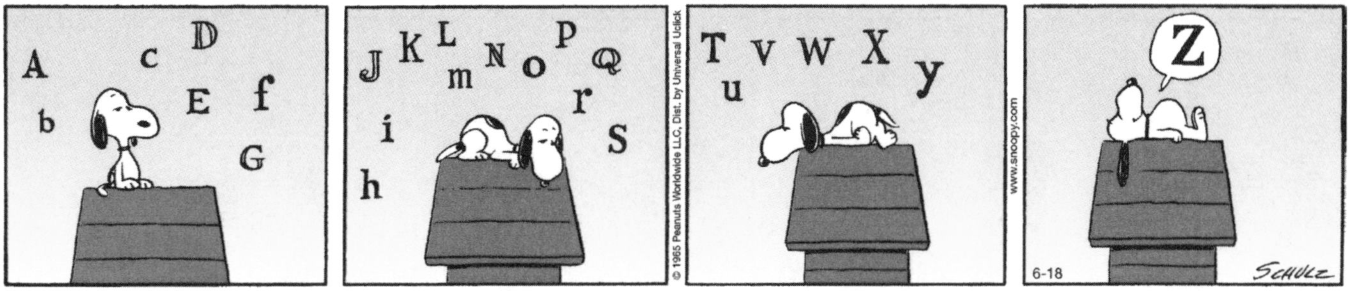
A b c D E f G
J K L m N o P Q i h r S
T u V W X y
Z
www.snoopy.com
6-18
SCHULZ

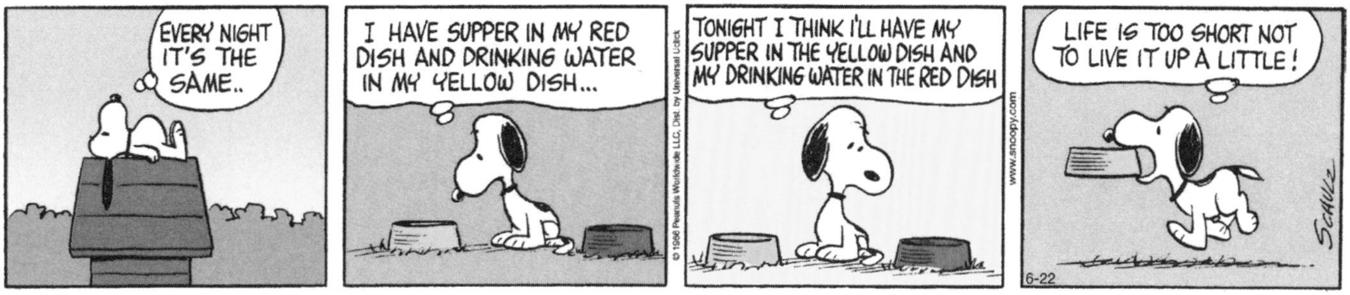
EVERY NIGHT IT'S THE SAME..
I HAVE SUPPER IN MY RED DISH AND DRINKING WATER IN MY YELLOW DISH...
TONIGHT I THINK I'LL HAVE MY SUPPER IN THE YELLOW DISH AND MY DRINKING WATER IN THE RED DISH
LIFE IS TOO SHORT NOT TO LIVE IT UP A LITTLE!
www.snoopy.com
6-22
SCHULZ

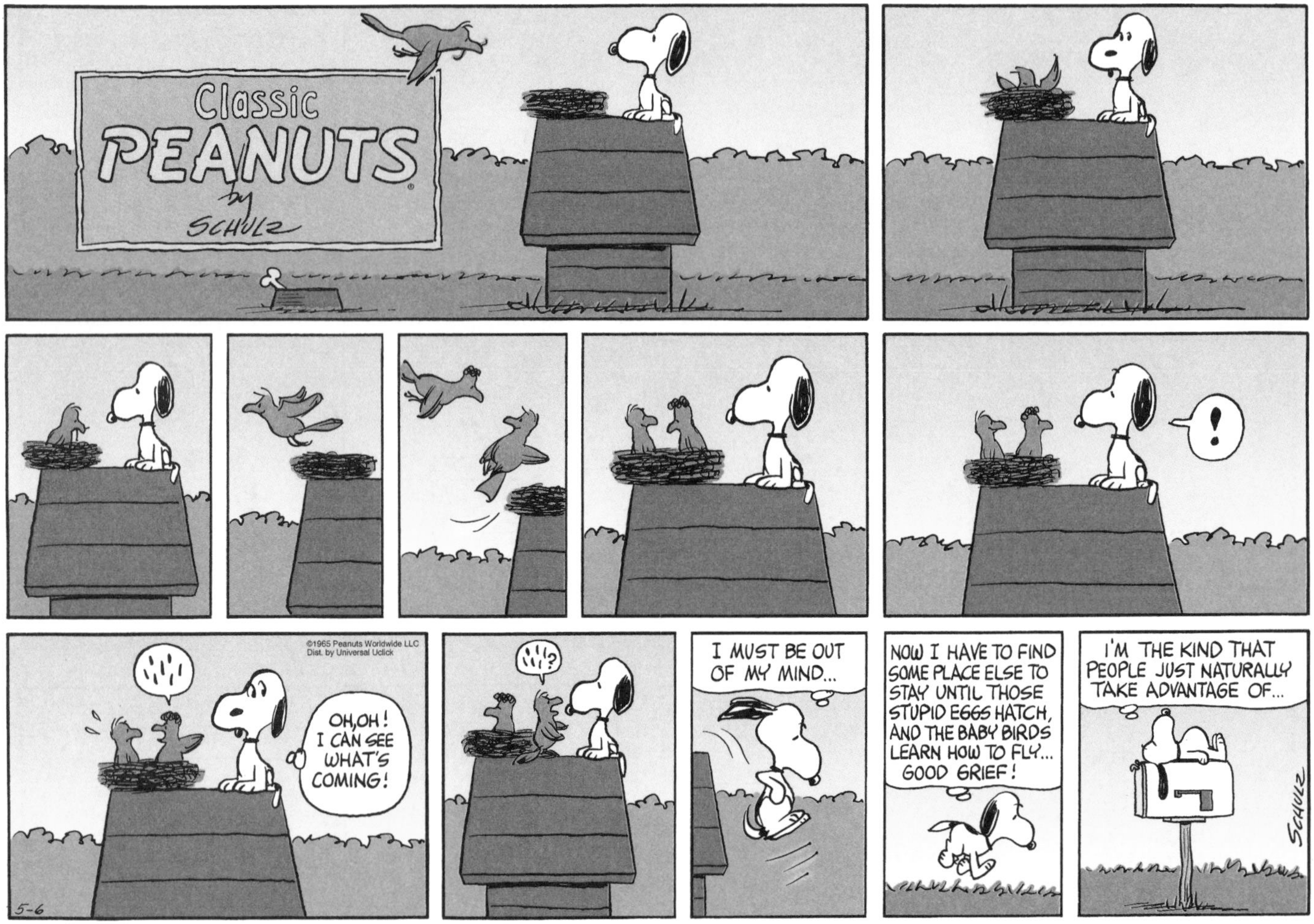
Classic
PEANUTS
by
SCHULZ
!
©1965 Peanuts Worldwide LLC
Dist. by Universal Uclick
OH,OH! I CAN SEE WHAT'S COMING!
I MUST BE OUT OF MY MIND...
NOW I HAVE TO FIND SOME PLACE ELSE TO STAY UNTIL THOSE STUPID EGGS HATCH, AND THE BABY BIRDS LEARN HOW TO FLY... GOOD GRIEF!
I'M THE KIND THAT PEOPLE JUST NATURALLY TAKE ADVANTAGE OF...
SCHULZ
5-6

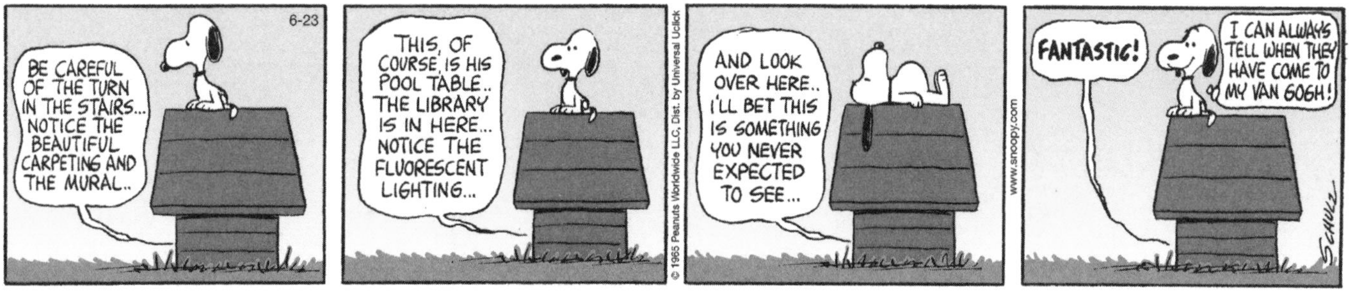
6-23
BE CAREFUL OF THE TURN IN THE STAIRS... NOTICE THE BEAUTIFUL CARPETING AND THE MURAL..
THIS, OF COURSE, IS HIS POOL TABLE.. THE LIBRARY IS IN HERE... NOTICE THE FLUORESCENT LIGHTING...
© 1965 Peanuts Worldwide LLC, Dist. by Universal Uclick
AND LOOK OVER HERE.. I'LL BET THIS IS SOMETHING YOU NEVER EXPECTED TO SEE...
www.snoopy.com
FANTASTIC!
I CAN ALWAYS TELL WHEN THEY HAVE COME TO MY VAN GOGH!
SCHULZ

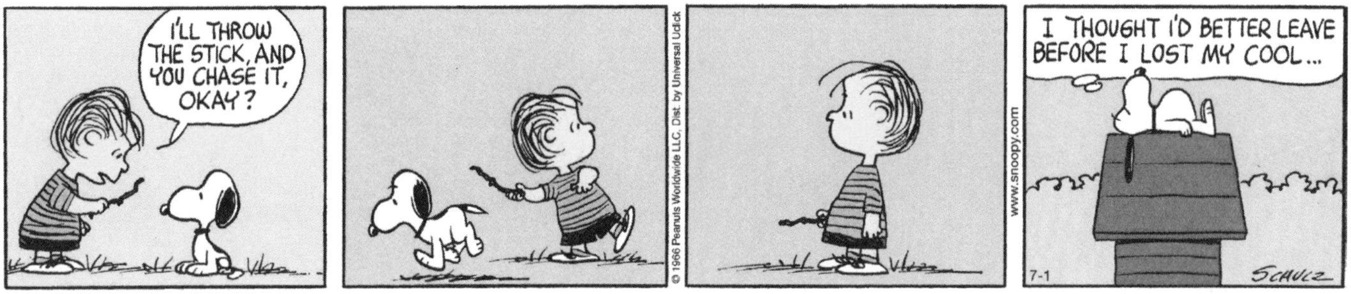
I'LL THROW THE STICK, AND YOU CHASE IT, OKAY?
© 1966 Peanuts Worldwide LLC, Dist. by Universal Uclick
www.snoopy.com
I THOUGHT I'D BETTER LEAVE BEFORE I LOST MY COOL...
7-1
SCHULZ

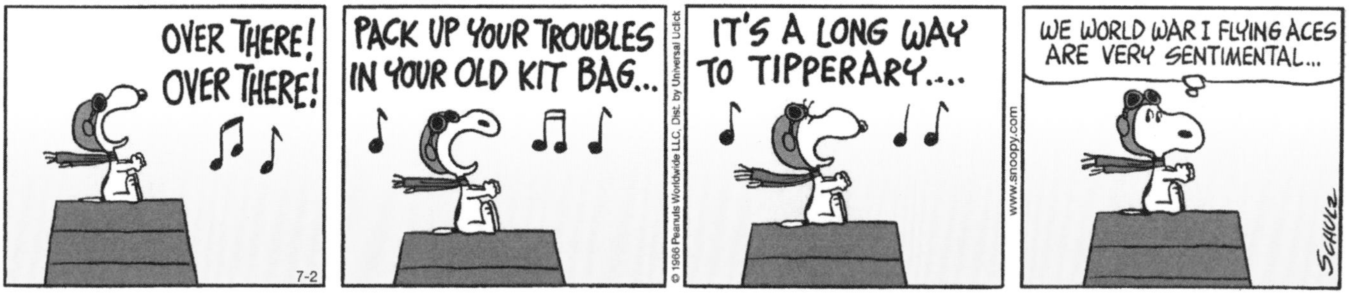
OVER THERE! OVER THERE!
7-2
PACK UP YOUR TROUBLES IN YOUR OLD KIT BAG...
© 1966 Peanuts Worldwide LLC, Dist. by Universal Uclick
IT'S A LONG WAY TO TIPPERARY....
www.snoopy.com
WE WORLD WAR I FLYING ACES ARE VERY SENTIMENTAL...
SCHULZ

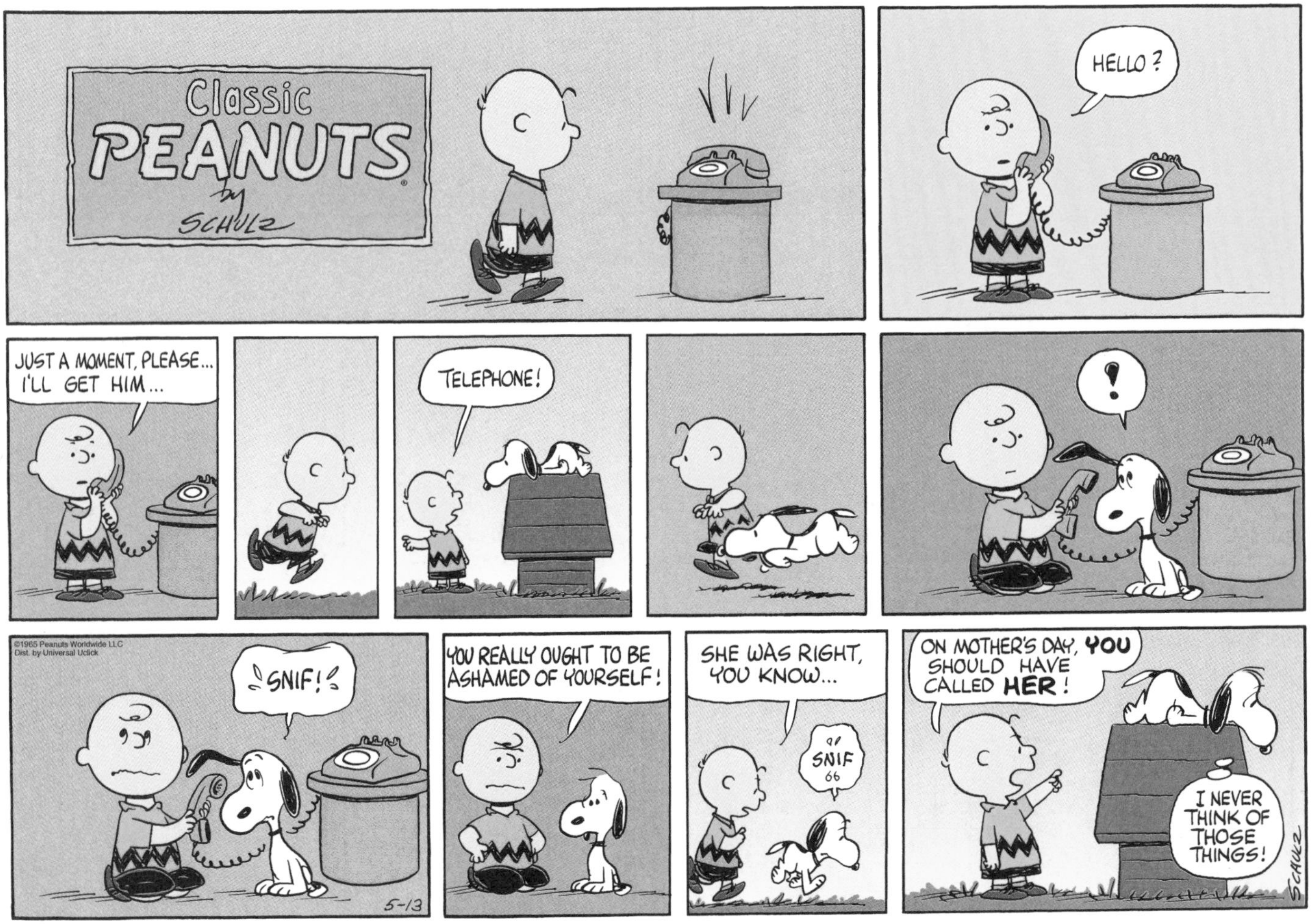
Classic PEANUTS by SCHULZ
HELLO?
JUST A MOMENT, PLEASE... I'LL GET HIM...
TELEPHONE!
!
©1965 Peanuts Worldwide LLC Dist. by Universal Uclick
SNIF!
5-13
YOU REALLY OUGHT TO BE ASHAMED OF YOURSELF!
SHE WAS RIGHT, YOU KNOW...
SNIF
ON MOTHER'S DAY, YOU SHOULD HAVE CALLED HER!
I NEVER THINK OF THOSE THINGS!
SCHULZ

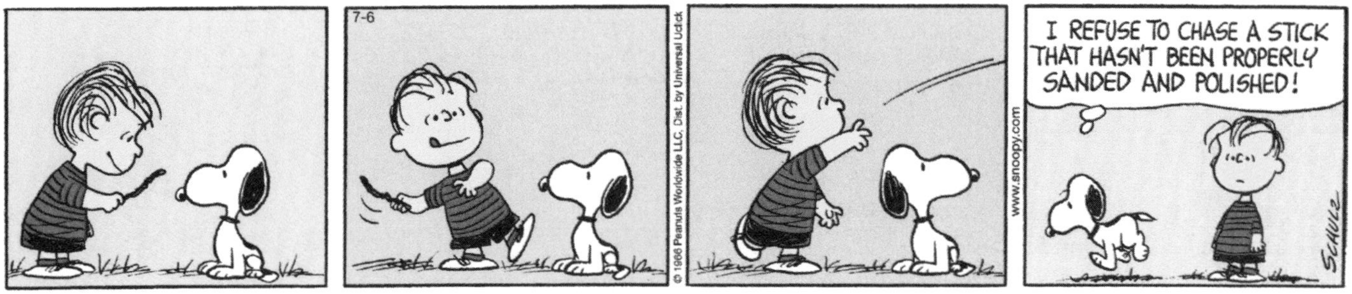
7-6
© 1966 Peanuts Worldwide LLC. Dist. by Universal Uclick
www.snoopy.com
I REFUSE TO CHASE A STICK THAT HASN'T BEEN PROPERLY SANDED AND POLISHED!
SCHULZ

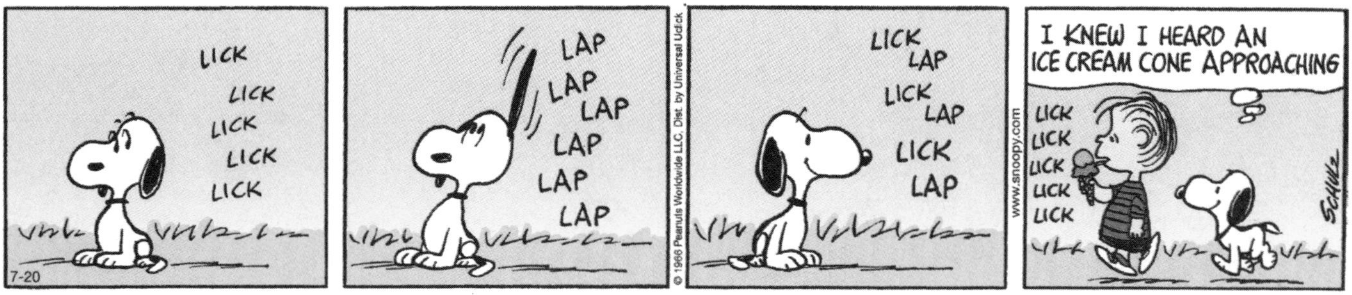
LICK LICK LICK LICK LICK
7-20
LAP LAP LAP LAP LAP LAP
© 1966 Peanuts Worldwide LLC. Dist. by Universal Uclick
LICK LAP LICK LAP LICK LAP
www.snoopy.com
I KNEW I HEARD AN ICE CREAM CONE APPROACHING
LICK LICK LICK LICK LICK
SCHULZ

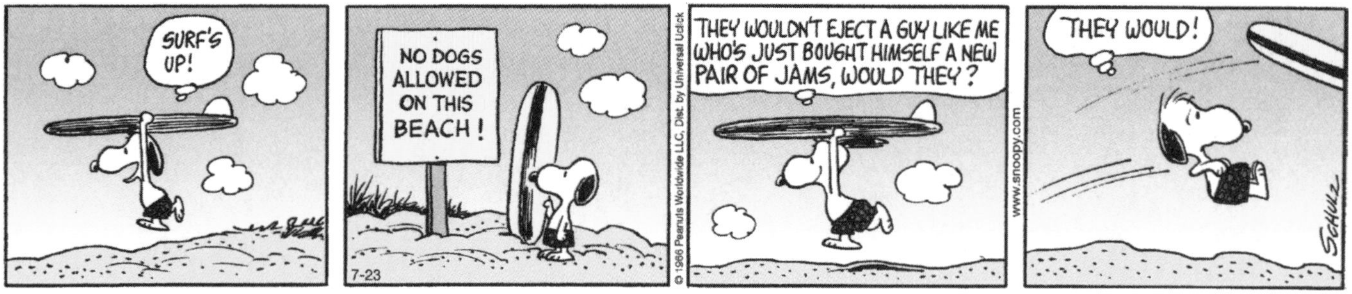
SURF'S UP!
NO DOGS ALLOWED ON THIS BEACH!
7-23
© 1966 Peanuts Worldwide LLC. Dist. by Universal Uclick
THEY WOULDN'T EJECT A GUY LIKE ME WHO'S JUST BOUGHT HIMSELF A NEW PAIR OF JAMS, WOULD THEY?
www.snoopy.com
THEY WOULD!
SCHULZ

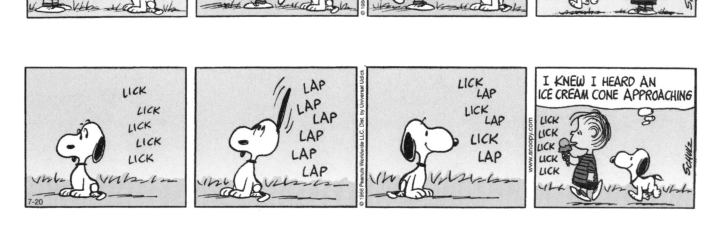

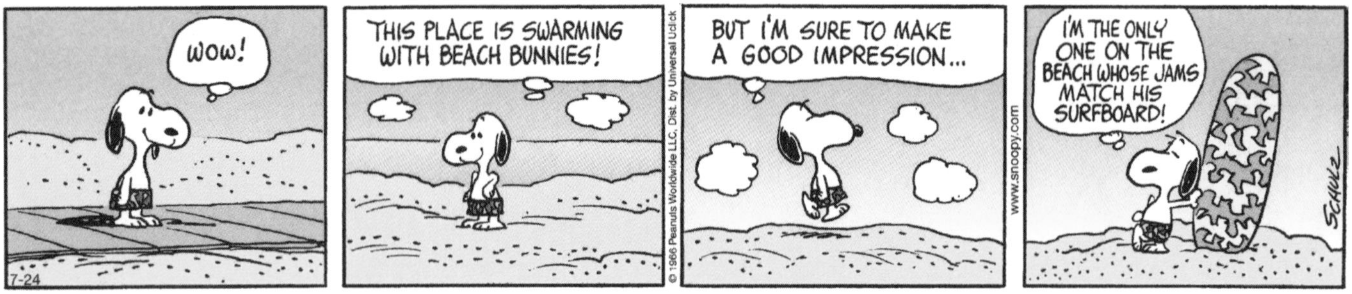
WOW!
THIS PLACE IS SWARMING WITH BEACH BUNNIES!
BUT I'M SURE TO MAKE A GOOD IMPRESSION...
I'M THE ONLY ONE ON THE BEACH WHOSE JAMS MATCH HIS SURFBOARD!
7-24
© 1966 Peanuts Worldwide LLC, Dist. by Universal Uclick
www.snoopy.com
SCHULZ

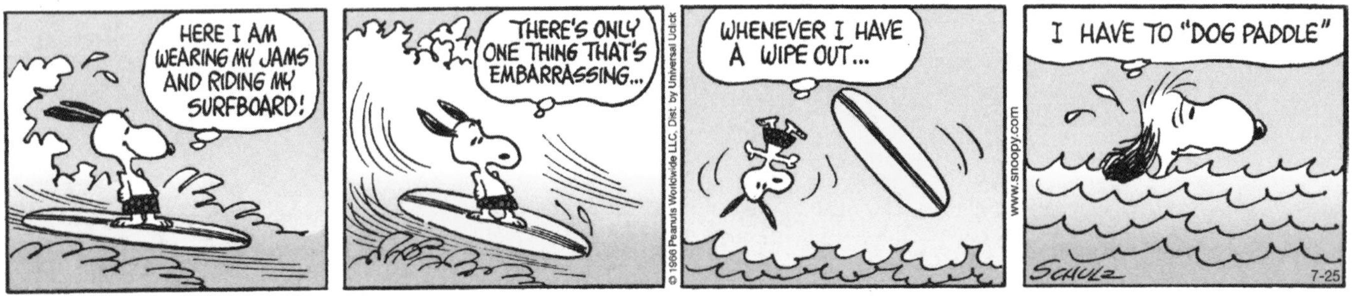
HERE I AM WEARING MY JAMS AND RIDING MY SURFBOARD!
THERE'S ONLY ONE THING THAT'S EMBARRASSING...
WHENEVER I HAVE A WIPE OUT...
I HAVE TO "DOG PADDLE"
7-25
© 1966 Peanuts Worldwide LLC, Dist. by Universal Uclick
www.snoopy.com
SCHULZ

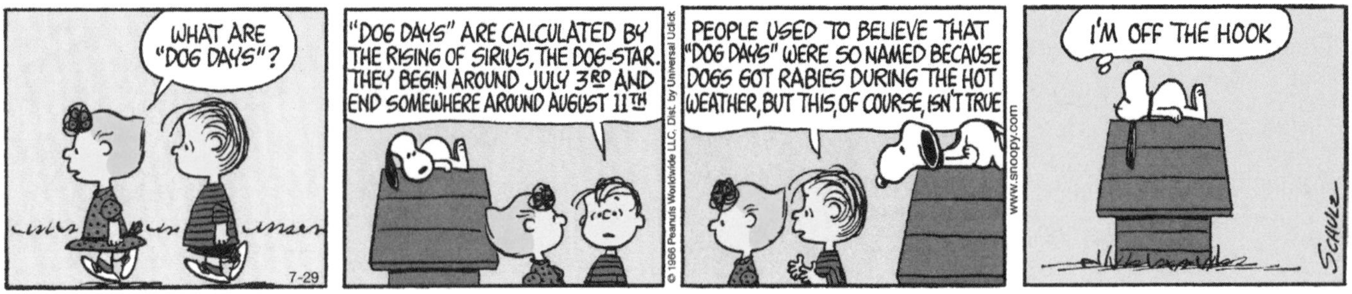
WHAT ARE "DOG DAYS"?
"DOG DAYS" ARE CALCULATED BY THE RISING OF SIRIUS, THE DOG-STAR. THEY BEGIN AROUND JULY 3RD AND END SOMEWHERE AROUND AUGUST 11TH
PEOPLE USED TO BELIEVE THAT "DOG DAYS" WERE SO NAMED BECAUSE DOGS GOT RABIES DURING THE HOT WEATHER, BUT THIS, OF COURSE, ISN'T TRUE
I'M OFF THE HOOK
7-29
© 1966 Peanuts Worldwide LLC, Dist. by Universal Uclick
www.snoopy.com
SCHULZ

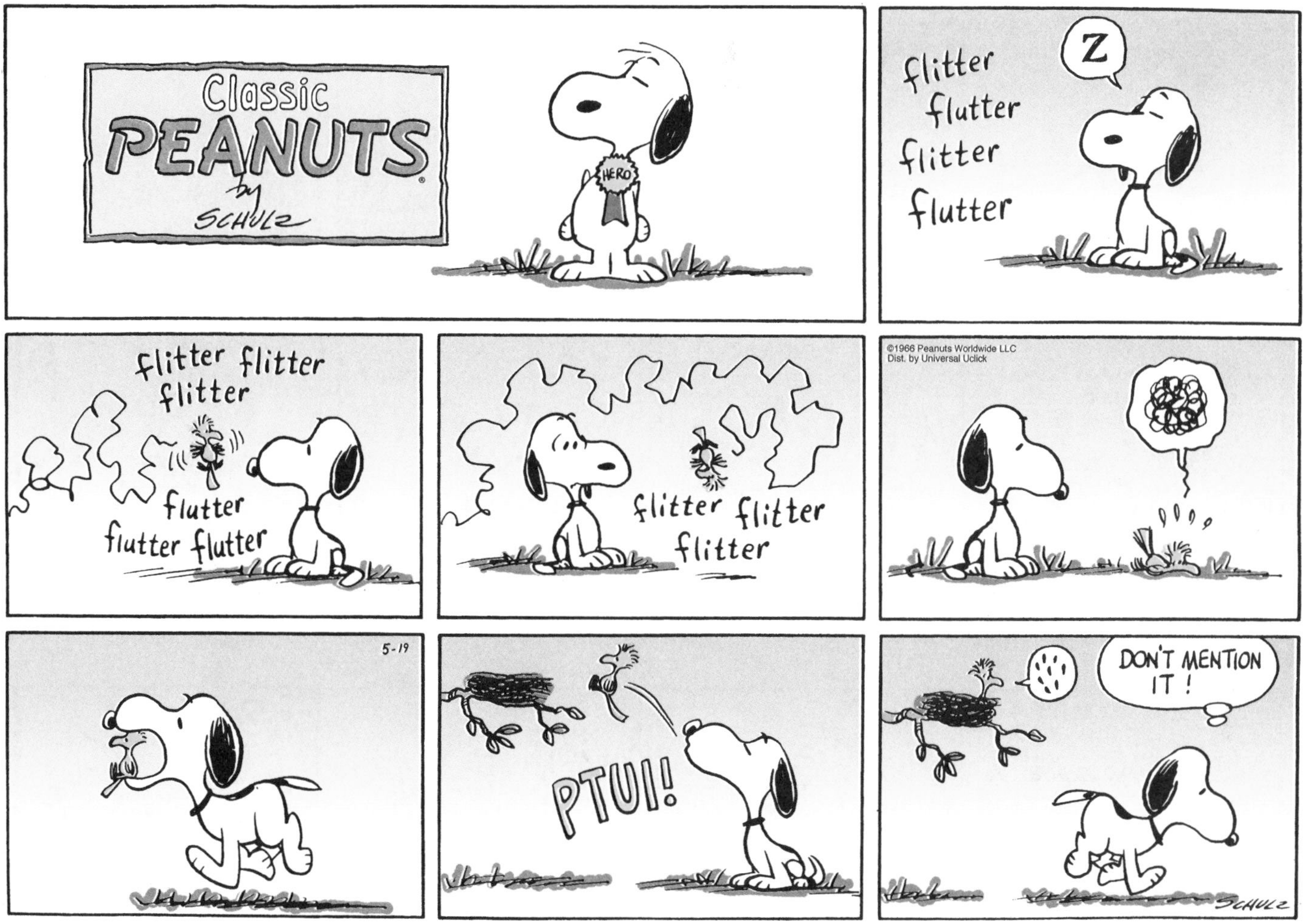
Classic
PEANUTS
by
SCHULZ
HERO
flitter
flutter
flitter
flutter
Z
flitter flitter
flitter
flutter
flutter flutter
flitter flitter
flitter
©1966 Peanuts Worldwide LLC
Dist. by Universal Uclick
5-19
PTUI!
DON'T MENTION IT!
SCHULZ

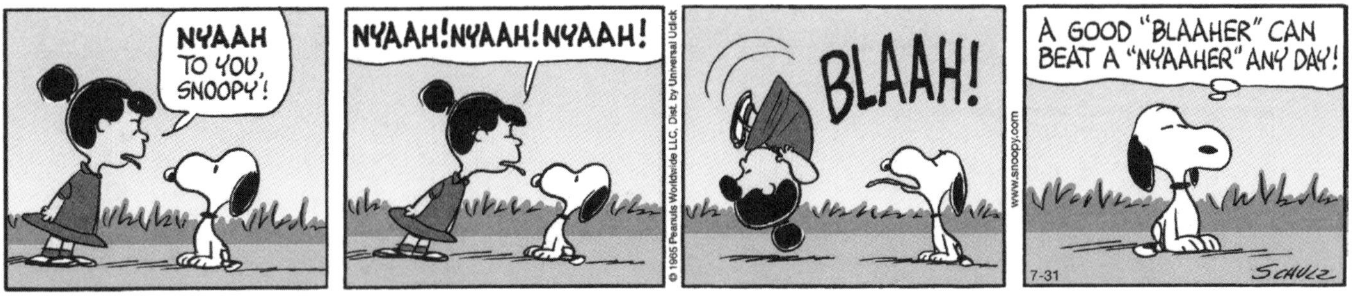
NYAAH TO YOU, SNOOPY!
NYAAH! NYAAH! NYAAH!
© 1965 Peanuts Worldwide LLC, Dist. by Universal Uclick
BLAAH!
www.snoopy.com
A GOOD "BLAAHER" CAN BEAT A "NYAAHER" ANY DAY!
7-31
SCHULZ

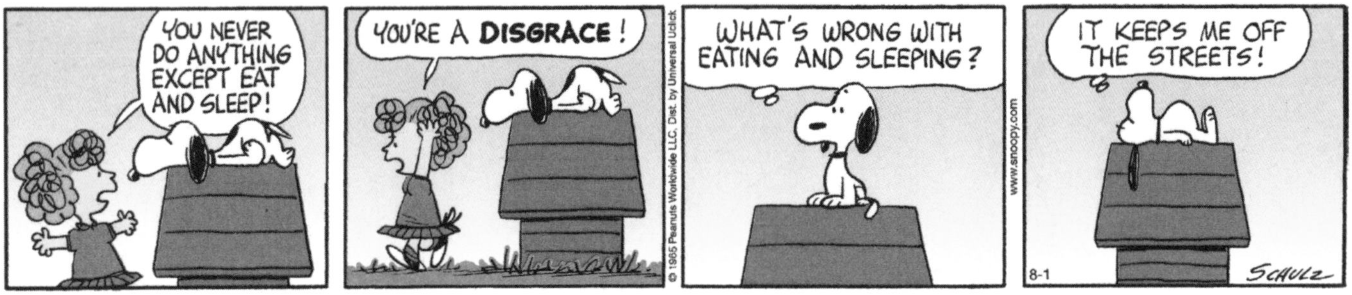
YOU NEVER DO ANYTHING EXCEPT EAT AND SLEEP!
YOU'RE A **DISGRACE**!
© 1965 Peanuts Worldwide LLC, Dist. by Universal Uclick
WHAT'S WRONG WITH EATING AND SLEEPING?
www.snoopy.com
IT KEEPS ME OFF THE STREETS!
8-1
SCHULZ

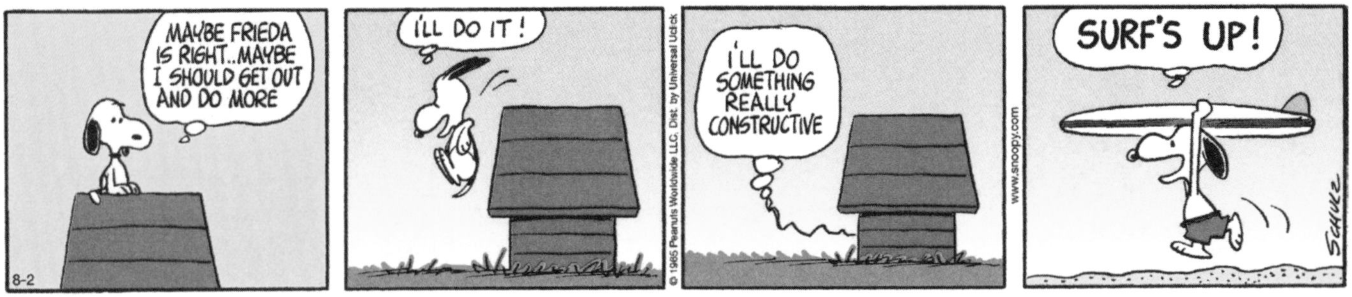
MAYBE FRIEDA IS RIGHT..MAYBE I SHOULD GET OUT AND DO MORE
8-2
I'LL DO IT!
© 1965 Peanuts Worldwide LLC, Dist. by Universal Uclick
I'LL DO SOMETHING REALLY CONSTRUCTIVE
www.snoopy.com
SURF'S UP!
SCHULZ

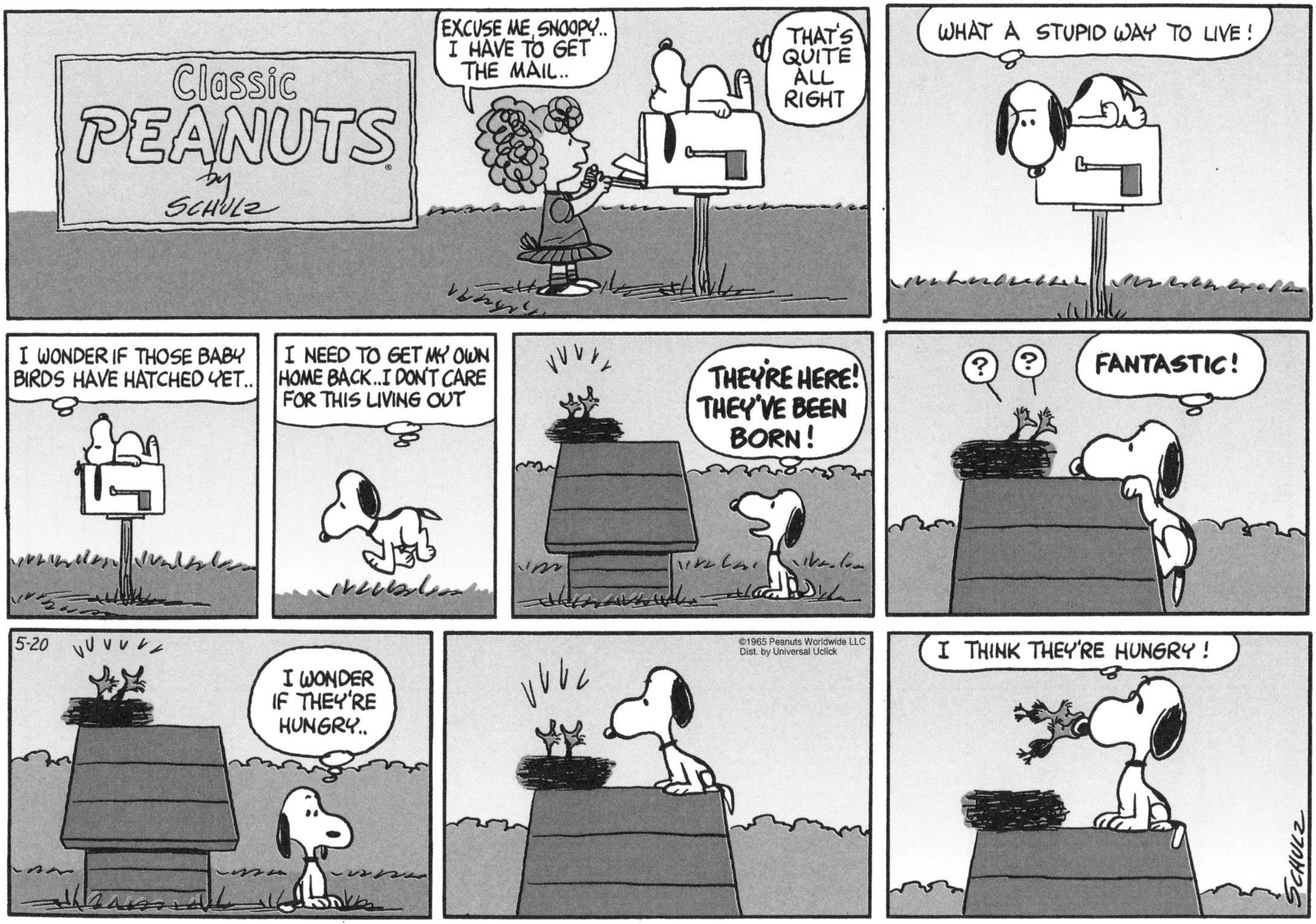
Classic PEANUTS by SCHULZ
EXCUSE ME, SNOOPY.. I HAVE TO GET THE MAIL..
THAT'S QUITE ALL RIGHT
WHAT A STUPID WAY TO LIVE!
I WONDER IF THOSE BABY BIRDS HAVE HATCHED YET..
I NEED TO GET MY OWN HOME BACK..I DON'T CARE FOR THIS LIVING OUT
THEY'RE HERE! THEY'VE BEEN BORN!
? ?
FANTASTIC!
5-20
I WONDER IF THEY'RE HUNGRY..
©1965 Peanuts Worldwide LLC
Dist. by Universal Uclick
I THINK THEY'RE HUNGRY!
SCHULZ

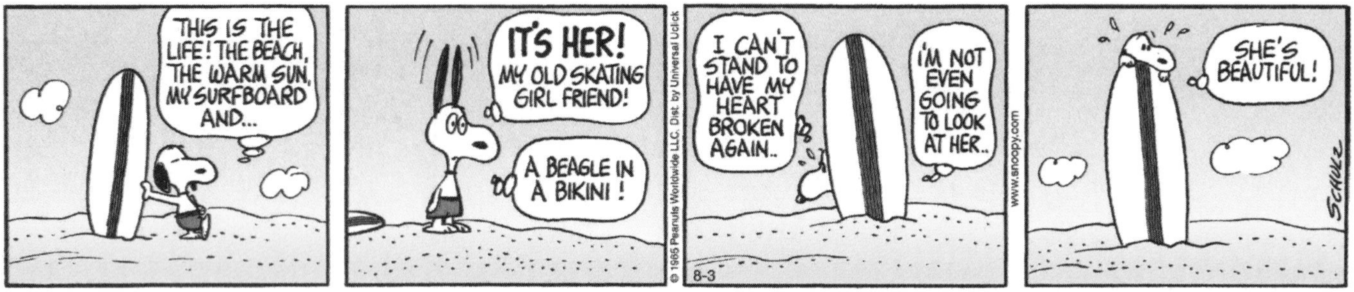
THIS IS THE LIFE! THE BEACH, THE WARM SUN, MY SURFBOARD AND...
IT'S HER! MY OLD SKATING GIRL FRIEND!
A BEAGLE IN A BIKINI!
© 1965 Peanuts Worldwide LLC, Dist. by Universal Uclick
I CAN'T STAND TO HAVE MY HEART BROKEN AGAIN..
I'M NOT EVEN GOING TO LOOK AT HER..
8-3
www.snoopy.com
SHE'S BEAUTIFUL!
SCHULZ

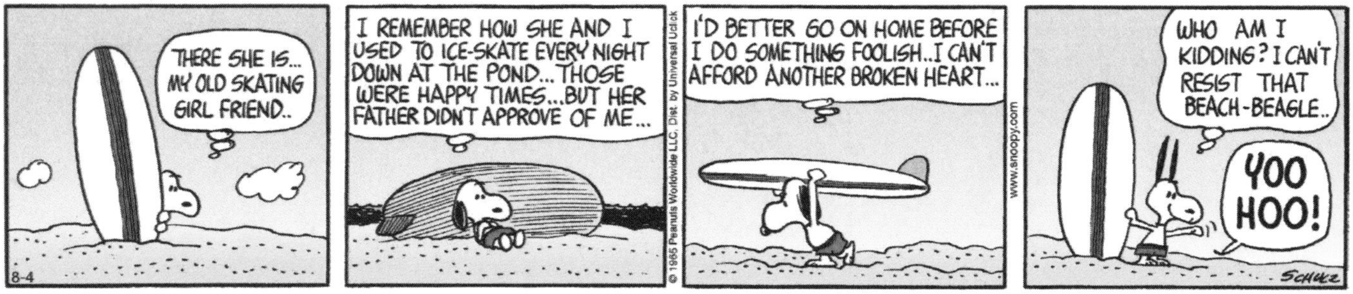
THERE SHE IS... MY OLD SKATING GIRL FRIEND..
8-4
I REMEMBER HOW SHE AND I USED TO ICE-SKATE EVERY NIGHT DOWN AT THE POND... THOSE WERE HAPPY TIMES... BUT HER FATHER DIDN'T APPROVE OF ME...
© 1965 Peanuts Worldwide LLC, Dist. by Universal Uclick
I'D BETTER GO ON HOME BEFORE I DO SOMETHING FOOLISH.. I CAN'T AFFORD ANOTHER BROKEN HEART...
www.snoopy.com
WHO AM I KIDDING? I CAN'T RESIST THAT BEACH-BEAGLE..
YOO HOO!
SCHULZ

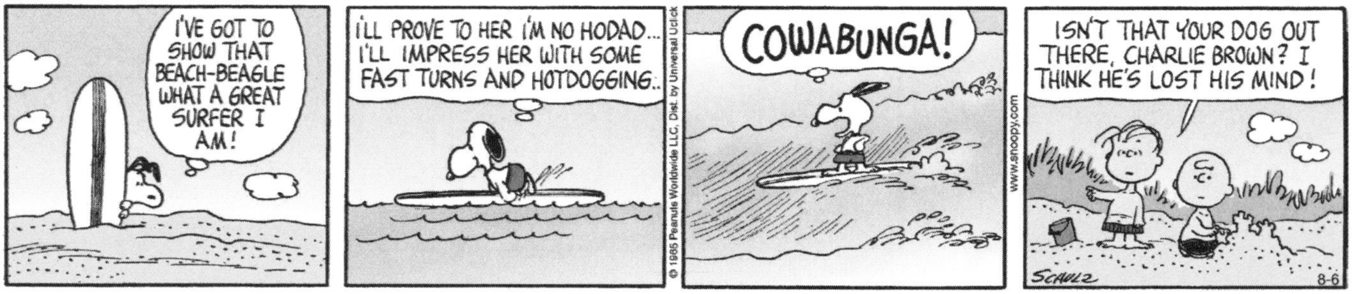
I'VE GOT TO SHOW THAT BEACH-BEAGLE WHAT A GREAT SURFER I AM!
I'LL PROVE TO HER I'M NO HODAD... I'LL IMPRESS HER WITH SOME FAST TURNS AND HOTDOGGING..
© 1965 Peanuts Worldwide LLC, Dist. by Universal Uclick
COWABUNGA!
www.snoopy.com
ISN'T THAT YOUR DOG OUT THERE, CHARLIE BROWN? I THINK HE'S LOST HIS MIND!
SCHULZ
8-6

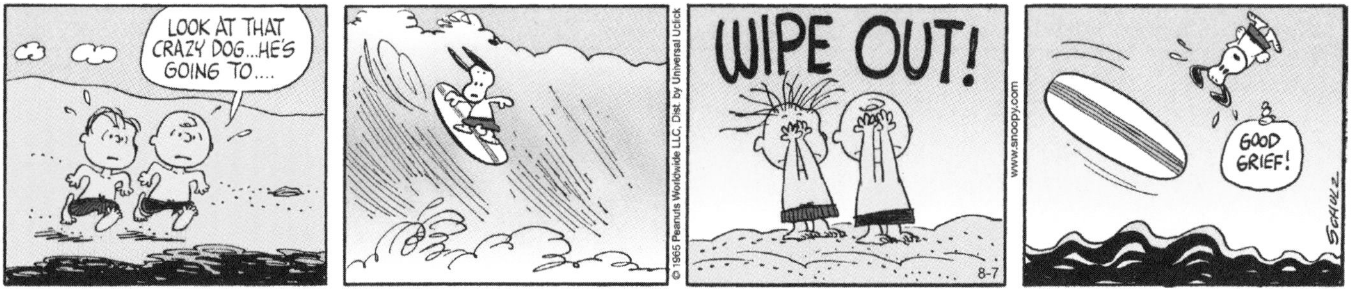
LOOK AT THAT CRAZY DOG...HE'S GOING TO....
WIPE OUT!
GOOD GRIEF!
© 1965 Peanuts Worldwide LLC, Dist. by Universal Uclick
www.snoopy.com
8-7
SCHULZ

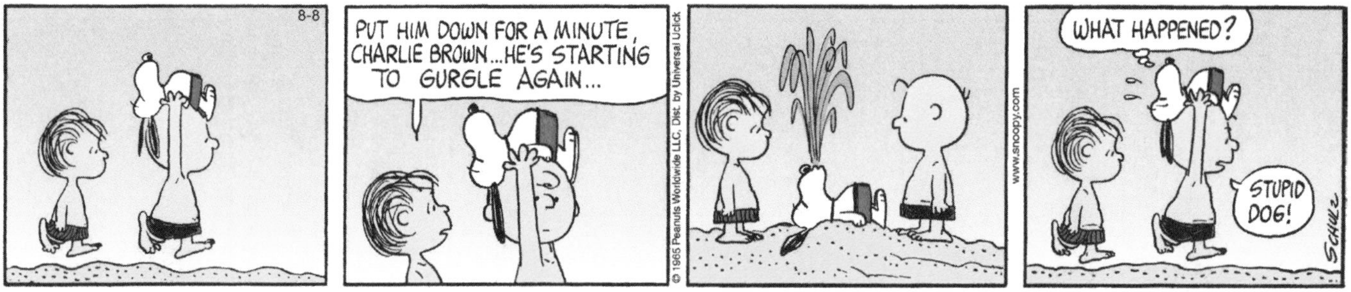
8-8
PUT HIM DOWN FOR A MINUTE, CHARLIE BROWN...HE'S STARTING TO GURGLE AGAIN...
WHAT HAPPENED?
STUPID DOG!
© 1965 Peanuts Worldwide LLC, Dist. by Universal Uclick
www.snoopy.com
SCHULZ

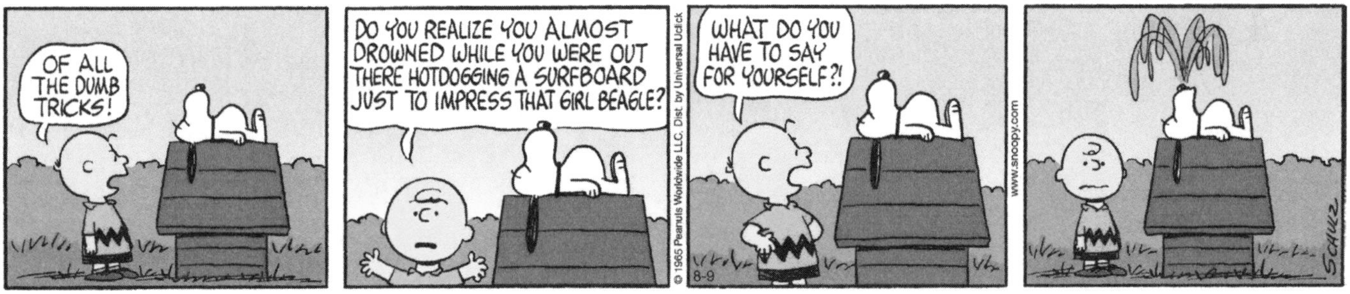
OF ALL THE DUMB TRICKS!
DO YOU REALIZE YOU ALMOST DROWNED WHILE YOU WERE OUT THERE HOTDOGGING A SURFBOARD JUST TO IMPRESS THAT GIRL BEAGLE?
WHAT DO YOU HAVE TO SAY FOR YOURSELF?!
© 1965 Peanuts Worldwide LLC, Dist. by Universal Uclick
www.snoopy.com
8-9
SCHULZ

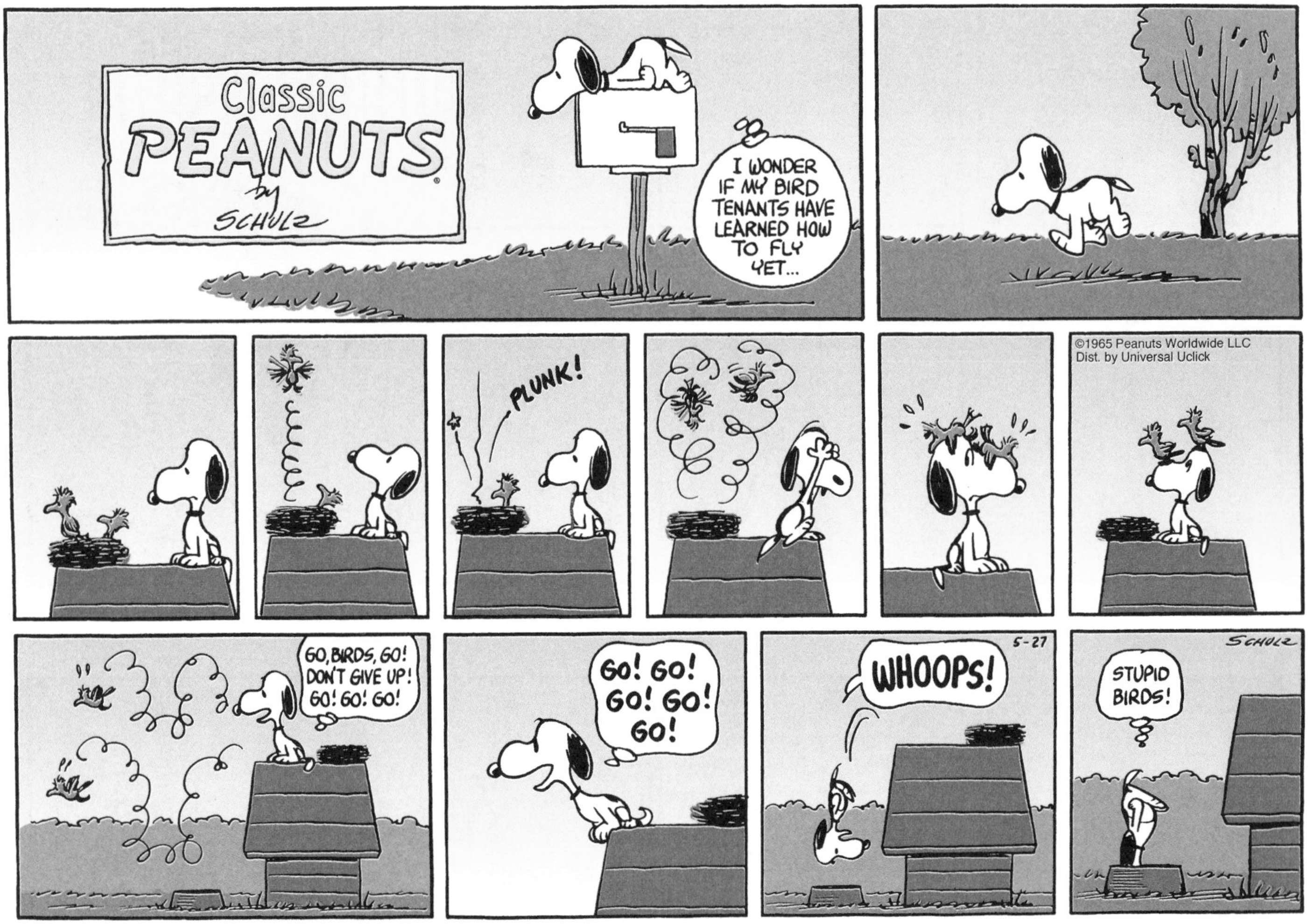
Classic
PEANUTS
by
SCHULZ
I WONDER IF MY BIRD TENANTS HAVE LEARNED HOW TO FLY YET...
©1965 Peanuts Worldwide LLC
Dist. by Universal Uclick
PLUNK!
GO, BIRDS, GO! DON'T GIVE UP! GO! GO! GO!
GO! GO! GO! GO! GO!
5-27
WHOOPS!
SCHULZ
STUPID BIRDS!

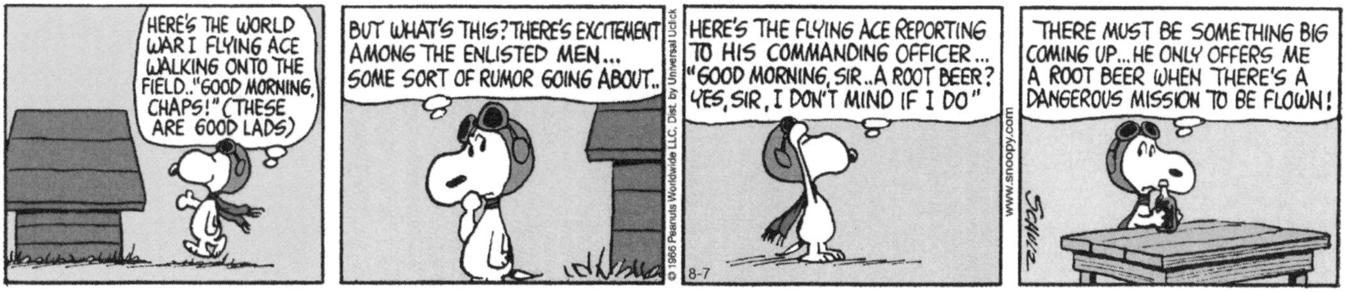
HERE'S THE WORLD WAR I FLYING ACE WALKING ONTO THE FIELD.."GOOD MORNING, CHAPS!" (THESE ARE GOOD LADS)
BUT WHAT'S THIS? THERE'S EXCITEMENT AMONG THE ENLISTED MEN... SOME SORT OF RUMOR GOING ABOUT..
© 1966 Peanuts Worldwide LLC, Dist. by Universal Uclick
HERE'S THE FLYING ACE REPORTING TO HIS COMMANDING OFFICER... "GOOD MORNING, SIR..A ROOT BEER? YES, SIR, I DON'T MIND IF I DO"
8-7
www.snoopy.com
THERE MUST BE SOMETHING BIG COMING UP...HE ONLY OFFERS ME A ROOT BEER WHEN THERE'S A DANGEROUS MISSION TO BE FLOWN!
SCHULZ

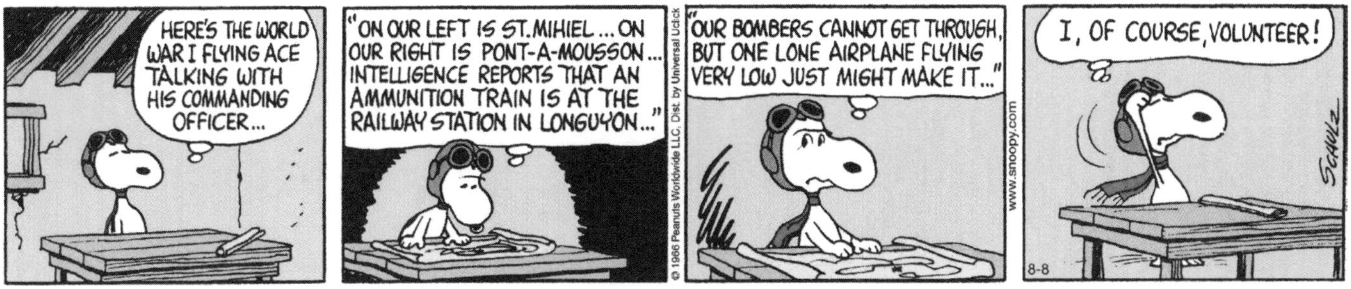
HERE'S THE WORLD WAR I FLYING ACE TALKING WITH HIS COMMANDING OFFICER...
"ON OUR LEFT IS ST. MIHIEL ... ON OUR RIGHT IS PONT-A-MOUSSON... INTELLIGENCE REPORTS THAT AN AMMUNITION TRAIN IS AT THE RAILWAY STATION IN LONGUYON..."
© 1966 Peanuts Worldwide LLC, Dist. by Universal Uclick
"OUR BOMBERS CANNOT GET THROUGH, BUT ONE LONE AIRPLANE FLYING VERY LOW JUST MIGHT MAKE IT..."
www.snoopy.com
I, OF COURSE, VOLUNTEER!
SCHULZ
8-8

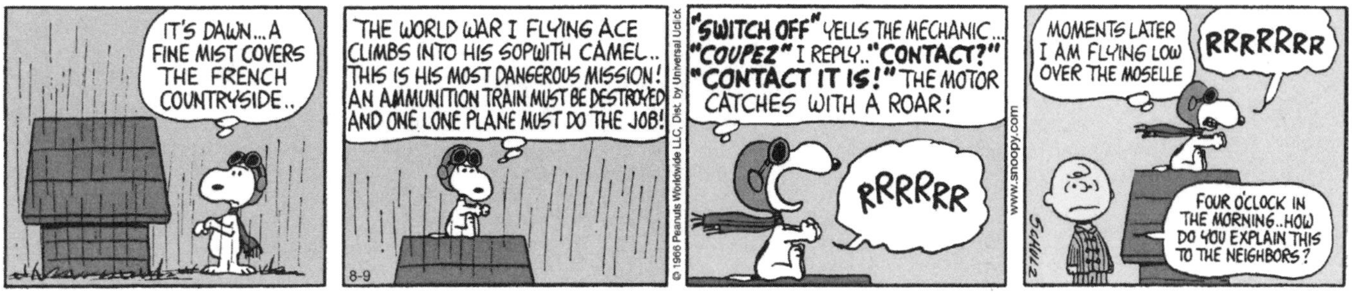
IT'S DAWN...A FINE MIST COVERS THE FRENCH COUNTRYSIDE..
THE WORLD WAR I FLYING ACE CLIMBS INTO HIS SOPWITH CAMEL.. THIS IS HIS MOST DANGEROUS MISSION! AN AMMUNITION TRAIN MUST BE DESTROYED AND ONE LONE PLANE MUST DO THE JOB!
8-9
© 1966 Peanuts Worldwide LLC, Dist. by Universal Uclick
"SWITCH OFF" YELLS THE MECHANIC... "COUPEZ" I REPLY.."CONTACT?" "CONTACT IT IS!" THE MOTOR CATCHES WITH A ROAR!
RRRRRR
www.snoopy.com
MOMENTS LATER I AM FLYING LOW OVER THE MOSELLE
RRRRRRR
SCHULZ
FOUR O'CLOCK IN THE MORNING..HOW DO YOU EXPLAIN THIS TO THE NEIGHBORS?

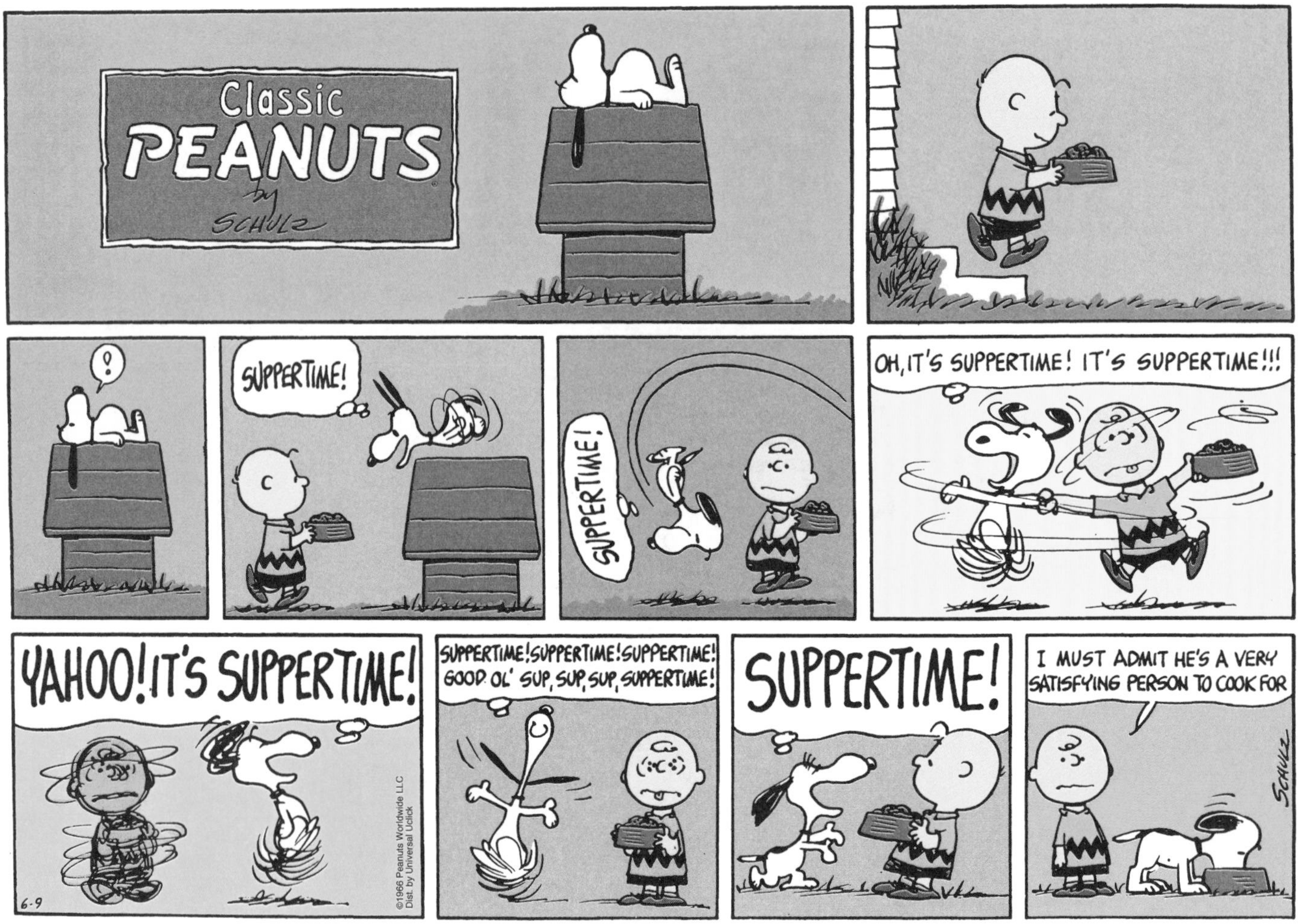
Classic
PEANUTS
by SCHULZ
!
SUPPERTIME!
SUPPERTIME!
OH, IT'S SUPPERTIME! IT'S SUPPERTIME!!!
YAHOO! IT'S SUPPERTIME!
6-9
©1966 Peanuts Worldwide LLC
Dist. by Universal Uclick
SUPPERTIME! SUPPERTIME! SUPPERTIME! GOOD OL' SUP, SUP, SUP, SUPPERTIME!
SUPPERTIME!
I MUST ADMIT HE'S A VERY SATISFYING PERSON TO COOK FOR
SCHULZ

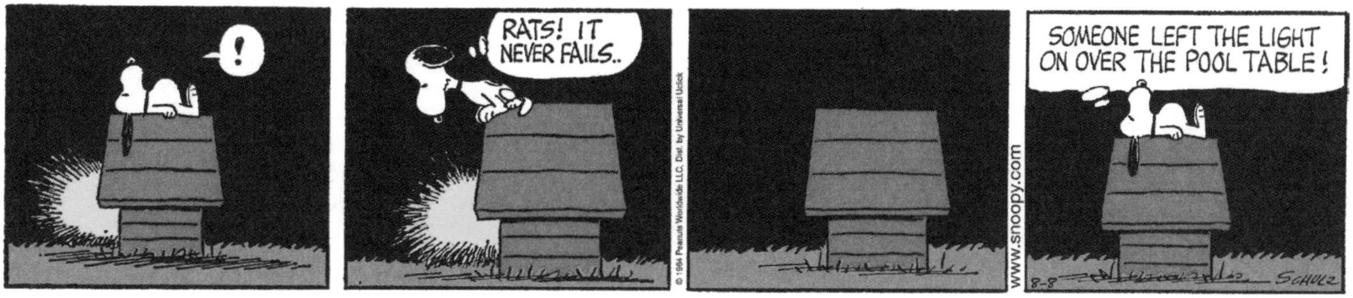
!
RATS! IT NEVER FAILS..
© 1964 Peanuts Worldwide LLC. Dist. by Universal Uclick
www.snoopy.com
SOMEONE LEFT THE LIGHT ON OVER THE POOL TABLE!
8-8
SCHULZ

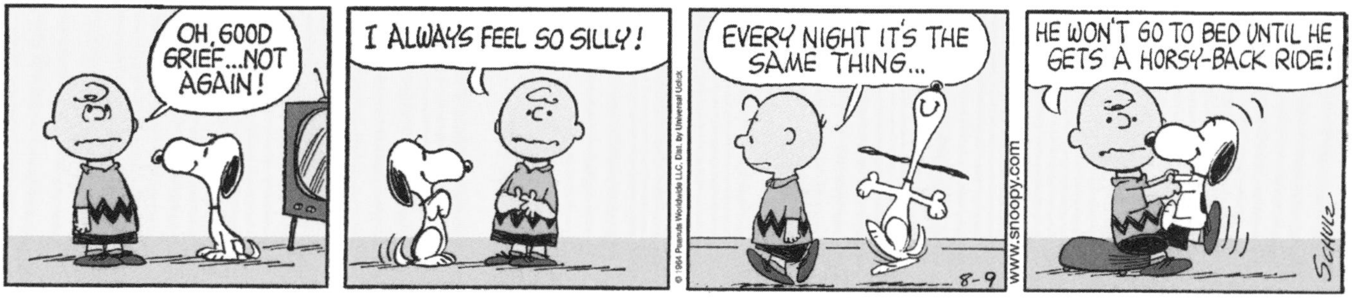
OH, GOOD GRIEF...NOT AGAIN!
I ALWAYS FEEL SO SILLY!
© 1964 Peanuts Worldwide LLC. Dist. by Universal Uclick
EVERY NIGHT IT'S THE SAME THING...
8-9
www.snoopy.com
HE WON'T GO TO BED UNTIL HE GETS A HORSY-BACK RIDE!
SCHULZ

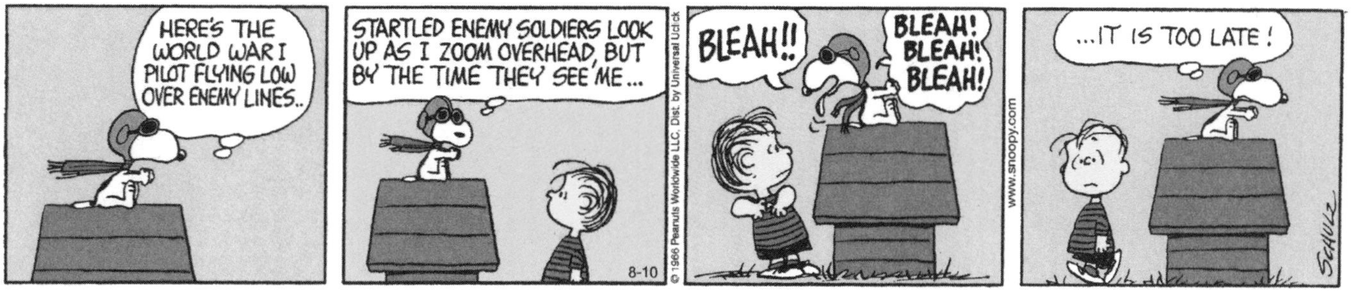
HERE'S THE WORLD WAR I PILOT FLYING LOW OVER ENEMY LINES..
STARTLED ENEMY SOLDIERS LOOK UP AS I ZOOM OVERHEAD, BUT BY THE TIME THEY SEE ME...
8-10
© 1966 Peanuts Worldwide LLC. Dist. by Universal Uclick
BLEAH!!
BLEAH! BLEAH! BLEAH!
www.snoopy.com
...IT IS TOO LATE!
SCHULZ

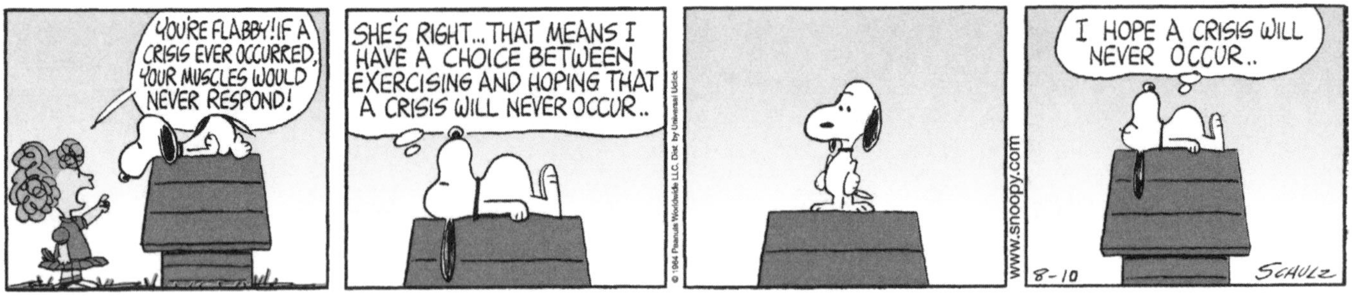
YOU'RE FLABBY! IF A CRISIS EVER OCCURRED, YOUR MUSCLES WOULD NEVER RESPOND!
SHE'S RIGHT... THAT MEANS I HAVE A CHOICE BETWEEN EXERCISING AND HOPING THAT A CRISIS WILL NEVER OCCUR..
© 1964 Peanuts Worldwide LLC. Dist. by Universal Uclick
www.snoopy.com
I HOPE A CRISIS WILL NEVER OCCUR..
8-10
SCHULZ

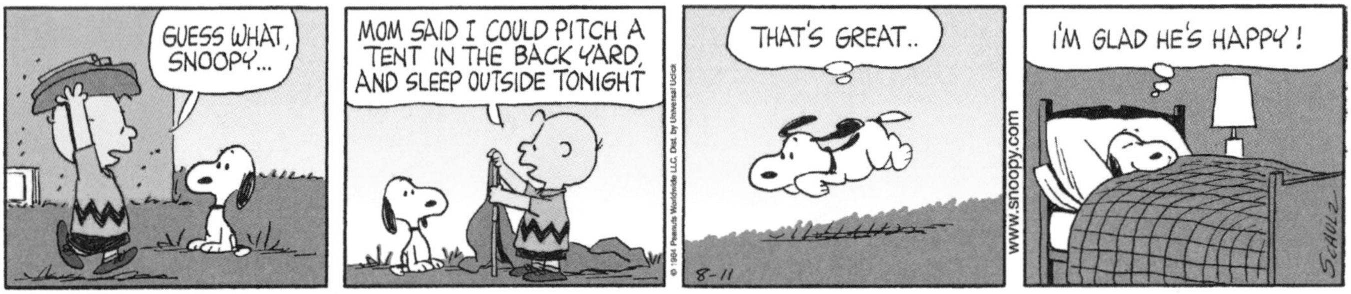
GUESS WHAT, SNOOPY...
MOM SAID I COULD PITCH A TENT IN THE BACK YARD, AND SLEEP OUTSIDE TONIGHT
© 1964 Peanuts Worldwide LLC. Dist. by Universal Uclick
THAT'S GREAT..
8-11
www.snoopy.com
I'M GLAD HE'S HAPPY!
SCHULZ

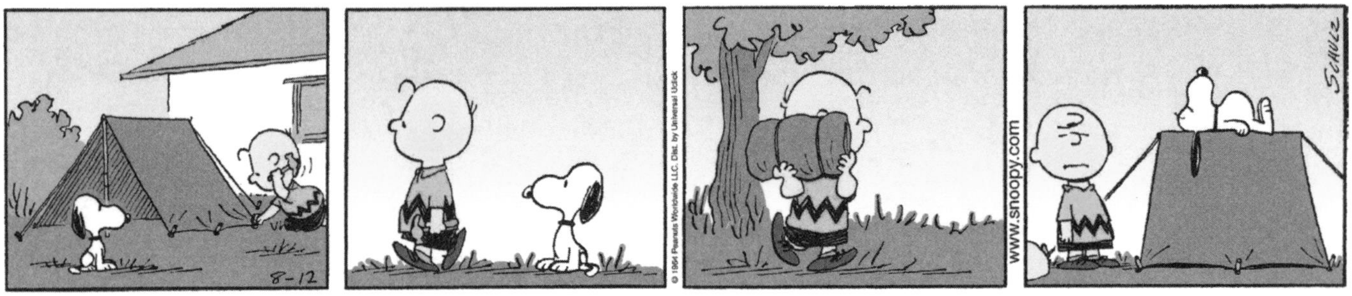
8-12
© 1964 Peanuts Worldwide LLC. Dist. by Universal Uclick
www.snoopy.com
SCHULZ

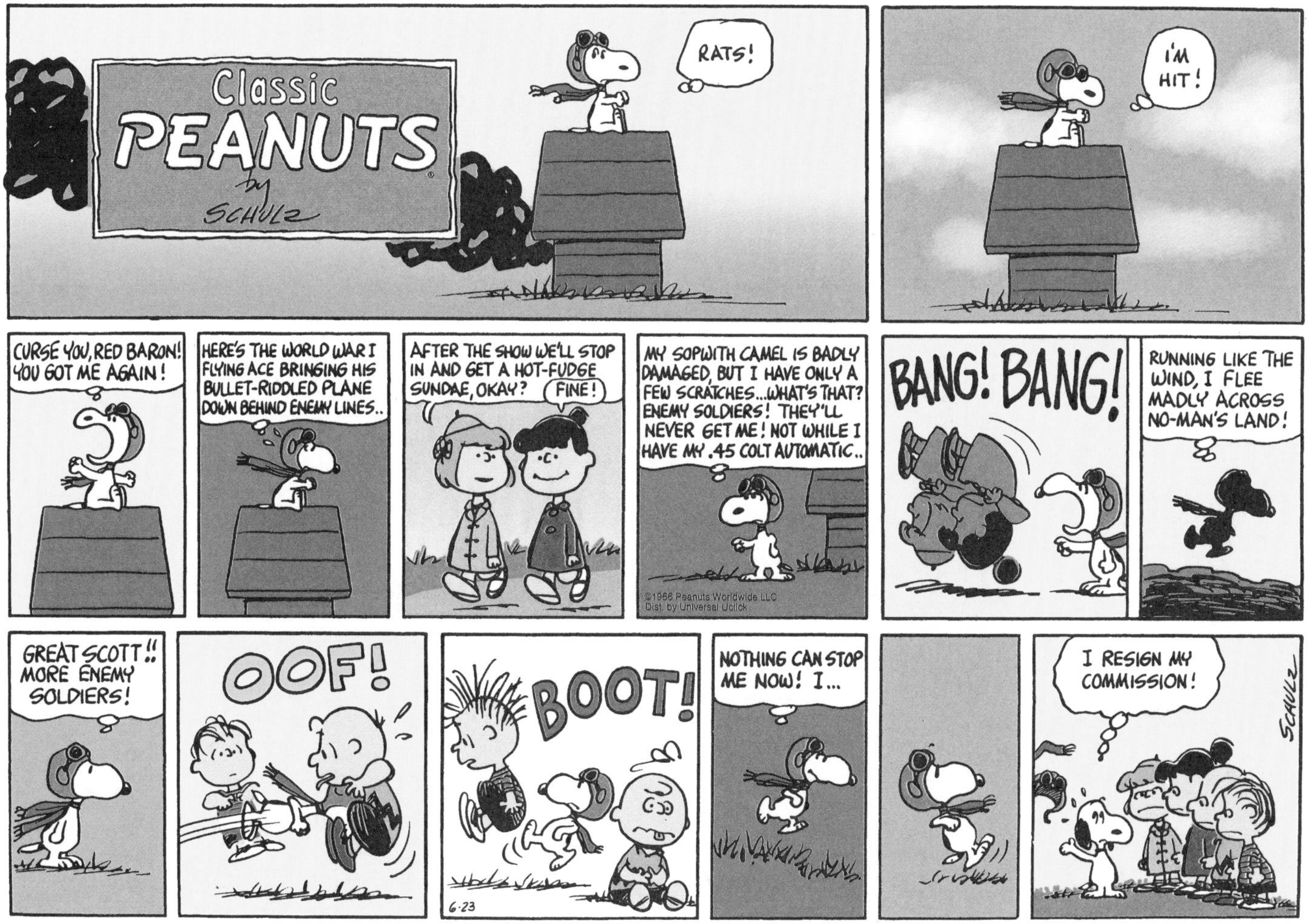
Classic
PEANUTS
by SCHULZ
RATS!
I'M HIT!
CURSE YOU, RED BARON! YOU GOT ME AGAIN!
HERE'S THE WORLD WAR I FLYING ACE BRINGING HIS BULLET-RIDDLED PLANE DOWN BEHIND ENEMY LINES..
AFTER THE SHOW WE'LL STOP IN AND GET A HOT-FUDGE SUNDAE, OKAY?
FINE!
MY SOPWITH CAMEL IS BADLY DAMAGED, BUT I HAVE ONLY A FEW SCRATCHES...WHAT'S THAT? ENEMY SOLDIERS! THEY'LL NEVER GET ME! NOT WHILE I HAVE MY .45 COLT AUTOMATIC..
©1966 Peanuts Worldwide LLC Dist. by Universal Uclick
BANG! BANG!
RUNNING LIKE THE WIND, I FLEE MADLY ACROSS NO-MAN'S LAND!
GREAT SCOTT!! MORE ENEMY SOLDIERS!
OOF!
BOOT!
6-23
NOTHING CAN STOP ME NOW! I...
I RESIGN MY COMMISSION!
SCHULZ

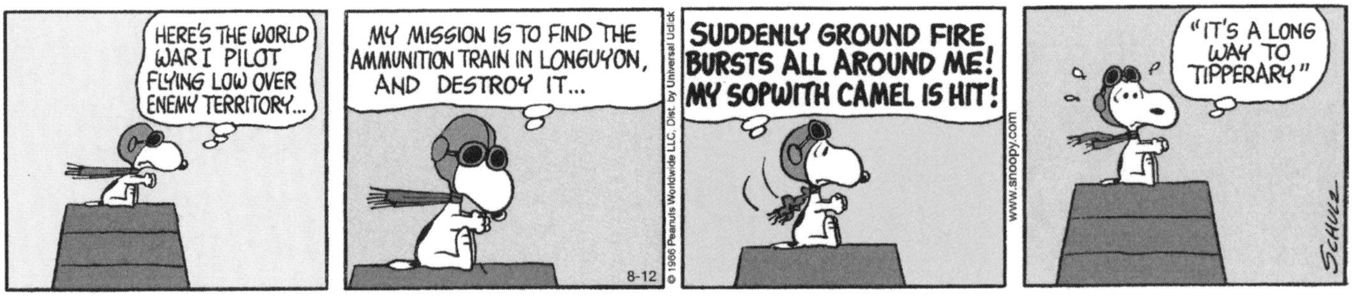
HERE'S THE WORLD WAR I PILOT FLYING LOW OVER ENEMY TERRITORY...
MY MISSION IS TO FIND THE AMMUNITION TRAIN IN LONGUYON, AND DESTROY IT...
8-12
© 1966 Peanuts Worldwide LLC, Dist. by Universal Uclick
SUDDENLY GROUND FIRE BURSTS ALL AROUND ME! MY SOPWITH CAMEL IS HIT!
www.snoopy.com
"IT'S A LONG WAY TO TIPPERARY"
SCHULZ

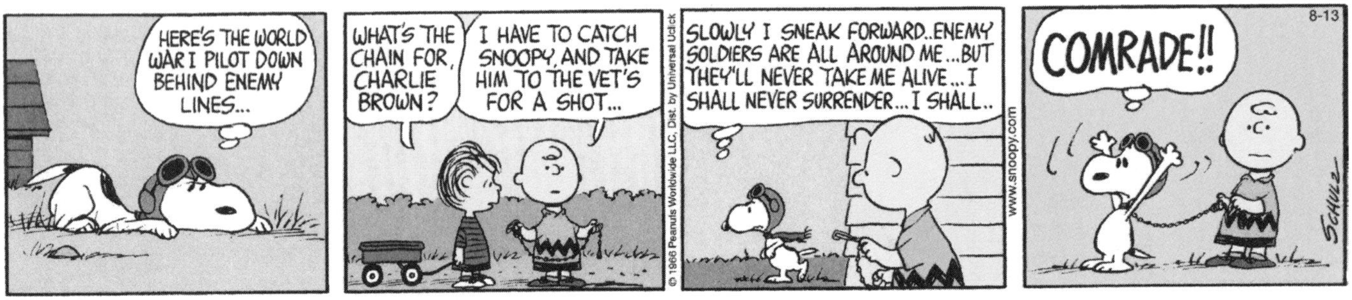
HERE'S THE WORLD WAR I PILOT DOWN BEHIND ENEMY LINES...
WHAT'S THE CHAIN FOR, CHARLIE BROWN?
I HAVE TO CATCH SNOOPY, AND TAKE HIM TO THE VET'S FOR A SHOT...
© 1966 Peanuts Worldwide LLC, Dist. by Universal Uclick
SLOWLY I SNEAK FORWARD..ENEMY SOLDIERS ARE ALL AROUND ME...BUT THEY'LL NEVER TAKE ME ALIVE...I SHALL NEVER SURRENDER...I SHALL..
www.snoopy.com
8-13
COMRADE!!
SCHULZ

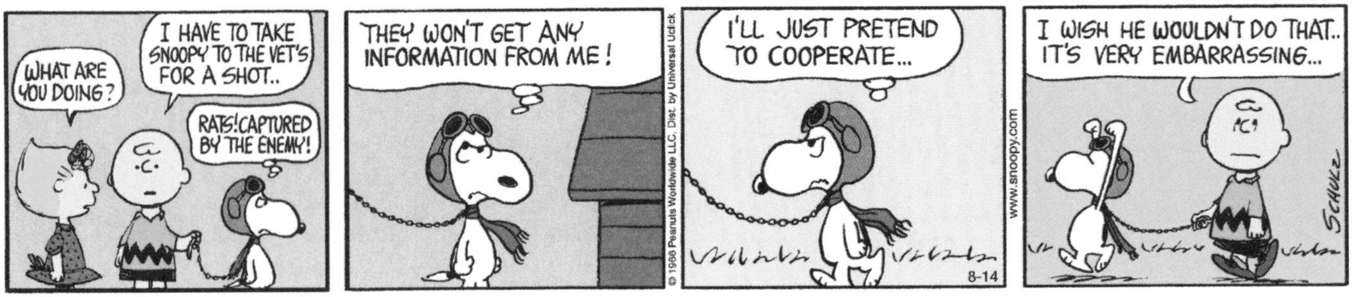
WHAT ARE YOU DOING?
I HAVE TO TAKE SNOOPY TO THE VET'S FOR A SHOT..
RATS! CAPTURED BY THE ENEMY!
THEY WON'T GET ANY INFORMATION FROM ME!
© 1966 Peanuts Worldwide LLC, Dist. by Universal Uclick
I'LL JUST PRETEND TO COOPERATE...
8-14
www.snoopy.com
I WISH HE WOULDN'T DO THAT.. IT'S VERY EMBARRASSING...
SCHULZ

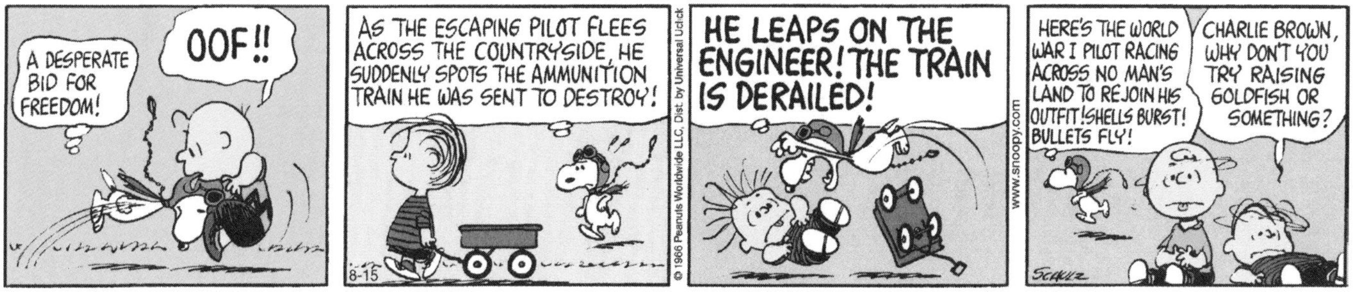
A DESPERATE BID FOR FREEDOM!
OOF!!
AS THE ESCAPING PILOT FLEES ACROSS THE COUNTRYSIDE, HE SUDDENLY SPOTS THE AMMUNITION TRAIN HE WAS SENT TO DESTROY!
8-15
© 1966 Peanuts Worldwide LLC, Dist. by Universal Uclick
HE LEAPS ON THE ENGINEER! THE TRAIN IS DERAILED!
www.snoopy.com
HERE'S THE WORLD WAR I PILOT RACING ACROSS NO MAN'S LAND TO REJOIN HIS OUTFIT! SHELLS BURST! BULLETS FLY!
CHARLIE BROWN, WHY DON'T YOU TRY RAISING GOLDFISH OR SOMETHING?
SCHULZ

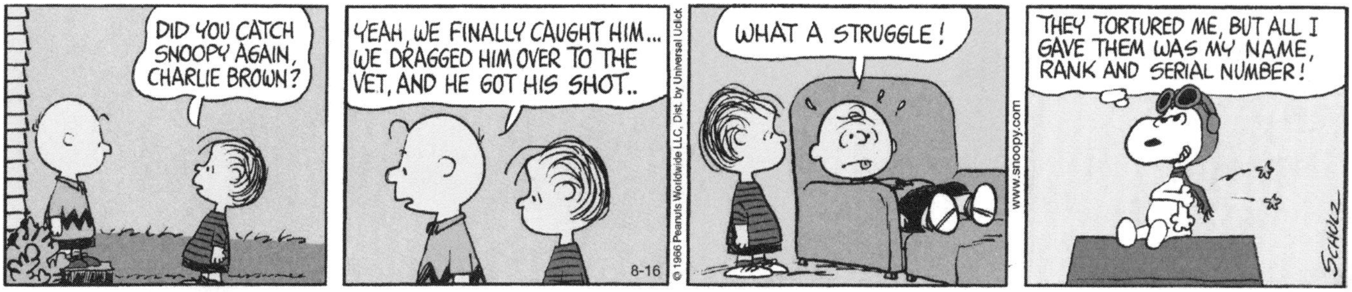
DID YOU CATCH SNOOPY AGAIN, CHARLIE BROWN?
YEAH, WE FINALLY CAUGHT HIM... WE DRAGGED HIM OVER TO THE VET, AND HE GOT HIS SHOT..
8-16
© 1966 Peanuts Worldwide LLC, Dist. by Universal Uclick
WHAT A STRUGGLE!
www.snoopy.com
THEY TORTURED ME, BUT ALL I GAVE THEM WAS MY NAME, RANK AND SERIAL NUMBER!
SCHULZ

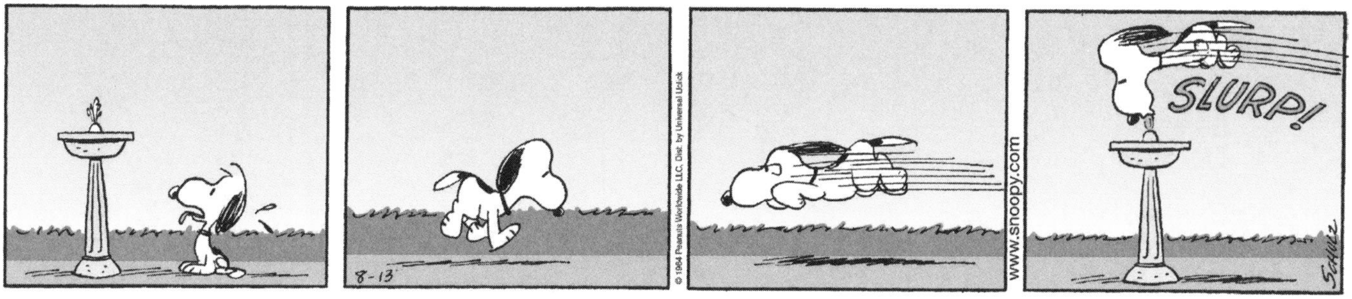
8-13
© 1964 Peanuts Worldwide LLC, Dist. by Universal Uclick
www.snoopy.com
SLURP!
SCHULZ

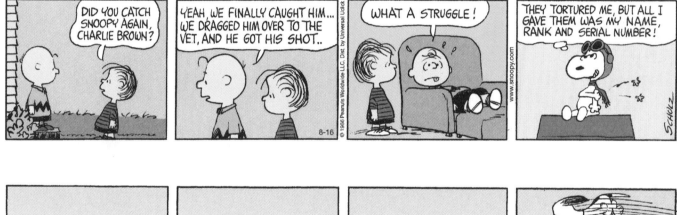

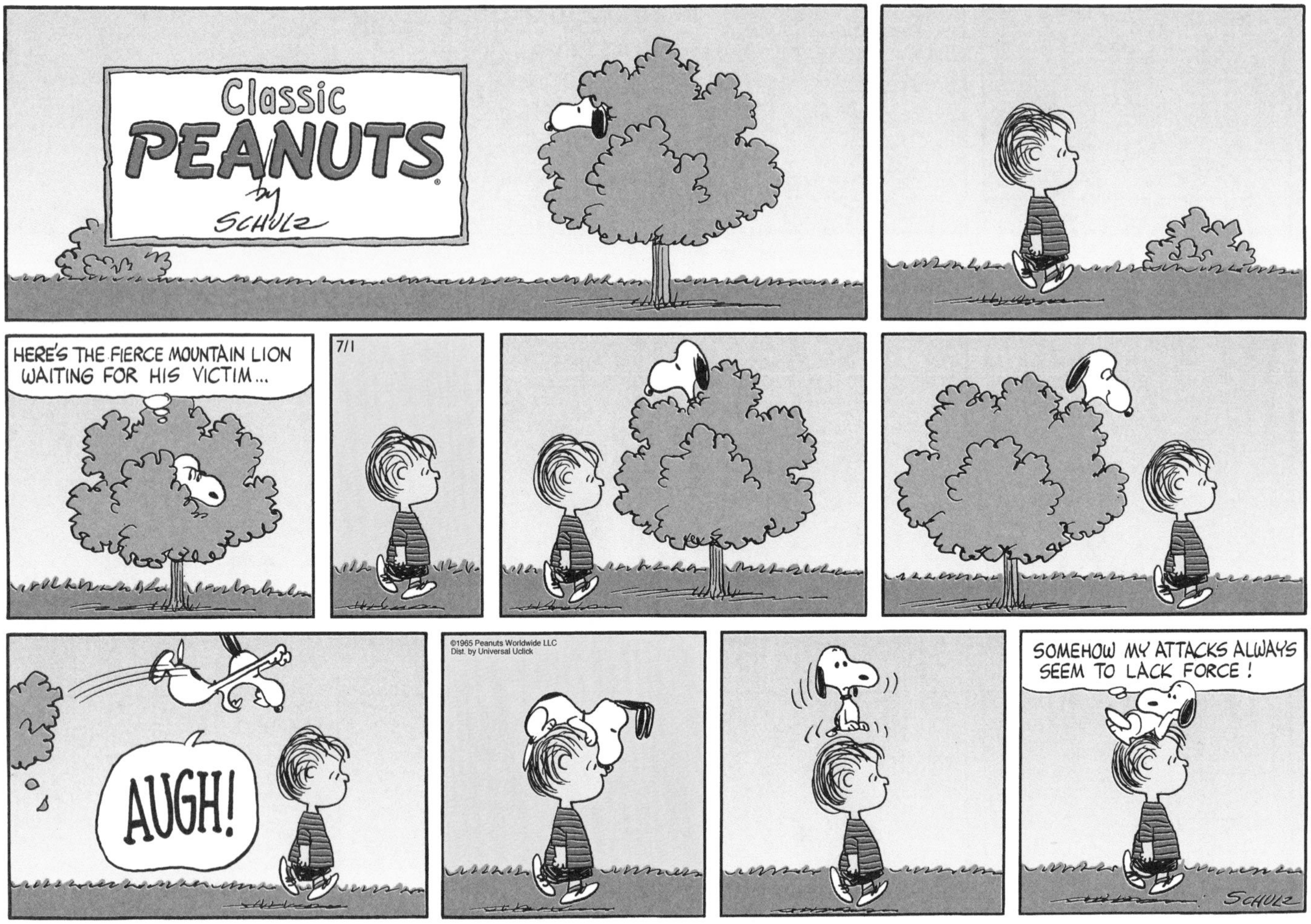
Classic
PEANUTS
by
SCHULZ
HERE'S THE FIERCE MOUNTAIN LION WAITING FOR HIS VICTIM...
7/1
AUGH!
©1965 Peanuts Worldwide LLC
Dist. by Universal Uclick
SOMEHOW MY ATTACKS ALWAYS SEEM TO LACK FORCE!
SCHULZ

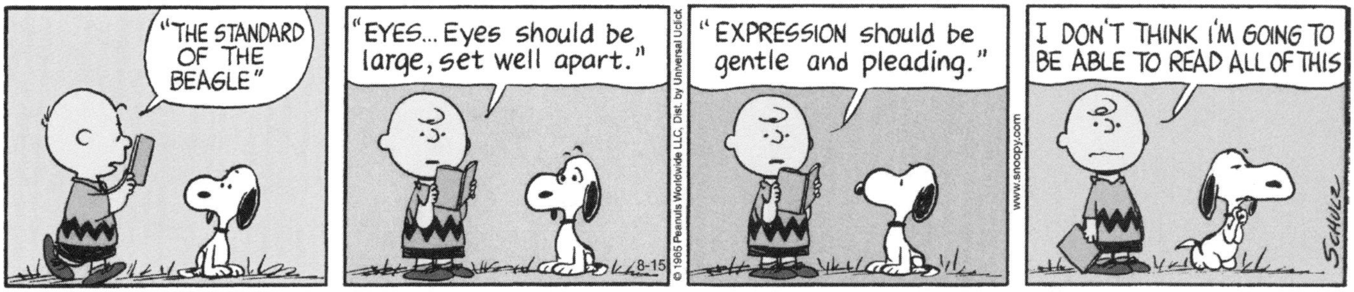
"THE STANDARD OF THE BEAGLE"
"EYES... Eyes should be large, set well apart."
"EXPRESSION should be gentle and pleading."
I DON'T THINK I'M GOING TO BE ABLE TO READ ALL OF THIS
8-15
© 1965 Peanuts Worldwide LLC. Dist. by Universal Uclick
www.snoopy.com
SCHULZ

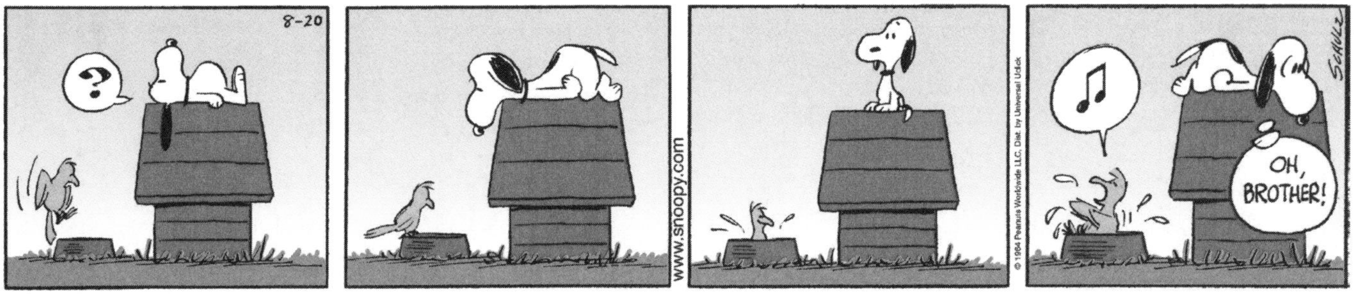
8-20
?
www.snoopy.com
♫
OH, BROTHER!
© 1964 Peanuts Worldwide LLC. Dist. by Universal Uclick
SCHULZ

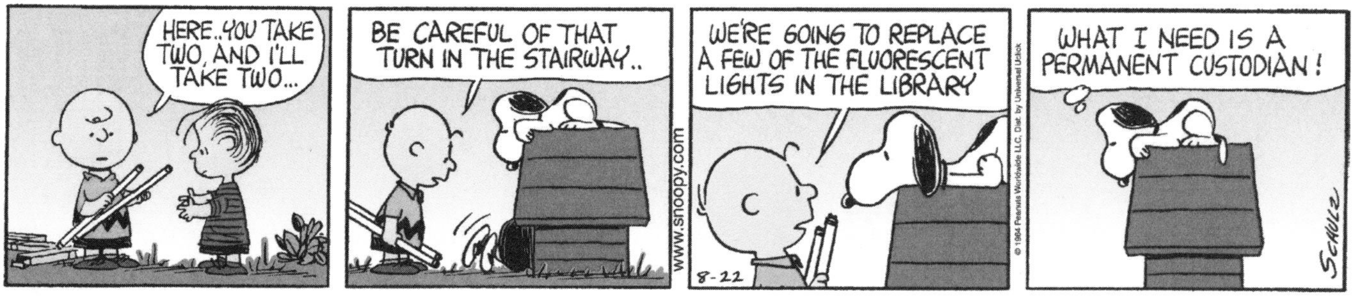
HERE..YOU TAKE TWO, AND I'LL TAKE TWO...
BE CAREFUL OF THAT TURN IN THE STAIRWAY..
www.snoopy.com
WE'RE GOING TO REPLACE A FEW OF THE FLUORESCENT LIGHTS IN THE LIBRARY
8-22
© 1964 Peanuts Worldwide LLC. Dist. by Universal Uclick
WHAT I NEED IS A PERMANENT CUSTODIAN!
SCHULZ

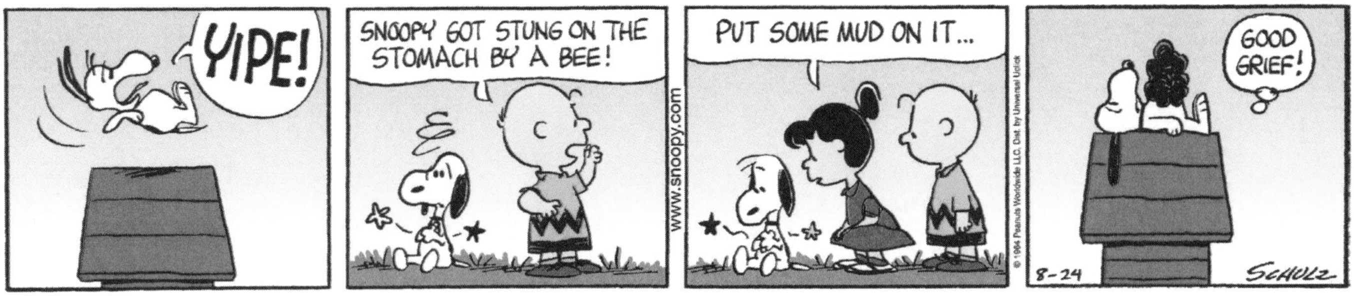
YIPE!
SNOOPY GOT STUNG ON THE STOMACH BY A BEE!
PUT SOME MUD ON IT...
GOOD GRIEF!
www.snoopy.com
8-24
SCHULZ

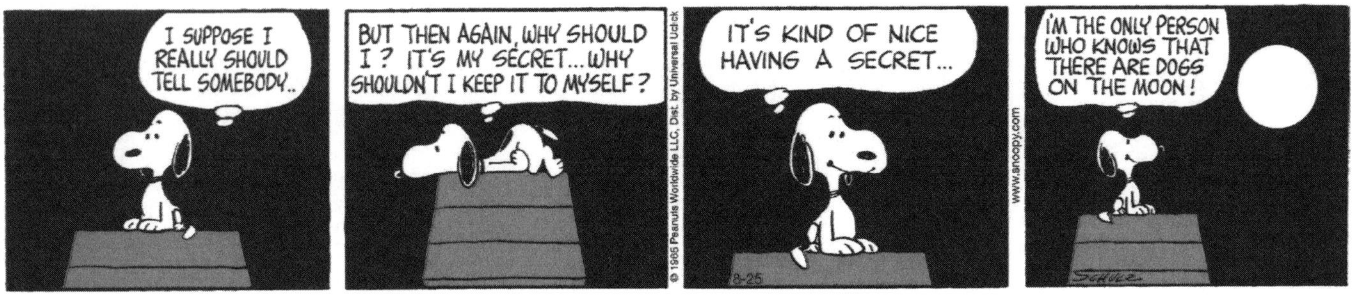
I SUPPOSE I REALLY SHOULD TELL SOMEBODY..
BUT THEN AGAIN, WHY SHOULD I? IT'S MY SECRET...WHY SHOULDN'T I KEEP IT TO MYSELF?
IT'S KIND OF NICE HAVING A SECRET...
I'M THE ONLY PERSON WHO KNOWS THAT THERE ARE DOGS ON THE MOON!
www.snoopy.com
8-25
SCHULZ

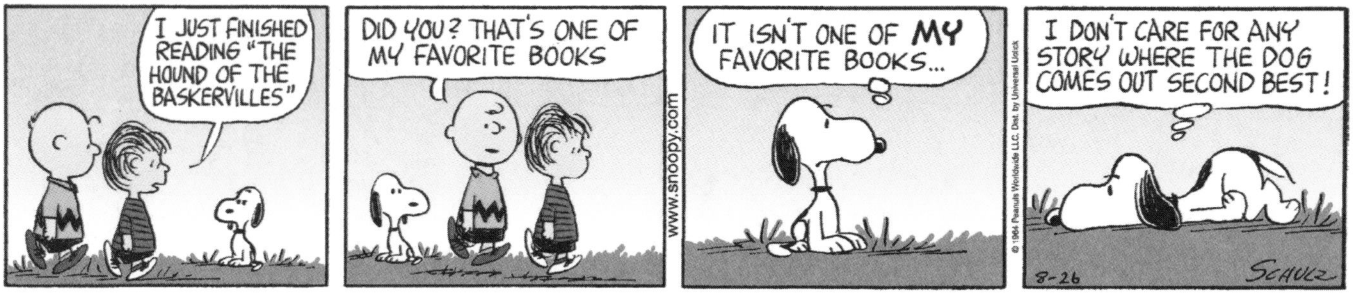
I JUST FINISHED READING "THE HOUND OF THE BASKERVILLES"
DID YOU? THAT'S ONE OF MY FAVORITE BOOKS
IT ISN'T ONE OF **MY** FAVORITE BOOKS...
I DON'T CARE FOR ANY STORY WHERE THE DOG COMES OUT SECOND BEST!
www.snoopy.com
8-26
SCHULZ

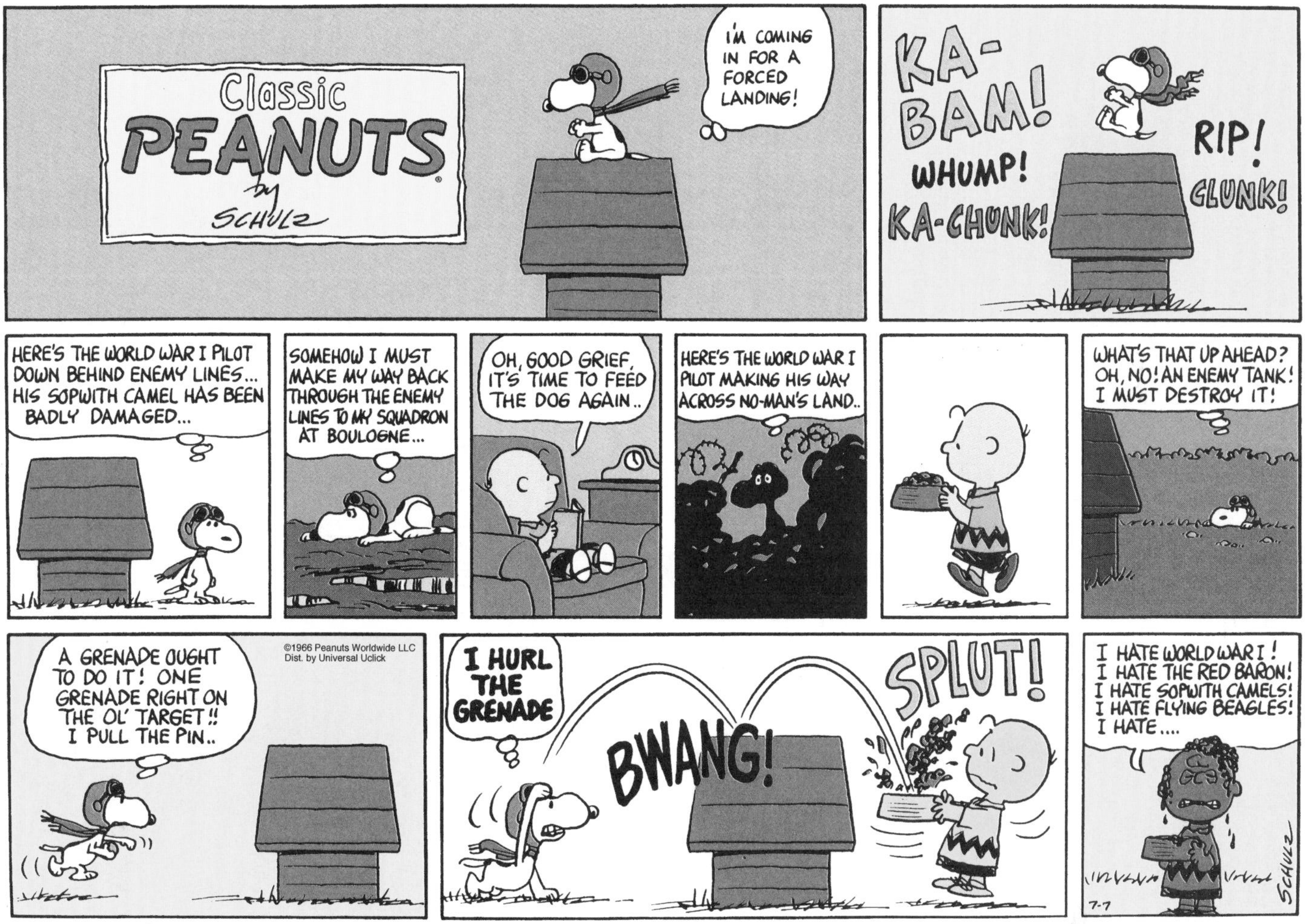

Classic PEANUTS by SCHULZ
I'M COMING IN FOR A FORCED LANDING!
KA-BAM!
WHUMP!
KA-CHUNK!
RIP!
GLUNK!
HERE'S THE WORLD WAR I PILOT DOWN BEHIND ENEMY LINES... HIS SOPWITH CAMEL HAS BEEN BADLY DAMAGED...
SOMEHOW I MUST MAKE MY WAY BACK THROUGH THE ENEMY LINES TO MY SQUADRON AT BOULOGNE...
OH, GOOD GRIEF, IT'S TIME TO FEED THE DOG AGAIN..
HERE'S THE WORLD WAR I PILOT MAKING HIS WAY ACROSS NO-MAN'S LAND..
WHAT'S THAT UP AHEAD? OH, NO! AN ENEMY TANK! I MUST DESTROY IT!
A GRENADE OUGHT TO DO IT! ONE GRENADE RIGHT ON THE OL' TARGET!! I PULL THE PIN..
©1966 Peanuts Worldwide LLC
Dist. by Universal Uclick
I HURL THE GRENADE
BWANG!
SPLUT!
I HATE WORLD WAR I! I HATE THE RED BARON! I HATE SOPWITH CAMELS! I HATE FLYING BEAGLES! I HATE....
7-7
SCHULZ

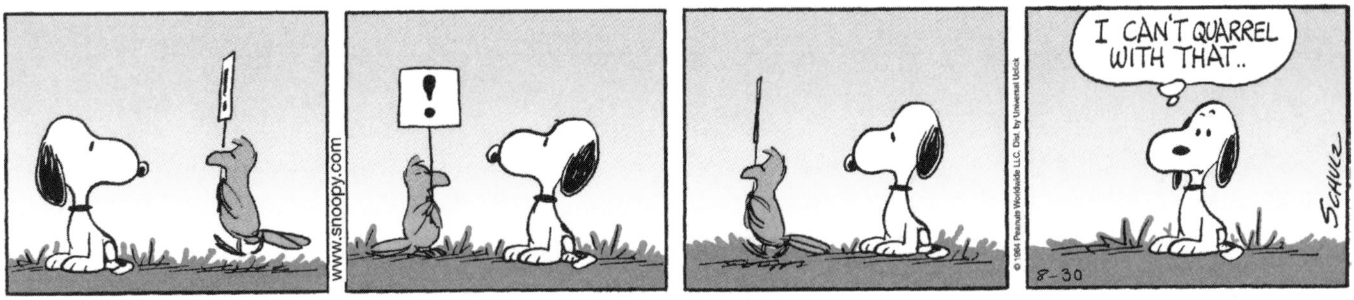
!
www.snoopy.com
!
© 1984 Peanuts Worldwide LLC, Dist. by Universal Uclick
I CAN'T QUARREL WITH THAT..
SCHULZ
8-30

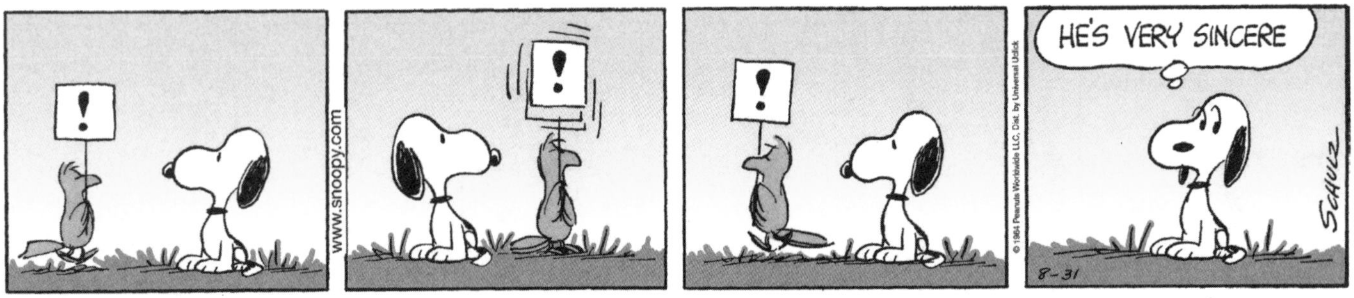
!
www.snoopy.com
!
!
© 1984 Peanuts Worldwide LLC, Dist. by Universal Uclick
HE'S VERY SINCERE
SCHULZ
8-31

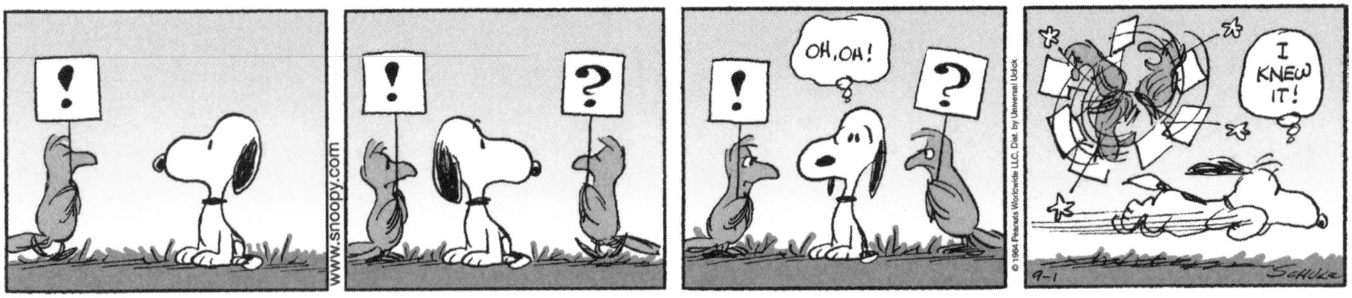
!
www.snoopy.com
!
?
!
OH, OH!
?
© 1984 Peanuts Worldwide LLC, Dist. by Universal Uclick
I KNEW IT!
9-1
SCHULZ

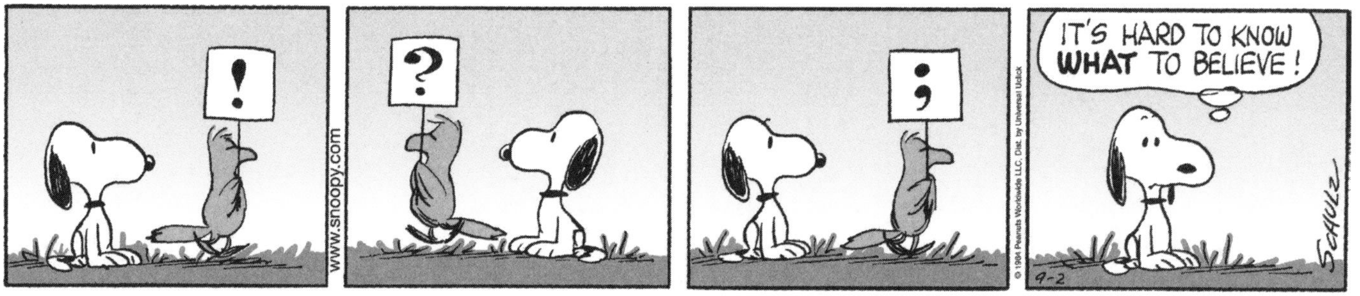
!
?
;
IT'S HARD TO KNOW WHAT TO BELIEVE!
www.snoopy.com
© 1984 Peanuts Worldwide LLC. Dist. by Universal Uclick
9-2
SCHULZ

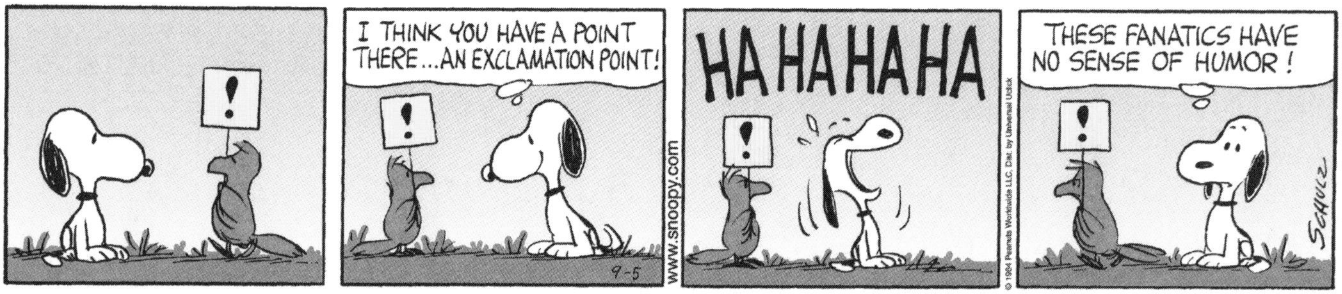
!
I THINK YOU HAVE A POINT THERE...AN EXCLAMATION POINT!
HA HA HA HA
THESE FANATICS HAVE NO SENSE OF HUMOR!
9-5
www.snoopy.com
© 1984 Peanuts Worldwide LLC. Dist. by Universal Uclick
SCHULZ

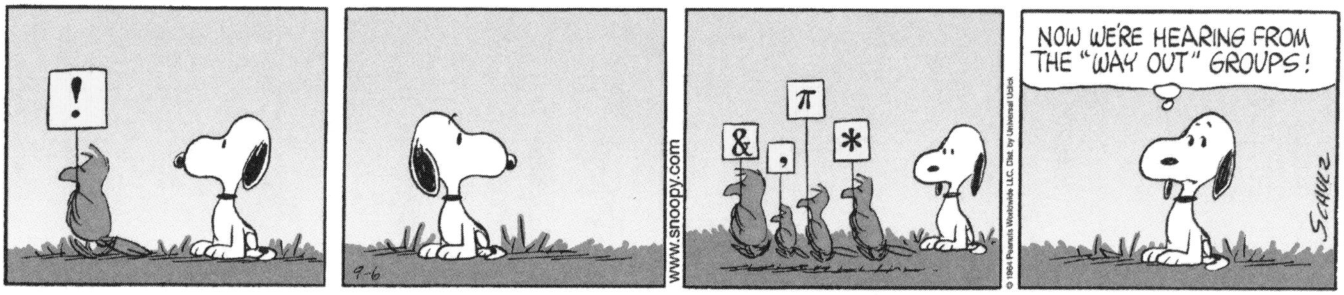
!
9-6
www.snoopy.com
& , π *
NOW WE'RE HEARING FROM THE "WAY OUT" GROUPS!
© 1984 Peanuts Worldwide LLC. Dist. by Universal Uclick
SCHULZ

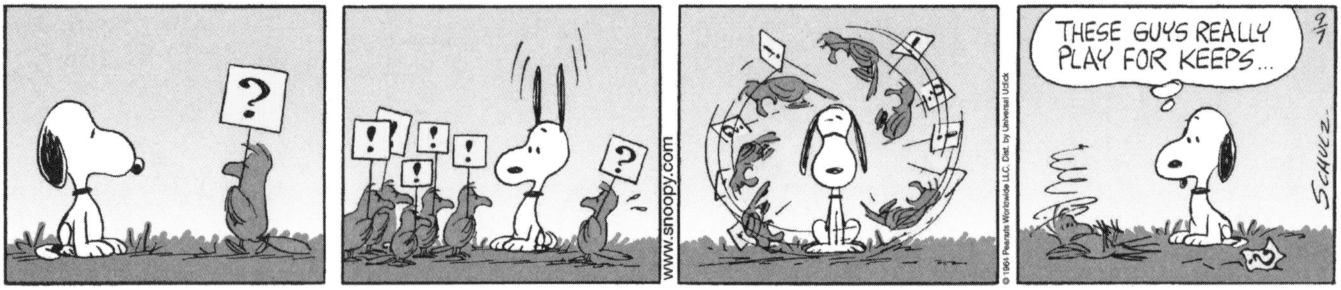
?
? ! ! ! ! ! ?
www.snoopy.com
© 1964 Peanuts Worldwide LLC. Dist. by Universal Uclick
THESE GUYS REALLY PLAY FOR KEEPS...
9/7
SCHULZ

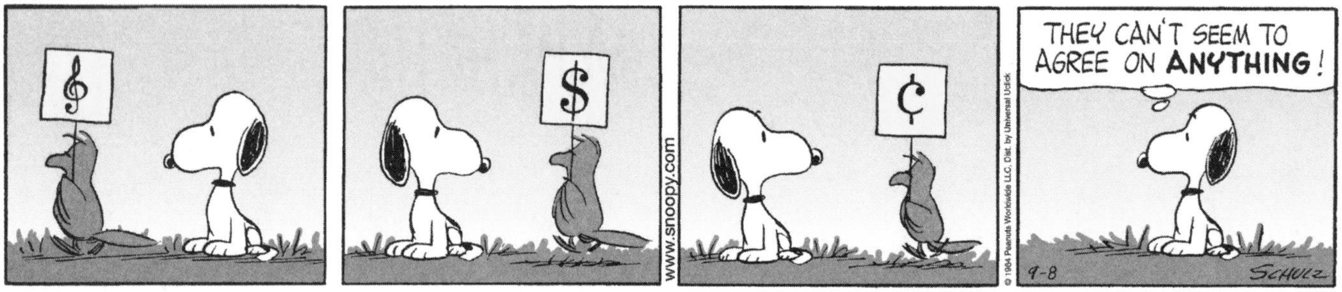
$
www.snoopy.com
¢
© 1964 Peanuts Worldwide LLC. Dist. by Universal Uclick
9-8
THEY CAN'T SEEM TO AGREE ON **ANYTHING**!
SCHULZ

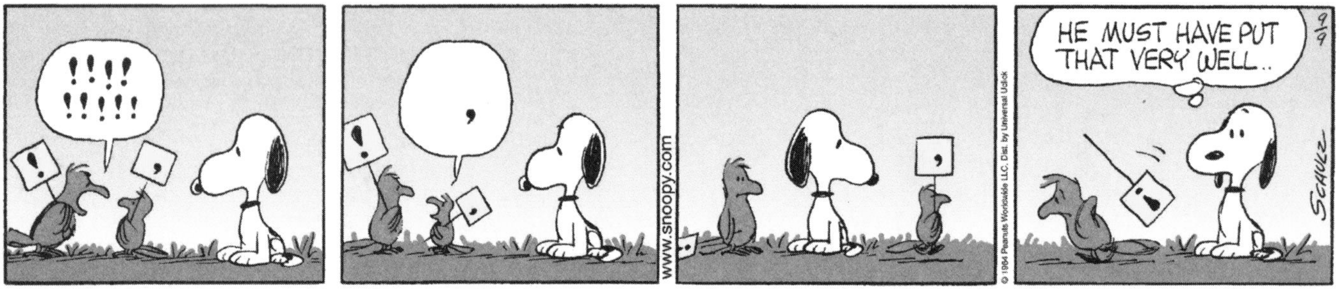
!!!!
!!!!!
!
,
!
,
www.snoopy.com
,
© 1964 Peanuts Worldwide LLC. Dist. by Universal Uclick
HE MUST HAVE PUT THAT VERY WELL..
9/9
SCHULZ

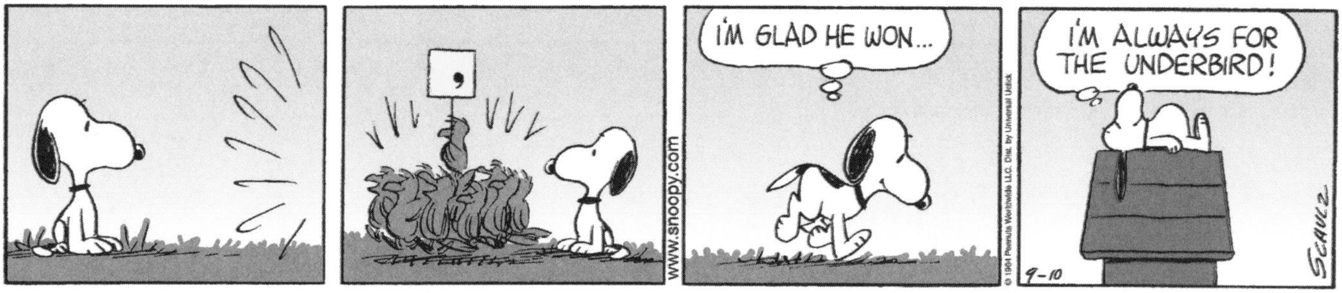
www.snoopy.com
I'M GLAD HE WON...
© 1964 Peanuts Worldwide LLC. Dist. by Universal Uclick
I'M ALWAYS FOR THE UNDERBIRD!
9-10
SCHULZ

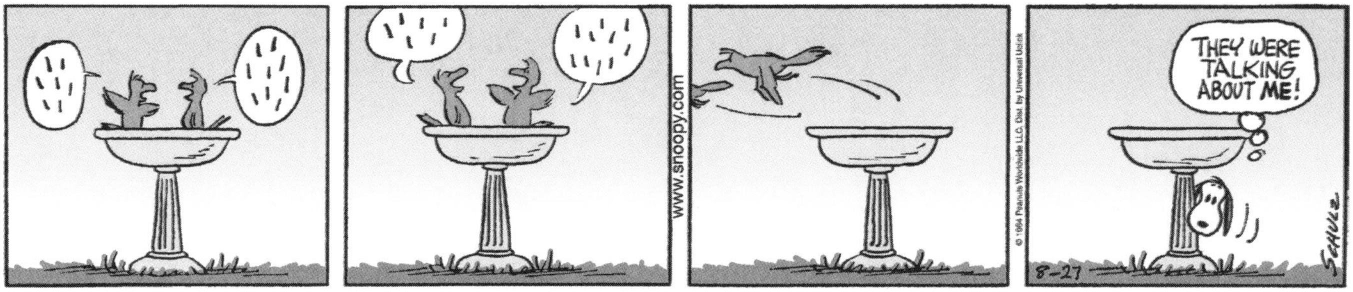
www.snoopy.com
© 1964 Peanuts Worldwide LLC. Dist. by Universal Uclick
THEY WERE TALKING ABOUT **ME**!
8-27
SCHULZ

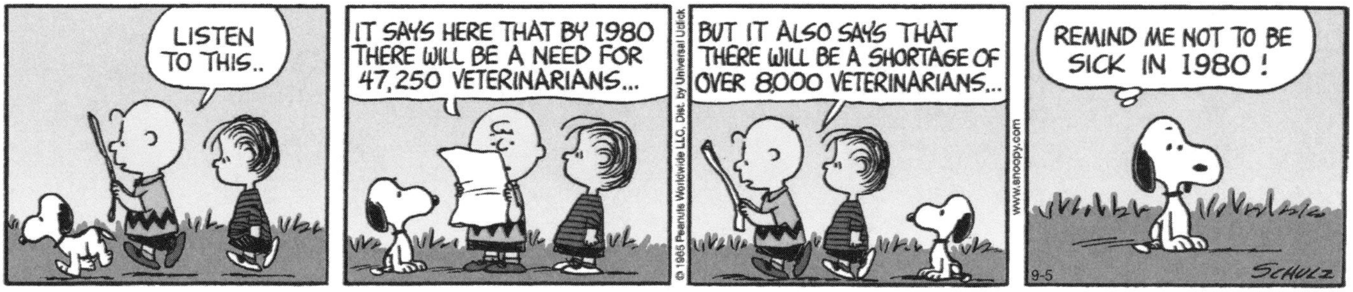
LISTEN TO THIS..
IT SAYS HERE THAT BY 1980 THERE WILL BE A NEED FOR 47,250 VETERINARIANS...
© 1965 Peanuts Worldwide LLC. Dist. by Universal Uclick
BUT IT ALSO SAYS THAT THERE WILL BE A SHORTAGE OF OVER 8,000 VETERINARIANS...
www.snoopy.com
REMIND ME NOT TO BE SICK IN 1980!
9-5
SCHULZ

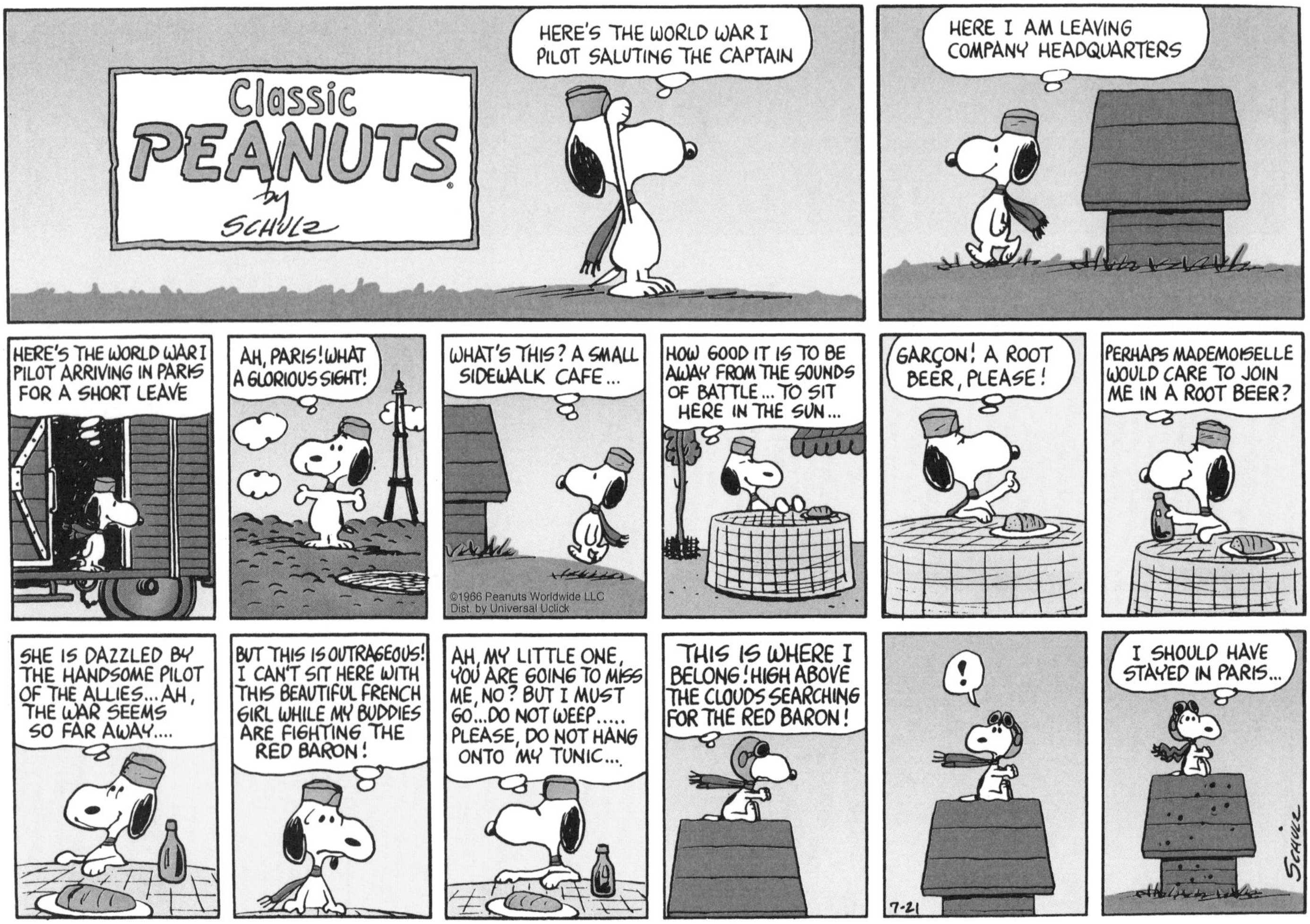
Classic PEANUTS by SCHULZ
HERE'S THE WORLD WAR I PILOT SALUTING THE CAPTAIN
HERE I AM LEAVING COMPANY HEADQUARTERS
HERE'S THE WORLD WAR I PILOT ARRIVING IN PARIS FOR A SHORT LEAVE
AH, PARIS! WHAT A GLORIOUS SIGHT!
WHAT'S THIS? A SMALL SIDEWALK CAFE...
©1966 Peanuts Worldwide LLC
Dist. by Universal Uclick
HOW GOOD IT IS TO BE AWAY FROM THE SOUNDS OF BATTLE... TO SIT HERE IN THE SUN...
GARÇON! A ROOT BEER, PLEASE!
PERHAPS MADEMOISELLE WOULD CARE TO JOIN ME IN A ROOT BEER?
SHE IS DAZZLED BY THE HANDSOME PILOT OF THE ALLIES... AH, THE WAR SEEMS SO FAR AWAY....
BUT THIS IS OUTRAGEOUS! I CAN'T SIT HERE WITH THIS BEAUTIFUL FRENCH GIRL WHILE MY BUDDIES ARE FIGHTING THE RED BARON!
AH, MY LITTLE ONE, YOU ARE GOING TO MISS ME, NO? BUT I MUST GO... DO NOT WEEP..... PLEASE, DO NOT HANG ONTO MY TUNIC...
THIS IS WHERE I BELONG! HIGH ABOVE THE CLOUDS SEARCHING FOR THE RED BARON!
!
7-21
I SHOULD HAVE STAYED IN PARIS...
SCHULZ

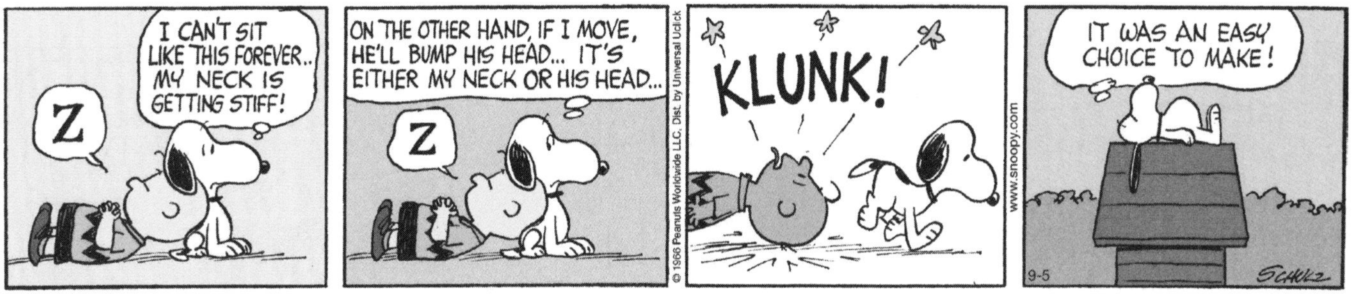
Z
I CAN'T SIT LIKE THIS FOREVER.. MY NECK IS GETTING STIFF!
Z
ON THE OTHER HAND, IF I MOVE, HE'LL BUMP HIS HEAD... IT'S EITHER MY NECK OR HIS HEAD...
© 1966 Peanuts Worldwide LLC, Dist. by Universal Uclick
KLUNK!
www.snoopy.com
IT WAS AN EASY CHOICE TO MAKE!
9-5
SCHULZ

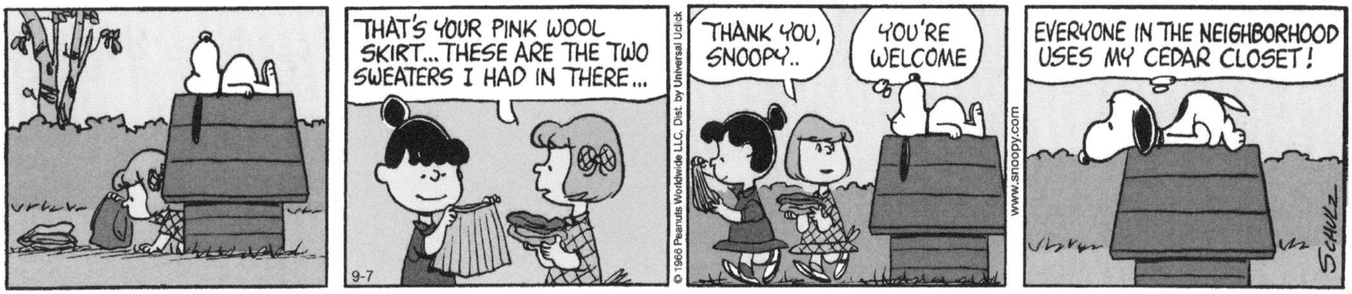
THAT'S YOUR PINK WOOL SKIRT...THESE ARE THE TWO SWEATERS I HAD IN THERE...
9-7
© 1966 Peanuts Worldwide LLC, Dist. by Universal Uclick
THANK YOU, SNOOPY..
YOU'RE WELCOME
www.snoopy.com
EVERYONE IN THE NEIGHBORHOOD USES MY CEDAR CLOSET!
SCHULZ

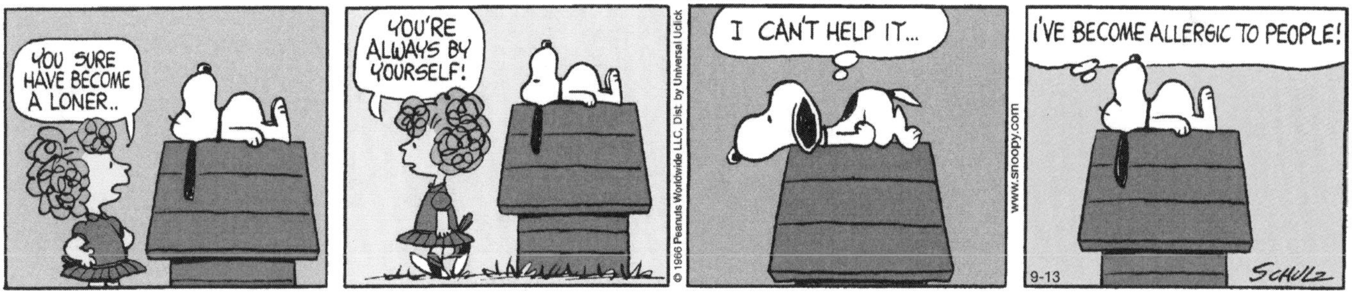
YOU SURE HAVE BECOME A LONER..
YOU'RE ALWAYS BY YOURSELF!
© 1966 Peanuts Worldwide LLC, Dist. by Universal Uclick
I CAN'T HELP IT...
www.snoopy.com
I'VE BECOME ALLERGIC TO PEOPLE!
9-13
SCHULZ

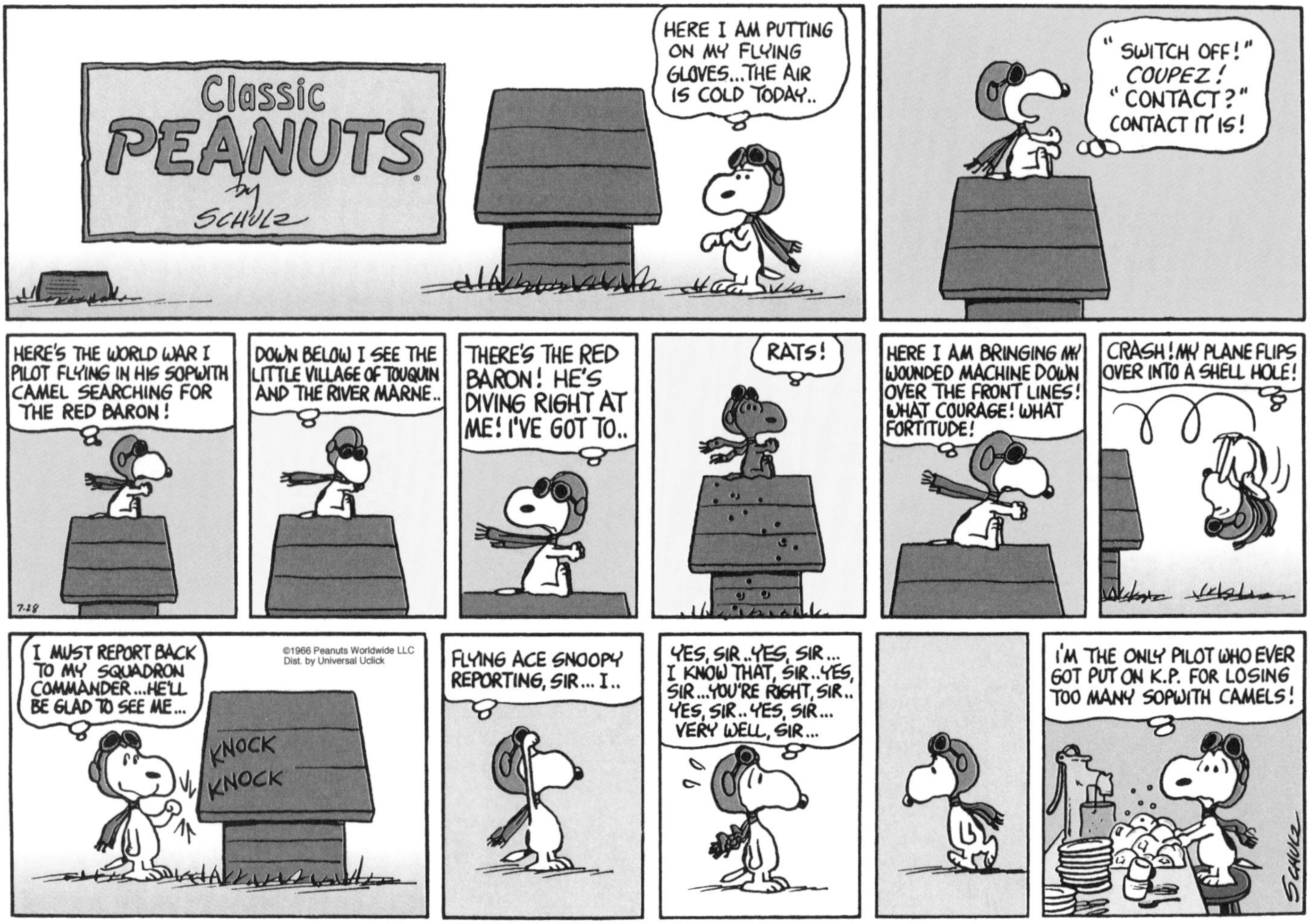
Classic PEANUTS by SCHULZ
HERE I AM PUTTING ON MY FLYING GLOVES...THE AIR IS COLD TODAY..
"SWITCH OFF!" COUPEZ! "CONTACT?" CONTACT IT IS!
HERE'S THE WORLD WAR I PILOT FLYING IN HIS SOPWITH CAMEL SEARCHING FOR THE RED BARON!
7-28
DOWN BELOW I SEE THE LITTLE VILLAGE OF TOUQUIN AND THE RIVER MARNE..
THERE'S THE RED BARON! HE'S DIVING RIGHT AT ME! I'VE GOT TO..
RATS!
HERE I AM BRINGING MY WOUNDED MACHINE DOWN OVER THE FRONT LINES! WHAT COURAGE! WHAT FORTITUDE!
CRASH! MY PLANE FLIPS OVER INTO A SHELL HOLE!
I MUST REPORT BACK TO MY SQUADRON COMMANDER...HE'LL BE GLAD TO SEE ME...
©1966 Peanuts Worldwide LLC
Dist. by Universal Uclick
KNOCK KNOCK
FLYING ACE SNOOPY REPORTING, SIR... I..
YES, SIR..YES, SIR... I KNOW THAT, SIR..YES, SIR...YOU'RE RIGHT, SIR.. YES, SIR..YES, SIR... VERY WELL, SIR...
I'M THE ONLY PILOT WHO EVER GOT PUT ON K.P. FOR LOSING TOO MANY SOPWITH CAMELS!
SCHULZ

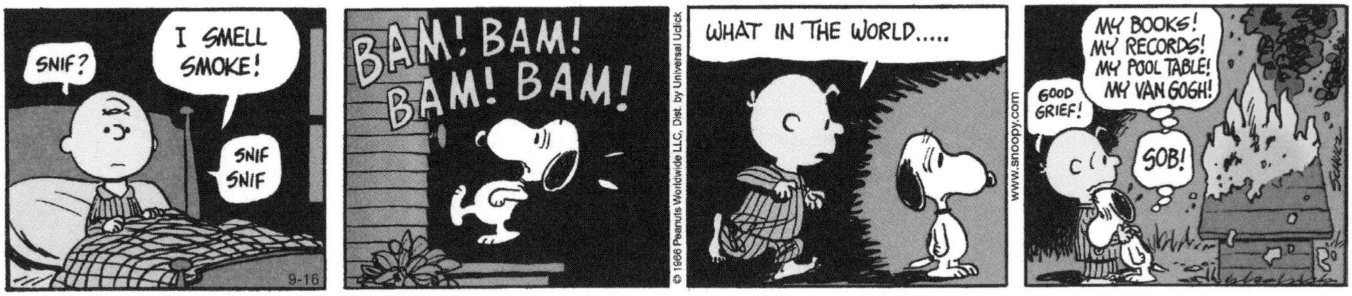
SNIF?
I SMELL SMOKE!
SNIF SNIF
9-16
BAM! BAM! BAM! BAM!
© 1966 Peanuts Worldwide LLC, Dist. by Universal Uclick
WHAT IN THE WORLD.....
www.snoopy.com
GOOD GRIEF!
MY BOOKS! MY RECORDS! MY POOL TABLE! MY VAN GOGH!
SOB!
SCHULZ

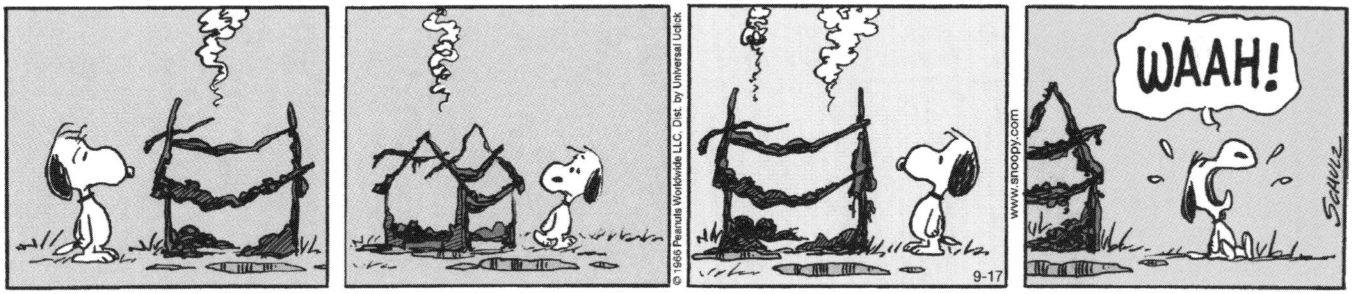
© 1966 Peanuts Worldwide LLC, Dist. by Universal Uclick
9-17
www.snoopy.com
WAAH!
SCHULZ

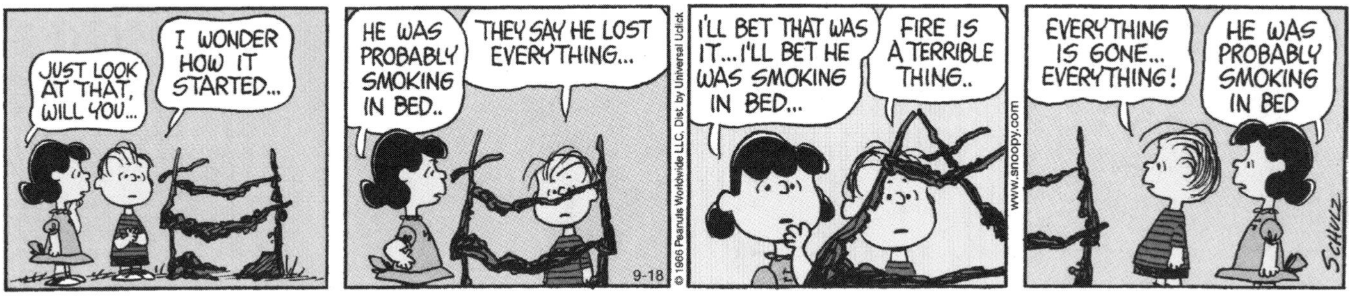
JUST LOOK AT THAT, WILL YOU...
I WONDER HOW IT STARTED...
HE WAS PROBABLY SMOKING IN BED..
THEY SAY HE LOST EVERYTHING...
9-18
© 1966 Peanuts Worldwide LLC, Dist. by Universal Uclick
I'LL BET THAT WAS IT...I'LL BET HE WAS SMOKING IN BED...
FIRE IS A TERRIBLE THING..
www.snoopy.com
EVERYTHING IS GONE... EVERYTHING!
HE WAS PROBABLY SMOKING IN BED
SCHULZ

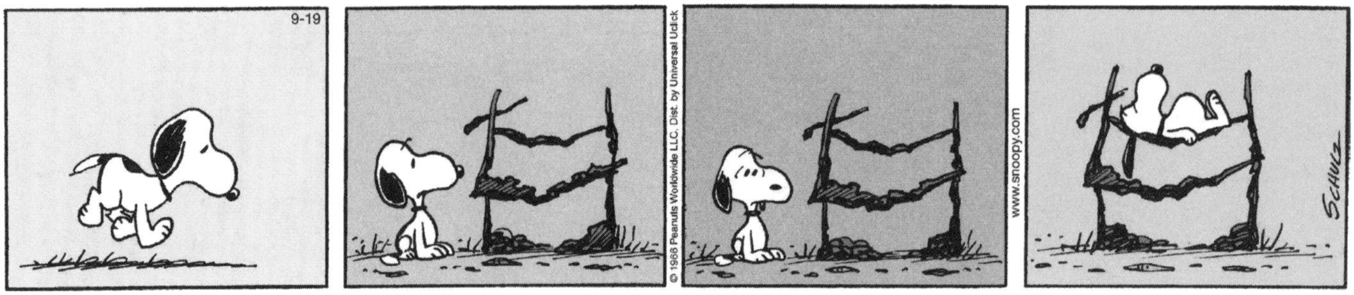
9-19
© 1966 Peanuts Worldwide LLC, Dist. by Universal Uclick
www.snoopy.com
SCHULZ

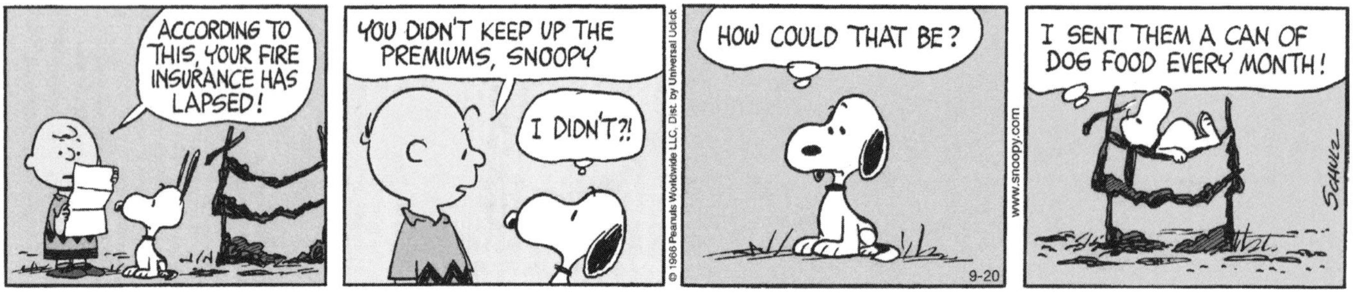
ACCORDING TO THIS, YOUR FIRE INSURANCE HAS LAPSED!
YOU DIDN'T KEEP UP THE PREMIUMS, SNOOPY
I DIDN'T?!
HOW COULD THAT BE?
I SENT THEM A CAN OF DOG FOOD EVERY MONTH!
9-20
© 1966 Peanuts Worldwide LLC, Dist. by Universal Uclick
www.snoopy.com
SCHULZ

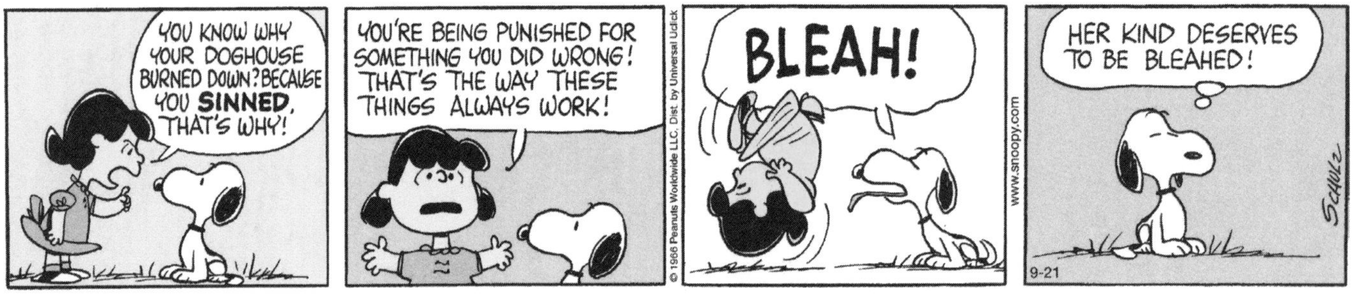
YOU KNOW WHY YOUR DOGHOUSE BURNED DOWN? BECAUSE YOU **SINNED**, THAT'S WHY!
YOU'RE BEING PUNISHED FOR SOMETHING YOU DID WRONG! THAT'S THE WAY THESE THINGS ALWAYS WORK!
BLEAH!
HER KIND DESERVES TO BE BLEAHED!
9-21
© 1966 Peanuts Worldwide LLC, Dist. by Universal Uclick
www.snoopy.com
SCHULZ

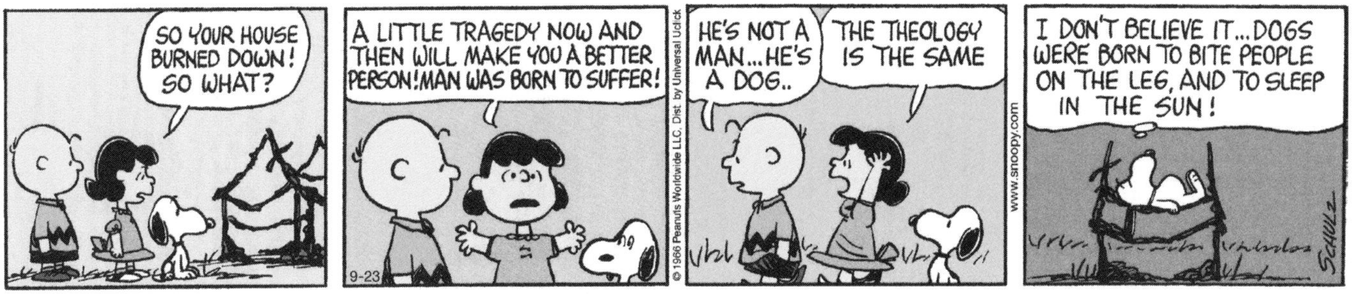
SO YOUR HOUSE BURNED DOWN! SO WHAT?
A LITTLE TRAGEDY NOW AND THEN WILL MAKE YOU A BETTER PERSON! MAN WAS BORN TO SUFFER!
9-23
© 1966 Peanuts Worldwide LLC, Dist. by Universal Uclick
HE'S NOT A MAN... HE'S A DOG..
THE THEOLOGY IS THE SAME
www.snoopy.com
I DON'T BELIEVE IT... DOGS WERE BORN TO BITE PEOPLE ON THE LEG, AND TO SLEEP IN THE SUN!
SCHULZ

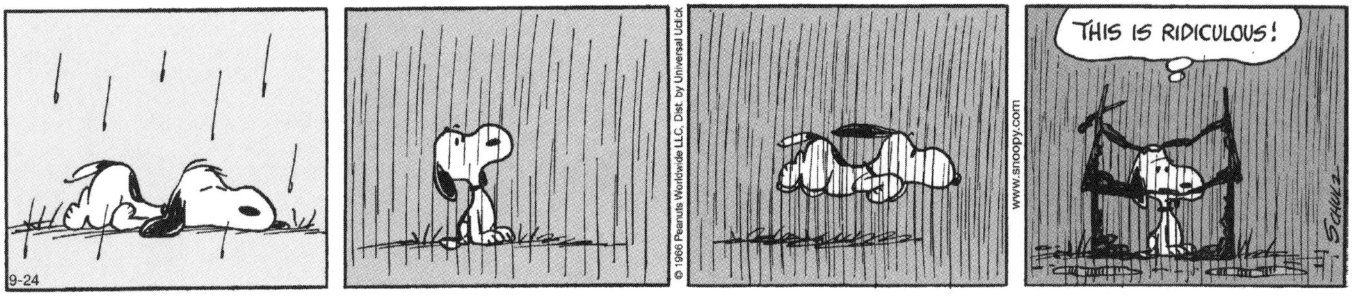
9-24
© 1966 Peanuts Worldwide LLC, Dist. by Universal Uclick
www.snoopy.com
THIS IS RIDICULOUS!
SCHULZ

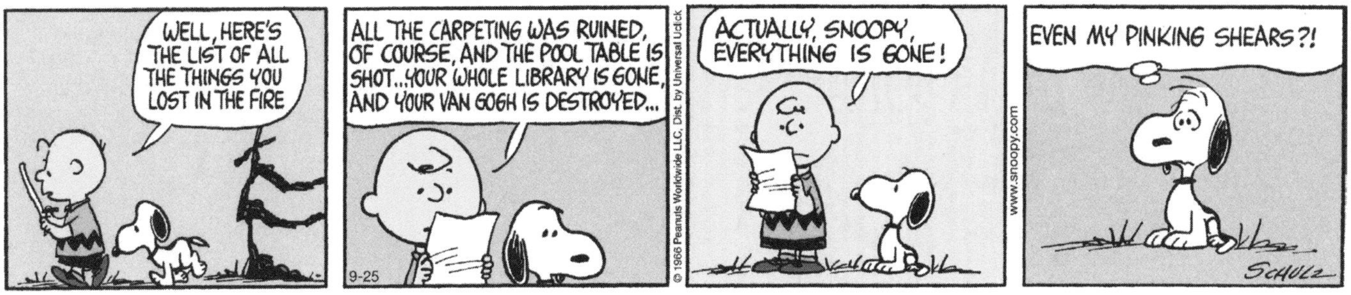
WELL, HERE'S THE LIST OF ALL THE THINGS YOU LOST IN THE FIRE
ALL THE CARPETING WAS RUINED, OF COURSE, AND THE POOL TABLE IS SHOT... YOUR WHOLE LIBRARY IS GONE, AND YOUR VAN GOGH IS DESTROYED...
9-25
© 1966 Peanuts Worldwide LLC, Dist. by Universal Uclick
ACTUALLY, SNOOPY, EVERYTHING IS GONE!
www.snoopy.com
EVEN MY PINKING SHEARS?!
SCHULZ

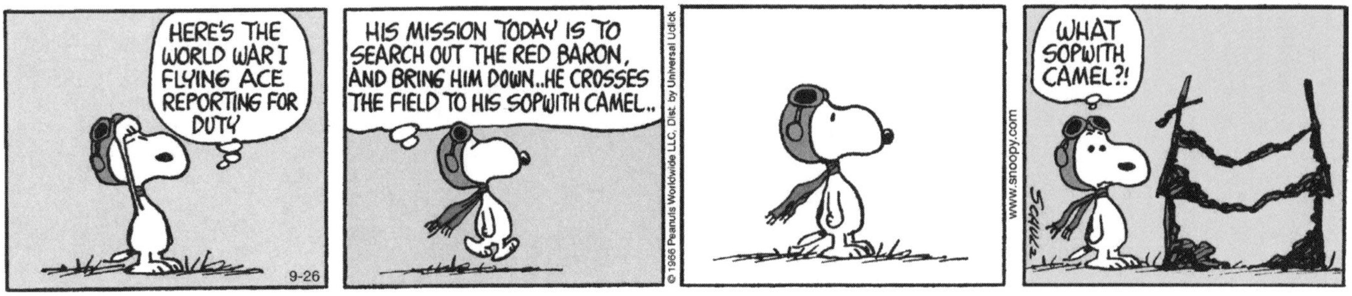
HERE'S THE WORLD WAR I FLYING ACE REPORTING FOR DUTY
9-26
HIS MISSION TODAY IS TO SEARCH OUT THE RED BARON, AND BRING HIM DOWN..HE CROSSES THE FIELD TO HIS SOPWITH CAMEL..
© 1966 Peanuts Worldwide LLC, Dist. by Universal Uclick
WHAT SOPWITH CAMEL?!
www.snoopy.com
SCHULZ

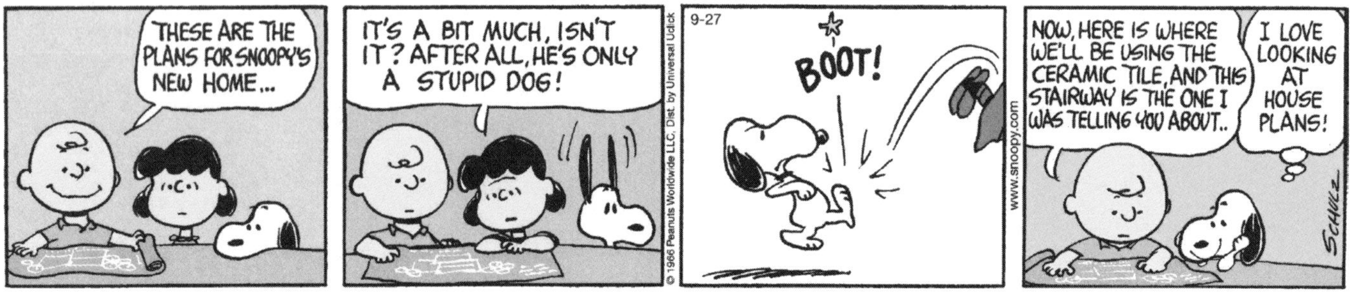
THESE ARE THE PLANS FOR SNOOPY'S NEW HOME...
IT'S A BIT MUCH, ISN'T IT? AFTER ALL, HE'S ONLY A STUPID DOG!
© 1966 Peanuts Worldwide LLC, Dist. by Universal Uclick
9-27
BOOT!
www.snoopy.com
NOW, HERE IS WHERE WE'LL BE USING THE CERAMIC TILE, AND THIS STAIRWAY IS THE ONE I WAS TELLING YOU ABOUT..
I LOVE LOOKING AT HOUSE PLANS!
SCHULZ

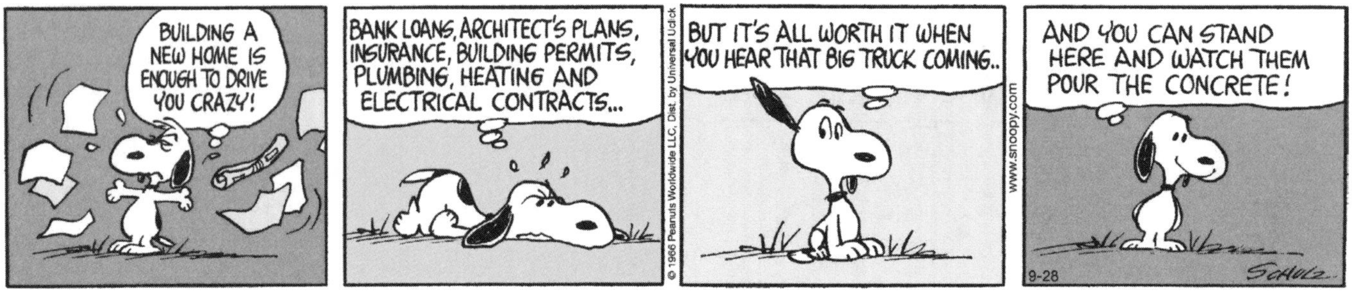
BUILDING A NEW HOME IS ENOUGH TO DRIVE YOU CRAZY!
BANK LOANS, ARCHITECT'S PLANS, INSURANCE, BUILDING PERMITS, PLUMBING, HEATING AND ELECTRICAL CONTRACTS...
© 1966 Peanuts Worldwide LLC, Dist. by Universal Uclick
BUT IT'S ALL WORTH IT WHEN YOU HEAR THAT BIG TRUCK COMING..
www.snoopy.com
AND YOU CAN STAND HERE AND WATCH THEM POUR THE CONCRETE!
9-28
SCHULZ

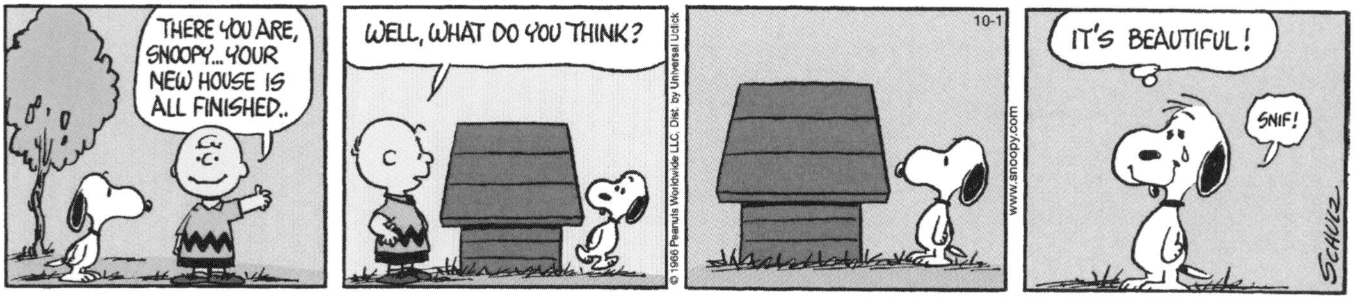
THERE YOU ARE, SNOOPY... YOUR NEW HOUSE IS ALL FINISHED..
WELL, WHAT DO YOU THINK?
© 1966 Peanuts Worldwide LLC, Dist. by Universal Uclick
10-1
www.snoopy.com
IT'S BEAUTIFUL!
SNIF!
SCHULZ

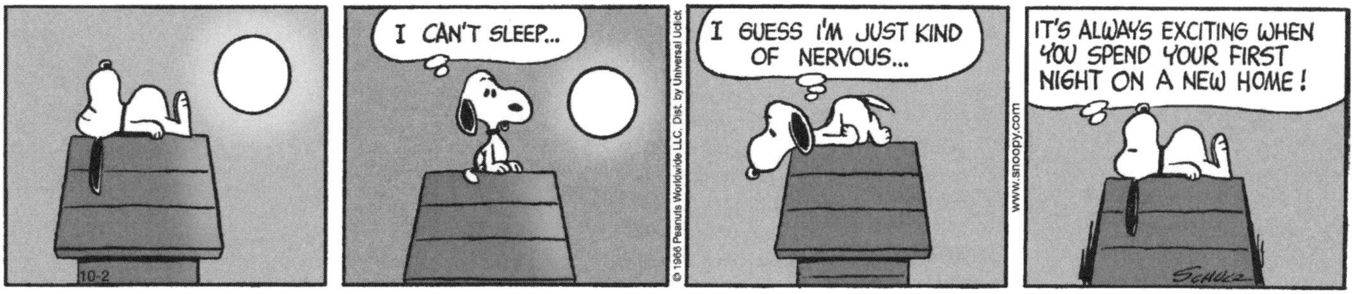
10-2
I CAN'T SLEEP...
© 1966 Peanuts Worldwide LLC, Dist. by Universal Uclick
I GUESS I'M JUST KIND OF NERVOUS...
www.snoopy.com
IT'S ALWAYS EXCITING WHEN YOU SPEND YOUR FIRST NIGHT ON A NEW HOME!
SCHULZ

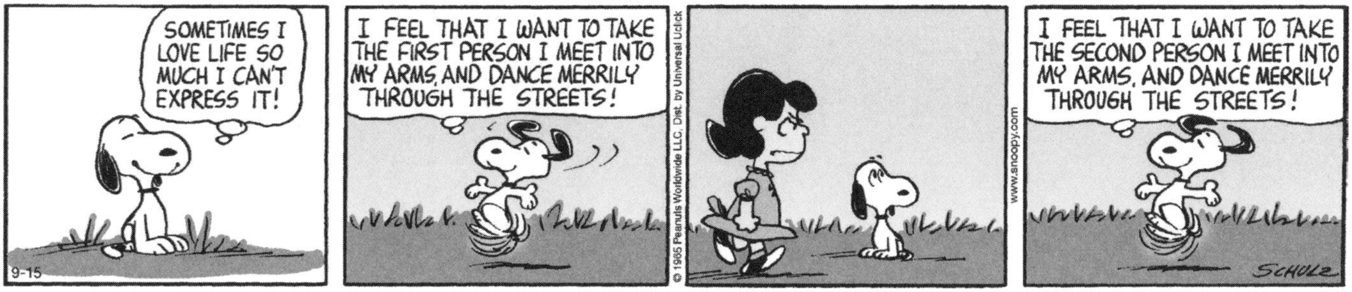
SOMETIMES I LOVE LIFE SO MUCH I CAN'T EXPRESS IT!
9-15
I FEEL THAT I WANT TO TAKE THE FIRST PERSON I MEET INTO MY ARMS, AND DANCE MERRILY THROUGH THE STREETS!
© 1965 Peanuts Worldwide LLC, Dist. by Universal Uclick
www.snoopy.com
I FEEL THAT I WANT TO TAKE THE SECOND PERSON I MEET INTO MY ARMS, AND DANCE MERRILY THROUGH THE STREETS!
SCHULZ

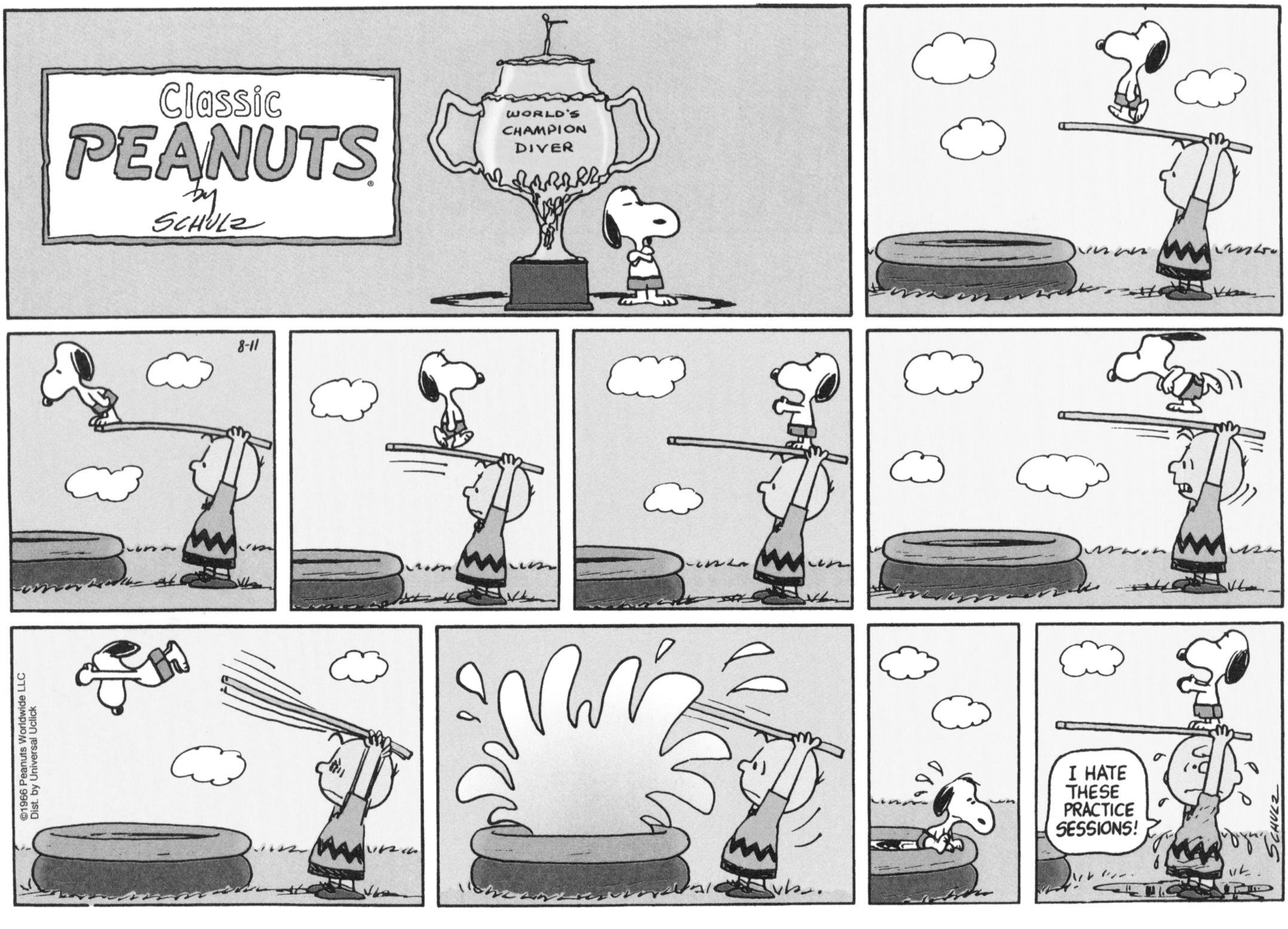
Classic
PEANUTS
by
SCHULZ
WORLD'S
CHAMPION
DIVER
8-11
©1966 Peanuts Worldwide LLC
Dist. by Universal Uclick
I HATE THESE PRACTICE SESSIONS!
SCHULZ

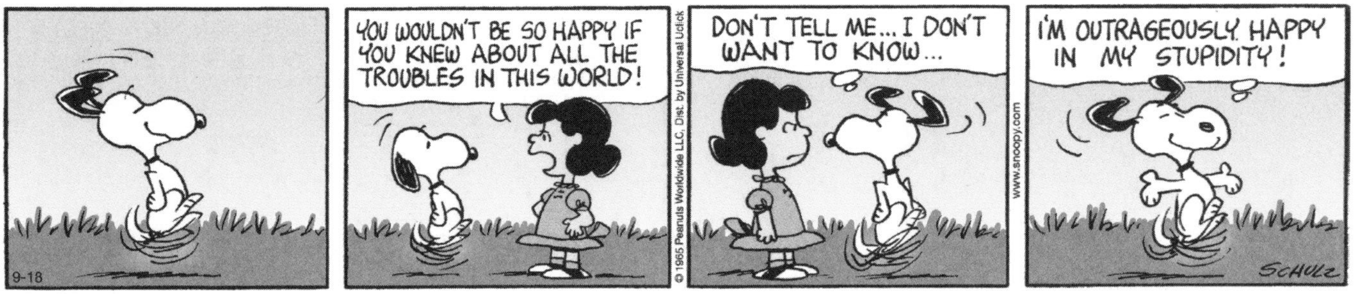
9-18
YOU WOULDN'T BE SO HAPPY IF YOU KNEW ABOUT ALL THE TROUBLES IN THIS WORLD!
DON'T TELL ME... I DON'T WANT TO KNOW...
I'M OUTRAGEOUSLY HAPPY IN MY STUPIDITY!
SCHULZ

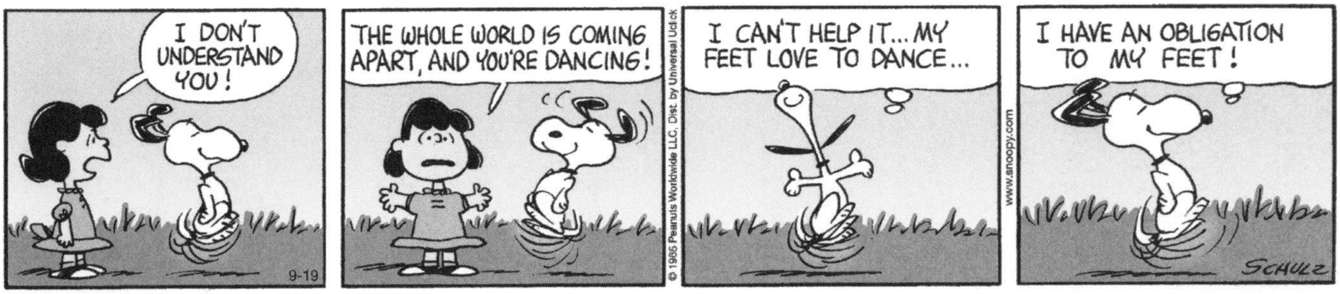
I DON'T UNDERSTAND YOU!
9-19
THE WHOLE WORLD IS COMING APART, AND YOU'RE DANCING!
I CAN'T HELP IT... MY FEET LOVE TO DANCE...
I HAVE AN OBLIGATION TO MY FEET!
SCHULZ

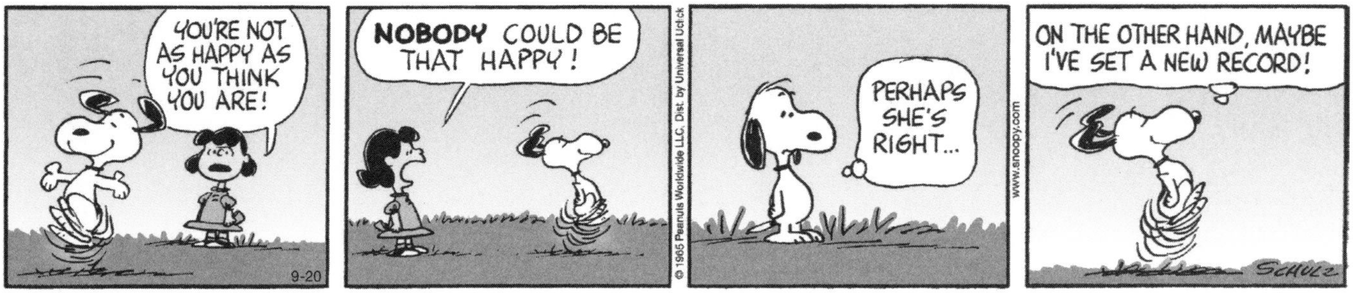
YOU'RE NOT AS HAPPY AS YOU THINK YOU ARE!
9-20
NOBODY COULD BE THAT HAPPY!
PERHAPS SHE'S RIGHT...
ON THE OTHER HAND, MAYBE I'VE SET A NEW RECORD!
SCHULZ

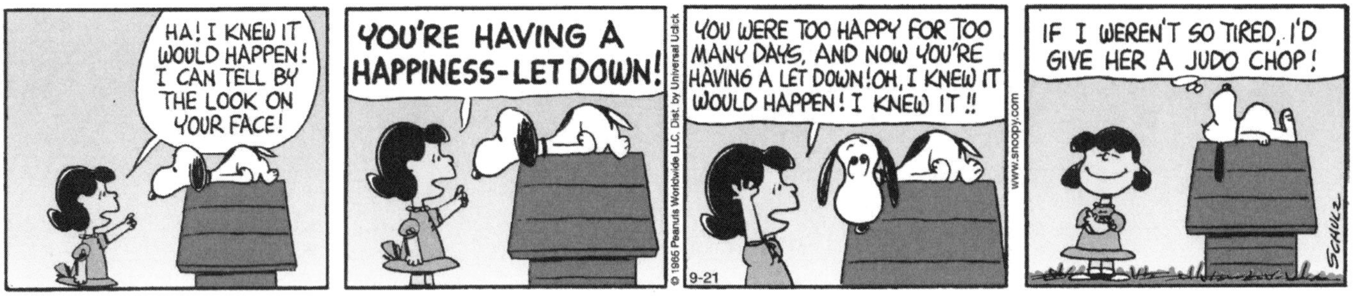
HA! I KNEW IT WOULD HAPPEN! I CAN TELL BY THE LOOK ON YOUR FACE!
YOU'RE HAVING A HAPPINESS-LET DOWN!
© 1965 Peanuts Worldwide LLC, Dist. by Universal Uclick
9-21
YOU WERE TOO HAPPY FOR TOO MANY DAYS, AND NOW YOU'RE HAVING A LET DOWN! OH, I KNEW IT WOULD HAPPEN! I KNEW IT!!
www.snoopy.com
IF I WEREN'T SO TIRED, I'D GIVE HER A JUDO CHOP!
SCHULZ

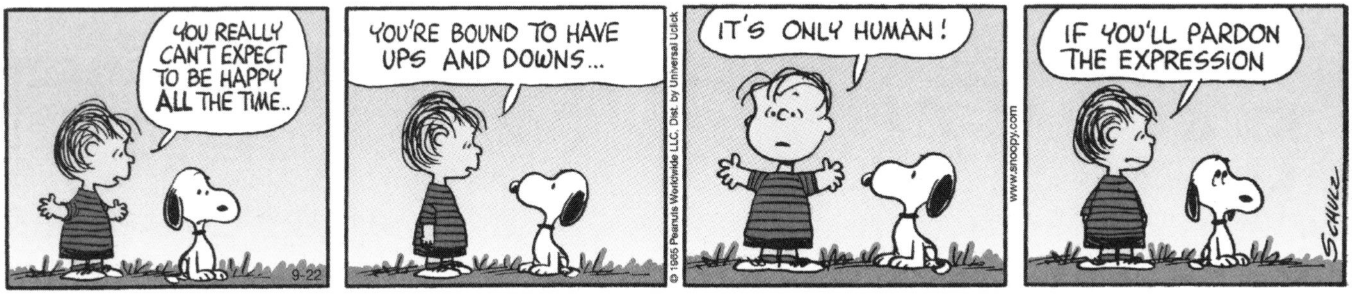
YOU REALLY CAN'T EXPECT TO BE HAPPY ALL THE TIME..
9-22
YOU'RE BOUND TO HAVE UPS AND DOWNS...
© 1965 Peanuts Worldwide LLC, Dist. by Universal Uclick
IT'S ONLY HUMAN!
www.snoopy.com
IF YOU'LL PARDON THE EXPRESSION
SCHULZ

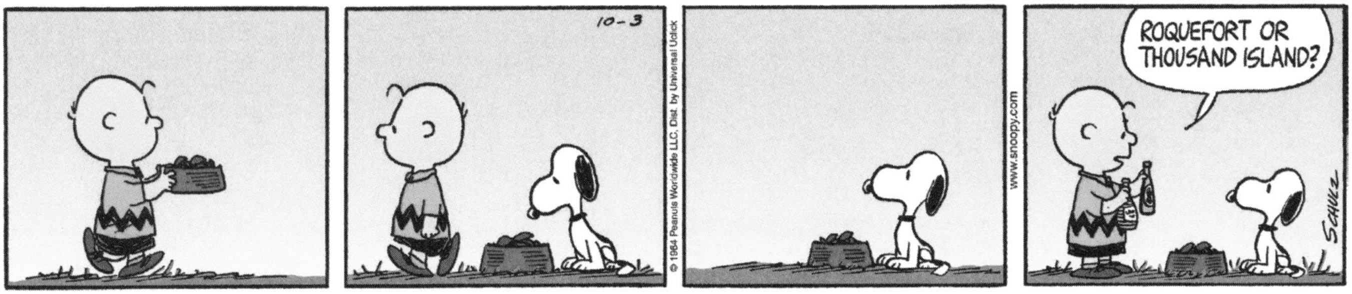
10-3
© 1964 Peanuts Worldwide LLC, Dist. by Universal Uclick
www.snoopy.com
ROQUEFORT OR THOUSAND ISLAND?
SCHULZ

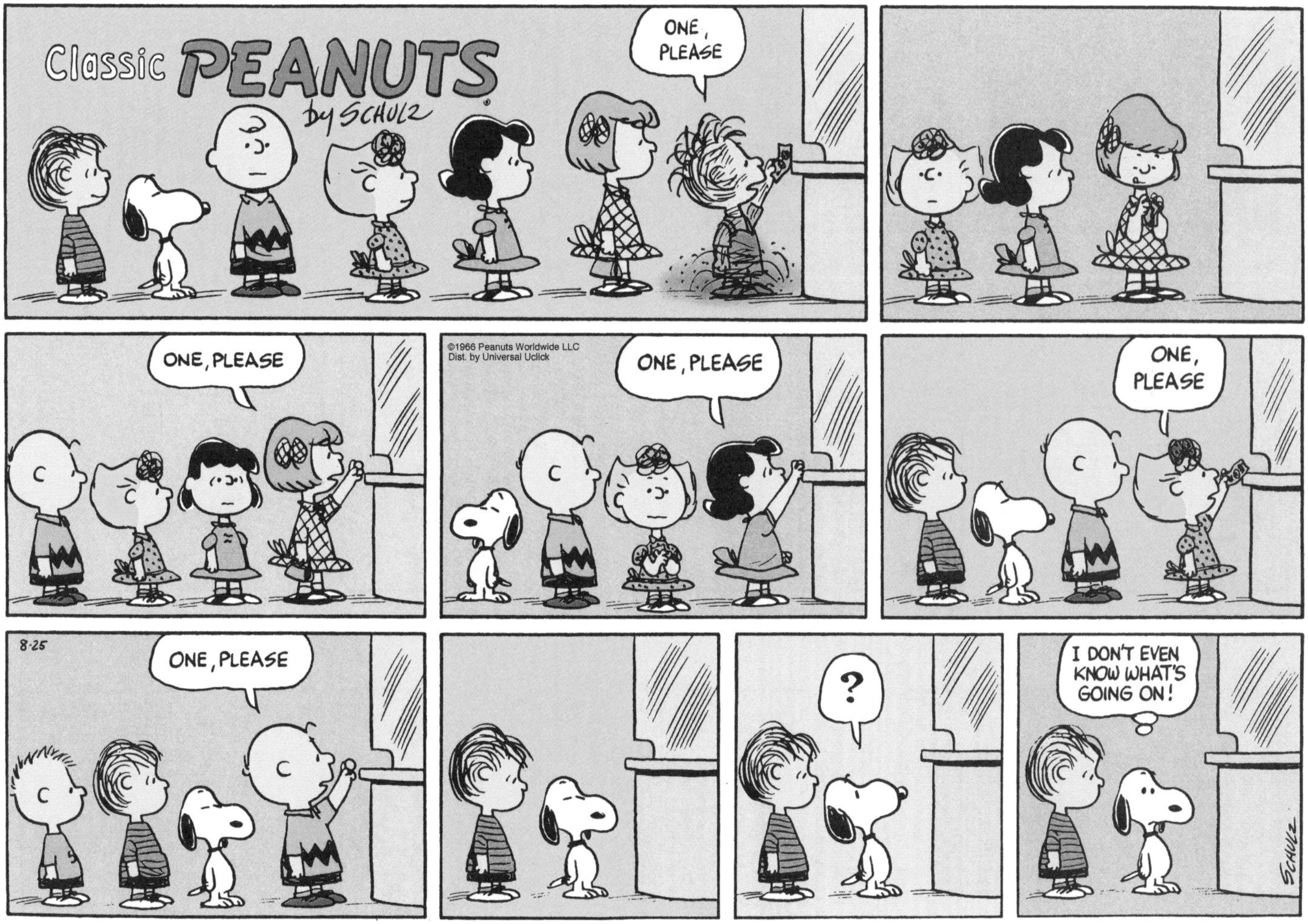
Classic PEANUTS
by SCHULZ
ONE, PLEASE
ONE, PLEASE
©1966 Peanuts Worldwide LLC
Dist. by Universal Uclick
ONE, PLEASE
ONE, PLEASE
8-25
ONE, PLEASE
?
I DON'T EVEN KNOW WHAT'S GOING ON!
SCHULZ

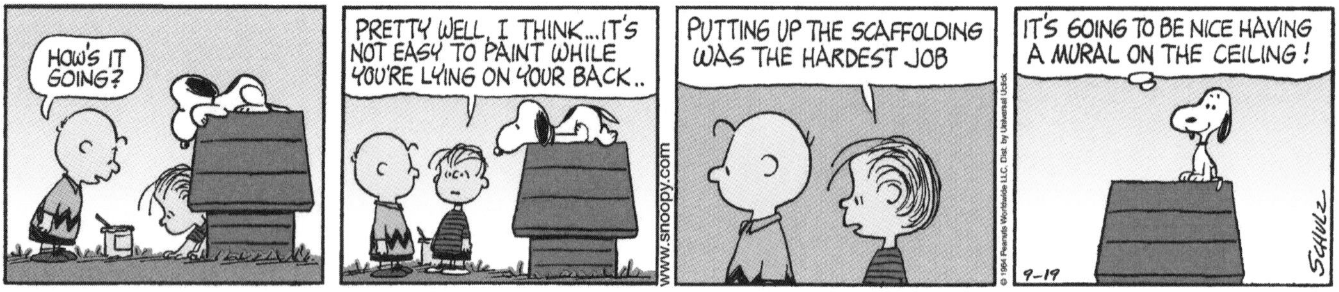
HOW'S IT GOING?
PRETTY WELL, I THINK...IT'S NOT EASY TO PAINT WHILE YOU'RE LYING ON YOUR BACK..
www.snoopy.com
PUTTING UP THE SCAFFOLDING WAS THE HARDEST JOB
© 1964 Peanuts Worldwide LLC. Dist. by Universal Uclick
IT'S GOING TO BE NICE HAVING A MURAL ON THE CEILING!
9-19
SCHULZ

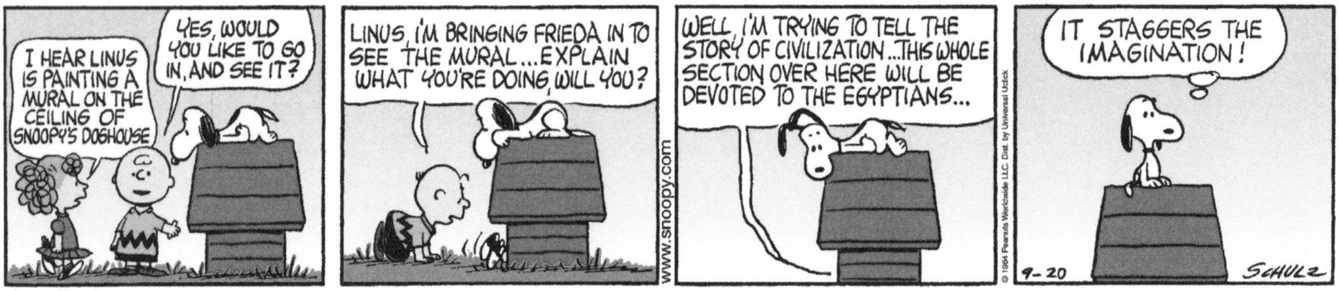
I HEAR LINUS IS PAINTING A MURAL ON THE CEILING OF SNOOPY'S DOGHOUSE
YES, WOULD YOU LIKE TO GO IN, AND SEE IT?
LINUS, I'M BRINGING FRIEDA IN TO SEE THE MURAL...EXPLAIN WHAT YOU'RE DOING, WILL YOU?
www.snoopy.com
WELL, I'M TRYING TO TELL THE STORY OF CIVILIZATION...THIS WHOLE SECTION OVER HERE WILL BE DEVOTED TO THE EGYPTIANS...
© 1964 Peanuts Worldwide LLC. Dist. by Universal Uclick
IT STAGGERS THE IMAGINATION!
9-20
SCHULZ

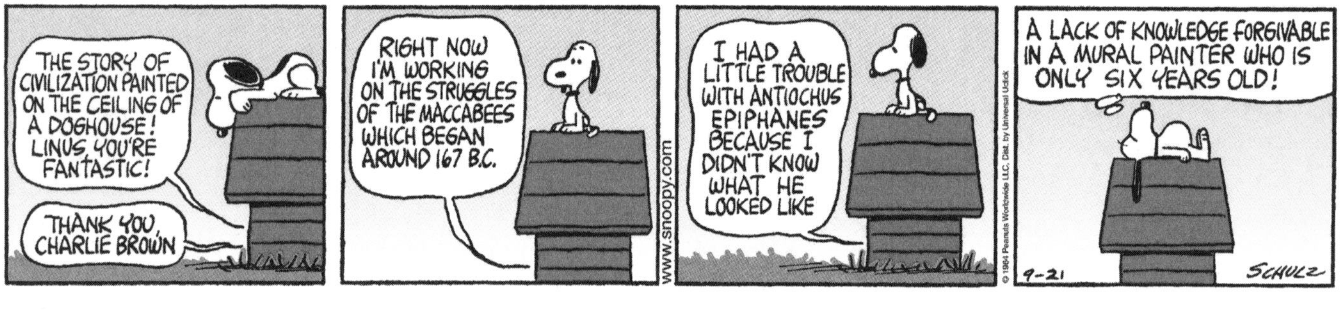
THE STORY OF CIVILIZATION PAINTED ON THE CEILING OF A DOGHOUSE! LINUS, YOU'RE FANTASTIC!
THANK YOU, CHARLIE BROWN
RIGHT NOW I'M WORKING ON THE STRUGGLES OF THE MACCABEES WHICH BEGAN AROUND 167 B.C.
www.snoopy.com
I HAD A LITTLE TROUBLE WITH ANTIOCHUS EPIPHANES BECAUSE I DIDN'T KNOW WHAT HE LOOKED LIKE
© 1964 Peanuts Worldwide LLC. Dist. by Universal Uclick
A LACK OF KNOWLEDGE FORGIVABLE IN A MURAL PAINTER WHO IS ONLY SIX YEARS OLD!
9-21
SCHULZ

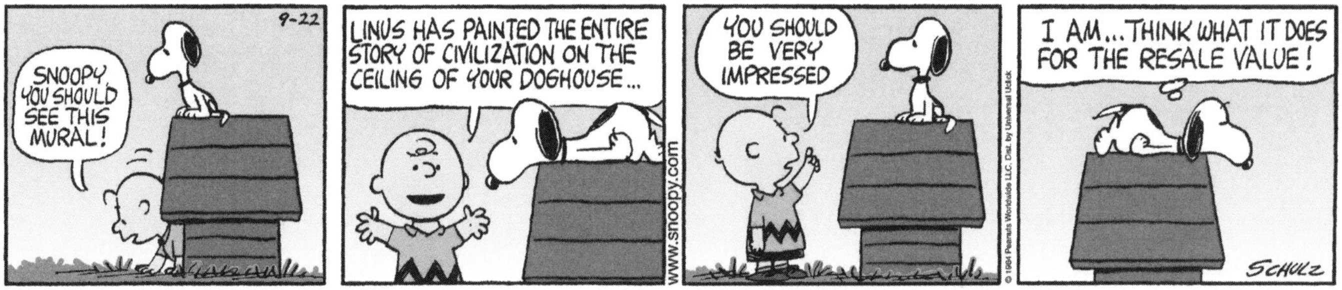
9-22
SNOOPY, YOU SHOULD SEE THIS MURAL!
LINUS HAS PAINTED THE ENTIRE STORY OF CIVILIZATION ON THE CEILING OF YOUR DOGHOUSE...
www.snoopy.com
YOU SHOULD BE VERY IMPRESSED
© 1964 Peanuts Worldwide LLC. Dist. by Universal Uclick
I AM...THINK WHAT IT DOES FOR THE RESALE VALUE!
SCHULZ

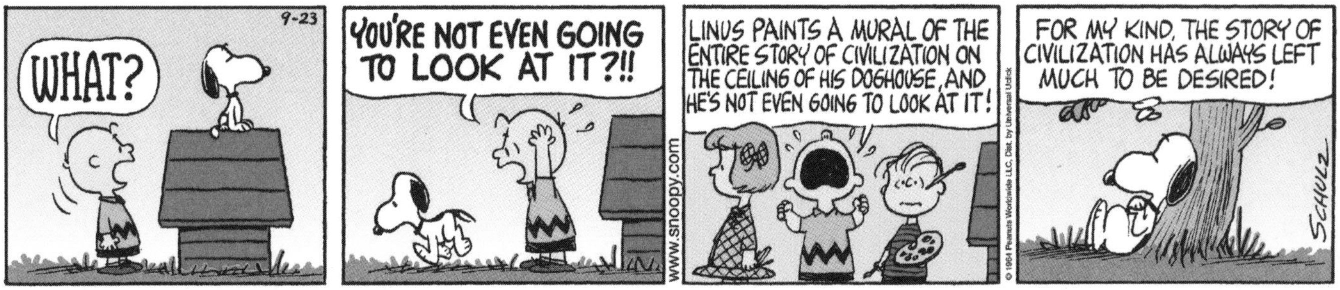
9-23
WHAT?
YOU'RE NOT EVEN GOING TO LOOK AT IT?!!
www.snoopy.com
LINUS PAINTS A MURAL OF THE ENTIRE STORY OF CIVILIZATION ON THE CEILING OF HIS DOGHOUSE, AND HE'S NOT EVEN GOING TO LOOK AT IT!
© 1964 Peanuts Worldwide LLC. Dist. by Universal Uclick
FOR MY KIND, THE STORY OF CIVILIZATION HAS ALWAYS LEFT MUCH TO BE DESIRED!
SCHULZ

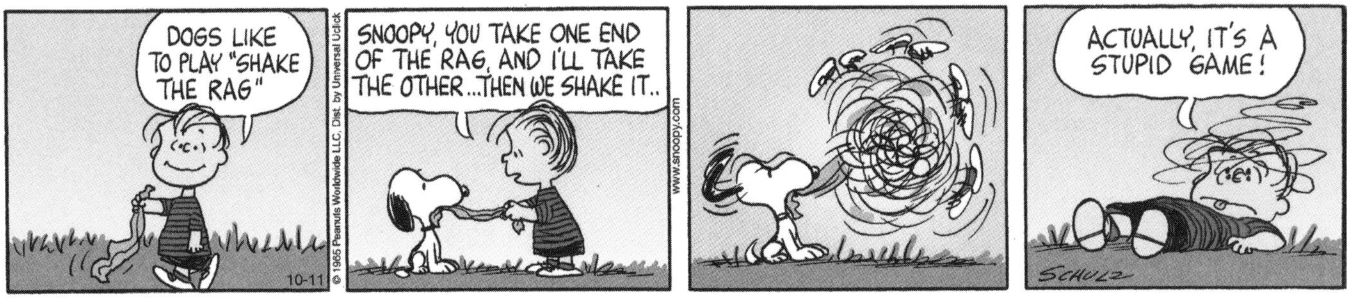
DOGS LIKE TO PLAY "SHAKE THE RAG"
10-11
© 1965 Peanuts Worldwide LLC. Dist. by Universal Uclick
SNOOPY, YOU TAKE ONE END OF THE RAG, AND I'LL TAKE THE OTHER...THEN WE SHAKE IT..
www.snoopy.com
ACTUALLY, IT'S A STUPID GAME!
SCHULZ

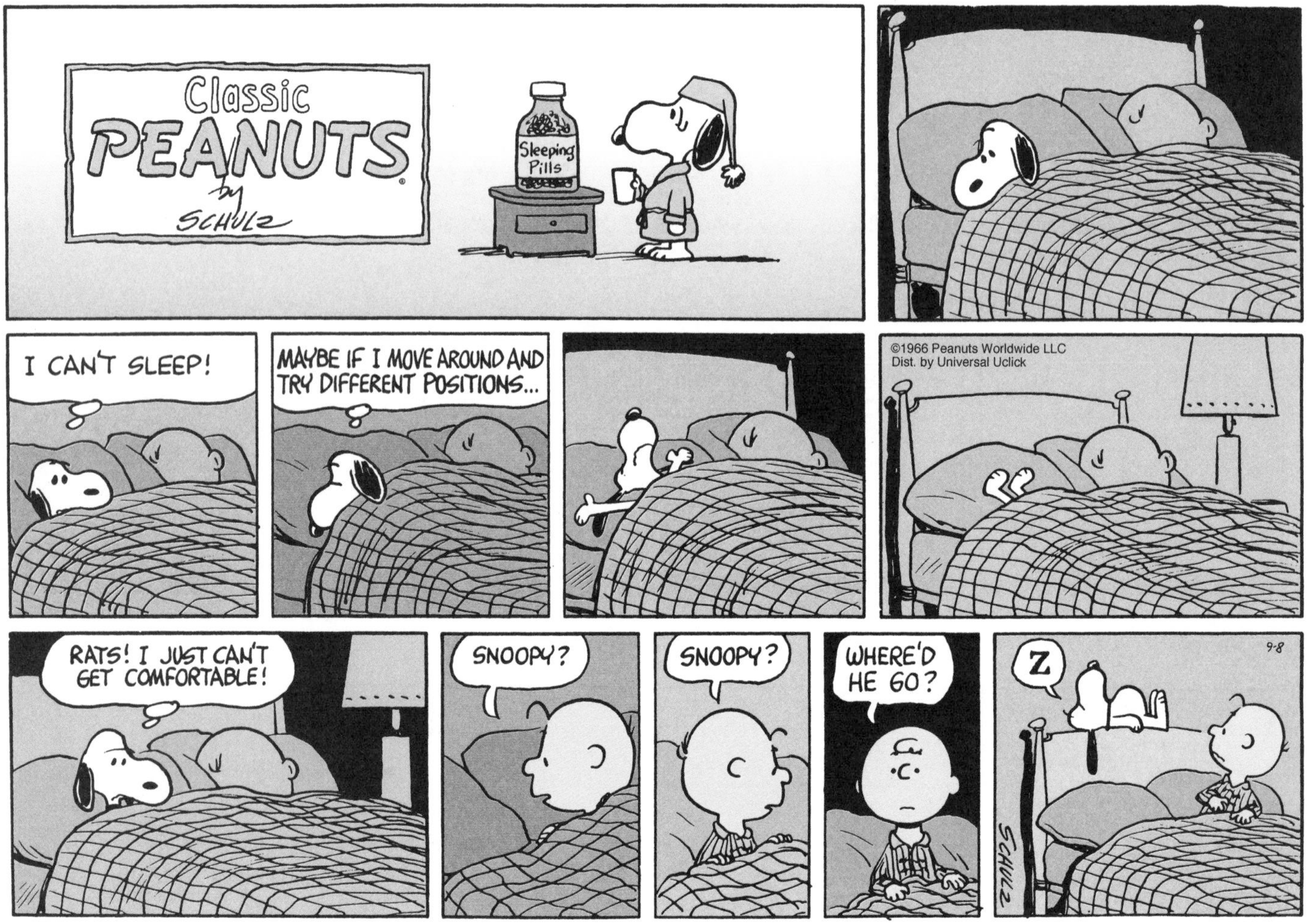
Classic PEANUTS by SCHULZ
Sleeping Pills
I CAN'T SLEEP!
MAYBE IF I MOVE AROUND AND TRY DIFFERENT POSITIONS...
©1966 Peanuts Worldwide LLC
Dist. by Universal Uclick
RATS! I JUST CAN'T GET COMFORTABLE!
SNOOPY?
SNOOPY?
WHERE'D HE GO?
Z
9-8
SCHULZ

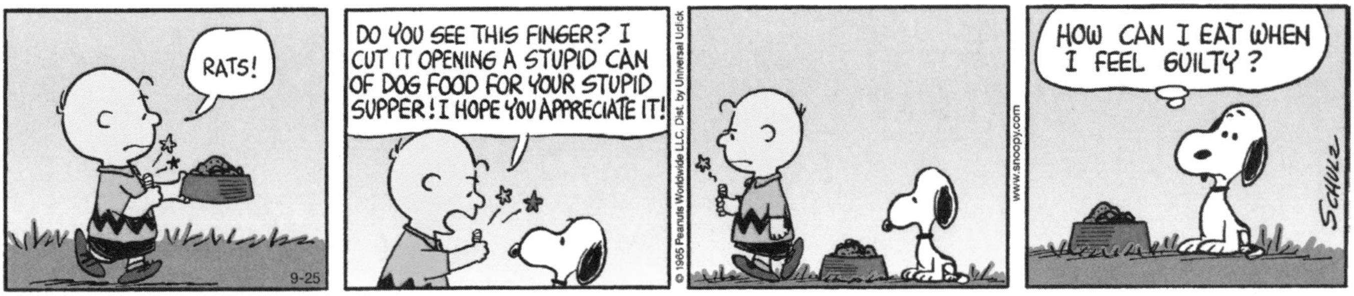
RATS!
9-25
DO YOU SEE THIS FINGER? I CUT IT OPENING A STUPID CAN OF DOG FOOD FOR YOUR STUPID SUPPER! I HOPE YOU APPRECIATE IT!
© 1965 Peanuts Worldwide LLC, Dist. by Universal Uclick
www.snoopy.com
HOW CAN I EAT WHEN I FEEL GUILTY?
SCHULZ

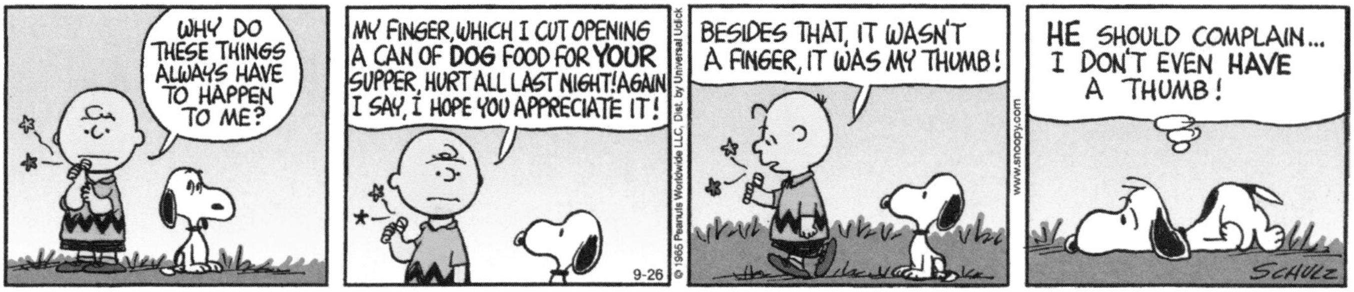
WHY DO THESE THINGS ALWAYS HAVE TO HAPPEN TO ME?
MY FINGER, WHICH I CUT OPENING A CAN OF **DOG** FOOD FOR **YOUR** SUPPER, HURT ALL LAST NIGHT! AGAIN I SAY, I HOPE YOU APPRECIATE IT!
9-26
© 1965 Peanuts Worldwide LLC, Dist. by Universal Uclick
BESIDES THAT, IT WASN'T A FINGER, IT WAS MY THUMB!
www.snoopy.com
HE SHOULD COMPLAIN... I DON'T EVEN **HAVE** A THUMB!
SCHULZ

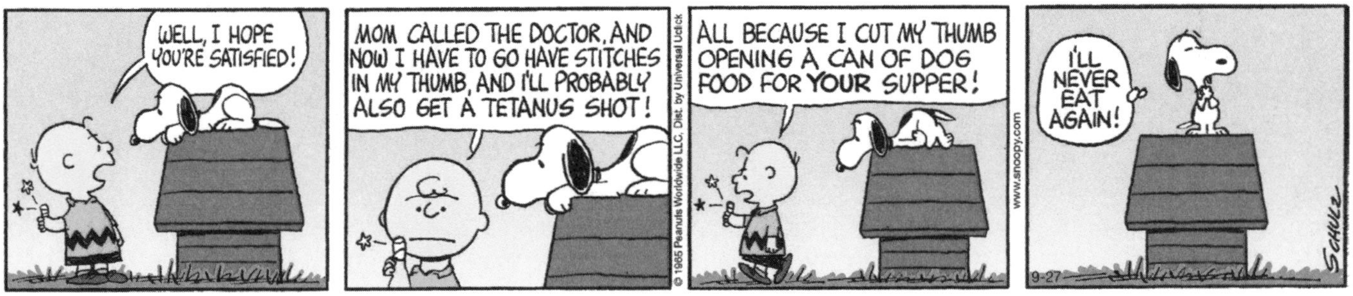
WELL, I HOPE YOU'RE SATISFIED!
MOM CALLED THE DOCTOR, AND NOW I HAVE TO GO HAVE STITCHES IN MY THUMB, AND I'LL PROBABLY ALSO GET A TETANUS SHOT!
© 1965 Peanuts Worldwide LLC, Dist. by Universal Uclick
ALL BECAUSE I CUT MY THUMB OPENING A CAN OF DOG FOOD FOR **YOUR** SUPPER!
www.snoopy.com
I'LL NEVER EAT AGAIN!
9-27
SCHULZ

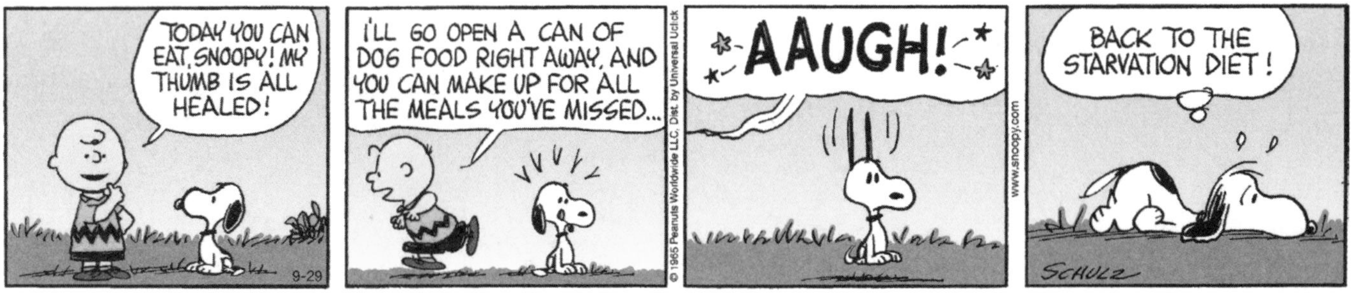
TODAY YOU CAN EAT, SNOOPY! MY THUMB IS ALL HEALED!
9-29
I'LL GO OPEN A CAN OF DOG FOOD RIGHT AWAY, AND YOU CAN MAKE UP FOR ALL THE MEALS YOU'VE MISSED...
© 1965 Peanuts Worldwide LLC. Dist. by Universal Uclick
AAUGH!
www.snoopy.com
BACK TO THE STARVATION DIET!
SCHULZ

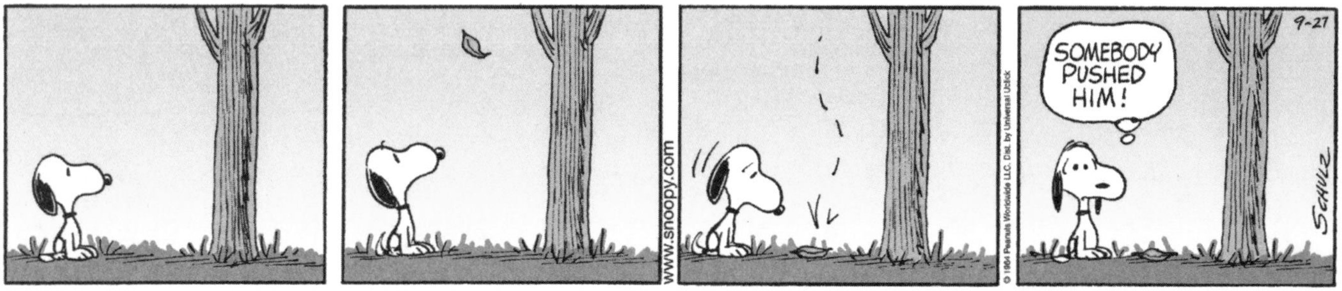
www.snoopy.com
© 1964 Peanuts Worldwide LLC. Dist. by Universal Uclick
9-27
SOMEBODY PUSHED HIM!
SCHULZ

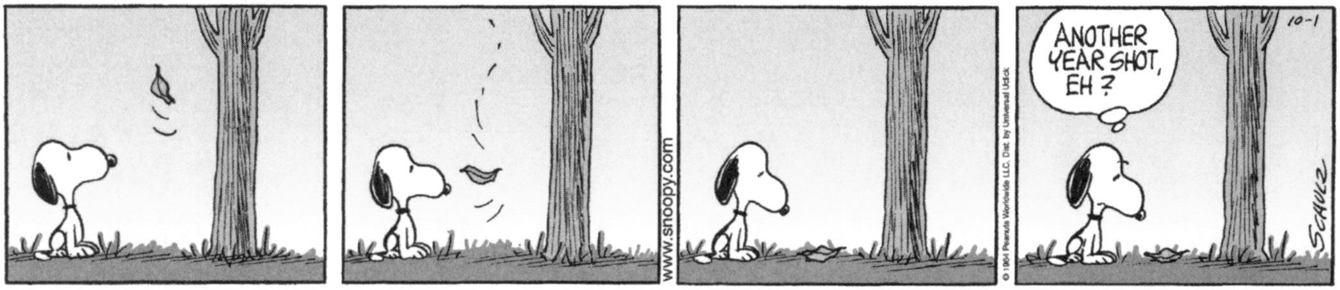
www.snoopy.com
© 1964 Peanuts Worldwide LLC. Dist. by Universal Uclick
10-1
ANOTHER YEAR SHOT, EH?
SCHULZ

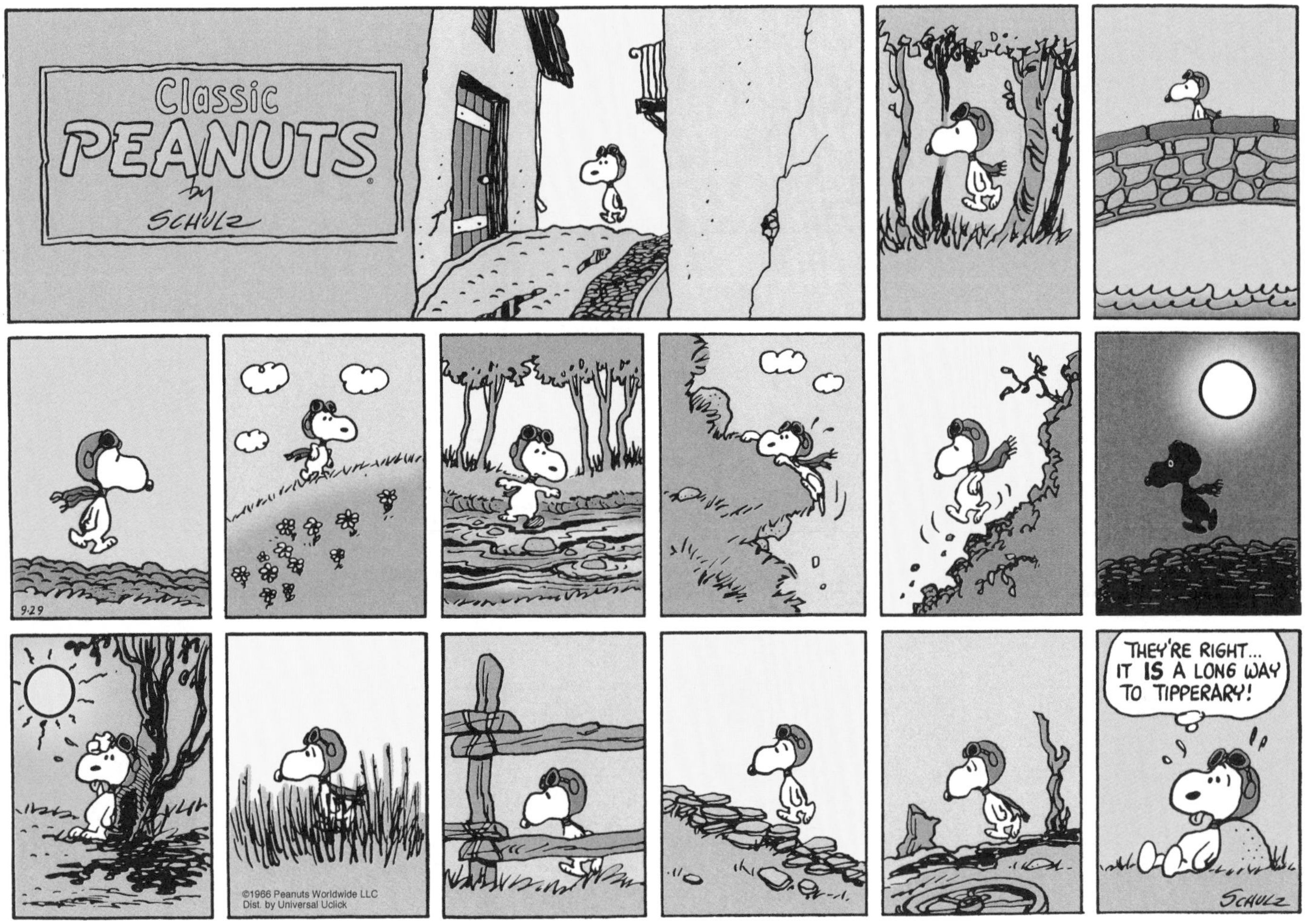
Classic PEANUTS by SCHULZ
9-29
©1966 Peanuts Worldwide LLC
Dist. by Universal Uclick
THEY'RE RIGHT... IT **IS** A LONG WAY TO TIPPERARY!
SCHULZ

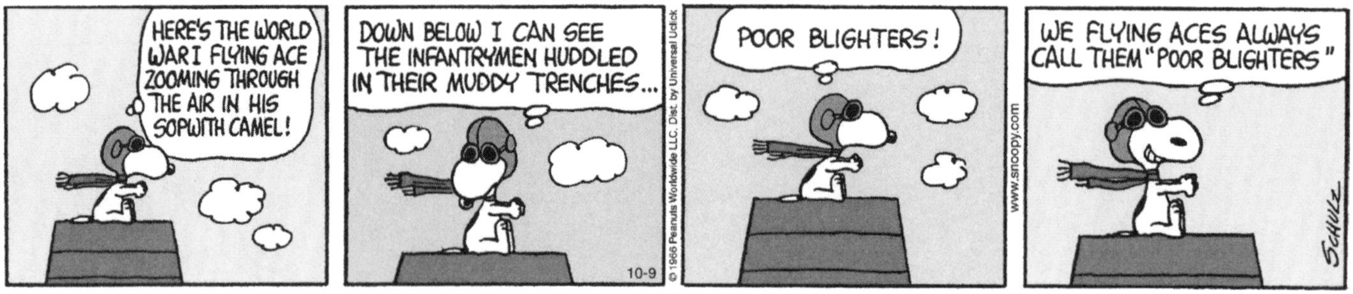
HERE'S THE WORLD WAR I FLYING ACE ZOOMING THROUGH THE AIR IN HIS SOPWITH CAMEL!
DOWN BELOW I CAN SEE THE INFANTRYMEN HUDDLED IN THEIR MUDDY TRENCHES...
10-9
© 1966 Peanuts Worldwide LLC. Dist. by Universal Uclick
POOR BLIGHTERS!
www.snoopy.com
WE FLYING ACES ALWAYS CALL THEM "POOR BLIGHTERS"
SCHULZ

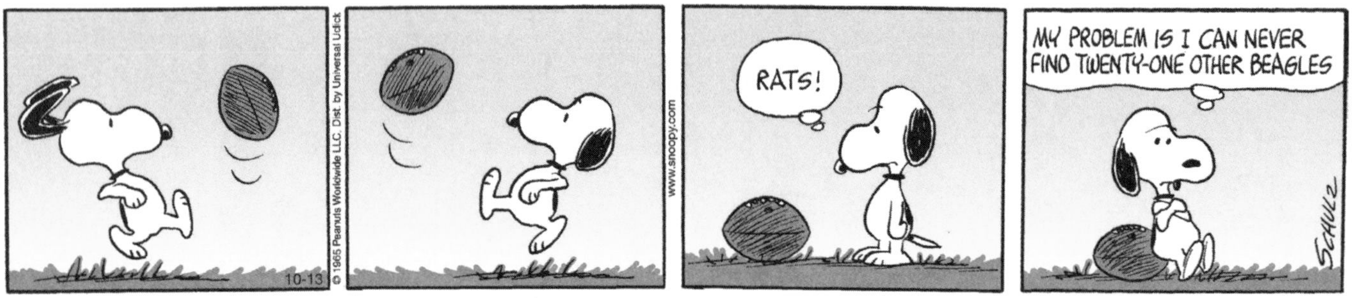
10-13
© 1965 Peanuts Worldwide LLC. Dist. by Universal Uclick
www.snoopy.com
RATS!
MY PROBLEM IS I CAN NEVER FIND TWENTY-ONE OTHER BEAGLES
SCHULZ

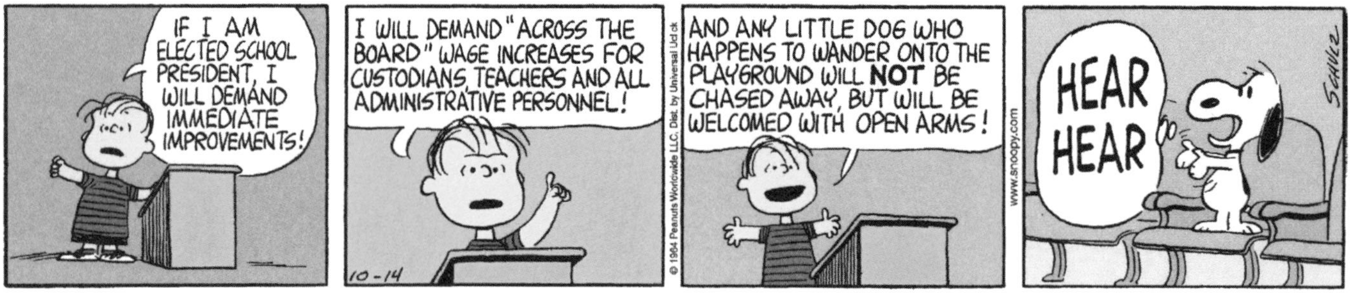
IF I AM ELECTED SCHOOL PRESIDENT, I WILL DEMAND IMMEDIATE IMPROVEMENTS!
I WILL DEMAND "ACROSS THE BOARD" WAGE INCREASES FOR CUSTODIANS, TEACHERS AND ALL ADMINISTRATIVE PERSONNEL!
10-14
© 1964 Peanuts Worldwide LLC. Dist. by Universal Uclick
AND ANY LITTLE DOG WHO HAPPENS TO WANDER ONTO THE PLAYGROUND WILL NOT BE CHASED AWAY, BUT WILL BE WELCOMED WITH OPEN ARMS!
www.snoopy.com
HEAR HEAR
SCHULZ

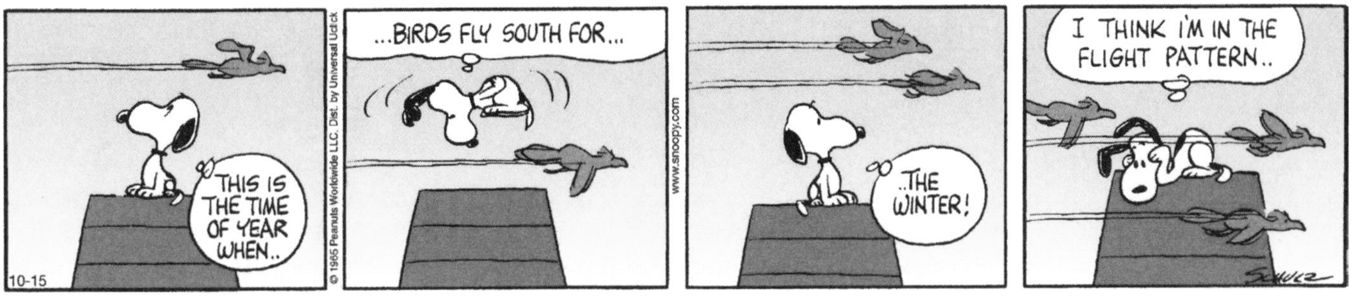
THIS IS THE TIME OF YEAR WHEN..
10-15
© 1965 Peanuts Worldwide LLC. Dist. by Universal Uclick
...BIRDS FLY SOUTH FOR...
www.snoopy.com
..THE WINTER!
I THINK I'M IN THE FLIGHT PATTERN..
SCHULZ

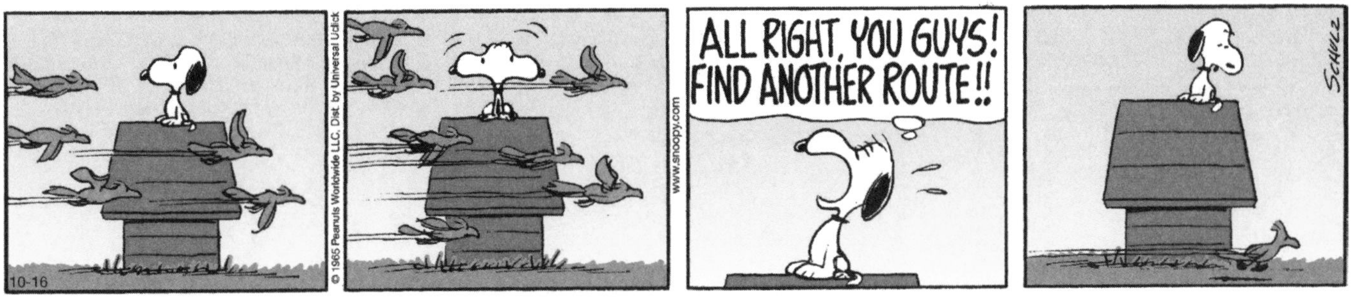
10-16
© 1965 Peanuts Worldwide LLC. Dist. by Universal Uclick
www.snoopy.com
ALL RIGHT, YOU GUYS! FIND ANOTHER ROUTE!!
SCHULZ

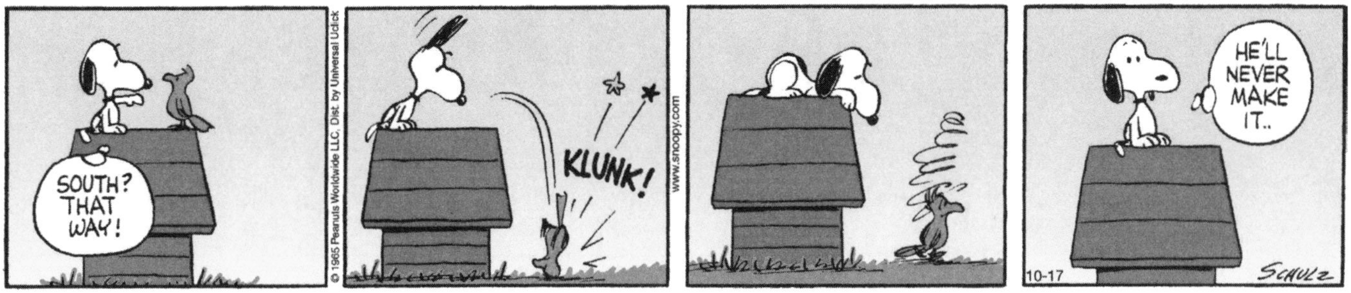
SOUTH? THAT WAY!
© 1965 Peanuts Worldwide LLC. Dist. by Universal Uclick
KLUNK!
www.snoopy.com
HE'LL NEVER MAKE IT..
10-17
SCHULZ

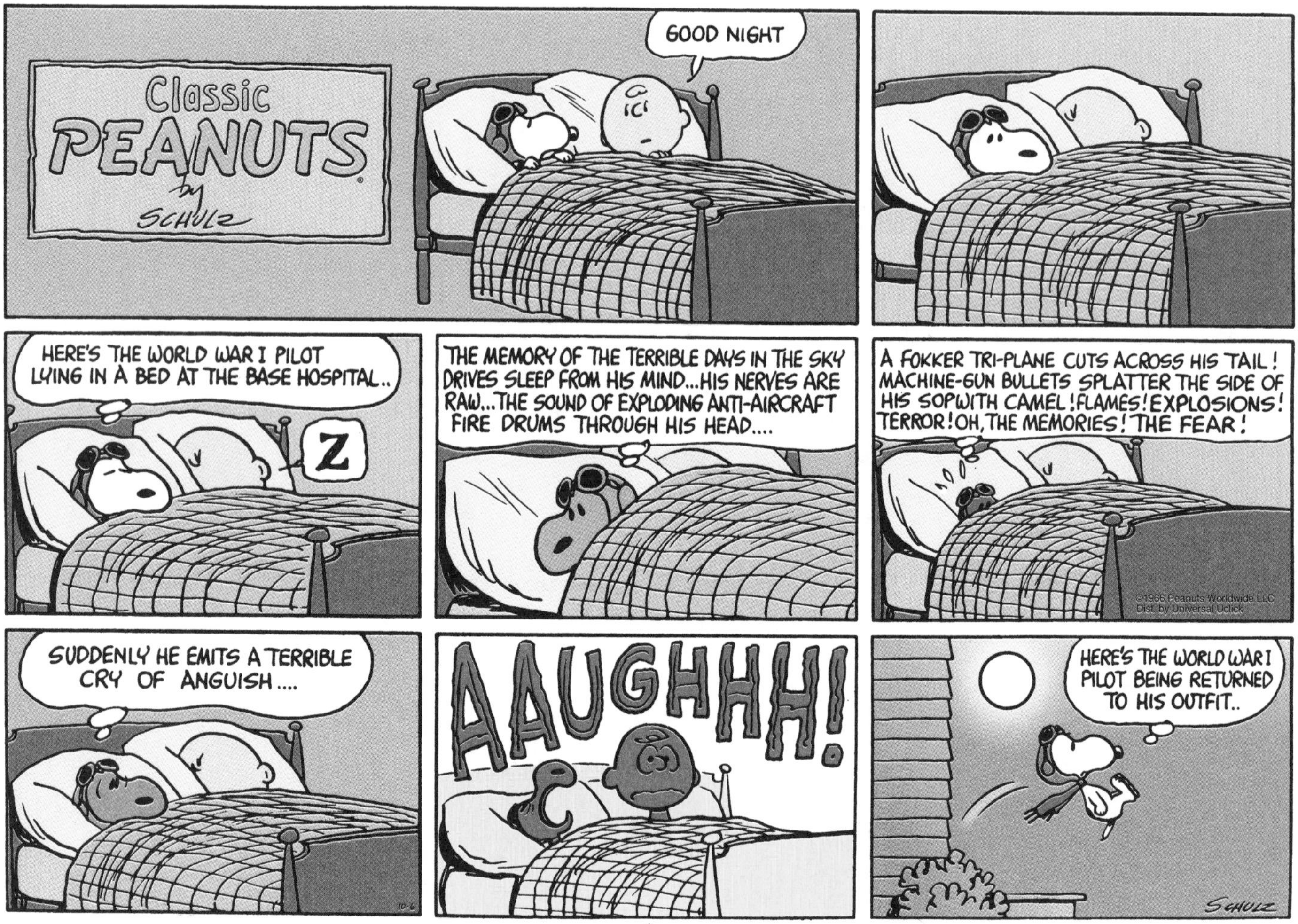
Classic PEANUTS by SCHULZ
GOOD NIGHT
HERE'S THE WORLD WAR I PILOT LYING IN A BED AT THE BASE HOSPITAL..
Z
THE MEMORY OF THE TERRIBLE DAYS IN THE SKY DRIVES SLEEP FROM HIS MIND...HIS NERVES ARE RAW...THE SOUND OF EXPLODING ANTI-AIRCRAFT FIRE DRUMS THROUGH HIS HEAD....
A FOKKER TRI-PLANE CUTS ACROSS HIS TAIL! MACHINE-GUN BULLETS SPLATTER THE SIDE OF HIS SOPWITH CAMEL! FLAMES! EXPLOSIONS! TERROR! OH, THE MEMORIES! THE FEAR!
©1966 Peanuts Worldwide LLC Dist. by Universal Uclick
SUDDENLY HE EMITS A TERRIBLE CRY OF ANGUISH....
AAUGHHH!
HERE'S THE WORLD WAR I PILOT BEING RETURNED TO HIS OUTFIT..
SCHULZ

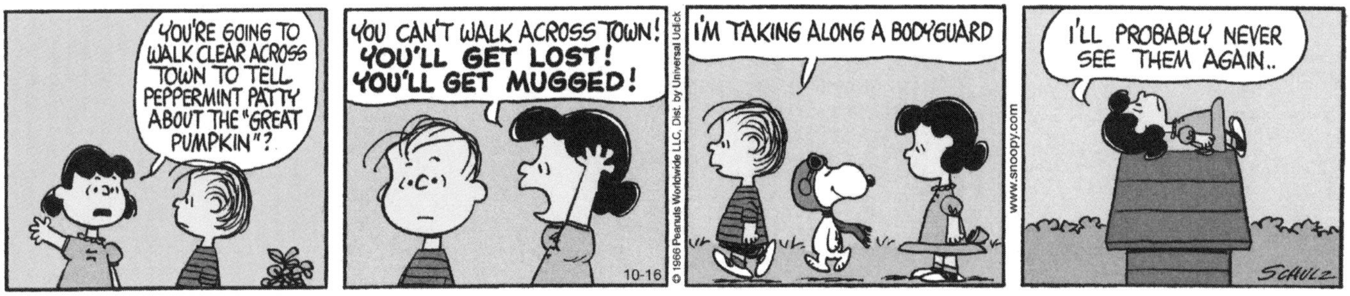
YOU'RE GOING TO WALK CLEAR ACROSS TOWN TO TELL PEPPERMINT PATTY ABOUT THE "GREAT PUMPKIN"?
YOU CAN'T WALK ACROSS TOWN! YOU'LL GET LOST! YOU'LL GET MUGGED!
10-16
© 1966 Peanuts Worldwide LLC, Dist. by Universal Uclick
I'M TAKING ALONG A BODYGUARD
www.snoopy.com
I'LL PROBABLY NEVER SEE THEM AGAIN..
SCHULZ

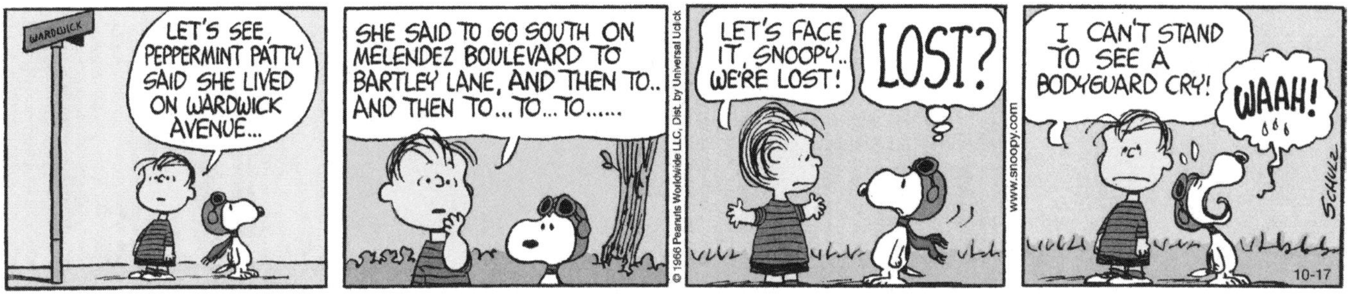
WARDWICK
LET'S SEE, PEPPERMINT PATTY SAID SHE LIVED ON WARDWICK AVENUE...
SHE SAID TO GO SOUTH ON MELENDEZ BOULEVARD TO BARTLEY LANE, AND THEN TO.. AND THEN TO...TO...TO......
© 1966 Peanuts Worldwide LLC, Dist. by Universal Uclick
LET'S FACE IT, SNOOPY.. WE'RE LOST!
LOST?
www.snoopy.com
I CAN'T STAND TO SEE A BODYGUARD CRY!
WAAH!
SCHULZ
10-17

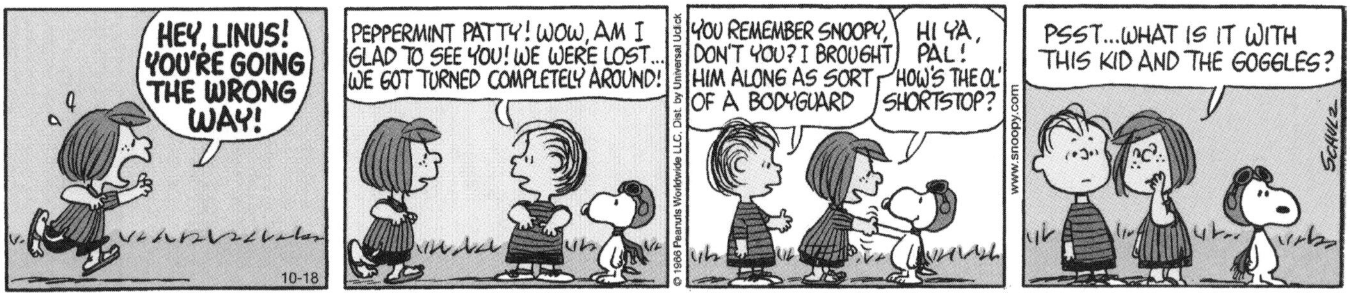
HEY, LINUS! YOU'RE GOING THE WRONG WAY!
10-18
PEPPERMINT PATTY! WOW, AM I GLAD TO SEE YOU! WE WERE LOST... WE GOT TURNED COMPLETELY AROUND!
© 1966 Peanuts Worldwide LLC, Dist. by Universal Uclick
YOU REMEMBER SNOOPY, DON'T YOU? I BROUGHT HIM ALONG AS SORT OF A BODYGUARD
HI YA, PAL! HOW'S THE OL' SHORTSTOP?
www.snoopy.com
PSST...WHAT IS IT WITH THIS KID AND THE GOGGLES?
SCHULZ

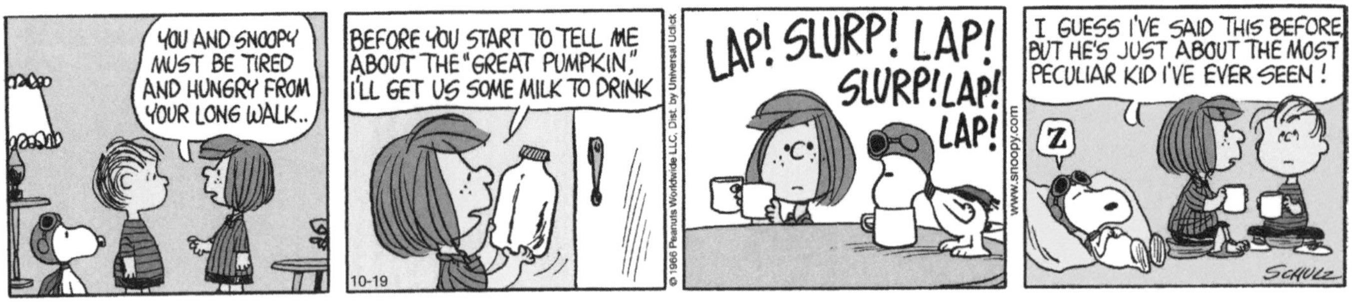
YOU AND SNOOPY MUST BE TIRED AND HUNGRY FROM YOUR LONG WALK..
BEFORE YOU START TO TELL ME ABOUT THE "GREAT PUMPKIN," I'LL GET US SOME MILK TO DRINK
10-19
© 1966 Peanuts Worldwide LLC, Dist. by Universal Uclick
LAP! SLURP! LAP! SLURP! LAP! LAP!
www.snoopy.com
I GUESS I'VE SAID THIS BEFORE, BUT HE'S JUST ABOUT THE MOST PECULIAR KID I'VE EVER SEEN!
Z
SCHULZ

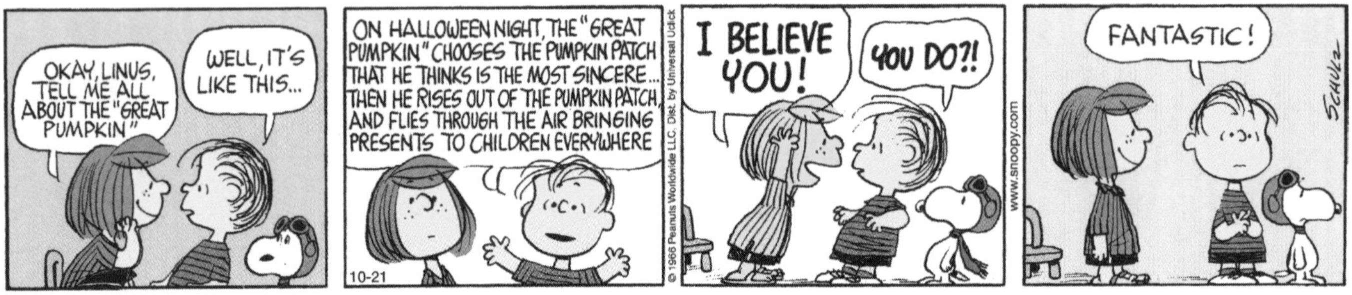
OKAY, LINUS, TELL ME ALL ABOUT THE "GREAT PUMPKIN"
WELL, IT'S LIKE THIS...
ON HALLOWEEN NIGHT, THE "GREAT PUMPKIN" CHOOSES THE PUMPKIN PATCH THAT HE THINKS IS THE MOST SINCERE... THEN HE RISES OUT OF THE PUMPKIN PATCH, AND FLIES THROUGH THE AIR BRINGING PRESENTS TO CHILDREN EVERYWHERE
10-21
© 1966 Peanuts Worldwide LLC, Dist. by Universal Uclick
I BELIEVE YOU!
YOU DO?!
www.snoopy.com
FANTASTIC!
SCHULZ

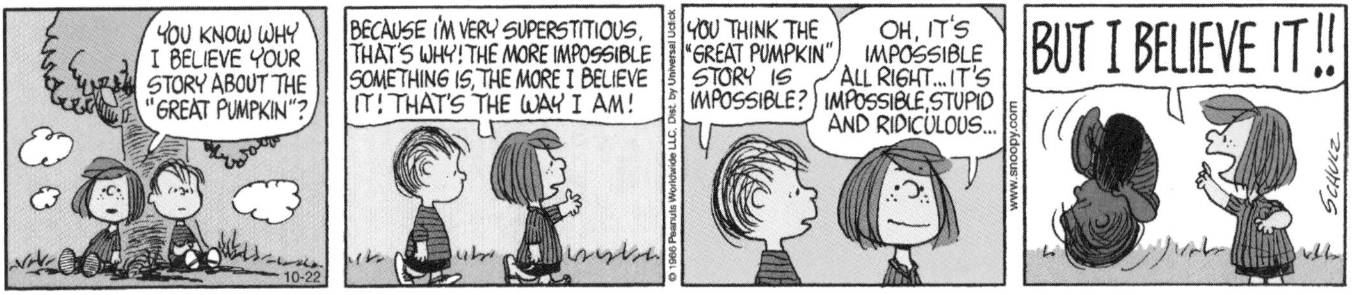
YOU KNOW WHY I BELIEVE YOUR STORY ABOUT THE "GREAT PUMPKIN"?
10-22
BECAUSE I'M VERY SUPERSTITIOUS, THAT'S WHY! THE MORE IMPOSSIBLE SOMETHING IS, THE MORE I BELIEVE IT! THAT'S THE WAY I AM!
© 1966 Peanuts Worldwide LLC, Dist. by Universal Uclick
YOU THINK THE "GREAT PUMPKIN" STORY IS IMPOSSIBLE?
OH, IT'S IMPOSSIBLE ALL RIGHT... IT'S IMPOSSIBLE, STUPID AND RIDICULOUS...
www.snoopy.com
BUT I BELIEVE IT!!
SCHULZ

ARE YOU SURE YOU CAN FIND YOUR WAY HOME NOW?
ABSOLUTELY! WE WON'T HAVE ANY TROUBLE AT ALL
HERE'S THE WORLD WAR I FLYING ACE RECEIVING HIS ORDERS...
10-23
SNOOPY HAS A GOOD SENSE OF DIRECTION, DON'T YOU, SNOOPY?
THE RED BARON HAS BEEN SIGHTED OVER CAMBRAI..I MUST BRING HIM DOWN!
I SAID, YOU CAN GET US HOME, CAN'T YOU, SNOOPY?
MY FAITHFUL MECHANICS ARE STANDING BY MY SOPWITH CAMEL...THEY ADMIRE MY CONFIDENT ATTITUDE...
IF YOU DON'T HEAR FROM US, SEND OUT A ST. BERNARD!
AS I WALK ACROSS THE FIELD TO MY PLANE, EVERYONE WAVES....I WAVE BACK.."SO LONG, CHAPS! SO LONG!"
SCHULZ

I'M A PHOTOGRAPHER FOR OUR SCHOOL PAPER, LINUS...
10-18
AS LONG AS YOU'RE RUNNING FOR SCHOOL PRESIDENT, WE'D LIKE A PICTURE OF YOU...
IN ORDER TO MAKE IT LOOK SORT OF "HOMEY," I THOUGHT WE'D POSE YOU WITH A DOG..
I'VE CHANGED MY MIND!
SCHULZ

THANKS FOR LETTING US PLAY POOL IN YOUR RECREATION ROOM, SNOOPY
INCIDENTALLY, A TIP CAME OFF OF ONE OF THE CUES SO I'M TAKING IT TO BE REPAIRED...
10-23
AND DON'T WORRY...I'LL SEE TO IT THAT THEY USE ONLY INDONESIAN WATER-BUFFALO HIDE...
I'M GLAD HE TOLD ME THAT... OTHERWISE, I WOULD HAVE STAYED AWAKE ALL NIGHT WORRYING..
SCHULZ

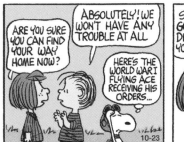

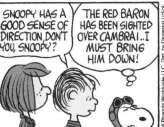

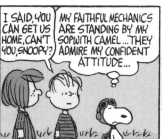

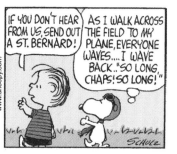

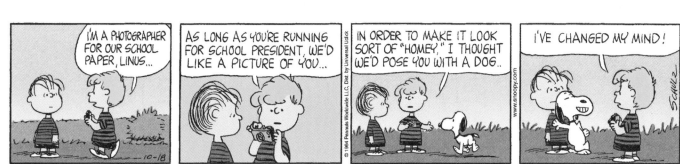

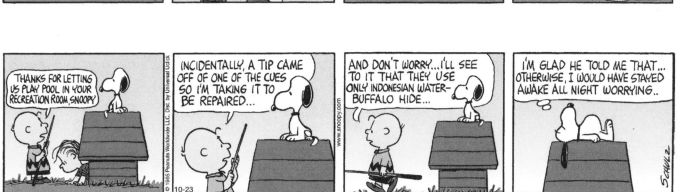

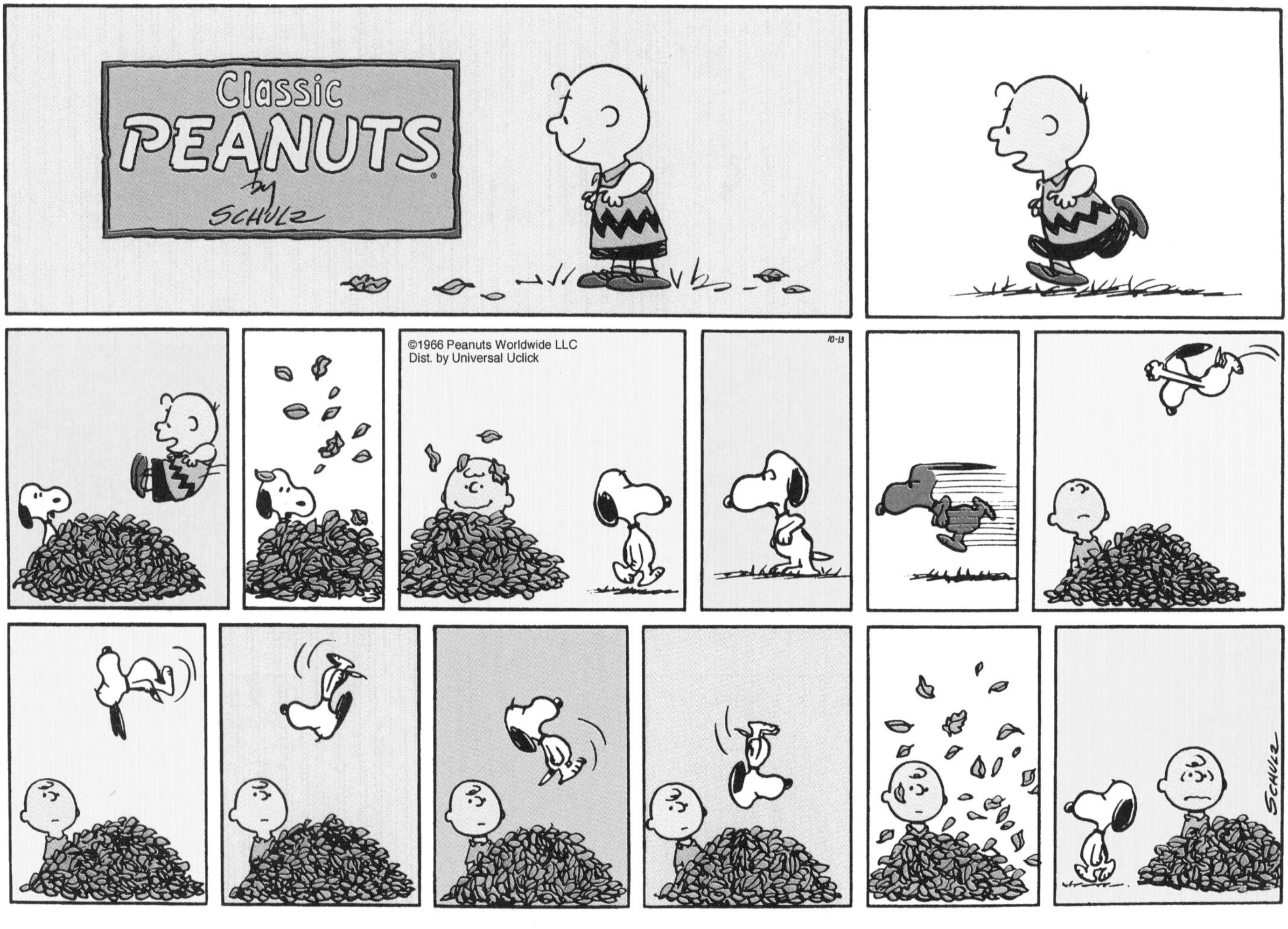
Classic
PEANUTS
by
SCHULZ
©1966 Peanuts Worldwide LLC
Dist. by Universal Uclick
10-13
SCHULZ

WHAT IN THE WORLD IS THAT, CHARLIE BROWN?
THIS IS SNOOPY'S SUPPER...I LIKE TO DRESS IT UP ONCE IN A WHILE....
I LIKE TO MAKE HIS MEAL LOOK INTERESTING...
10-24
© 1965 Peanuts Worldwide LLC. Dist. by Universal Uclick
www.snoopy.com
SCHULZ

10-27
THE GREAT PUMPKIN IS COMING!
SEE YOUR LOCAL PUMPKIN PATCH FOR DETAILS
© 1964 Peanuts Worldwide LLC. Dist. by Universal Uclick
www.snoopy.com
SCHULZ

THERE'S NOT ENOUGH ROOM UNDER HERE FOR ALL THREE OF US!
10-28
© 1966 Peanuts Worldwide LLC. Dist. by Universal Uclick
www.snoopy.com
I KNEW THEY'D FEEL GUILTY!
SCHULZ

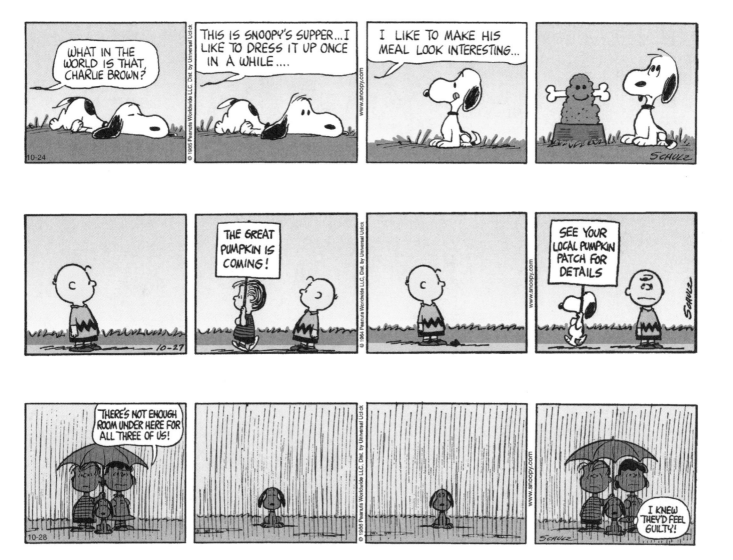

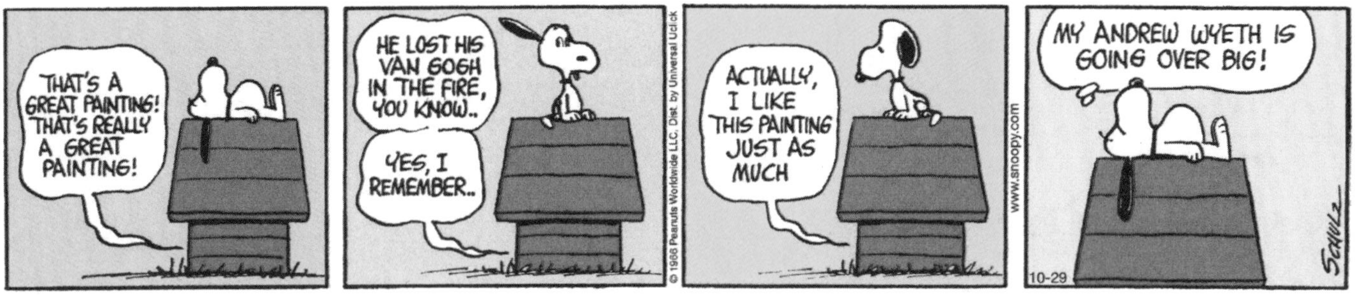
THAT'S A GREAT PAINTING! THAT'S REALLY A GREAT PAINTING!
HE LOST HIS VAN GOGH IN THE FIRE, YOU KNOW..
YES, I REMEMBER..
ACTUALLY, I LIKE THIS PAINTING JUST AS MUCH
MY ANDREW WYETH IS GOING OVER BIG!
10-29
SCHULZ

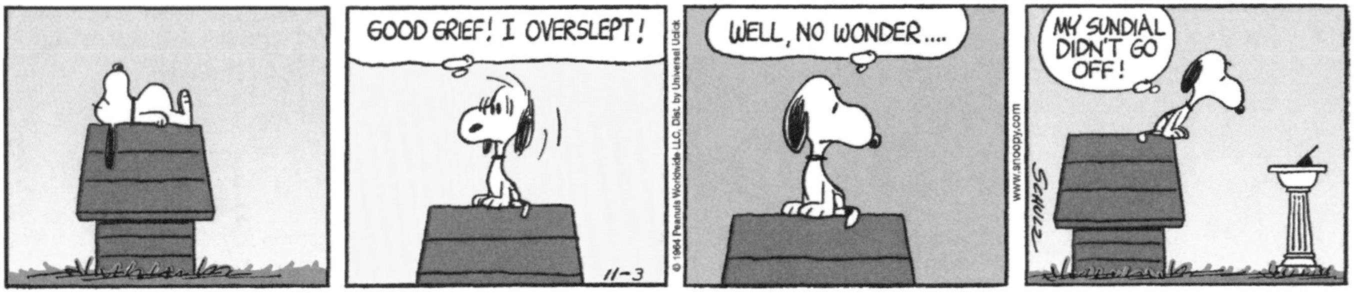
GOOD GRIEF! I OVERSLEPT!
11-3
WELL, NO WONDER....
MY SUNDIAL DIDN'T GO OFF!
SCHULZ

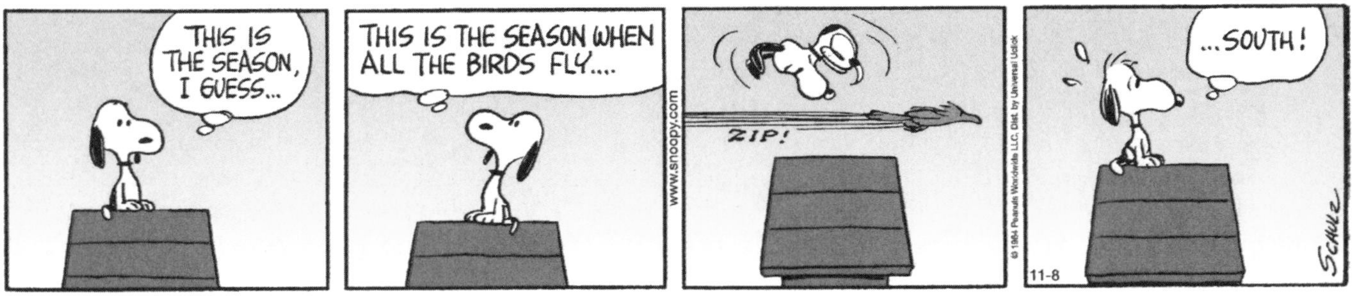
THIS IS THE SEASON, I GUESS...
THIS IS THE SEASON WHEN ALL THE BIRDS FLY....
ZIP!
...SOUTH!
11-8
SCHULZ

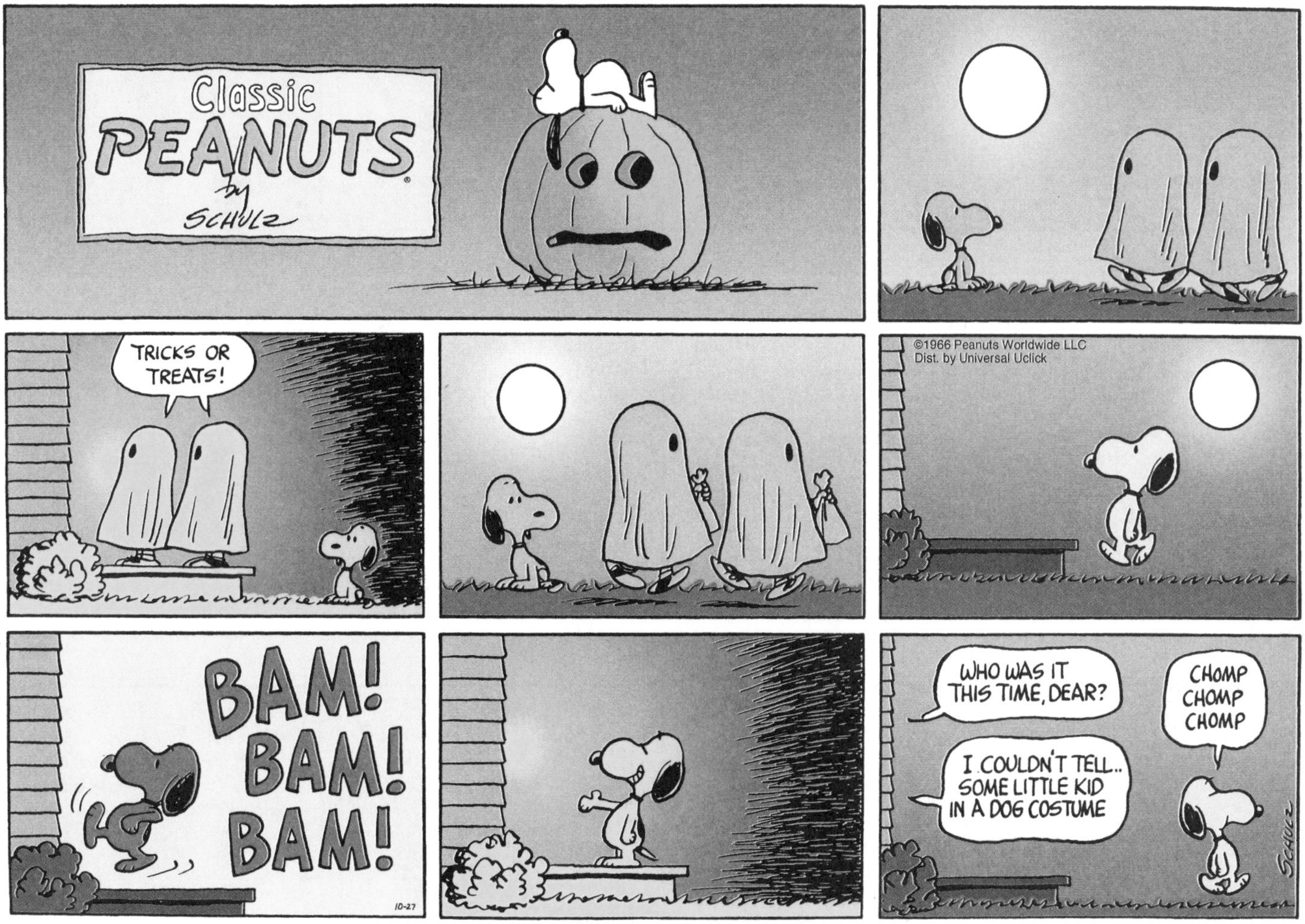
Classic PEANUTS by SCHULZ
TRICKS OR TREATS!
©1966 Peanuts Worldwide LLC
Dist. by Universal Uclick
BAM! BAM! BAM!
10-27
WHO WAS IT THIS TIME, DEAR?
I COULDN'T TELL.. SOME LITTLE KID IN A DOG COSTUME
CHOMP CHOMP CHOMP
SCHULZ

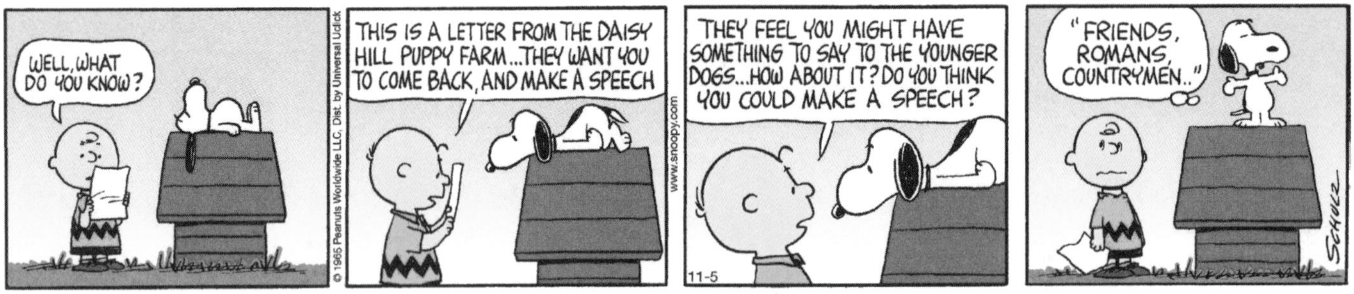
WELL, WHAT DO YOU KNOW?
© 1965 Peanuts Worldwide LLC, Dist. by Universal Uclick
THIS IS A LETTER FROM THE DAISY HILL PUPPY FARM...THEY WANT YOU TO COME BACK, AND MAKE A SPEECH
www.snoopy.com
THEY FEEL YOU MIGHT HAVE SOMETHING TO SAY TO THE YOUNGER DOGS...HOW ABOUT IT? DO YOU THINK YOU COULD MAKE A SPEECH?
11-5
"FRIENDS, ROMANS, COUNTRYMEN.."
SCHULZ

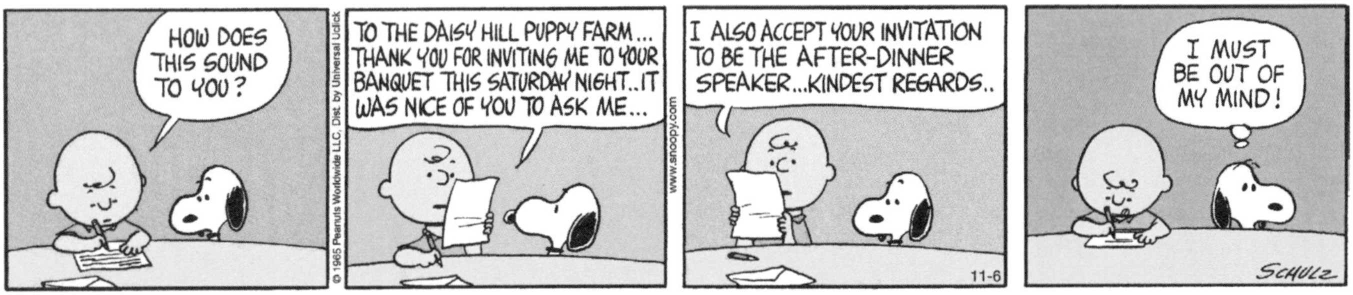
HOW DOES THIS SOUND TO YOU?
© 1965 Peanuts Worldwide LLC, Dist. by Universal Uclick
TO THE DAISY HILL PUPPY FARM... THANK YOU FOR INVITING ME TO YOUR BANQUET THIS SATURDAY NIGHT..IT WAS NICE OF YOU TO ASK ME...
www.snoopy.com
I ALSO ACCEPT YOUR INVITATION TO BE THE AFTER-DINNER SPEAKER...KINDEST REGARDS..
11-6
I MUST BE OUT OF MY MIND!
SCHULZ

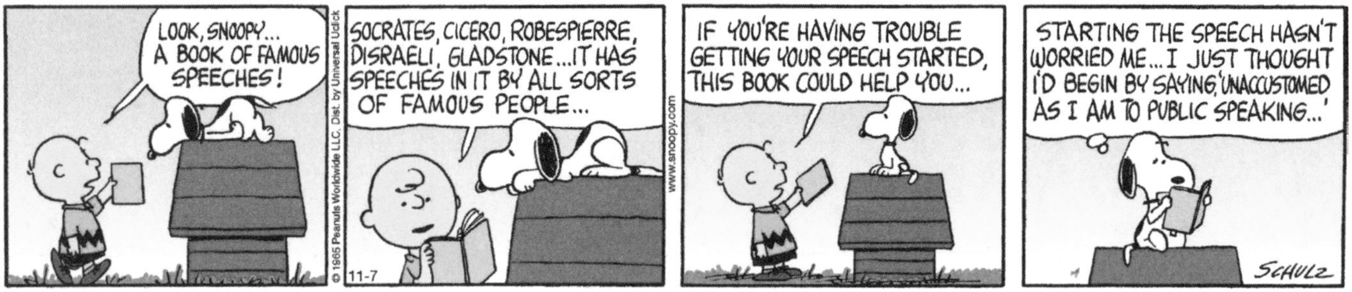
LOOK, SNOOPY... A BOOK OF FAMOUS SPEECHES!
© 1965 Peanuts Worldwide LLC, Dist. by Universal Uclick
11-7
SOCRATES, CICERO, ROBESPIERRE, DISRAELI, GLADSTONE...IT HAS SPEECHES IN IT BY ALL SORTS OF FAMOUS PEOPLE...
www.snoopy.com
IF YOU'RE HAVING TROUBLE GETTING YOUR SPEECH STARTED, THIS BOOK COULD HELP YOU...
STARTING THE SPEECH HASN'T WORRIED ME...I JUST THOUGHT I'D BEGIN BY SAYING, 'UNACCUSTOMED AS I AM TO PUBLIC SPEAKING...'
SCHULZ

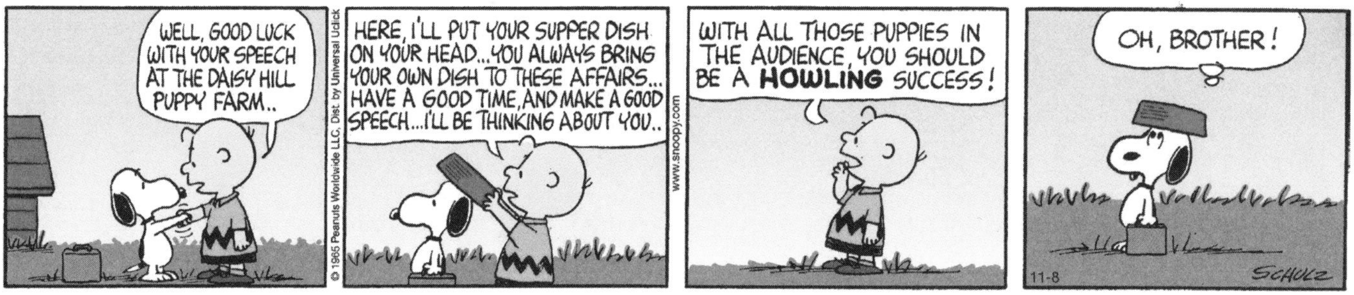
WELL, GOOD LUCK WITH YOUR SPEECH AT THE DAISY HILL PUPPY FARM..
© 1965 Peanuts Worldwide LLC, Dist. by Universal Uclick
HERE, I'LL PUT YOUR SUPPER DISH ON YOUR HEAD...YOU ALWAYS BRING YOUR OWN DISH TO THESE AFFAIRS... HAVE A GOOD TIME, AND MAKE A GOOD SPEECH...I'LL BE THINKING ABOUT YOU..
www.snoopy.com
WITH ALL THOSE PUPPIES IN THE AUDIENCE, YOU SHOULD BE A **HOWLING** SUCCESS!
OH, BROTHER!
11-8
SCHULZ

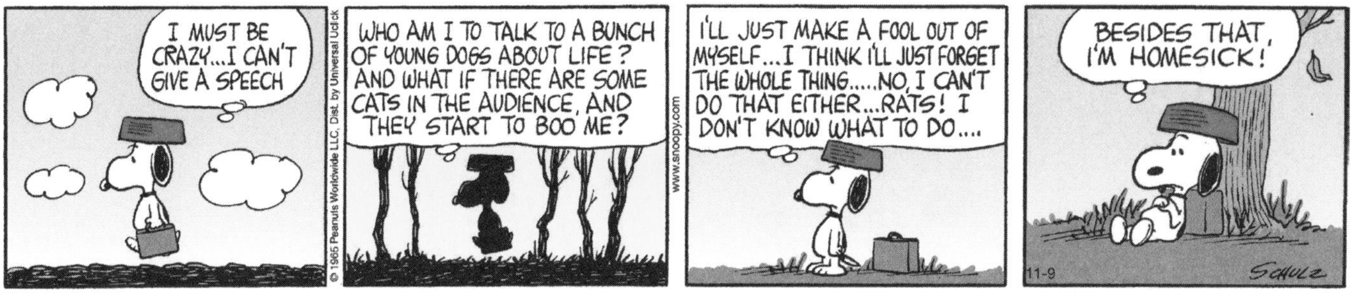
I MUST BE CRAZY...I CAN'T GIVE A SPEECH
© 1965 Peanuts Worldwide LLC, Dist. by Universal Uclick
WHO AM I TO TALK TO A BUNCH OF YOUNG DOGS ABOUT LIFE? AND WHAT IF THERE ARE SOME CATS IN THE AUDIENCE, AND THEY START TO BOO ME?
www.snoopy.com
I'LL JUST MAKE A FOOL OUT OF MYSELF...I THINK I'LL JUST FORGET THE WHOLE THING.....NO, I CAN'T DO THAT EITHER...RATS! I DON'T KNOW WHAT TO DO....
BESIDES THAT, I'M HOMESICK!
11-9
SCHULZ

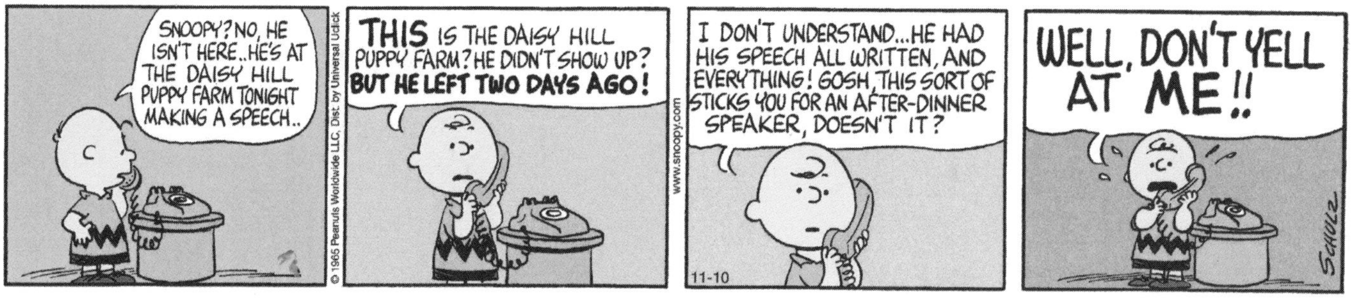
SNOOPY? NO, HE ISN'T HERE..HE'S AT THE DAISY HILL PUPPY FARM TONIGHT MAKING A SPEECH..
© 1965 Peanuts Worldwide LLC, Dist. by Universal Uclick
THIS IS THE DAISY HILL PUPPY FARM? HE DIDN'T SHOW UP? **BUT HE LEFT TWO DAYS AGO!**
www.snoopy.com
I DON'T UNDERSTAND...HE HAD HIS SPEECH ALL WRITTEN, AND EVERYTHING! GOSH, THIS SORT OF STICKS YOU FOR AN AFTER-DINNER SPEAKER, DOESN'T IT?
11-10
WELL, DON'T YELL AT **ME**!!
SCHULZ

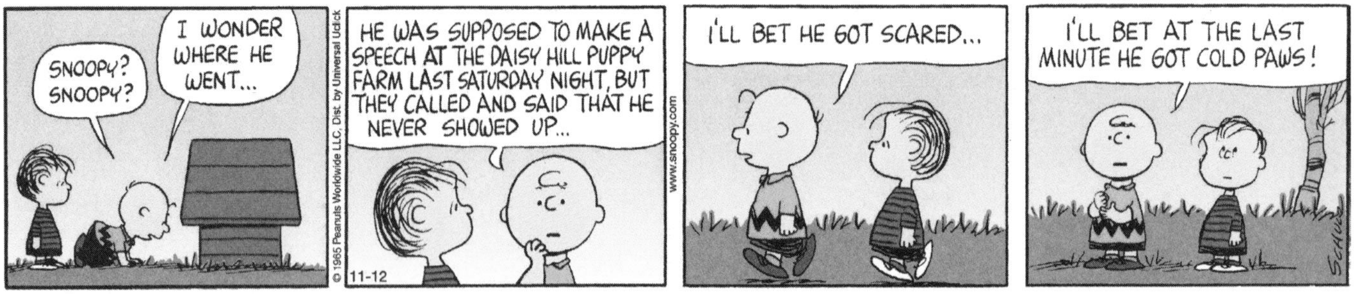
SNOOPY? SNOOPY?
I WONDER WHERE HE WENT...
© 1965 Peanuts Worldwide LLC, Dist. by Universal Uclick
HE WAS SUPPOSED TO MAKE A SPEECH AT THE DAISY HILL PUPPY FARM LAST SATURDAY NIGHT, BUT THEY CALLED AND SAID THAT HE NEVER SHOWED UP...
11-12
www.snoopy.com
I'LL BET HE GOT SCARED...
I'LL BET AT THE LAST MINUTE HE GOT COLD PAWS!
SCHULZ

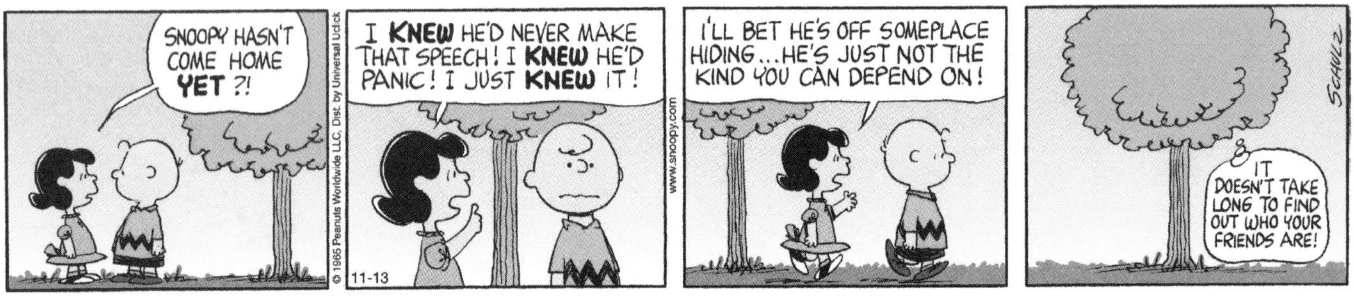
SNOOPY HASN'T COME HOME **YET** ?!
© 1965 Peanuts Worldwide LLC, Dist. by Universal Uclick
I **KNEW** HE'D NEVER MAKE THAT SPEECH! I **KNEW** HE'D PANIC! I JUST **KNEW** IT!
11-13
www.snoopy.com
I'LL BET HE'S OFF SOMEPLACE HIDING...HE'S JUST NOT THE KIND YOU CAN DEPEND ON!
SCHULZ
IT DOESN'T TAKE LONG TO FIND OUT WHO YOUR FRIENDS ARE!

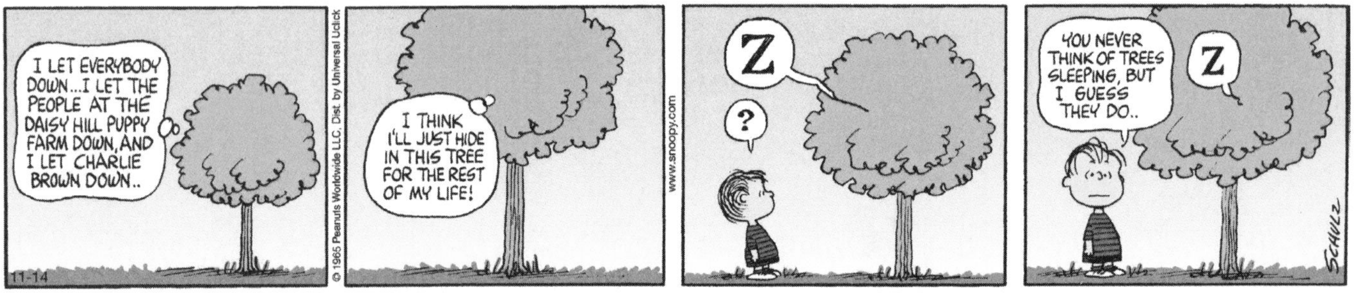
I LET EVERYBODY DOWN...I LET THE PEOPLE AT THE DAISY HILL PUPPY FARM DOWN, AND I LET CHARLIE BROWN DOWN..
11-14
© 1965 Peanuts Worldwide LLC, Dist. by Universal Uclick
I THINK I'LL JUST HIDE IN THIS TREE FOR THE REST OF MY LIFE!
www.snoopy.com
Z
?
YOU NEVER THINK OF TREES SLEEPING, BUT I GUESS THEY DO..
Z
SCHULZ

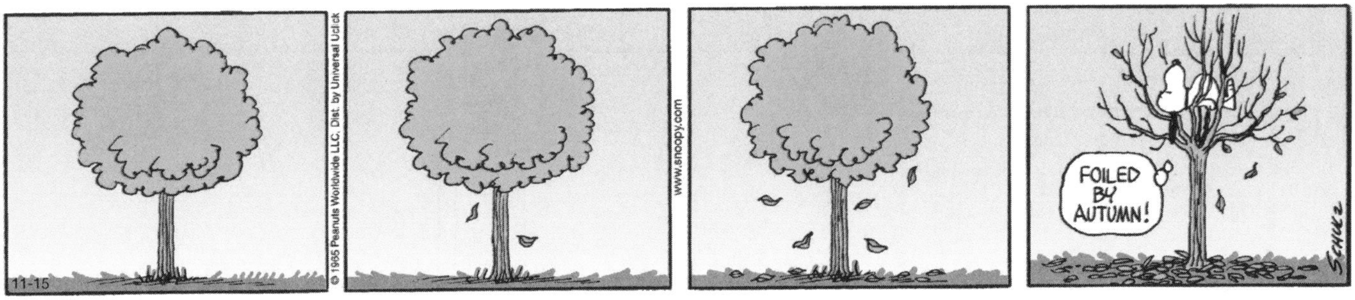
11-15
© 1965 Peanuts Worldwide LLC. Dist. by Universal Uclick
www.snoopy.com
FOILED BY AUTUMN!
SCHULZ

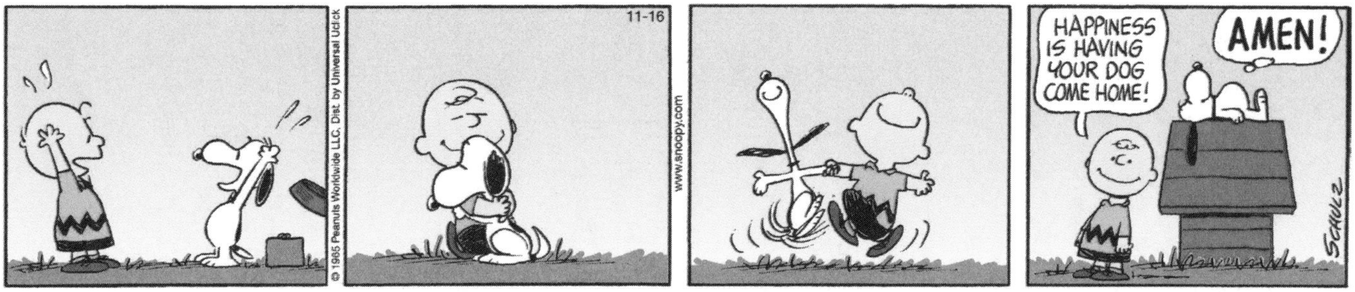
© 1965 Peanuts Worldwide LLC. Dist. by Universal Uclick
11-16
www.snoopy.com
HAPPINESS IS HAVING YOUR DOG COME HOME!
AMEN!
SCHULZ

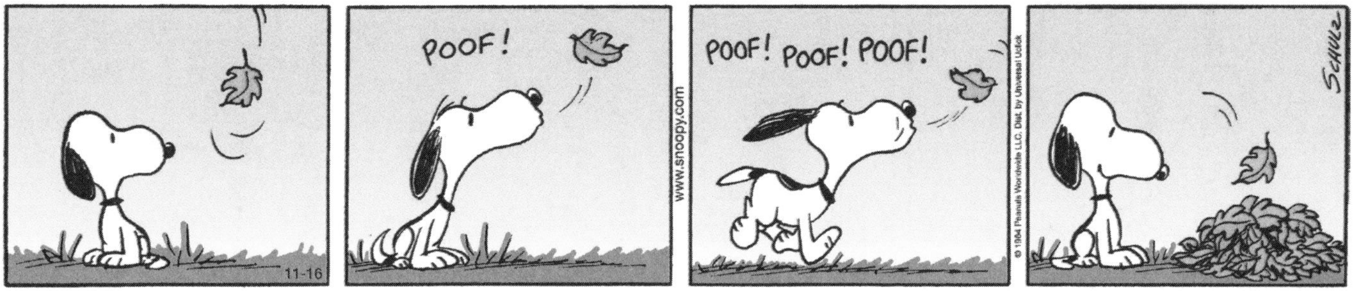
11-16
POOF!
www.snoopy.com
POOF! POOF! POOF!
© 1964 Peanuts Worldwide LLC. Dist. by Universal Uclick
SCHULZ

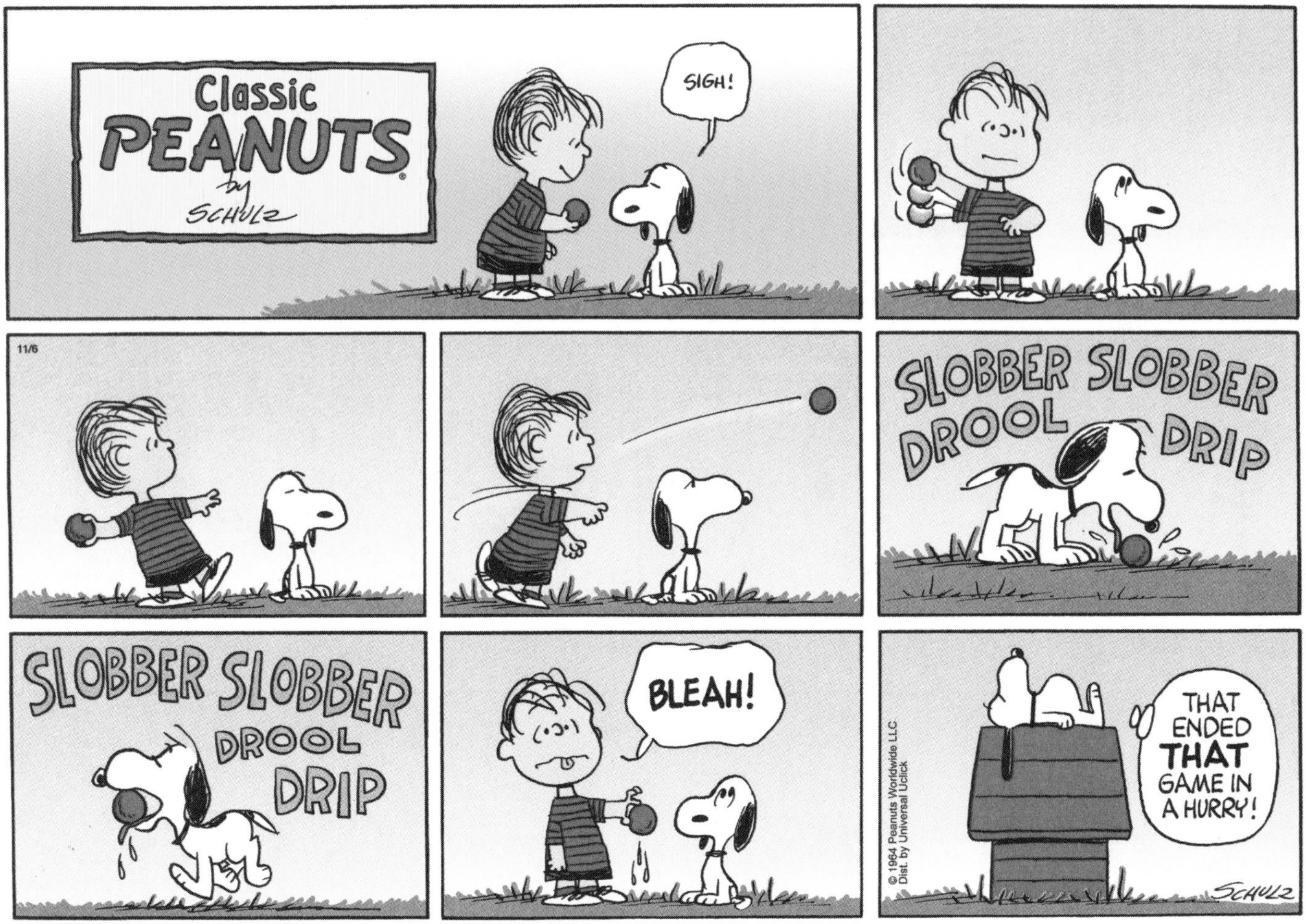
Classic PEANUTS by SCHULZ
SIGH!
11/6
SLOBBER SLOBBER DROOL DRIP
SLOBBER SLOBBER DROOL DRIP
BLEAH!
© 1964 Peanuts Worldwide LLC
Dist. by Universal Uclick
THAT ENDED THAT GAME IN A HURRY!
SCHULZ

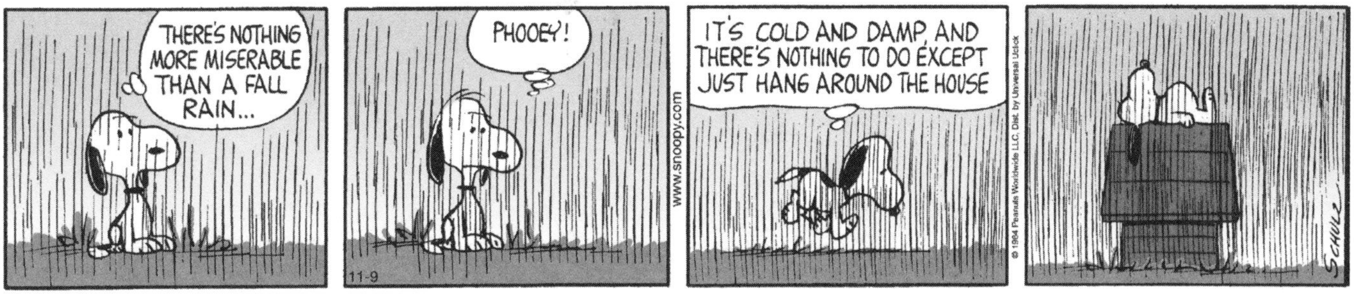
THERE'S NOTHING MORE MISERABLE THAN A FALL RAIN...
11-9
PHOOEY!
www.snoopy.com
IT'S COLD AND DAMP, AND THERE'S NOTHING TO DO EXCEPT JUST HANG AROUND THE HOUSE
© 1964 Peanuts Worldwide LLC. Dist. by Universal Uclick
SCHULZ

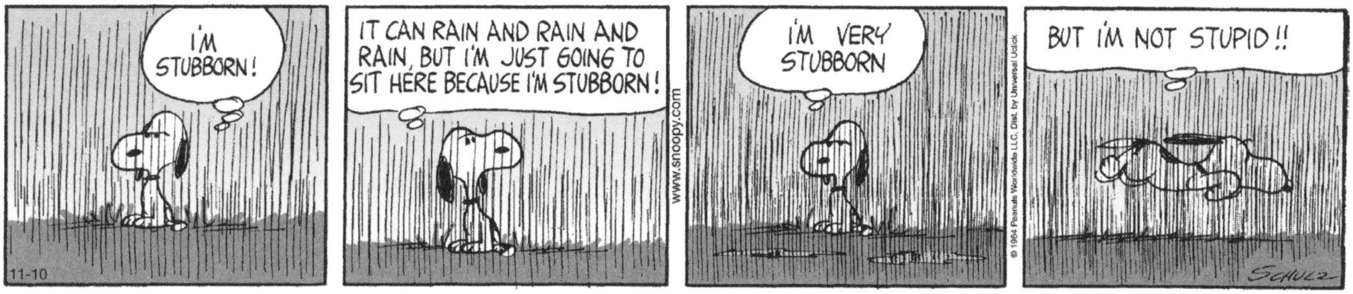
I'M STUBBORN!
11-10
IT CAN RAIN AND RAIN AND RAIN, BUT I'M JUST GOING TO SIT HERE BECAUSE I'M STUBBORN!
www.snoopy.com
I'M VERY STUBBORN
© 1964 Peanuts Worldwide LLC. Dist. by Universal Uclick
BUT I'M NOT STUPID!!
SCHULZ

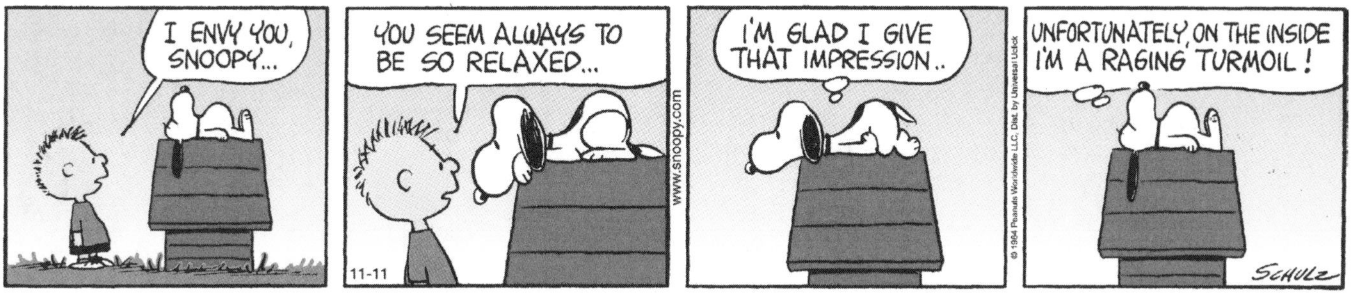
I ENVY YOU, SNOOPY...
YOU SEEM ALWAYS TO BE SO RELAXED...
11-11
www.snoopy.com
I'M GLAD I GIVE THAT IMPRESSION..
© 1964 Peanuts Worldwide LLC. Dist. by Universal Uclick
UNFORTUNATELY, ON THE INSIDE I'M A RAGING TURMOIL!
SCHULZ

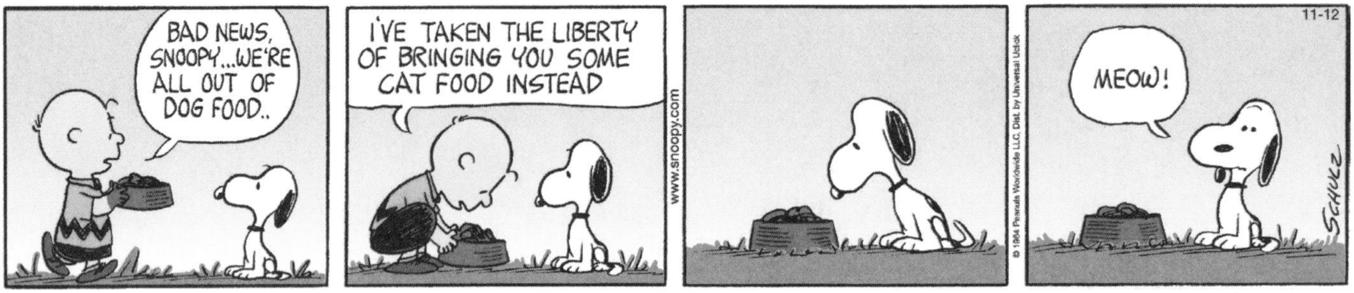
BAD NEWS, SNOOPY...WE'RE ALL OUT OF DOG FOOD..
I'VE TAKEN THE LIBERTY OF BRINGING YOU SOME CAT FOOD INSTEAD
www.snoopy.com
© 1964 Peanuts Worldwide LLC. Dist. by Universal Uclick
11-12
MEOW!
SCHULZ

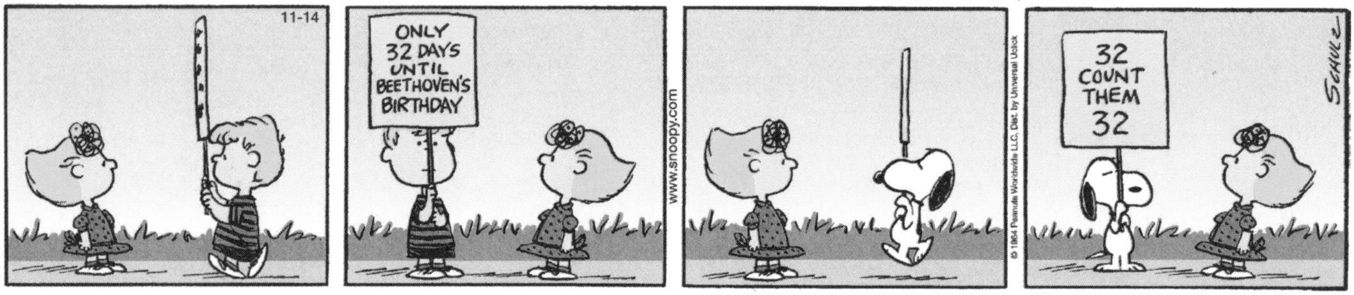
11-14
ONLY 32 DAYS UNTIL BEETHOVEN'S BIRTHDAY
www.snoopy.com
© 1964 Peanuts Worldwide LLC. Dist. by Universal Uclick
32 COUNT THEM 32
SCHULZ

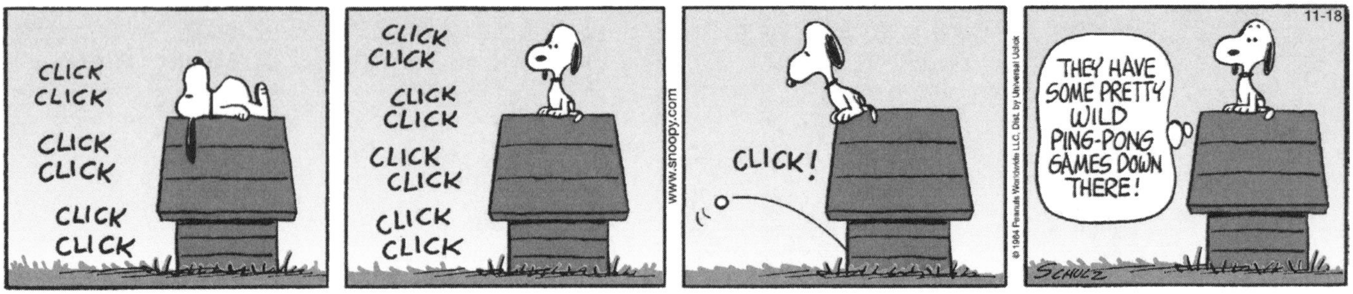
CLICK CLICK
CLICK CLICK
CLICK CLICK
CLICK CLICK
CLICK CLICK
CLICK CLICK
CLICK CLICK
www.snoopy.com
CLICK!
© 1964 Peanuts Worldwide LLC. Dist. by Universal Uclick
11-18
THEY HAVE SOME PRETTY WILD PING-PONG GAMES DOWN THERE!
SCHULZ

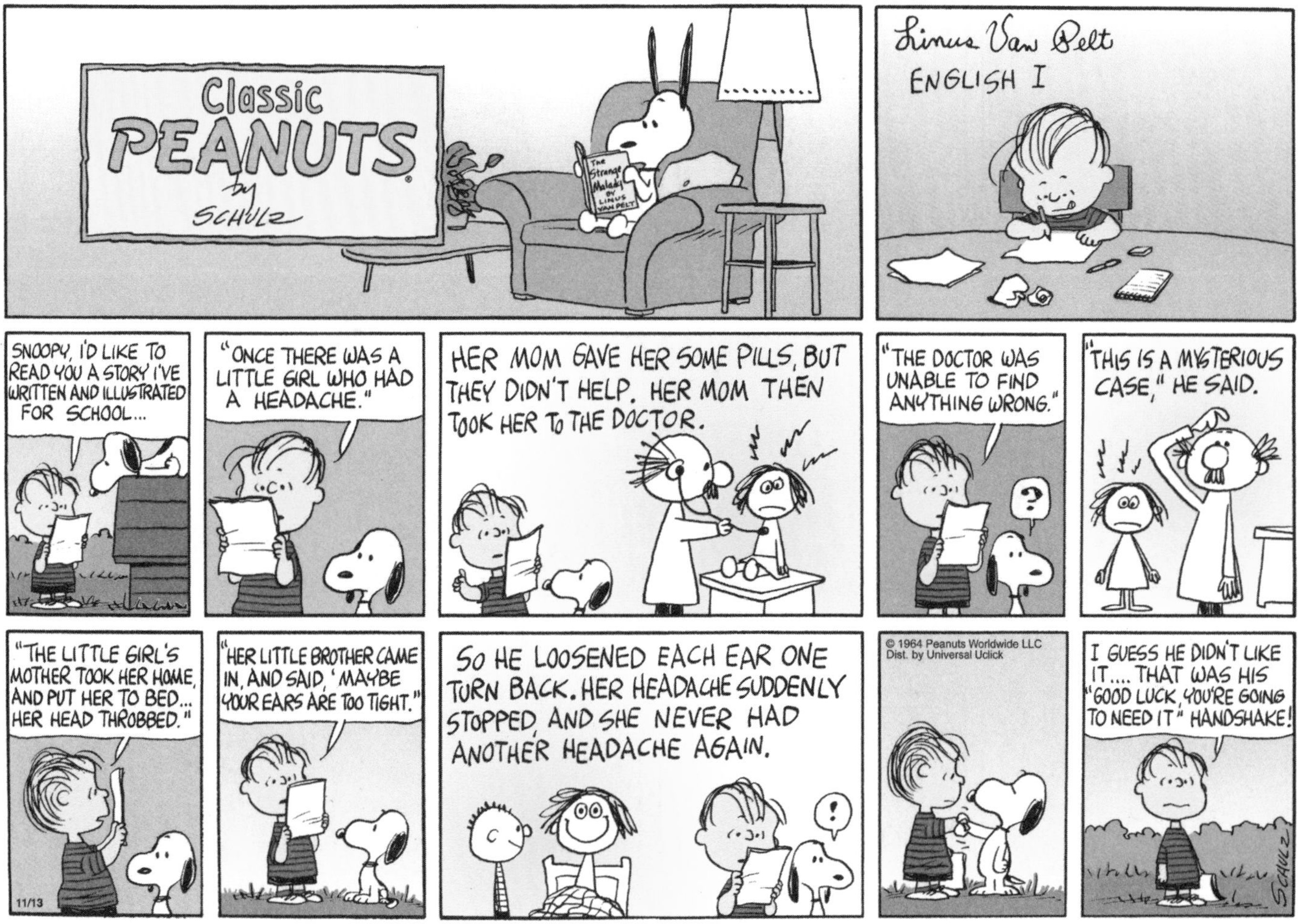
Classic PEANUTS by SCHULZ
The Strange Malady BY LINUS VAN PELT
Linus Van Pelt
ENGLISH I
SNOOPY, I'D LIKE TO READ YOU A STORY I'VE WRITTEN AND ILLUSTRATED FOR SCHOOL...
"ONCE THERE WAS A LITTLE GIRL WHO HAD A HEADACHE."
HER MOM GAVE HER SOME PILLS, BUT THEY DIDN'T HELP. HER MOM THEN TOOK HER TO THE DOCTOR.
"THE DOCTOR WAS UNABLE TO FIND ANYTHING WRONG."
?
"THIS IS A MYSTERIOUS CASE," HE SAID.
"THE LITTLE GIRL'S MOTHER TOOK HER HOME, AND PUT HER TO BED... HER HEAD THROBBED."
11/13
"HER LITTLE BROTHER CAME IN, AND SAID, 'MAYBE YOUR EARS ARE TOO TIGHT.'"
SO HE LOOSENED EACH EAR ONE TURN BACK. HER HEADACHE SUDDENLY STOPPED, AND SHE NEVER HAD ANOTHER HEADACHE AGAIN.
!
© 1964 Peanuts Worldwide LLC
Dist. by Universal Uclick
I GUESS HE DIDN'T LIKE IT.... THAT WAS HIS "GOOD LUCK, YOU'RE GOING TO NEED IT" HANDSHAKE!
SCHULZ

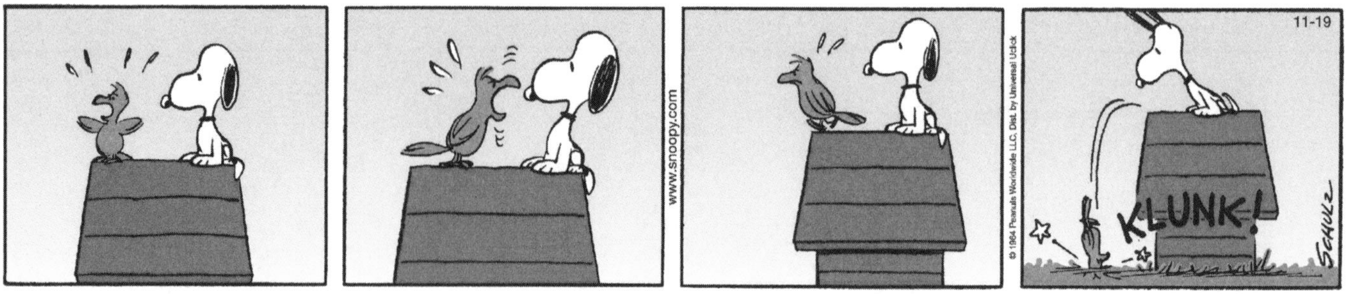
www.snoopy.com
© 1964 Peanuts Worldwide LLC, Dist. by Universal Uclick
11-19
KLUNK!
SCHULZ

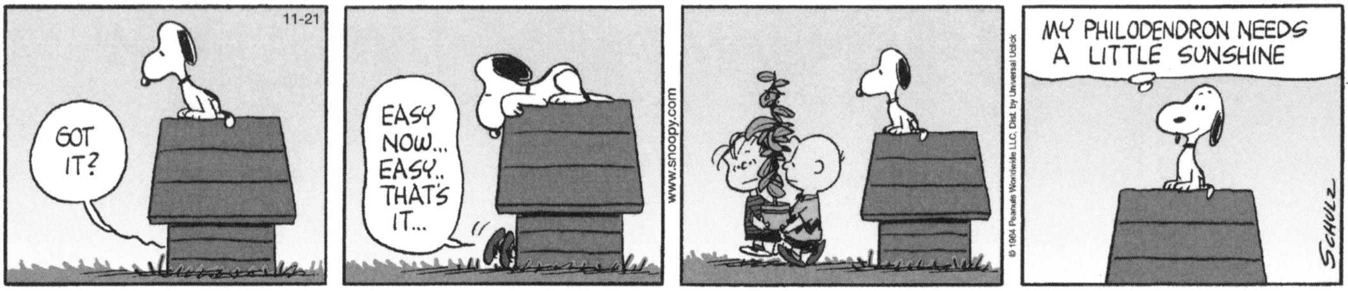
11-21
GOT IT?
EASY NOW... EASY.. THAT'S IT...
www.snoopy.com
© 1964 Peanuts Worldwide LLC, Dist. by Universal Uclick
MY PHILODENDRON NEEDS A LITTLE SUNSHINE
SCHULZ

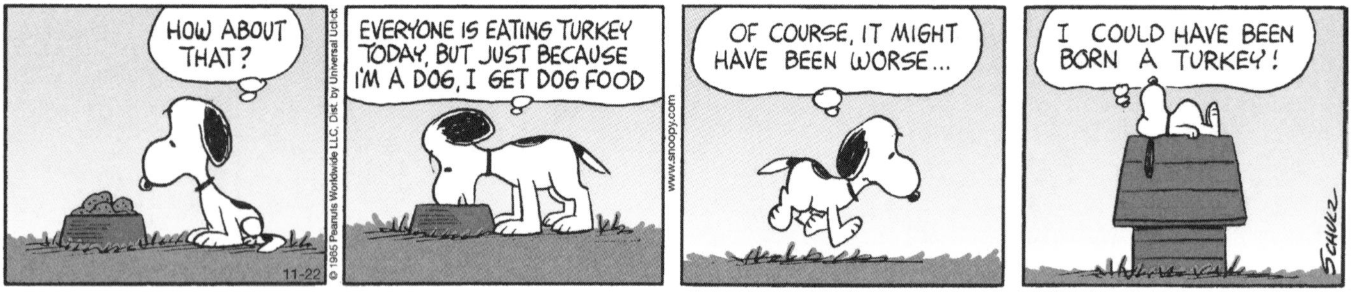
HOW ABOUT THAT?
11-22
© 1965 Peanuts Worldwide LLC, Dist. by Universal Uclick
EVERYONE IS EATING TURKEY TODAY, BUT JUST BECAUSE I'M A DOG, I GET DOG FOOD
www.snoopy.com
OF COURSE, IT MIGHT HAVE BEEN WORSE...
I COULD HAVE BEEN BORN A TURKEY!
SCHULZ

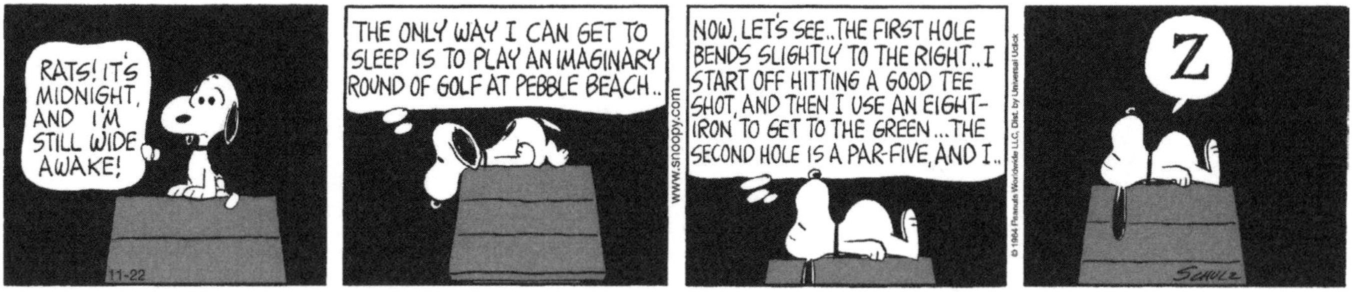
11-22
RATS! IT'S MIDNIGHT, AND I'M STILL WIDE AWAKE!
THE ONLY WAY I CAN GET TO SLEEP IS TO PLAY AN IMAGINARY ROUND OF GOLF AT PEBBLE BEACH..
www.snoopy.com
NOW, LET'S SEE..THE FIRST HOLE BENDS SLIGHTLY TO THE RIGHT..I START OFF HITTING A GOOD TEE SHOT, AND THEN I USE AN EIGHT-IRON TO GET TO THE GREEN...THE SECOND HOLE IS A PAR-FIVE, AND I..
© 1964 Peanuts Worldwide LLC, Dist. by Universal Uclick
Z
SCHULZ

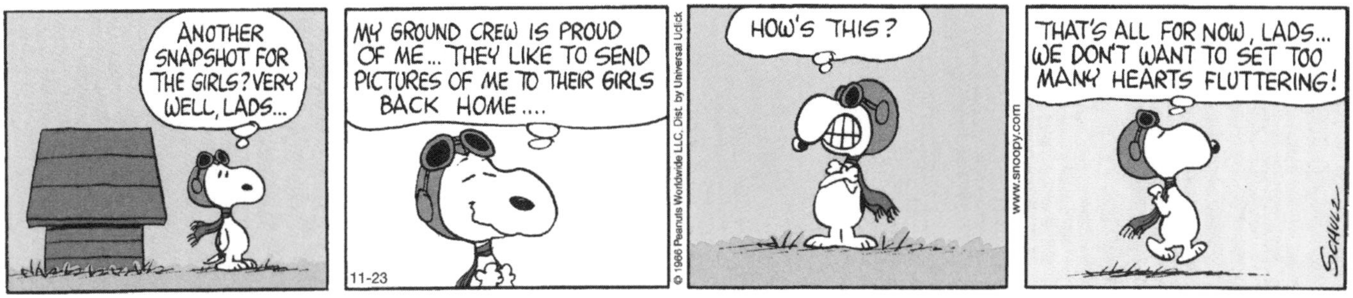
ANOTHER SNAPSHOT FOR THE GIRLS? VERY WELL, LADS...
MY GROUND CREW IS PROUD OF ME... THEY LIKE TO SEND PICTURES OF ME TO THEIR GIRLS BACK HOME....
11-23
© 1966 Peanuts Worldwide LLC, Dist. by Universal Uclick
HOW'S THIS?
www.snoopy.com
THAT'S ALL FOR NOW, LADS... WE DON'T WANT TO SET TOO MANY HEARTS FLUTTERING!
SCHULZ

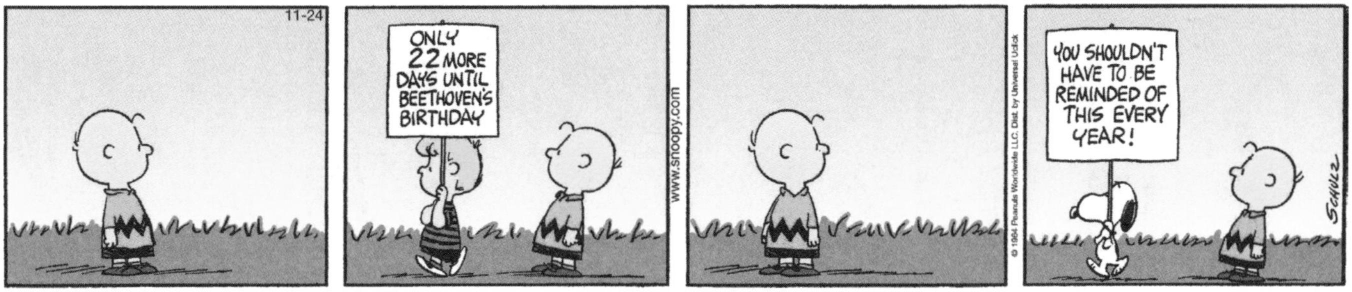
11-24
ONLY 22 MORE DAYS UNTIL BEETHOVEN'S BIRTHDAY
www.snoopy.com
© 1964 Peanuts Worldwide LLC, Dist. by Universal Uclick
YOU SHOULDN'T HAVE TO BE REMINDED OF THIS EVERY YEAR!
SCHULZ

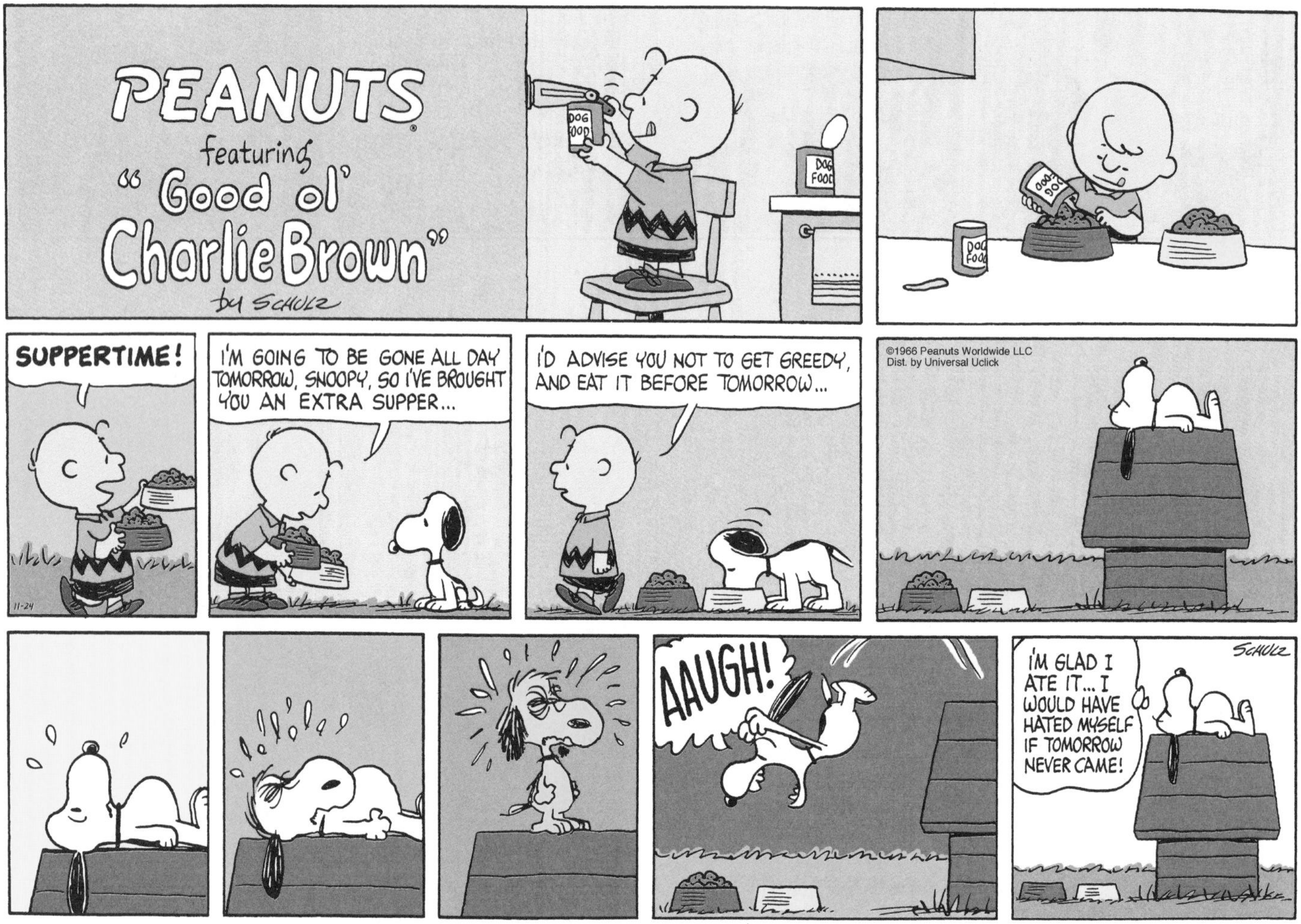
PEANUTS
featuring
"Good ol' Charlie Brown"
by SCHULZ
DOG FOOD
DOG FOOD
DOG FOOD
DOG FOOD
SUPPERTIME!
I'M GOING TO BE GONE ALL DAY TOMORROW, SNOOPY, SO I'VE BROUGHT YOU AN EXTRA SUPPER...
I'D ADVISE YOU NOT TO GET GREEDY, AND EAT IT BEFORE TOMORROW...
©1966 Peanuts Worldwide LLC
Dist. by Universal Uclick
AAUGH!
I'M GLAD I ATE IT... I WOULD HAVE HATED MYSELF IF TOMORROW NEVER CAME!
SCHULZ

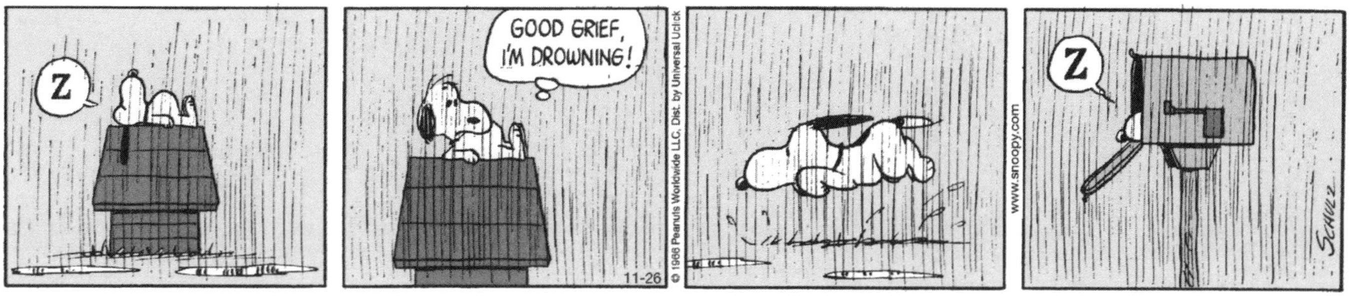
Z
GOOD GRIEF, I'M DROWNING!
11-26
© 1986 Peanuts Worldwide LLC, Dist. by Universal Uclick
www.snoopy.com
Z
SCHULZ

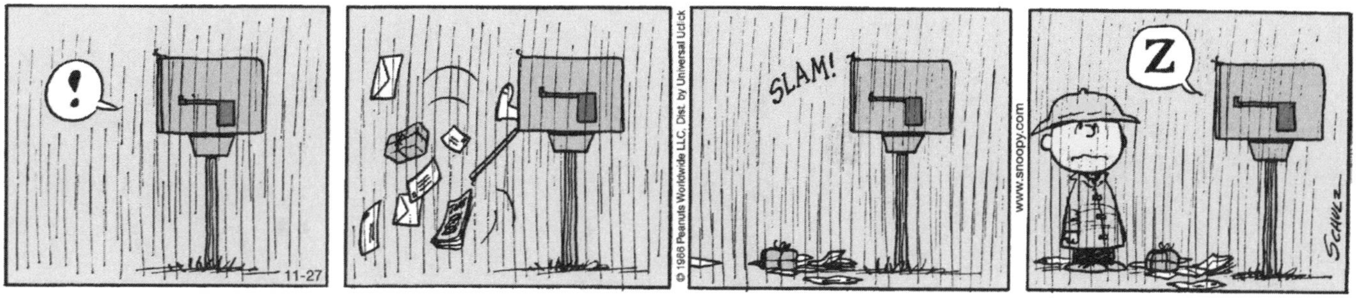
!
11-27
© 1986 Peanuts Worldwide LLC, Dist. by Universal Uclick
SLAM!
www.snoopy.com
Z
SCHULZ

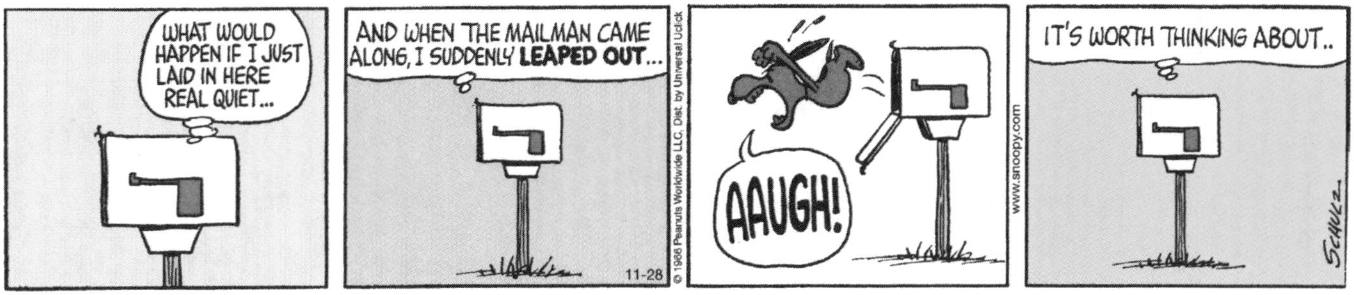
WHAT WOULD HAPPEN IF I JUST LAID IN HERE REAL QUIET...
AND WHEN THE MAILMAN CAME ALONG, I SUDDENLY **LEAPED OUT**...
11-28
© 1986 Peanuts Worldwide LLC, Dist. by Universal Uclick
AAUGH!
www.snoopy.com
IT'S WORTH THINKING ABOUT..
SCHULZ

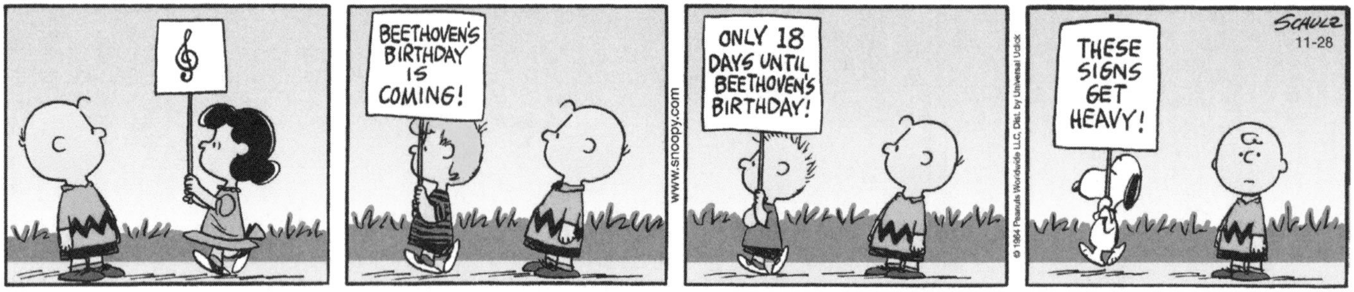
BEETHOVEN'S BIRTHDAY IS COMING!
ONLY 18 DAYS UNTIL BEETHOVEN'S BIRTHDAY!
THESE SIGNS GET HEAVY!
SCHULZ 11-28
www.snoopy.com
© 1964 Peanuts Worldwide LLC, Dist. by Universal Uclick

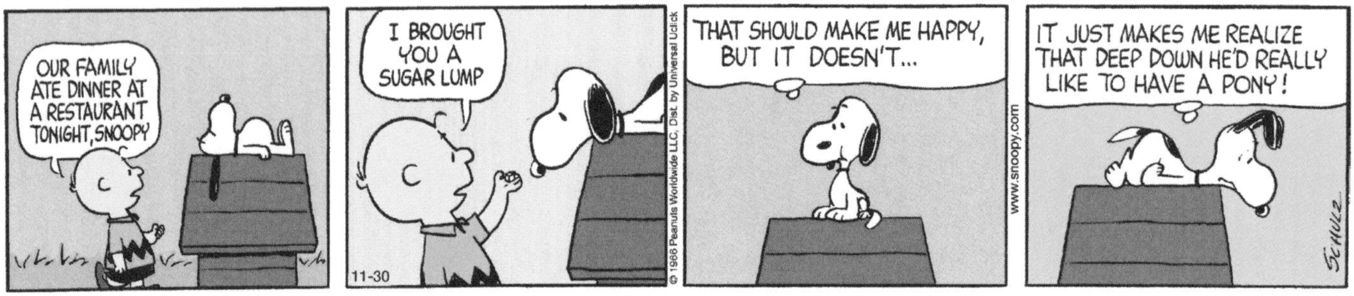
OUR FAMILY ATE DINNER AT A RESTAURANT TONIGHT, SNOOPY
I BROUGHT YOU A SUGAR LUMP
11-30
THAT SHOULD MAKE ME HAPPY, BUT IT DOESN'T...
IT JUST MAKES ME REALIZE THAT DEEP DOWN HE'D REALLY LIKE TO HAVE A PONY!
SCHULZ
© 1966 Peanuts Worldwide LLC, Dist. by Universal Uclick
www.snoopy.com

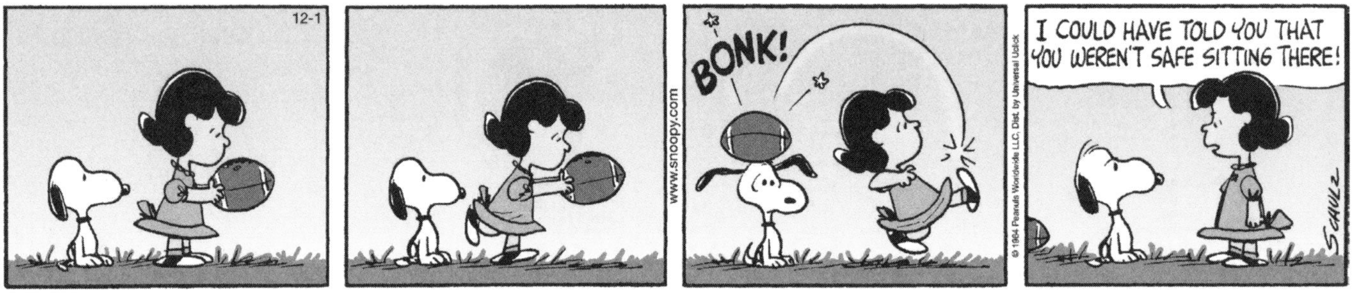
12-1
BONK!
I COULD HAVE TOLD YOU THAT YOU WEREN'T SAFE SITTING THERE!
SCHULZ
www.snoopy.com
© 1964 Peanuts Worldwide LLC, Dist. by Universal Uclick

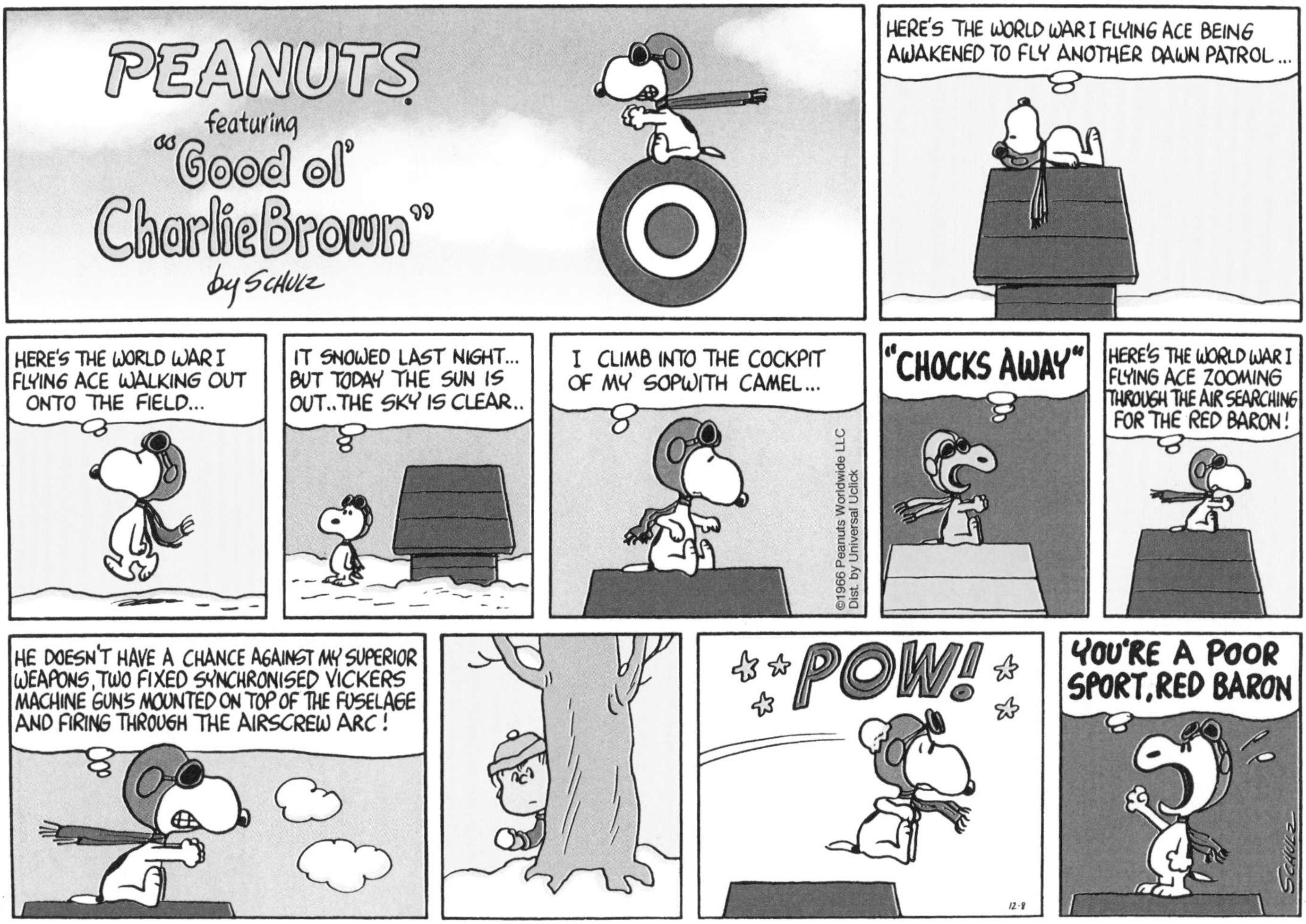
PEANUTS
featuring
"Good ol' Charlie Brown"
by SCHULZ
HERE'S THE WORLD WAR I FLYING ACE BEING AWAKENED TO FLY ANOTHER DAWN PATROL...
HERE'S THE WORLD WAR I FLYING ACE WALKING OUT ONTO THE FIELD...
IT SNOWED LAST NIGHT... BUT TODAY THE SUN IS OUT..THE SKY IS CLEAR..
I CLIMB INTO THE COCKPIT OF MY SOPWITH CAMEL...
©1966 Peanuts Worldwide LLC
Dist. by Universal Uclick
"CHOCKS AWAY"
HERE'S THE WORLD WAR I FLYING ACE ZOOMING THROUGH THE AIR SEARCHING FOR THE RED BARON!
HE DOESN'T HAVE A CHANCE AGAINST MY SUPERIOR WEAPONS, TWO FIXED SYNCHRONISED VICKERS MACHINE GUNS MOUNTED ON TOP OF THE FUSELAGE AND FIRING THROUGH THE AIRSCREW ARC!
POW!
12-8
YOU'RE A POOR SPORT, RED BARON
SCHULZ

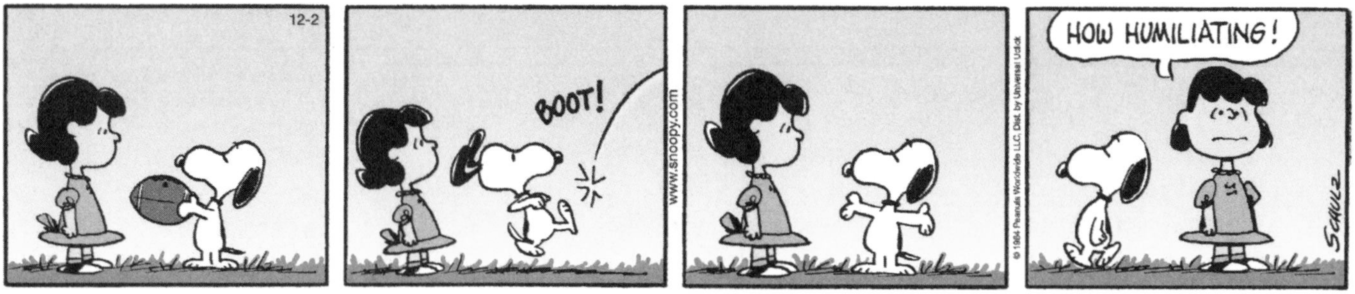
12-2
BOOT!
www.snoopy.com
© 1964 Peanuts Worldwide LLC. Dist. by Universal Uclick
HOW HUMILIATING!
SCHULZ

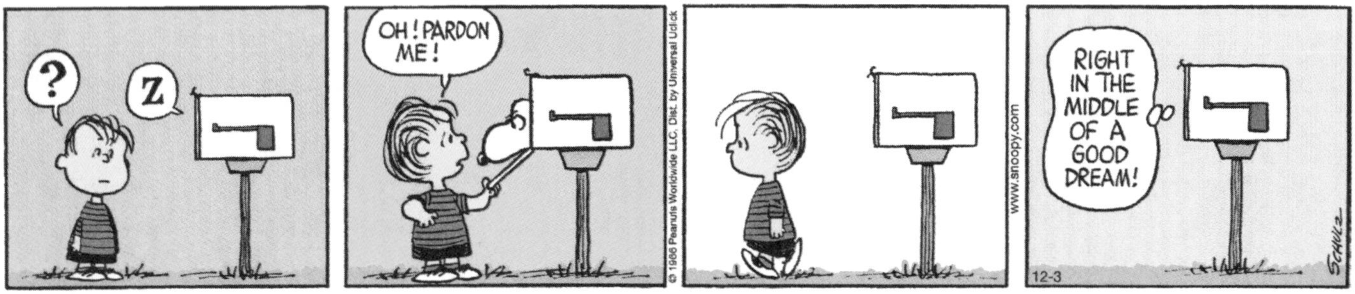
?
Z
OH! PARDON ME!
© 1966 Peanuts Worldwide LLC. Dist. by Universal Uclick
www.snoopy.com
RIGHT IN THE MIDDLE OF A GOOD DREAM!
12-3
SCHULZ

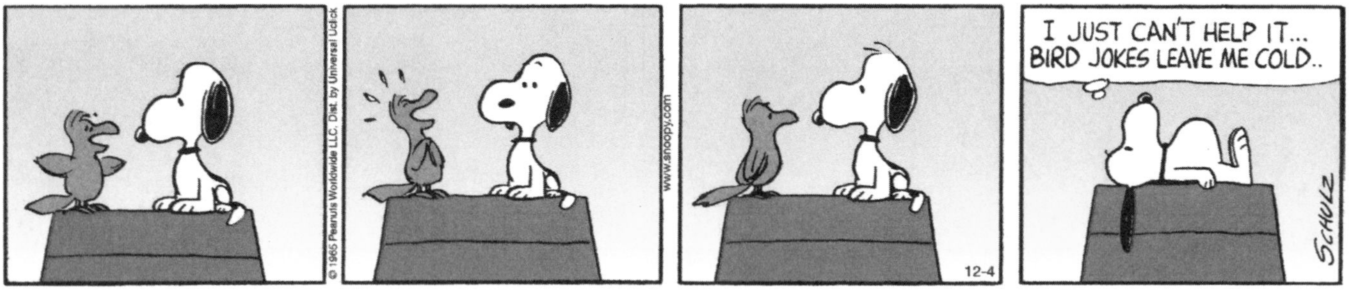
© 1965 Peanuts Worldwide LLC. Dist. by Universal Uclick
www.snoopy.com
12-4
I JUST CAN'T HELP IT... BIRD JOKES LEAVE ME COLD..
SCHULZ

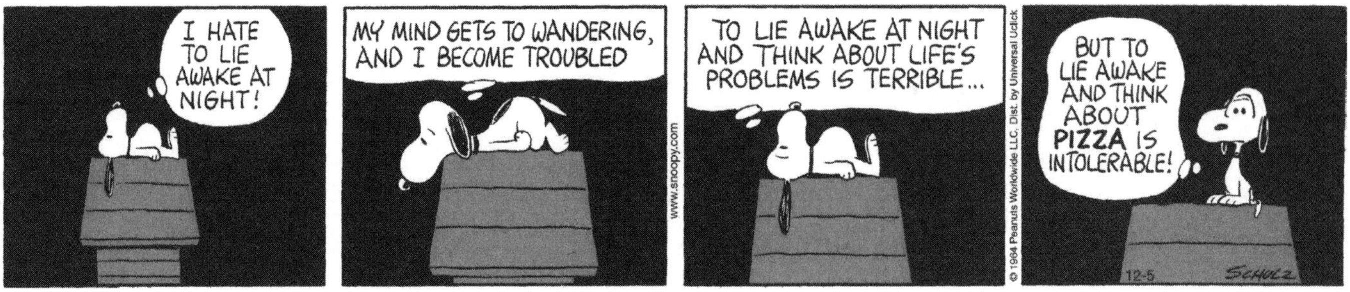
I HATE TO LIE AWAKE AT NIGHT!
MY MIND GETS TO WANDERING, AND I BECOME TROUBLED
TO LIE AWAKE AT NIGHT AND THINK ABOUT LIFE'S PROBLEMS IS TERRIBLE...
BUT TO LIE AWAKE AND THINK ABOUT **PIZZA** IS INTOLERABLE!
www.snoopy.com
© 1964 Peanuts Worldwide LLC. Dist. by Universal Uclick
12-5
SCHULZ

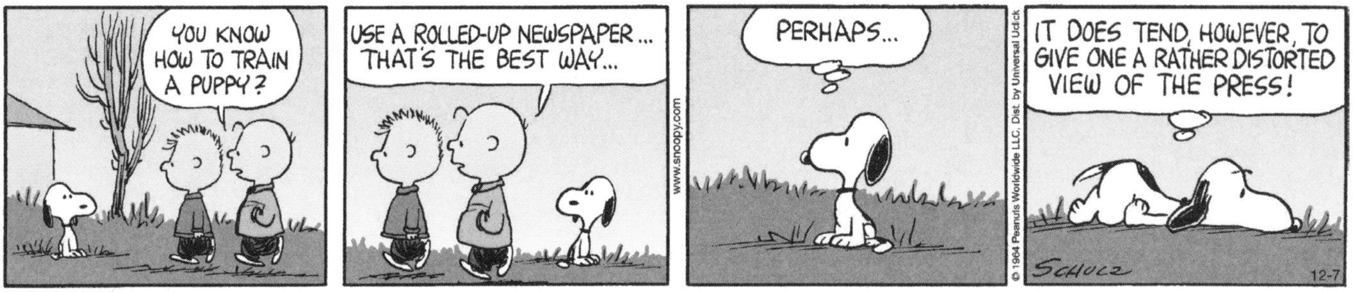
YOU KNOW HOW TO TRAIN A PUPPY?
USE A ROLLED-UP NEWSPAPER... THAT'S THE BEST WAY...
PERHAPS...
IT DOES TEND, HOWEVER, TO GIVE ONE A RATHER DISTORTED VIEW OF THE PRESS!
www.snoopy.com
© 1964 Peanuts Worldwide LLC. Dist. by Universal Uclick
SCHULZ
12-7

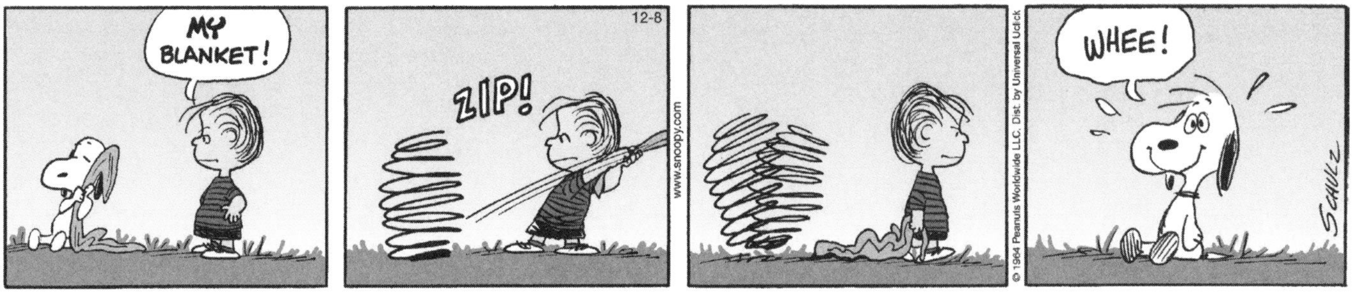
MY BLANKET!
12-8
ZIP!
WHEE!
www.snoopy.com
© 1964 Peanuts Worldwide LLC. Dist. by Universal Uclick
SCHULZ

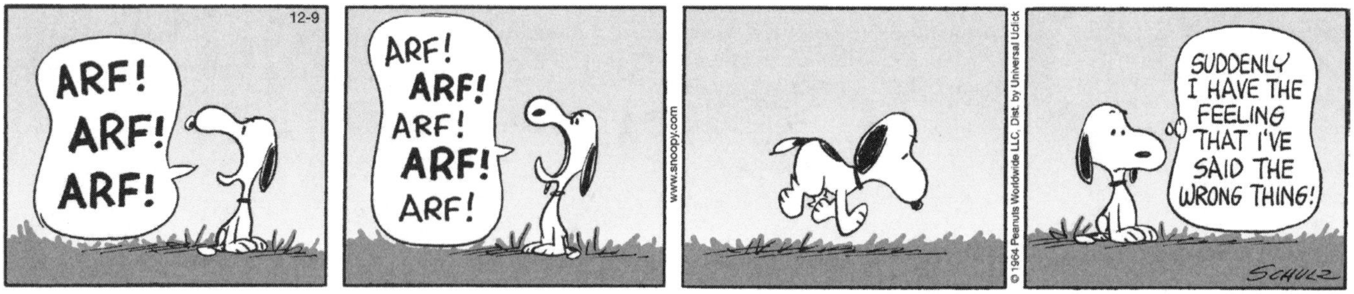
12-9
ARF! ARF! ARF!
ARF! ARF! ARF! ARF! ARF!
SUDDENLY I HAVE THE FEELING THAT I'VE SAID THE WRONG THING!
www.snoopy.com
© 1964 Peanuts Worldwide LLC. Dist. by Universal Uclick
SCHULZ

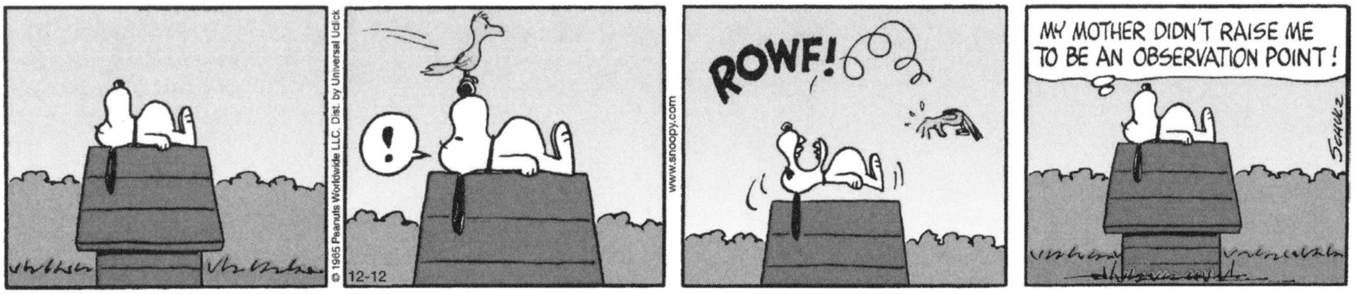
© 1965 Peanuts Worldwide LLC. Dist. by Universal Uclick
12-12
!
www.snoopy.com
ROWF!
MY MOTHER DIDN'T RAISE ME TO BE AN OBSERVATION POINT!
SCHULZ

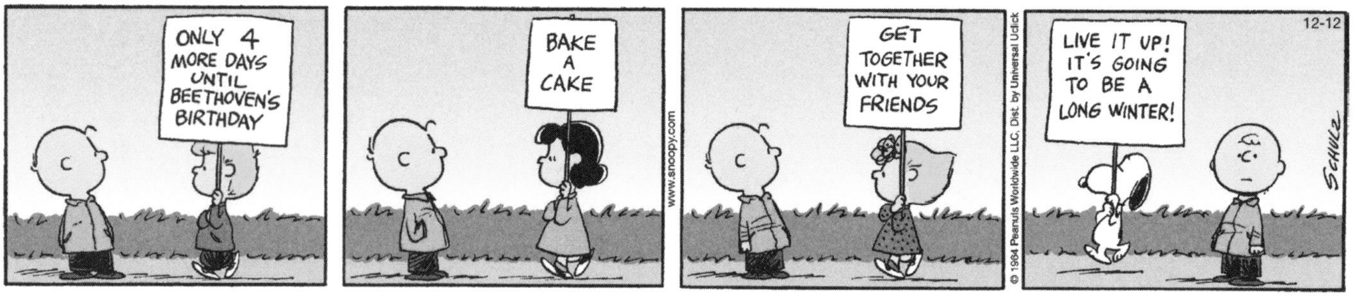
ONLY 4 MORE DAYS UNTIL BEETHOVEN'S BIRTHDAY
BAKE A CAKE
www.snoopy.com
GET TOGETHER WITH YOUR FRIENDS
© 1964 Peanuts Worldwide LLC. Dist. by Universal Uclick
12-12
LIVE IT UP! IT'S GOING TO BE A LONG WINTER!
SCHULZ

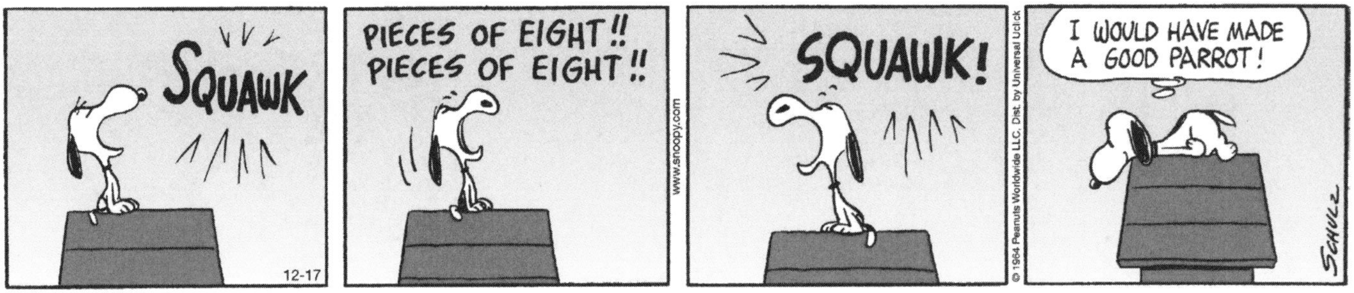
SQUAWK
12-17
PIECES OF EIGHT!! PIECES OF EIGHT!!
www.snoopy.com
SQUAWK!
© 1964 Peanuts Worldwide LLC, Dist. by Universal Uclick
I WOULD HAVE MADE A GOOD PARROT!
SCHULZ

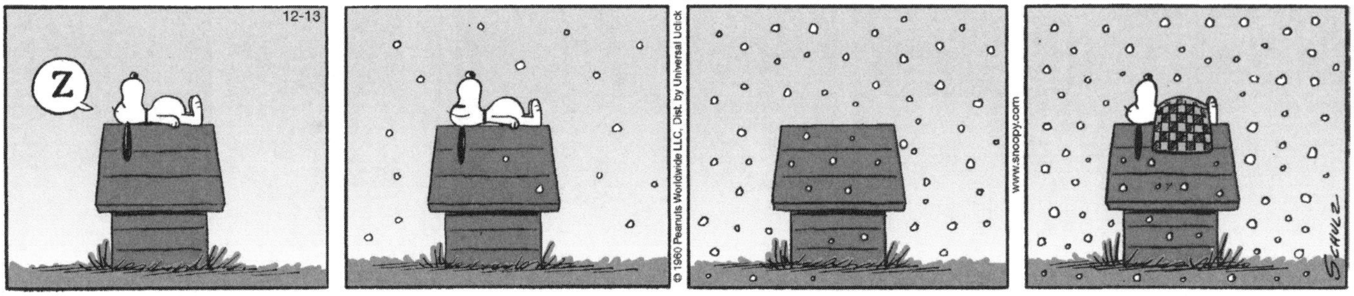
12-13
Z
© 1960 Peanuts Worldwide LLC, Dist. by Universal Uclick
www.snoopy.com
SCHULZ

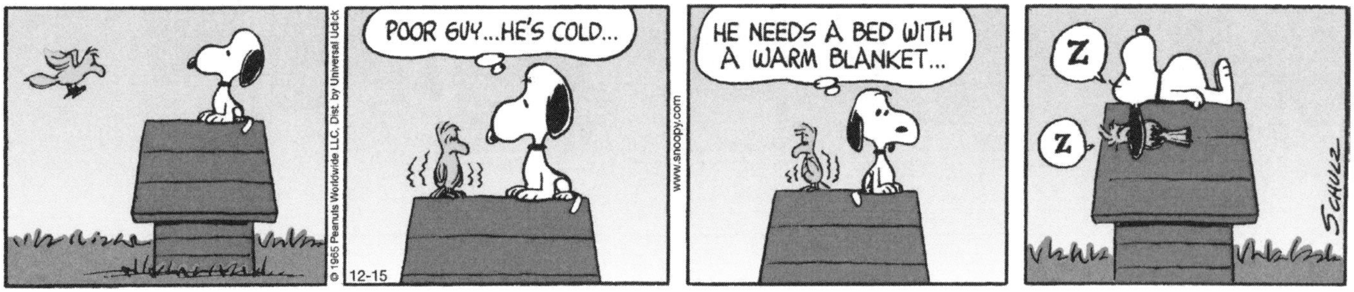
© 1965 Peanuts Worldwide LLC, Dist. by Universal Uclick
POOR GUY...HE'S COLD...
12-15
www.snoopy.com
HE NEEDS A BED WITH A WARM BLANKET...
Z
Z
SCHULZ

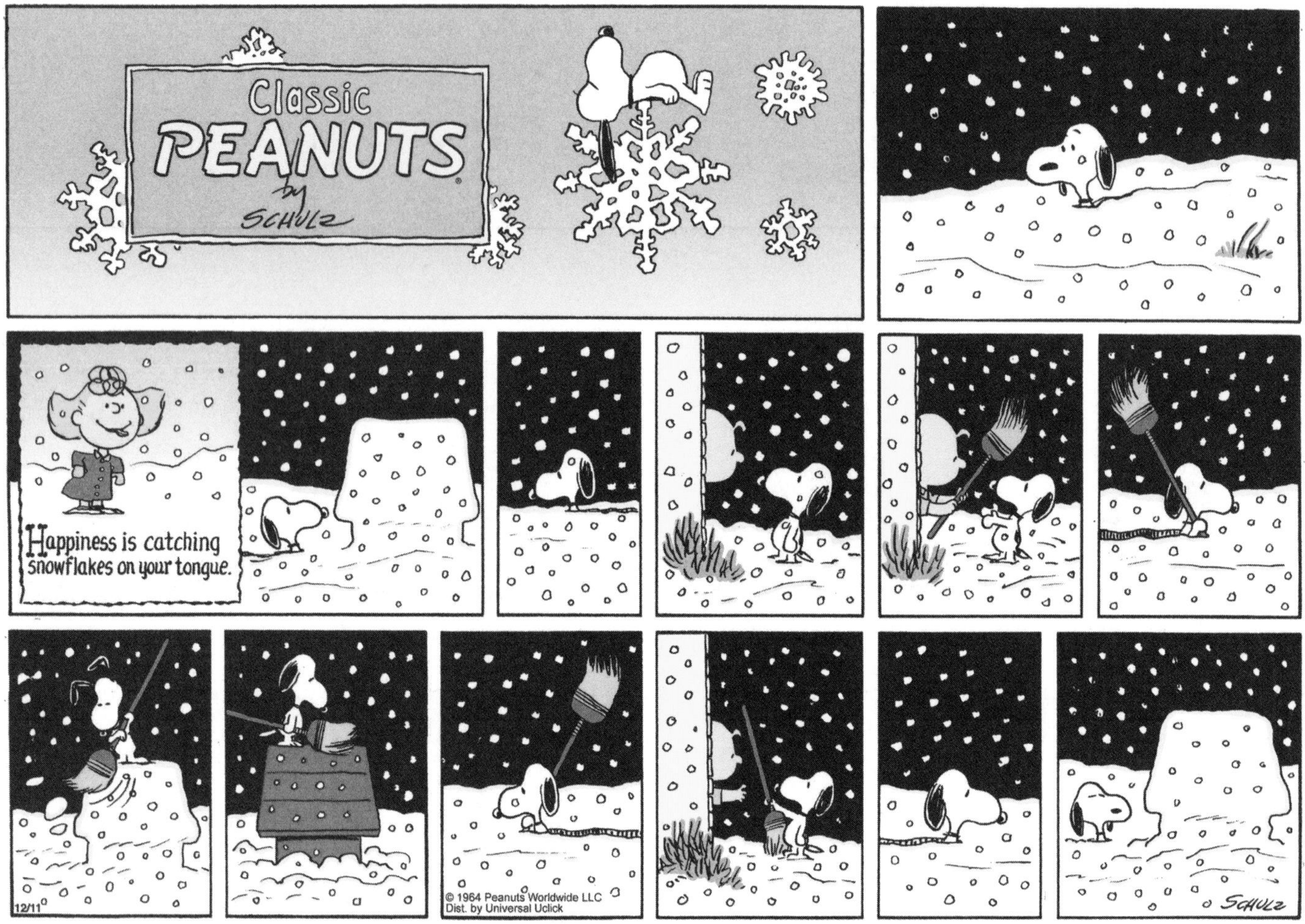
Classic
PEANUTS
by
SCHULZ
Happiness is catching snowflakes on your tongue.
12/11
© 1964 Peanuts Worldwide LLC
Dist. by Universal Uclick
SCHULZ

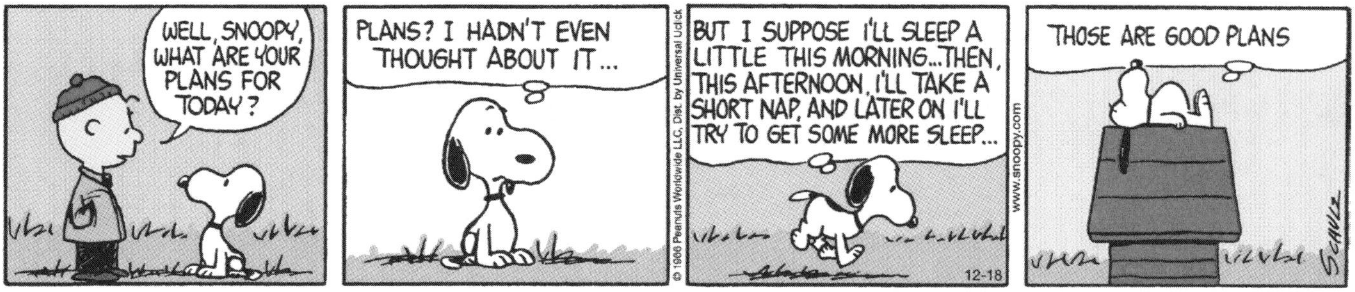
WELL, SNOOPY, WHAT ARE YOUR PLANS FOR TODAY?
PLANS? I HADN'T EVEN THOUGHT ABOUT IT...
BUT I SUPPOSE I'LL SLEEP A LITTLE THIS MORNING...THEN, THIS AFTERNOON, I'LL TAKE A SHORT NAP, AND LATER ON I'LL TRY TO GET SOME MORE SLEEP...
12-18
www.snoopy.com
THOSE ARE GOOD PLANS
SCHULZ

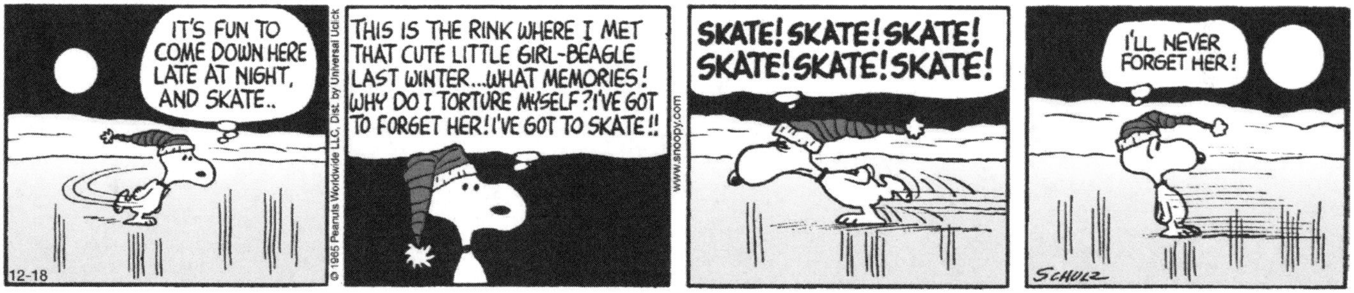
IT'S FUN TO COME DOWN HERE LATE AT NIGHT, AND SKATE..
12-18
THIS IS THE RINK WHERE I MET THAT CUTE LITTLE GIRL-BEAGLE LAST WINTER...WHAT MEMORIES! WHY DO I TORTURE MYSELF? I'VE GOT TO FORGET HER! I'VE GOT TO SKATE!!
www.snoopy.com
SKATE! SKATE! SKATE! SKATE! SKATE! SKATE!
I'LL NEVER FORGET HER!
SCHULZ

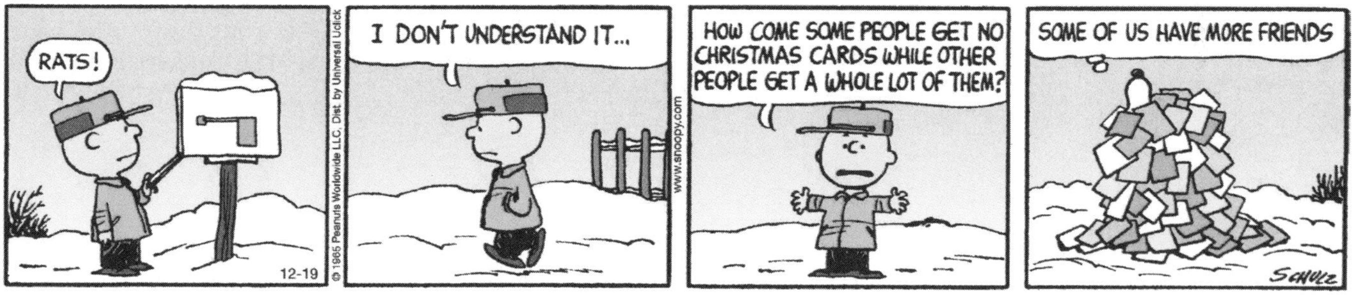
RATS!
12-19
I DON'T UNDERSTAND IT...
www.snoopy.com
HOW COME SOME PEOPLE GET NO CHRISTMAS CARDS WHILE OTHER PEOPLE GET A WHOLE LOT OF THEM?
SOME OF US HAVE MORE FRIENDS
SCHULZ

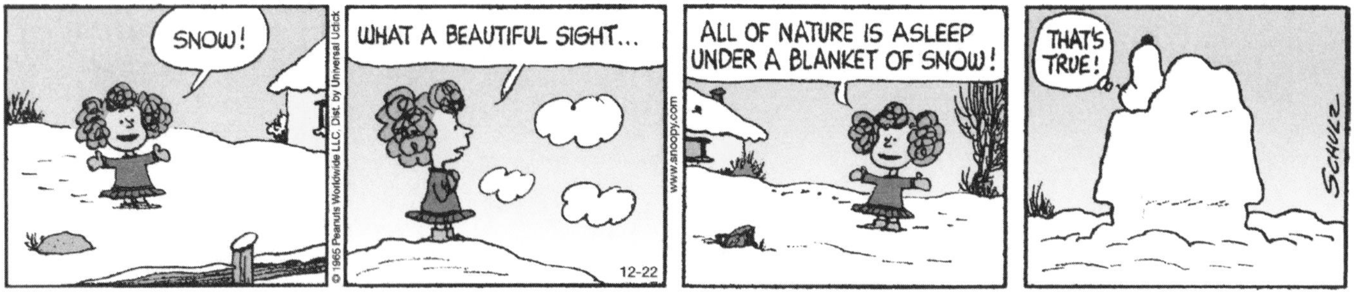
SNOW!
© 1965 Peanuts Worldwide LLC. Dist. by Universal Uclick
WHAT A BEAUTIFUL SIGHT...
12-22
www.snoopy.com
ALL OF NATURE IS ASLEEP UNDER A BLANKET OF SNOW!
THAT'S TRUE!
SCHULZ

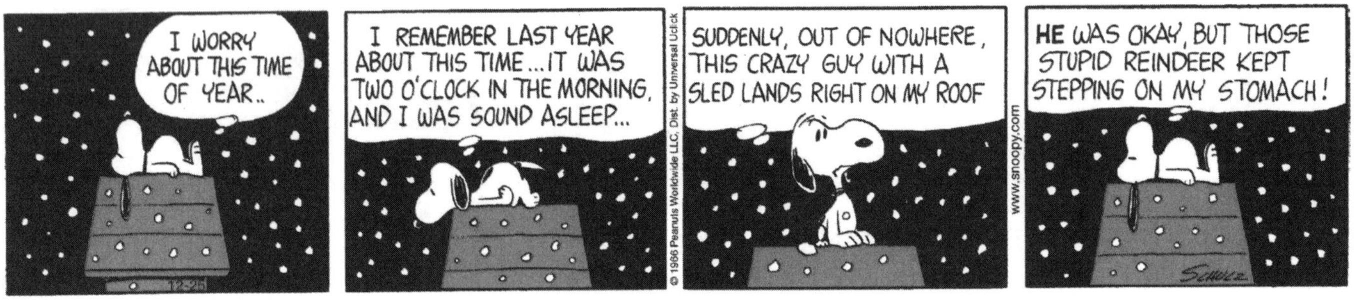
I WORRY ABOUT THIS TIME OF YEAR..
I REMEMBER LAST YEAR ABOUT THIS TIME...IT WAS TWO O'CLOCK IN THE MORNING, AND I WAS SOUND ASLEEP...
© 1966 Peanuts Worldwide LLC. Dist. by Universal Uclick
SUDDENLY, OUT OF NOWHERE, THIS CRAZY GUY WITH A SLED LANDS RIGHT ON MY ROOF
www.snoopy.com
HE WAS OKAY, BUT THOSE STUPID REINDEER KEPT STEPPING ON MY STOMACH!
SCHULZ

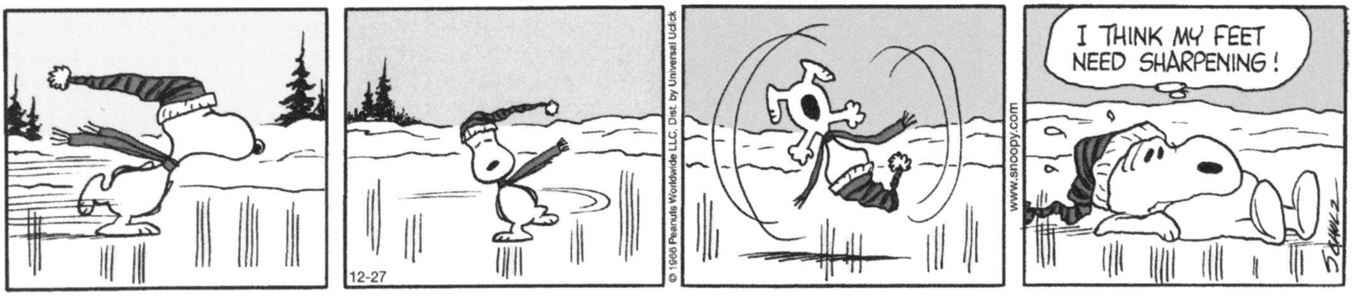
12-27
© 1966 Peanuts Worldwide LLC. Dist. by Universal Uclick
www.snoopy.com
I THINK MY FEET NEED SHARPENING!
SCHULZ

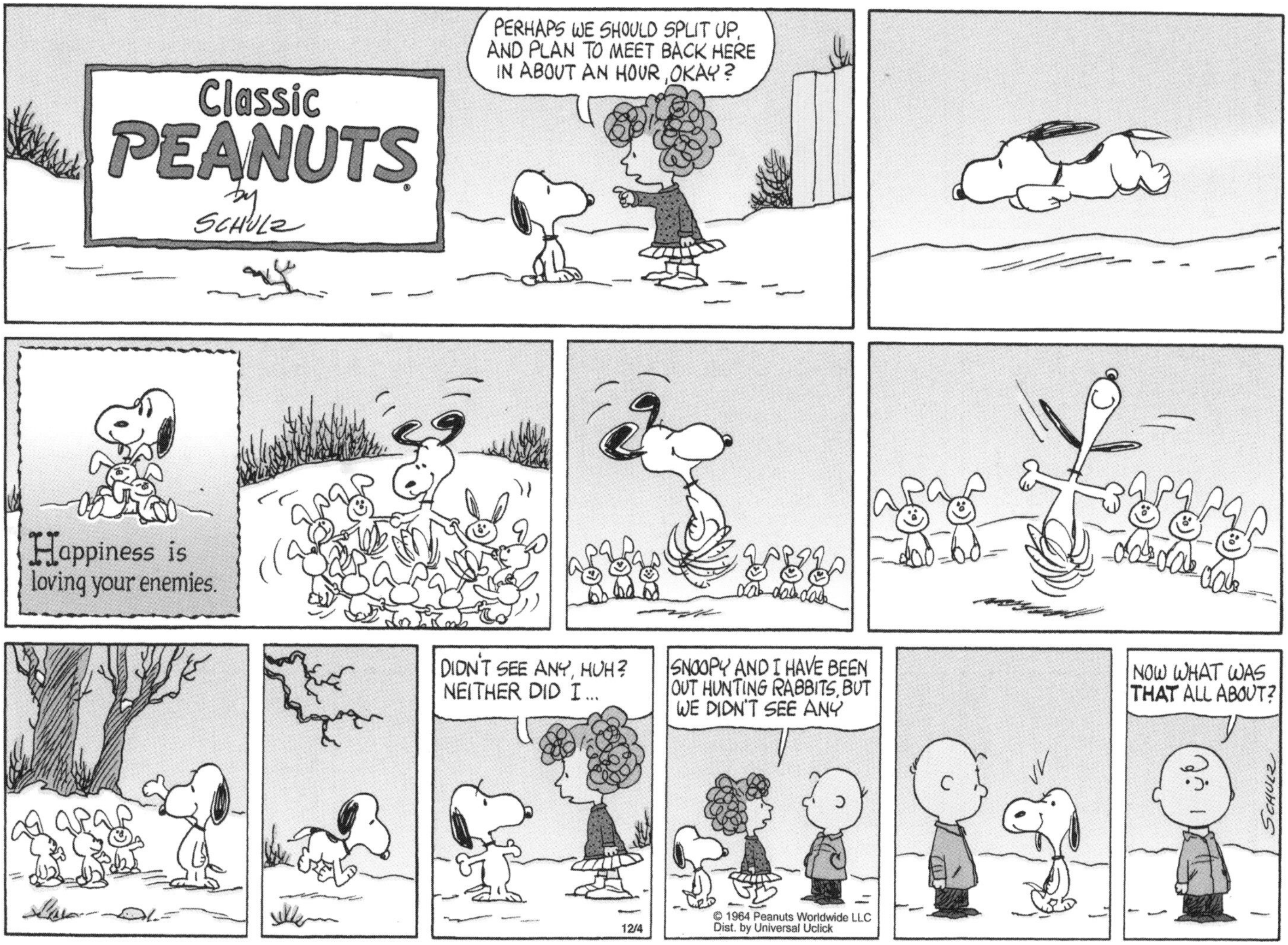
Classic PEANUTS by SCHULZ
PERHAPS WE SHOULD SPLIT UP, AND PLAN TO MEET BACK HERE IN ABOUT AN HOUR, OKAY?
Happiness is loving your enemies.
DIDN'T SEE ANY, HUH? NEITHER DID I...
12/4
SNOOPY AND I HAVE BEEN OUT HUNTING RABBITS, BUT WE DIDN'T SEE ANY
© 1964 Peanuts Worldwide LLC
Dist. by Universal Uclick
NOW WHAT WAS THAT ALL ABOUT?
SCHULZ

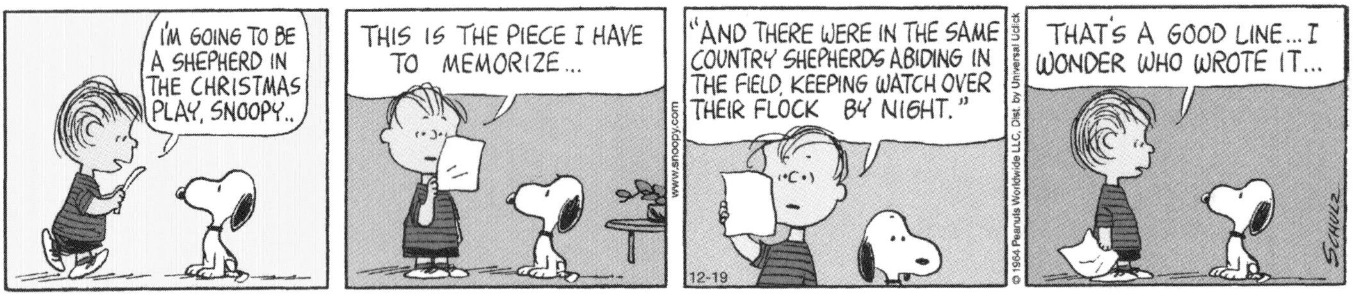
I'M GOING TO BE A SHEPHERD IN THE CHRISTMAS PLAY, SNOOPY..
THIS IS THE PIECE I HAVE TO MEMORIZE...
"AND THERE WERE IN THE SAME COUNTRY SHEPHERDS ABIDING IN THE FIELD, KEEPING WATCH OVER THEIR FLOCK BY NIGHT."
THAT'S A GOOD LINE... I WONDER WHO WROTE IT...
12-19
© 1964 Peanuts Worldwide LLC, Dist. by Universal Uclick
www.snoopy.com
SCHULZ

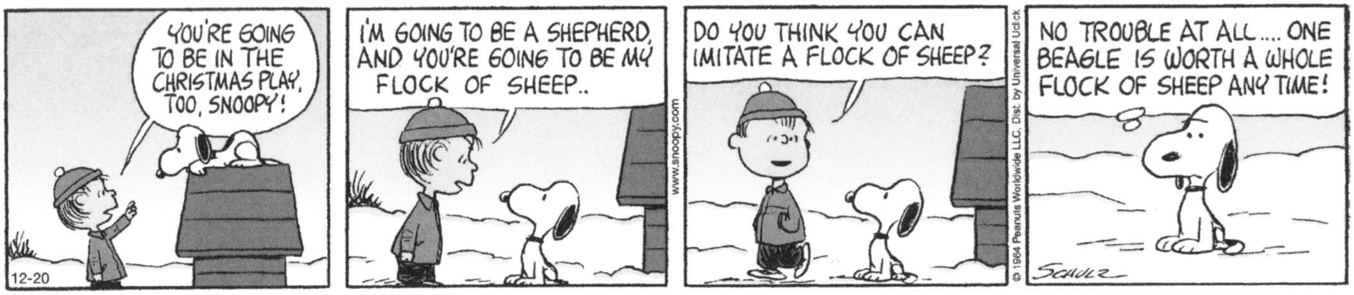
YOU'RE GOING TO BE IN THE CHRISTMAS PLAY, TOO, SNOOPY!
I'M GOING TO BE A SHEPHERD, AND YOU'RE GOING TO BE MY FLOCK OF SHEEP..
DO YOU THINK YOU CAN IMITATE A FLOCK OF SHEEP?
NO TROUBLE AT ALL.... ONE BEAGLE IS WORTH A WHOLE FLOCK OF SHEEP ANY TIME!
12-20
© 1964 Peanuts Worldwide LLC, Dist. by Universal Uclick
www.snoopy.com
SCHULZ

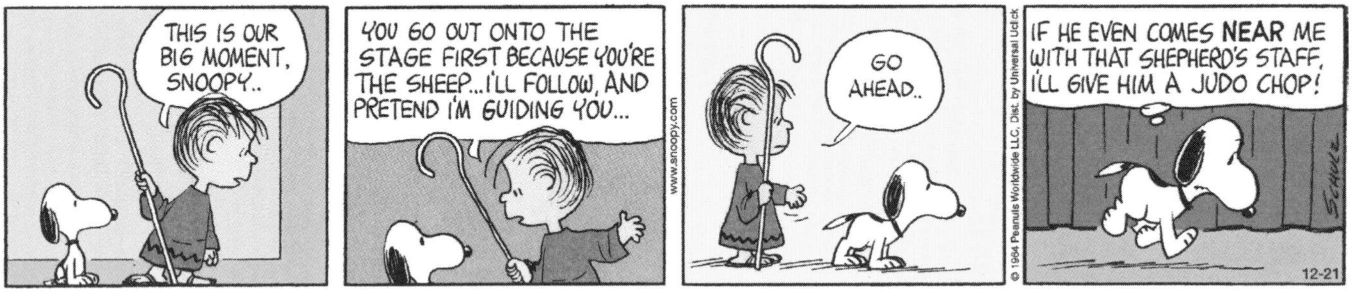
THIS IS OUR BIG MOMENT, SNOOPY..
YOU GO OUT ONTO THE STAGE FIRST BECAUSE YOU'RE THE SHEEP... I'LL FOLLOW, AND PRETEND I'M GUIDING YOU...
GO AHEAD..
IF HE EVEN COMES **NEAR** ME WITH THAT SHEPHERD'S STAFF, I'LL GIVE HIM A JUDO CHOP!
12-21
© 1964 Peanuts Worldwide LLC, Dist. by Universal Uclick
www.snoopy.com
SCHULZ

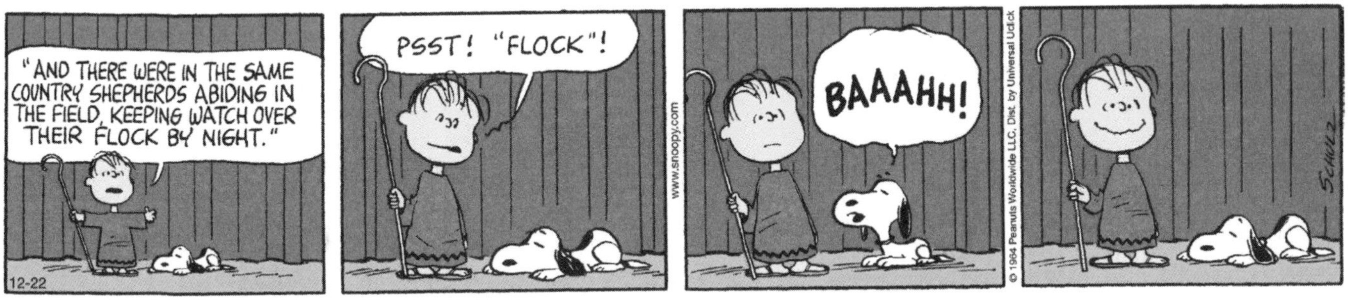
"AND THERE WERE IN THE SAME COUNTRY SHEPHERDS ABIDING IN THE FIELD, KEEPING WATCH OVER THEIR FLOCK BY NIGHT."
12-22
PSST! "FLOCK"!
www.snoopy.com
BAAAHH!
© 1964 Peanuts Worldwide LLC, Dist. by Universal Uclick
SCHULZ

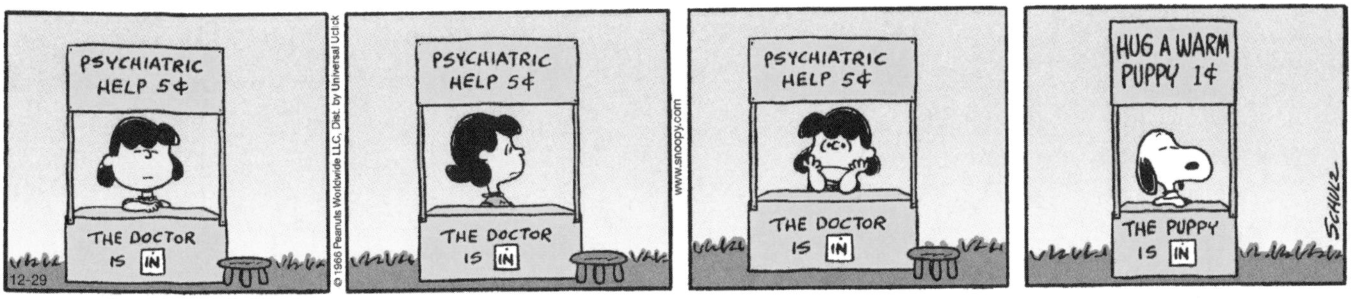
PSYCHIATRIC HELP 5¢
THE DOCTOR IS IN
12-29
© 1966 Peanuts Worldwide LLC, Dist. by Universal Uclick
PSYCHIATRIC HELP 5¢
THE DOCTOR IS IN
www.snoopy.com
PSYCHIATRIC HELP 5¢
THE DOCTOR IS IN
HUG A WARM PUPPY 1¢
THE PUPPY IS IN
SCHULZ

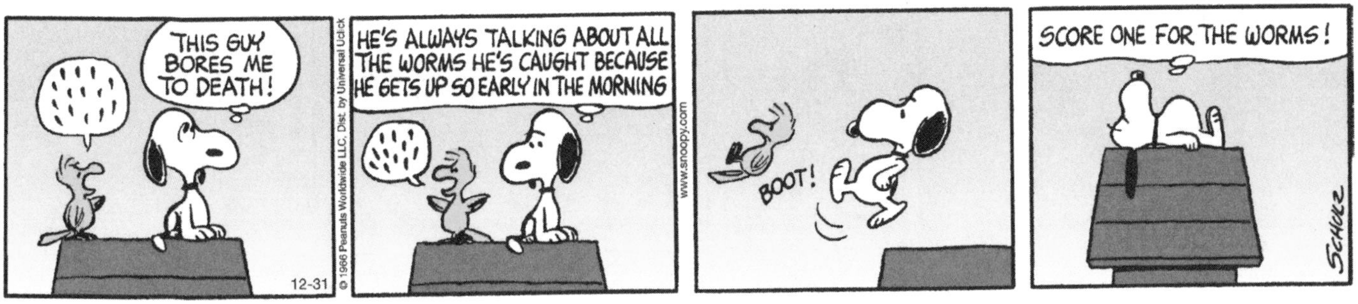
THIS GUY BORES ME TO DEATH!
12-31
© 1966 Peanuts Worldwide LLC, Dist. by Universal Uclick
HE'S ALWAYS TALKING ABOUT ALL THE WORMS HE'S CAUGHT BECAUSE HE GETS UP SO EARLY IN THE MORNING
www.snoopy.com
BOOT!
SCORE ONE FOR THE WORMS!
SCHULZ

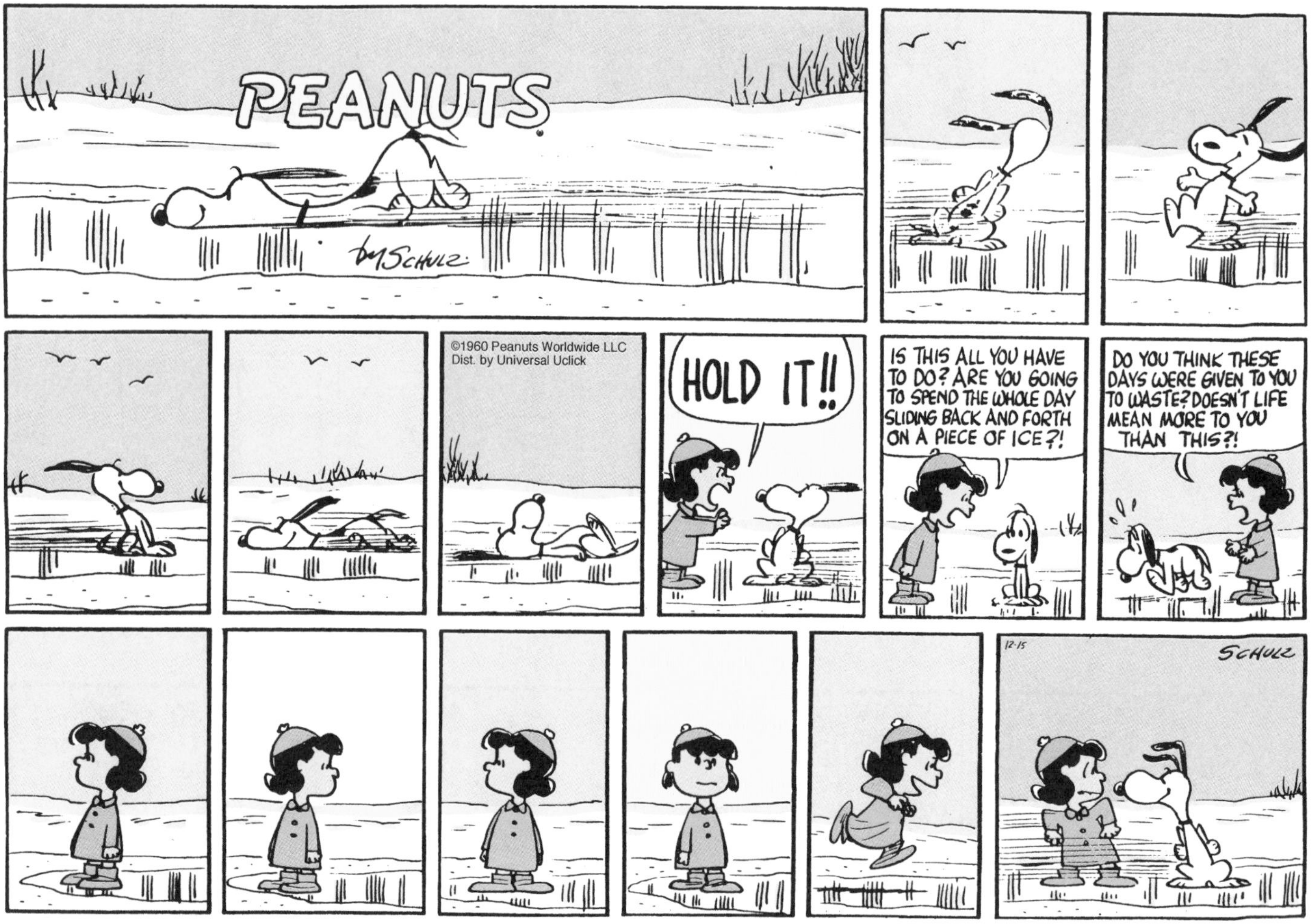
PEANUTS
by SCHULZ
©1960 Peanuts Worldwide LLC
Dist. by Universal Uclick
HOLD IT!!
IS THIS ALL YOU HAVE TO DO? ARE YOU GOING TO SPEND THE WHOLE DAY SLIDING BACK AND FORTH ON A PIECE OF ICE?!
DO YOU THINK THESE DAYS WERE GIVEN TO YOU TO WASTE? DOESN'T LIFE MEAN MORE TO YOU THAN THIS?!
12-15
SCHULZ

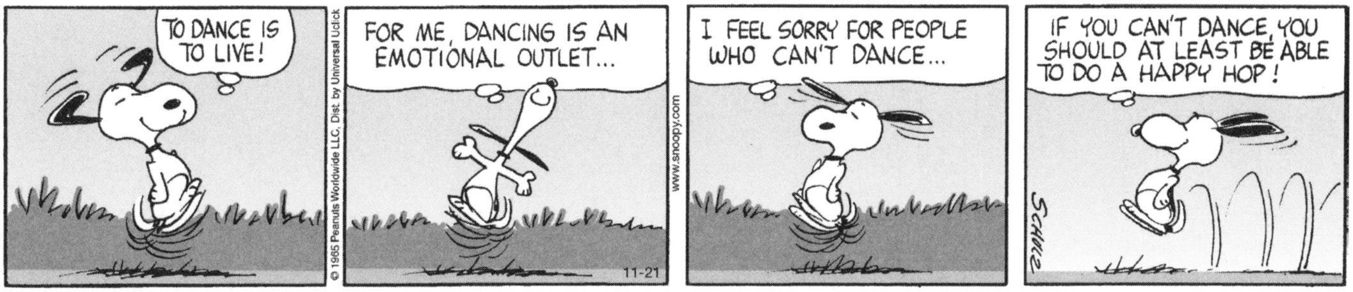

TO DANCE IS TO LIVE!
FOR ME, DANCING IS AN EMOTIONAL OUTLET...
I FEEL SORRY FOR PEOPLE WHO CAN'T DANCE...
IF YOU CAN'T DANCE, YOU SHOULD AT LEAST BE ABLE TO DO A HAPPY HOP!
SCHULZ
11-21
© 1965 Peanuts Worldwide LLC, Dist. by Universal Uclick
www.snoopy.com